Comparative Tax Systems: Europe, Canada, and Japan

Comparative Tax Systems: Europe, Canada, and Japan

Joseph A. Pechman, Editor
The Brookings Institution

Contributing Authors

Krister Andersson
Laura Castellucci
Flip de Kam
Annette Dengel, translated by Birgit Schneider
M. Homma, T. Maeda, and K. Hashimoto
Harry M. Kitchen
Jean-Louis Lienard, Kenneth C. Messere, and Jeffrey Owens
Nick Morris
Joseph A. Pechman

Tax Analysts
Arlington, Virginia
1987

Tax Analysts, Arlington, Virginia, 22213
Copyright 1987 by Joseph A. Pechman. All rights reserved.
Printed in the United States of America

Library of Congress Catalog Card Number: 87-50143
ISBN 0-918255-05-8

Library of Congress Cataloging-in-Publication Data

Comparative Tax Systems.

    Includes bibliographies and index.
    Contents: Introduction / Joseph A. Pechman — Sweden / by Krister
Andersson — Netherlands / by Flip de Kam — France / by Jean-Louis Lienard,
Kenneth C. Messere, and Jeffrey Owens — Italy / by Laura Castellucci — Federal
Republic of Germany / by Annette Dengel, translated by Birgit Schneider —
United Kingdom / by Nick Morris — Canada / by Harry M. Kitchen — Japan / by
M Homma, T. Maeda, and K. Hashimoto
    1. Taxation—Europe.   2. Taxation—Japan.   3. Taxation—Canada.
    I. Pechman, Joseph A., 1918-   II. Andersson, Krister. III. de Kam,
Flip.   IV. Lienard, Jean-Louis, Messere, Kenneth C., and Owens, Jeffrey.
V. Castellucci, Laura.   VI. Dengel, Annette, translated by Birgit Schneider.
VII. Morris, Nick.   VIII. Kitchen, Harry M.   IX. Homma, M., Maeda, J.,
and Hashimoto, K.
HJ2599.5.C65   1987   336.2   87-50143
ISBN 0-918255-05-8

Foreword

The idea of tax reform has been sweeping the western world. Tax systems almost everywhere are widely regarded as unfair, inefficient, and unnecessarily complicated. The recent experience with tax reform in the United States has greatly impressed our friends and trading partners, and tax structures are being reexamined by government and private groups to see how they can be improved. The purpose of this volume is to explain the basic features of the tax systems in Europe, Canada, and Japan, so that their need for reform and future progress can be evaluated. Since it was impractical to cover all of Europe, six countries—Sweden, the Netherlands, France, Italy, West Germany, and the United Kingdom—were selected as representative of current tax practice on that continent.

Each country chapter was prepared by a resident expert or experts, following a uniform outline to permit comparisons among them. The chapters describe the tax systems as they were in mid-1986. My introduction, which identifies the major issues and the solutions being considered, was prepared on the basis of discussions in the summer of 1986 with key tax officials and tax experts from each country. I am grateful to each of the authors and to the many people—too numerous to mention—who took the time and effort to educate me on the intricacies of the tax law and the realities of tax politics in their countries.

I also wish to acknowledge the assistance of Melissa Burman, who prepared the manuscript for publication, and Paul Doster and M.B. Brewer, who were responsible for the composition and layout of the volume.

The research on this volume was supported by the Brookings Institution, with grants from the German Marshall Fund and the Alfred P. Sloan Foundation. The views expressed are those of the authors and should not be attributed to the Brookings Institution or to the two supporting foundations.

Joseph A. Pechman
The Brookings Institution
February, 1987

Contents

List of Tables and Figures

1. Public Expenditure, 1955-1985
2. The Public Sector of the Netherlands Economy, 1985
3. Income Redistribution Through the Public Sector, 1977
4. Main Deductions and Exemptions, 1985
5. Distribution of Deductions and Exemptions by Socio-economic Group, 1985
6. Distribution of Deductions and Exemptions by Taxable Income Class, 1985
7. Other Taxes Levied by Central Government, 1985
8. Rates of Estate Tax and Gift Tax, 1985
9. Financing the Social Insurance, 1985
10. Contributions for General Insurance, 1985
11. Contributions for Employee Insurance Programs, 1985
12. Burden of Personal Income Tax and Social Insurance Contributions at Selected Income Levels, 1985
13. Labor Cost, Gross and Net Wage of an Average Production Worker, 1985
14. Burden of Income Tax and Social Insurance Contributions, 1979
15. Burden of Income Tax and Social Insurance Contributions, 1981
16. Rate Scale Options Presented by Tax Simplification Commission
17. Frequency Distribution of Change in Disposable Income Through Proposals of the Tax Simplification Commission
18. Change in Disposable Income Through Proposals of the Tax Simplification Commission, by Income Class
19. Change in Disposable Income Through Proposals of the Tax Simplification Commission, by Socioeconomic Group
20. Budgetary Consequences of Proposals of the Tax Simplification Commission

Figures and Examples
1. Example 1: Rates and Contribution Ceiling of the Five General Social Insurances, 1985
2. Figure 1: Economic Incidence of the Corporate Income Tax, 1973
3. Figure 2: Economic Incidence of All Social Insurance Contributions, 1973
4. Figure 3: Taxpayers Classified According to Highest Applicable Rate Scale of the Income Levy, 1985

CHAPTER **1**

Introduction: Recent Developments

Joseph A. Pechman

INTRODUCTION

Taxation is usually an important item on the policy agenda of most western countries, but it is now receiving unusual attention almost everywhere. In part, this reflects the general dissatisfaction with the heavy burden of taxation which accompanied the rise in expenditures during the 1960s and 1970s. It also reflects a widely held view that tax systems in the western world are unfair and inefficient. The recent passage of a comprehensive tax reform in the United States has also had a tremendous influence on the thinking of key opinion leaders inside and outside governments about the practicality of tax reform.

I visited six European countries and Canada in the Spring and Summer of 1986 to learn first hand what the major tax issues were and the solutions that are being considered. During the same year, I also had an opportunity to discuss tax developments with many Japanese visitors to the United States. I met with government and opposition leaders, tax officials, businessmen, and tax experts in the private sector and in the academic community. I had at my disposal the papers in this volume which describe the major features of the tax systems of each country, so that I had a basis for engaging in discussions about technical tax matters with the local tax experts. I was cordially received everywhere and the discussions were frank, stimulating, and informative. As a result, I believe I was able to identify the key issues and to learn how they are likely to be resolved.

The countries included in this survey are Sweden, the Netherlands, France, Italy, West Germany, the United Kingdom, Canada, and Japan. Taxes are higher in Europe and Canada than in the United States, ranging in 1984 from 33.7 percent of gross domestic product in Canada to 50.5 percent in Sweden. The comparable figure for the United States was 29 percent (table 1). Japan, with 27 percent, is rapidly approaching the United States in total tax burden. All the European countries relied much more heavily on payroll and consumption taxes than the United States and Japan. Except for Canada, the maximum individual income tax rates in these countries were higher than those levied in the United States even before the tax reform bill was passed and they are much higher now that the bill has passed (table 2). The corporation tax rates were about the same as, or higher than, in the United States before the reform; the United Kingdom has already reduced its corporate rate to 35 percent, but the rates in the other countries will be much higher after the U.S. reform takes effect (table 3).

Although the tax structures and major tax problems differ greatly, a number of common themes emerged in the discussions:

1. Except in Italy, West Germany, and Japan, the statutes provide for automatic adjustment of individual income tax rate brackets and exemptions for inflation. Yet the adjustments were either omitted or reduced frequently to avoid the revenue reductions that would otherwise take place. There is little evidence that indexation restrained the growth in government expenditures as expected by its proponents. Now that the inflation has moderated, indexation is being eliminated or replaced by partial adjustments for price change.

2. There is great diversity in the tax treatment of the family in these countries. West Germany splits income between husband and wife for tax purposes, while France uses a quotient system which provides half-splitting for children as well. The other countries generally tax earnings of married couples separately to each spouse and arbitrarily allocate investment income among the spouses (either dividing it equally or taxing it to the spouse with the higher marginal tax rate). Although tax officials recognize that these arrangements produce anamolies, they are reluctant to change them because of the fear of antagonizing women's groups who generally support separate taxation of husband and wife or some form of income splitting.

3. Like the United States, Sweden and the Netherlands levy separate corporate and individual income taxes, so that dividends are in effect taxed twice. All the others attempt to "integrate" the two taxes by reducing the corporate tax rate on distributed earnings, enacting some form of dividend relief at the individual level, or both. Such relief was provided in Canada, Italy, and Japan even when no corporate tax had been paid on the distributed earnings. To remedy this defect, Italy has adopted an "advance corporate tax" similar to the tax levied in France, West Germany and the United Kingdom to bring the tax on distributed profits up to the statutory level. Canada is avoiding the advance corporate tax; instead, it has reduced the dividend tax credit from 50 percent

to 33-1/3 percent. Japan has taken no action to avoid giving tax credits for dividends when no tax has been paid at the corporate level.

4. Every country has experimented with tax incentives for investment, but tax rates on investment differ greatly. Julian Alworth of the Bank for International Settlements has estimated that, assuming zero inflation, the effective marginal tax rate on investment in 1985 was -15 percent in Italy, as compared with 33 percent in the United Kingdom, 48 percent in France, 60 percent in West Germany, and 74 percent in the Netherlands.

5. There is growing disenchantment almost everywhere with investment incentives. Opinion is widespread that they distort the allocation of resources and generate numerous inequities among industries and firms. Britain has already replaced immediate expensing of plant and equipment with more realistic depreciation rates and lowered the corporate rate. Canada is phasing out its investment tax credit and reducing the corporate tax rate. Now that the United States has also eliminated its investment tax credit and lowered its corporate tax rate to 34 percent, other countries are reconsidering the structure and rates of their corporate taxes.

6. Incentives to encourage personal saving through the tax system are also universal. In addition to tax deferral for employer contributions to employee pension plans, the devices include IRA-type deductions for individuals with earned income, exemptions for small amounts of interest and dividends, flat tax rates on interest and dividends far below the ordinary tax rates, deductions for life insurance premiums, favorable treatment of investments in small business enterprises and many others. Capital gains on financial transactions are either wholly tax-exempt or taxable at preferential rates. Tax officials recognize that these provisions distort the allocation of saving, complicate the income tax, and favor high-income taxpayers. But they are reluctant to curtail these preferences even if the tax rates are reduced at the same time, because of the fear of political repercussions.

7. Payroll tax rates are extremely high in Europe by U.S. standards. The payroll taxes are needed to finance social security systems that are much more extensive than the U.S. system. Demographics will create difficult financing problems for the retirement systems, but action to solve this problem is being deferred everywhere.

8. The value-added tax (VAT) continues to be a mainstay of the European tax system. In most countries, there are numerous exemptions and a variety of tax rates that complicate administration, but very little is being done to simplify matters. Canada is planning to substitute a value-added tax for its manufacturers'

excise tax, but it is considering what it calls a "business transfer tax" (BTT), rather than the type of tax used in Europe. Under the BTT, business firms calculate value added by subtracting purchases from sales, whereas under the European VAT each firm calculates the tax on is total sales and then takes credit for the taxes paid by their suppliers. Japan is also planning to introduce a value-added tax in order to reduce its budget deficit.

9. Several of the European countries impose an annual tax on net wealth as well as a tax on bequests and gifts. The yield of these taxes is small, because wealth is often undervalued for tax purposes, exemptions are provided for farmers and small businesses, and there are many ways to avoid the taxes. The Chirac government in France has eliminated the wealth tax and Canada has withdrawn completely from the estate tax.

10. Because they are open economies, Europe, Canada, and Japan are extremely sensitive to tax policies in other countries. On the one hand, they are reluctant to eliminate tax preferences for saving and domestic investment for fear that capital will flow abroad. On the other hand, they are impressed with the success of tax reform in the United States, particularly the large reduction in tax rates it provided. Although they feel pressure to reform their tax systems, it is not clear whether they will in fact have the political will to follow the lead of the United States.

The following summaries of the discussions I had in each country provide more detail on these developments.

I. Sweden

Sweden has the highest tax burden in the world. Individual income tax rates range from 34 percent to a maximum of 80 percent and the corporation tax rate is 52 percent. Payroll taxes and the VAT are also high by international standards. Sweden is now considering a modest reduction in the top individual income tax rate and upward revisions in the capital gains tax. It is also studying the role of corporate income taxation in its tax system.

1. Indexation

The tax brackets and personal exemptions were fully indexed in 1979, but the law was followed only in 1979, 1980, and 1982. Indexation was abandoned in 1985, largely because of the revenue consequences. Social Democrats opposed indexation, because (they argued) it was most advantageous to high-income taxpayers. The tax base has not been indexed, except for the calculation of capital gains on owner-occupied homes. The purchase price of homes is indexed beginning in the fifth year after occupancy.

2. Treatment of the Family

All political parties support separate taxation of husband and wife, which was enacted to achieve equality between spouses. Investment income of a couple was taxable to the spouse with the higher income, but in 1987 there will be separate taxation of investment income as well. No concern was expressed about the use of gifts and other devices to split investment income between husband and wife. Nor was there any concern about the inequality of tax burdens among couples with equal incomes. In addition to separate filing, subsidized day care is available only to families with two working spouses or single-parent families.

3. The Corporate Tax

The classical system of corporate taxation (that is, separate taxation of corporate and individual income) is used in Sweden, and there is no pressure to relieve the so-called "double taxation." One reason is that the corporate tax is not a big tax (considering the generous allowances for investment), so that double taxation is not large. Moreover, business managers prefer to keep the money at the corporate level for reinvestment purposes, and oppose any tax measure that would pressure them to increase distributions. However, relief is provided for dividends paid on newly issued shares and by unlisted corporations.

4. Taxation of Income from Capital

There is considerable diversity of opinion about how to make the Swedish tax system more neutral. Some propose elimination of the individual income tax on capital income entirely, on the ground that the deduction for interest is larger than capital income for top-bracket taxpayers so that the net tax on capital income is negative. Others propose either a consumption expenditure tax or a labor income tax, combined with a more effective tax on wealth. There is also interest in Sweden in a Danish reform, which taxes net capital income separately from labor income at a flat 50 percent rate (thus limiting the tax value of interest deductions to 50 percent). Such a system would increase taxes on capital income in Sweden.

Homeowners also have negative income from their investment. Assessed values to compute imputed rent are substantially below true value and full deduction is allowed for mortgage interest. To limit the revenue loss, deficits on capital income can only be deducted at a maximum rate of 50 percent, except that up to SK 30,000 (about $4,500) may be deducted at above the 50 percent rate for owner-occupied homes.

There is general agreement that the deductions for saving encourage people to funnel their savings into tax-exempt forms (e.g., insurance). But there is no evidence on whether the tax incentives have had any effect on total private saving. In fact, personal saving has declined sharply as a ratio to GNP. There are now 2.7 million savings accounts built up by the tax-exemption of interest on these accounts, but there is no way to estimate how much this type of saving has been substituted for other forms. The government would like to move toward a simpler and broader tax base with lower rates, but is discouraged by the political problems.

Everybody agrees that the tax treatment of capital income is *not* viable for the long run. Several official committees are working on alternatives, including committees on the corporate tax, the capital gains tax, and the expenditure tax. The maximum tax rate will be reduced from 80 percent to 75 percent by 1988. The government will move slowly in other areas, because it does not want to jeopardize economic expansion.

5. The Tax Free Investment and Profit-Sharing Funds

Swedish firms are permitted to set aside up to 50 percent of their profits tax free in funds that may be used later for investment purposes, when permission is granted by the government. These funds were successful in stabilizing the time profile of investment over the business cycle in the 1950s and 1960s. Since then, they have been used as general stimulants to investment, since firms have no trouble getting permission to use the funds at almost any time. (Firms are, in effect, permitted a tax free write-off of investment at the time the investment is made to the extent that it is financed out of an investment fund). What will happen to this device depends on the forthcoming review of the corporate tax.

The profit-sharing funds were introduced at the insistence of the trade union movement. They are financed in part by a 0.2 percent tax on payrolls and in part by a tax on *real* profits, i.e., profits after real depreciation. (This is the only place in the tax system where depreciation is adjusted for inflation.) The government is committed to continue payment of taxes into these funds until 1990.

In practice, workers have not benefitted directly from the profit-sharing funds. The funds are required to pay three percent of their capital each year into the public pension system and thus benefit workers indirectly. The investment managers have, in some instances, pursued an aggressive investment policy. Some people believe that the recent stock market boom has been attributable in part to the infusion of this new money into the stock market.

6. Wealth Taxes

The annual net wealth tax is levied at rates ranging from 1.5 percent to 3.0 percent. Undervaluations of owner-occupied homes, real estate, farms, and small businesses have greatly reduced the effectiveness of this tax. The tax is not effective in reaching very many wealthy people because the sum of income and wealth taxes cannot exceed 80 percent of taxable income (75 percent when the maximum rate will be cut to that level in 1988). Inheritance and gift taxes are not integrated and their yield is also relatively small. The effect of the wealth taxes on the distribution of income and wealth has, therefore, been small.

7. Payroll Taxes

Payroll taxes now average 36 percent of wages and salaries and are used to finance the large transfer system as well as the public pension system. The public approves the use of payroll taxes in this way, because it would be impossible to impose an additional load onto the individual income tax.

The social security system is on a pay-as-you-go basis, and the system will be self-financing for some years to come with moderate reductions in benefits or increases in taxes. However, the demographics will change radically in the 21st century, and some revisions in the underlying financial system will be made. Because other matters are more urgent, no changes are expected in the years immediately ahead.

8. Tax Reform

The government has just completed a tax revision program, which will reduce individual income tax rates to a maximum of 75 percent. Next on the agenda will be an upward revision of the capital gains tax. The committee on the corporate tax will report next year, so that a revision of the corporate tax will not be on the agenda until 1988. The tax experts in the Ministry of Finance would like to broaden the income tax base and lower the tax rates, but nothing definite has yet been decided. As already noted, the Danish tax reform is mentioned frequently and there is great interest in the U.S. tax reform.

Beginning in 1987 (for incomes in 1986), Sweden will embark on a novel system of tax assessment. The government will calculate the amount of income subject to tax for each taxpayer from records sent in by employers, financial institutions, and corporations. The taxpayer will certify that he accepts the government calculation and the government will then calculate and assess the tax. The tax authorities are confident that they can administer the system effectively through its computer system.

II. The Netherlands

Individual income tax rates in the Netherlands range from 16 percent to 72 percent, but numerous tax preferences reduce effective rates—especially for recipients of investment income. The government is now preoccupied with a proposed simplification of its individual income and payroll tax systems, but little consideration is being given to broadening the income tax bases.

1. Indexation

Automatic indexation of the brackets and family allowances has been in effect since 1971. But in many years, the government has cut back indexation to 80 percent—and in some cases, 60 percent—of the increase in the consumer price index. This was particularly true during the years of high inflation, when transfer payments were fully indexed and revenue needs were great. The indexation provision remains in the law, even though it does not have much significance now that price increases have subsided.

2. Treatment of the Family

Married persons are taxed separately on their earned income, but the investment income of the couple is taxed to the spouse with the higher marginal rate. People who share a household and pool their income are treated like married couples, though unmarried couples attempt to persuade the tax authorities that they consume independently. This system is strongly entrenched because of the strength of the women's rights movement. Tax authorities and tax experts recognize that under this system couples with the same total income can pay substantially different taxes but they do not intend to suggest any changes in it because it is popular politically. Nor is there a demand from the public to equalize the tax on married couples with the same income.

3. The Corporate Tax

The Dutch use the classical corporation tax system because there are several very large multinational corporations based in Holland and it is an open economy. They would prefer to avoid the problems of restricting dividend credits to domestic shareholders and of imposing advance corporation tax in cases where the corporation has been paying no tax. (This is a substantial possibility because of the use of the Dutch Antilles as tax havens by their multinational companies.)

4. Investment and Capital Income

Capital income is very lightly taxed in the Netherlands because (a) the corporation tax is low, (b) capital gains on the sales of securities are exempt from tax, (c) houses are assessed at 60 percent of market value for purposes of calculating imputed rent, while mortgage interest is fully deductible, (d) small deductions are allowed for interest and dividends and a large deduction for insurance premiums, (e) all other interest is fully deductible, and (f) the wealth tax plus income tax is limited to 80 percent of *taxable* income, no matter how low taxable incomes may have been driven by the deductions for interest and insurance premiums. Although the tax on capital is low (or perhaps even negative), nobody has taken the trouble to calculate the net tax burden on capital income.

Some people in the Netherlands believe that capital gains should be taxed and that a limit should be placed on the deduction for interest expense. However, they are in the distinct minority. Tax officials and private tax experts alike prefer to leave capital gains untaxed, partly because they do not agree that limits can be placed on capital losses and interest deductions and partly because they are worried about a flight of capital abroad. Even the Social Democrats have not been urging taxation of capital gains.

Officially, depreciation is calculated according to "conventional accounting standards." In practice, it is negotiated between the tax inspector and the business. Depreciation allowances seem to be more generous than economic depreciation, in conformity with court decisions that have tended to give considerable weight to the inadequacy of historical depreciation during periods of inflation. In addition to depreciation, there is an investment tax credit of 12.5 percent on buildings as well as machinery.

The Dutch recognize the considerable non-uniformity with which they treat different assets and industries and the many distortions in investment patterns that result. I found no one in the Netherlands who was concerned about these distortions.

5. Wealth Tax

As already noted, the wealth tax is not very effective because of the undervaluation of property and the maximum effective rate of wealth plus income tax on taxable income. Moreover, the rate is relatively low (0.8 percent) and the tax threshold relatively high. The inheritance taxes also yield very little revenue, mainly because the tax thresholds are high. There does not seem to be any interest in improving the wealth taxes, despite the long social democratic tradition in the country.

6. Tax Reform

A prestigious Tax Reform Commission issued a major report at the end of May, 1986, dealing with simplification of the complicated income tax and social security tax system. The commission proposed integration of income and social security taxes at a flat rate of 40 percent on a wide first bracket, after which progression would rise to 65 or 70 percent. The 40 percent rate would apply to 88 percent of the taxpayers. This revision would enable the tax authorities to dispense with tax returns for many taxpayers with income subject to withholding, probably two to three million out of the seven million total.

The Commission did not make any proposals to broaden the tax base, although some of its members believe that the Dutch should follow the U.S. example. However, political leaders and tax officials are hesitant about going in this direction on the usual grounds (such a reform will "hurt" too many important taxpayer groups; transition problems are difficult; the public will not accept reforms that deny them cherished tax advantages, and so on). Moreover, because public expenditures are high, most observers believe that rates cannot be brought down very far even with substantial base-broadening.

III. France

The French have relatively high individual income tax rates (the maximum rate is 65 percent), but they collect only a small amount of revenue from the income tax because numerous deductions and tax credits erode the tax base. The Chirac government has already eliminated the wealth tax and expects to reduce the top income tax rate to 50 percent. However, significant reform of the income taxes is not in the offing. In fact, the government has been adding new tax preferences, rather than curtailing them.

1. Indexation

The French tax law has called for indexation of the tax brackets and the personal exemptions since the 1960s, but the provision has been modified frequently for budgetary or political reasons. Between 1974 and 1981, indexation was confined to the lower brackets. Since 1981, indexation has been fully implemented, and surtaxes were used to raise revenues. This is the honest way to raise additional revenues, but extremely painful. The surtaxes have now been eliminated, and it is expected that indexation will be continued.

2. Treatment of the Family

A quotient system was adopted in 1945 to encourage family formation. Under this system, income is split not only with spouses but also with children (with weights of 0.5 for the children). A (low) ceiling on the tax benefit for splitting was imposed by the Socialists in 1981. (All families are now entitled to the benefit of income splitting between the spouses. The ceiling is imposed on the *additional* benefit of splitting with children.)

The major criticism of the quotient system is that two unmarried parents—each with one child—each have a quotient of two (or a total of four), whereas a married couple with two children has a quotient of three. Some change may be made to remedy this problem, but nobody expects any fundamental changes in the quotient system. Unlike other European countries, there is no significant movement toward separate filing by spouses in France.

3. The Corporate Tax

The French imputation system for dividends seems to be very popular with all groups. The credit (*avoir fiscal*) is calculated at 50 percent of dividends received, which was equivalent to one-half of the corporate tax rate until recently when the corporate rate was reduced to 45 percent. If the profits distributed as dividends do not bear the full corporate tax, the corporation must pay an equalization tax (*precompte*) to bring the tax on distributed profits up to that level. The dividend credit was not changed when the corporate rate was reduced to 45 percent, which means that the effective dividend relief was raised from 50 percent of the corporate tax to 61 percent. The Chirac government would support further increases in dividend relief if it were not for the budgetary constraint.

4. Investment and Capital Income

The French are familiar with the calculations made in the United States and the United Kingdom of the cost of capital, but have not made such calculations for France. They are aware that their business tax system is not neutral among assets and industries, but don't seem to mind it. As one expert put it, "the French tax system is not neutral *by design.*"

Capital income is taxed lightly in France, if at all. Capital gains are subject to a flat rate of 16 percent: contributions to pension plans are deductible without limit; modest deductions are allowed for life insurance premiums and mortgage interest; and favorable treatment is accorded to investments in risk capital investment funds. However, none of the political parties proposes any significant reforms in this area.

5. Wealth Tax

The Chirac government has already eliminated the wealth tax beginning in 1987. The yield of the tax was low for the usual reasons: a high taxable threshold, undervaluation of taxable wealth, exemptions for works of art, and evasion. The Socialists still support a wealth tax, but recognize that it is a difficult tax to implement. The yield of the inheritance and gift taxes in France is also disappointing for similar reasons.

6. The Payroll Tax

French payroll taxes were 58 percent of the average manufacturing wage in 1984. The payroll taxes are heavy in France because they are easy to collect and are invisible to the average citizen. The high payroll taxes and tax incentives for investment may have encouraged companies to substitute capital for labor, a possibility that is particularly disturbing in an economy where unemployment remains high. However, no other source of revenue is readily available to finance the French social security system.

7. Tax Reform

The Chirac government has announced its intention to reduce the top-bracket individual income tax rate to 58 percent in 1986 and to 50 percent by 1989. It has also said that it will cut the corporate tax rate to 42 percent by 1988. But it has not proposed any othe major changes in the tax structure. A reform of the *tax professionalle* (a local payroll tax) is expected, but not much more. The U.S. experience with tax reform will have some influence on professional opinion in France, but nobody expects it to affect French tax policy significantly. In fact, some tax experts fear a new wave of tax expenditures, as the new government attempts to appeal to major political groups (farmers, small businessmen, low income groups, etc.). The French seem to be quite happy with their tax system, which relies heavily on the VAT and payroll taxes for most of their revenues.

France is probably the only country in the world which does not collect the personal income tax currently through withholding. But there is no interest in moving toward a current payment system.

IV. Italy

Italy is noted for the high degree of noncompliance of its citizens with its major taxes. In addition, numerous special deductions and tax credits have narrowed the tax bases of both the corporation and individual income taxes. Nevertheless, significant changes do not seem to be in the offing, because the coalition government is too weak to overcome the political obstacles to tax reform.

1. Indexation

The Italians have not formally indexed their tax brackets or their personal exemptions. The reason given was that it was necessary to have a high degree of fiscal drag during the period of high inflation. They did raise the personal exemptions, however, in order to preserve the minimum taxable threshold in real terms. More recently, they have introduced deductions for wage earners and reduced bottom bracket rates as part of their income policy to restrain the growth of wages. By avoiding indexation of brackets, the yield of the personal income tax rose much faster in Italy than in most other European countries. There is a considerable body of expert opinion that favors increasing reliance on indirect taxes, but this is difficult because of political constraints.

2. Treatment of the Family

Husband and wife have been allowed to file separate returns since 1977. Investment income is divided equally between the spouses. There are no deductions for children under the income tax, but family allowances are provided through the social security system. There seems to be no interest in changing the system.

3. The Corporate Tax

Italy provides a full tax credit for the corporate tax at the individual level. Prior to 1983, this credit was allowed whether or not taxes were actually paid by the corporation. To remedy this defect, a "balancing tax" was levied at the corporate level to require payment of tax when dividends are paid out of tax preferences. This tax operates like the advance corporate tax in France and the United Kingdom. There is no evidence of any dissatisfaction with this system now that the balancing tax is in place.

4. Investment and Capital Income

Italian officials are aware that their tax system is unnecessarily complicated and distorts the allocation of investment. (Italy has a system of grants to industry for investment in the South, as well as accelerated depreciation.) Italian academics and tax officials were not surprised to learn that the average marginal tax on investment in Italy is negative. They also agreed that the tax distortions in their system must be very large, but no one seemed disturbed about them. Italians *like* to use tax devices to promote economic objectives, even if they generate distortions.

There are several types of preferences for saving in the Italian tax system: (1) non-dividend income from private financial assets is subject to a variety of flat withholding rates, all of them much lower than the top bracket rates (for example, the withholding rate for interest on private bonds is 12.5 percent); (2) interest on government bonds is taxable to individuals at a low flat rate (12.5 percent beginning in 1987); and (3) capital gains on financial securities are tax-exempt. The Italian saving rate has been very high for years, but there is no way to determine whether the tax system has been a major factor. Everybody, including the Minister of Finance, recognizes that something should be done about this hodge-podge. But the government is restrained by the fear of antagonizing important pressure groups. The "primary deficit"— i.e., the deficit *excluding* interest payments on the debt—exceeds five percent of GNP.

5. Wealth Tax

Italy has no wealth tax, but it does tax gifts and inheritances. However, tax avoidance is easy and rates are low. Since the entire tax system is probably regressive, it increases the concentration of income and wealth. The political left is concerned about this, but is powerless to do much about it.

6. The Payroll Tax

Italian payroll taxes ranged from 48 percent in the handicrafts to 56 percent in industry in 1985. Payrolls are taxed so heavily because Italy relies on them to pay for its social security system, which provides a wide range of benefits for retirement, disability, unemployment compensation, family allowances and health. The subsidy to capital (see above) and the heavy tax on labor income may reduce the demand for labor, but nobody has tried to measure this effect.

Italians in and out of the government recognize that the Italian social security system is too generous, but very little is being done about it. Health benefits will probably be limited, to restrain the growth in health expenditures and to encourage economy in the use of health services. The retirement system is run on a pay-as-you-go basis, and demography will soon make the tax burden excessive. But the government is not facing up to the inevitability of reductions in retirement benefits. Payroll taxes probably will not be increased because they are already high.

7. Tax Reform

Because the coalition government is weak, a frontal assault on tax preferences to achieve equity and reduce distortions is not in the cards. A long-overdue reform of the local tax system was turned down by parliament on a vote of no-confidence in the Craxi coalition. Tax experts in the government and the universities admire the U.S. tax reform, but they do not believe it can be duplicated in Italy.

V. West Germany

West Germany is reducing its marginal income tax rates, but is retaining the top bracket rate of 56 percent. Despite numerous features that erode the tax bases, very little attention is being paid to improving the equity and efficiency of the individual and corporation income taxes.

1. Indexation

West Germany has not indexed its personal exemptions and tax brackets because of its fear of inflation. It is generally agreed that inflation must be avoided at all costs. Indexation, it is feared, would weaken the resolve of the government to combat inflation.

Nevertheless, the lack of indexation has produced some unhappy results. The personal exemptions have lagged behind inflation and they now amount to about one-half of the minimum subsistence level, and the marginal tax rates for middle class workers have increased sharply. Reductions in marginal tax rates and doubling of the personal exemptions have been enacted (to take effect in two stages by January 1, 1988) to ameliorate these problems.

2. Treatment of the Family

Income splitting was adopted in the early 1950s after a Supreme Court decision ruled that the West German Constitution required equality of tax treatment of taxpayers before and after marriage. There seems to be no significant opposition to this method of taxing the family. Single persons have not complained about their high tax rates relative to the rates of a married person with a non-working spouse; and there is no special treatment for single heads of household. In fact, per capita splitting (along the French lines) has been discussed, but the government is not in favor of this approach because of the large revenue implications. Benefits for children are being provided instead by a generous child care deduction.

3. The Corporate Tax

The present split-rate tax on corporate profits was adopted in 1977, after a thorough discussion of the pros and cons. Retained profits are taxed at 56 percent and distributed profits at 36 percent. The shareholder is granted a tax credit against his individual income tax for the 36 percent paid at the corporate level. A wide political consensus developed to tax distributed profits less heavily than retained profits, partly for equity reasons and partly to promote a wider distribution of corporate shares. Relief was given at the individual level to avoid giving tax benefits to foreigners. (About 45 percent of the stock of West German corporations is in the hands of foreign shareholders.) There is no evidence that dividend relief has increased the number of shareholders or the amount of equity financing by shareholders.

4. Investment and Capital Income

It is generally understood that the special tax concessions and preferences for investment create major distortions in the economy. The interest deduction is also a major problem, just as in the United States. The government and most academics believe that

the distortions should be reduced by eliminating the tax preferences and reducing the tax rates. Despite the tax breaks, the
average marginal tax rate on income from new investment is
higher in West Germany than in most other countries. (As noted
above, Alworth has estimated that the effective marginal tax rate
on investment in West Germany was 60 percent in 1985.) This is
not well known in West Germany.

Provisions in the tax law intended to promote saving include
special deductions for life insurance and saving for housing; a
small deduction for "capital-forming payments" to employees; a
bonus for the construction of a dwelling; and complete exemption
of capital gains on securities. Saving by West German households
is high, but there is little evidence to suggest that tax preferences
have been a major factor in promoting such saving. Most experts
believe that the saving incentives should be eliminated (except for
the capital gains preference), but there is no political will to
change the status quo.

Although the distortions created by the saving and investment
incentives are well recognized, the Germans, like other Europeans,
fear that heavier taxation of investment income will encourage
capital flight. Hence, they are reluctant to eliminate these preferences, even though they recognize that this would permit them to
lower the top marginal tax rates. The Social Democrats are in
favor of removing preferences and taxing capital gains, but they
are not very vigorous in their support for drastic changes in the tax
law.

5. Wealth Tax

The wealth tax does not raise much revenue because taxpayers
underreport their wealth, the exemption is high, and the rates are
low. It has, therefore, had very little effect on the concentration of
income and wealth. (A peculiar feature of the West German wealth
tax system is that the capital of corporations is subject to wealth
tax both at the Federal and local levels.) The inheritance and gift
taxes are not very effective for the same reasons.

6. The Payroll Tax

The payroll tax on wages of the average employee is about 31
percent, half of which is paid by the employer and half by the
employee. Although this rate is lower than in most other European
countries, the Germans recognize that it is high, discouraging the
use of labor and encouraging workers to work in the hidden
economy. Politicians and fiscal experts agree that these rates

should come down, but payroll taxes cannot be reduced unless social security benefits are cut.

Demography will create enormous fiscal problems for the West German retirement system early in the twenty-first century. The Chancellor has stated that people should be allowed to work until they are 68 years of age, but he did not suggest that full benefits should be delayed until that age. No action on this question is expected in the immediate future, largely because the finances of the public retirement system are in good shape for the short run.

7. Tax Reform

The second stage of the tax cut enacted in 1985 is set to go into effect on January 1, 1988, when marginal tax rates will be reduced by up to 5.5 percentage points (and by another 0.5 percentage points for each child). However, the top marginal rate will remain at 56 percent. Beyond this change, the government has announced its intention to move toward a "linear" rate of progression to flatten the tax rates in the middle income brackets (that rose sharply in the 1970s as a result of bracket creep).

A major difficulty with tightening the preferences for saving is that the government has no way to check nonwithheld incomes because financial institutions are not required to report investment income to the government. As a result, there is a great deal of underreporting of taxable interest income. Nothing is being done about this problem because of the fetish of Germans about disclosure of personal information to the government.

A tax advisory commission will soon recommend to the Minister of Finance substitution of a VAT of the income type for the local business tax. (This tax is partly a tax on business profits and partly a tax on the assets of business enterprises.) Business opposes such a change and the national government does not seem to be interested either.

The radical tax reform in the United States is widely discussed in West Germany. Government officials and tax experts are impressed, but there is considerable skepticism about the political feasibility of such an approach in West Germany.

VI. The United Kingdom

The U.K. Government led the United States by two years in curtailing tax incentives for investment and reducing the corporation tax rate. Yet, it displays little interest in improving the bases of the income taxes in other respects. In fact, it has recently added a number of tax expenditures and has proposed a tax subsidy for private profit-sharing plans to encourage more flexible wage and hiring practices.

1. Indexation

In the United Kingdom, the law provides for annual automatic adjustment of the personal allowance and tax rate brackets for inflation, unless Parliament decides otherwise. In practice, the allowances have been adjusted occasionally and the rate brackets have been adjusted only rarely.

2. Treatment of the Family

Britain's treatment of the family is an anachronism dating back to the time when wives remained at home and husbands were regarded as the head of the family. The incomes of husbands and wives are taxed jointly (except that they may elect separate taxation on earnings), but a working wife is allowed a personal exemption which is not "transferable" to (i.e., cannot be used by) the husband. The result is that a two-earner couple has 2.6 exemptions (if the wife's earnings exceed her exemption), a one-earner couple 1.6 exemptions, and a single person one exemption.

The government has proposed that a wife's exemption should be "transferable" to the husband even if she has no earned income. To correct for the discrimination against single people, it is presumed that the single person's exemption would be raised (to, say, half that of a married couple with two earners). Since transferable exemptions would be costly, the government has hesitated to implement the scheme. Moreover, many tax experts oppose transferable exemptions, because it would in effect *raise* the marginal tax rates on the spouse with the lower earnings (since an additional dollar would be fully taxed). In addition, there is a great deal of support for independent taxation of husband and wife. The result has been that the government has deferred consideration of its plan, and no action on the issue is expected until after the next election.

3. Investment and Capital Income

Two years ago, the conservative government phased out expensing of plant and equipment expenditures and used the revenue to reduce the corporation income tax rate to 35 percent. The two-year transition period ended on April 30, 1986. Curiously, there was very little opposition from the business community at the time this radical change was made. However, some economists and members of the business community worry that the elimination of the investment incentive will discourage investment. (So far, there has been no effect, because business was encouraged to invest during the transition period when a partial benefit from expensing was still granted.) A significant reduction in capital outlays in the last half of 1986 and in 1987 would cause considerable agitation to restore the tax incentive for investment. However, the government says it has no intention to capitulate.

Despite paying lip-service to the idea of a comprehensive income tax, the present government has narrowed the tax base by providing new incentives for saving and equity investment. The capital gains tax has been reduced by gradual increases in the amount of capital gains that are exempt from tax (it is now £5,900); in addition, since 1982 gains have been adjusted for inflation. A new scheme to encourage venture capital investment was put in place in 1984, and in 1986 another scheme to encourage individuals to invest in corporate stock was introduced. Finally, business and partnership losses generated by large interest deductions may be used to reduce taxable wage and salary income of individual investors. The net tax on capital income is, therefore, minimal, even if it isn't negative. A few tax experts worry about this state of affairs, but no action is in prospect to stop the erosion of the tax base.

4. Social Security

Britain started with a flat retirement benefit, and added a wage related feature (called SERPS) about fifteen years ago. Because the wage-related feature was actuarially unsound, last year the government proposed to eliminate SERPS and to mandate private portable and indexed pensions as a substitute. This proposal met with opposition from all quarters, including the insurance companies, and the government has now withdrawn it. Instead, it has reduced benefits to be provided by SERPS somewhat. However, the system will be in great financial difficulties after the turn of the century, when the number of retirees per worker will be at a peak. The government has deferred action on this issue until the furor over its misguided attempt to scuttle SERPS subsides.

5. Tax Reform

The government continues to support further reduction in tax rates, but does not couple this recommendation with base-broadening. Thus, the amount of rate reduction it can afford is limited, given the budgetary constraints. Knowledgable people in England admire the progress being made in the United States on tax reform, but they do not believe that the U.S. experience can be duplicated in Britain. In particular, I did not find anybody who thought that capital gains would ever be taxed like ordinary income in Britain. Most experts agree that the numerous savings incentives should be eliminated, but the government is actually going in the opposite direction.

A new plan to encourage profit-sharing in private industry was proposed by the government on July 15, 1986. This plan implements in a modest way the restructuring of employee compensation to promote greater flexibility in wage and hiring practices, along the lines originally proposed by Martin Weitzman of MIT. The government plan (called PRP: profit related pay) would provide a tax-exemption for one-fourth of any compensation received under a profit arrangement, up to five percent of regular compensation or £1,000, whichever is smaller. The plan will be implemented in 1987 if the reactions of business, labor, and the public are favorable and if there is assurance that a significant number of firms will take advantage of the scheme.

The government has also proposed a radical revision of local government taxation, which has not been well received. The main source of local government tax revenues are the "rates" imposed on households and business enterprises. These rates are similar to a property tax, except that they are expressed as a percentage of the rental value of the property rather than its market or assessed value. Like the property tax, the rates are criticized because they are based on outdated rental values and discriminate among different properties.

The government proposes to replace the rates for households by a poll tax (initially £50 per person) and to introduce a uniform business rate system throughout the country which would be distributed to local authorities on a per capita basis. The block grant system would also be revised to provide grants on the basis of "need" alone. Finally, a safety net grant system would be enacted to ensure that no local authority would lose or gain in the first year of transition to the new system. The safety net grants would in subsequent years remain at a constant cash level, which means that their value would be gradually eroded by inflation. The government proposal has been criticized on grounds of fairness both among households and different communities. (The government claims that the poll tax is no more regressive than the rates paid by households, but this is hotly disputed.) The proposal seems to be dormant and is not likely to be introduced before the next election.

VII. Canada

Canada has recently reduced its corporation tax rates and eliminated its investment tax credit. It has also introduced a generous life-time exemption of $500,000 for capital gains. The major tax reform now under serious consideration is the substitution of a business transfer tax for the manufacturer's excise tax. The government is considering tax base broadening and individual income tax rate reductions along U.S. lines, but the Minister of Finance would have to reverse his field to implement such an approach.

1. Indexation

Canada indexed the personal exemptions and individual income tax rate brackets between 1974 and 1985. Proponents expected indexation to restrain the growth of expenditures, but expenditures continued to rise at a rapid rate and the deficit is now at a very high level.

Even though it was generally popular, indexation was limited recently to raise revenues. Beginning in 1986, the adjustment will amount to the excess of the change in the consumer price index over three percent.

Indexation never applied to personal taxation of capital income or to corporate taxation. Ad hoc anti-inflationary tax provisions (e.g., accelerated depreciation, low taxes or no taxes on capital gains) created more problems, but the only attempt to adjust the tax base for inflation (by combining indexation with full taxation of real capital gains of assets held in special accounts) got nowhere. There are no pressures yet to restore full indexation of the exemptions and rate brackets because inflation has moderated.

2. Treatment of the Family

The Canadian individual income tax is levied on an individual basis; and there is little support for converting to a family base. Nobody seems to be concerned that taxpayers split their income with their spouses to minimize tax liability. Problems in individual taxation are more evident at the low end of income scale—where there is poor integration of taxes and transfers. The government expects to prepare a white paper on taxes and transfers.

3. Capital Gains

The 1985 budget introduced a lifetime exemption for realized capital gains, with a phase-in over a six-year period. The exemption begins at $10,000 per taxpayer in 1985 and rises to $500,000 in 1989. Capital gains above these limits are taxed at half the rates on ordinary income. Opinion is almost unanimous that this generous treatment of capital gains will have serious revenue consequences. Investment counselors are already advising clients to take advantage of the lifetime capital gains exemption now because of the possibility of changes. There are already shifts of property within the family to cash in on multiple lifetime exemptions.

4. The Corporate Tax

The corporate tax rate in Canada is being reduced from 46 percent to 43 percent (from 43 percent to 40 percent in manufacturing) by 1989. Canadian recipients of dividends from Canadian corporations are allowed a dividend credit to reduce the double taxation of dividends. Dividends are grossed up by 50 percent and the taxpayer deducts the gross-up as a tax credit against his final tax. Beginning in 1987, the dividend credit will be reduced from 50 percent to 33-1/3 percent to avoid giving relief where corporate tax was not paid. This reduction in the dividend rate was combined with a reduction in the tax rate on small corporations. As a result, the present situation (at the Federal level) is approximately full integration for small companies, underintegration for large taxpaying companies, and overintegration for large non-taxpaying companies. Taking into account provincial taxes, the position is less clear-cut. For example, there is overintegration at the small business level in Ontario and Quebec.

The major problem of the system is that dividend tax credits are given whether or not corporate taxes are paid, thus giving rise to the overintegration problem. An advance corporate tax along European lines would deal with the problem, but Canadians want to avoid giving the credit to foreign shareholders. Moreover, dividend relief is regarded primarily as an incentive measure (to promote equity investment) and only secondarily as a device to eliminate double taxation.

5. Investment and Capital Income

As in most countries, Canada provides investment incentives through the tax system. The incentives include an investment tax credit of seven percent (10 percent for designated slow growth areas and 20 percent for the Atlantic provinces and the Gaspe). The credit will be phased out beginning in 1987, except for investment in the slow growth areas, the Atlantic provinces and the Gaspe.

In the 1986 budget, the Minister of Finance justified elimination of the investment credit on the ground that it is desirable to reduce disparities in effective tax rates across types of assets and industries. Business in general is not upset about the elimination of the credit, particularly since it was coupled with a cut in the corporate rate from 43 to 40 percent for manufacturing corporations and from 46 percent to 40 percent for other corporations (to be phased in between 1987 and 1989) and generous treatment of R&D will remain.

Manufacturing corporations are subject to a corporate rate that is three percentage points lower than the general rate. The lower rate on manufacturing was a direct response to the adoption of DISC (and later FISC) in the United States.

The Canadian income tax contains a number of provisions designed to promote saving. Employer contributions to registered pension plans (RRPs) are not taxable up to $3,500 a year per employee; employees are allowed to contribute an equal amount tax-free. For workers not covered by pension plans, deductions are allowed for contributions to registered retirement savings plans (RRSP) up to $7,000 of earned income.

Tax-exempt limits on employee contributions to RRPs and RRSPs are being increased gradually from $7,000 in 1986 to $15,550 in 1990. In addition, $1,000 of interest and dividend income from Canadian sources and the first $1,000 of pension income are not taxed.

It is not clear whether the incentives for saving have accomplished their objectives. Some tax experts believe that total saving has not increased as a result of the tax incentives. However, the share of savings in sheltered form (mostly retirement savings) has increased sharply, and support for the retirement saving provisions is widespread.

6. Estate Tax

The Federal government withdrew from death and gift taxes in 1972 because it was frustrated in trying to administer them in a

Federal-provincial system. Since then, all the provinces except Quebec have dropped them in competition with one another. Curiously, in contrast to the United States and Europe, capital gains transferred by gift or at death are taxed in Canada, although they will be exempt in large part as a result of the lifetime exemption.

Even though there is no estate tax, it is argued that capital is *not* taxed relatively lightly in Canada. When all forms of taxes on capital income (i.e., personal, corporate, and property) are taken into account, the total effective marginal tax rate on capital income is close to 50 percent. However, these calculations were made *before* the recent changes in the tax law, in particular before the corporate rate was reduced, the lifetime exemption for capital gains was introduced, and the limits on employee contributions to pension plans were raised.

There is little concern in Canada about increasing concentration of wealth. In fact, the Minister of Finance has said that there are not enough rich people in Canada.

7. The Value-Added Tax

A general consumption tax is being seriously considered in Canada as a substitute for the manufacturers excise tax, which introduces distortions and is bitterly resented by manufacturers. The tax being considered is the business transfer tax (BTT)—a value-added tax which is calculated by subtracting purchases from sales to obtain value added. Experts in the government believe that this type of tax is easier to administer than the invoice-type VAT, which is used in all European countries. Moreover, VAT is unacceptable because of the opposition of the provinces, all of which levy a retail sales tax.

8. The Social Security System

There is a great deal of emphasis on private pensions in Canada, as well as on social security. Canada will have the same social security problems as the United States in the 21st century, but nobody seems to worry about this.

9. Tax Reform

As already noted, major tax changes are already scheduled to take place over the next few years. The investment credit is being eliminated and the corporate tax rates are being lowered. The capital gains tax is being sharply reduced by the introduction of the $500,000 lifetime exemption. The introduction of a BTT has been temporarily deferred for political reasons, but the government is still interested in this type of tax. Action along the lines of the tax reform in the United States is supported by tax experts inside and outside the government, but the government has been moving in the opposite direction since it took office in 1983. However, the Canadians are impressed by the impending reductions of the individual and corporate tax rates in the United States and are planning to cut their own rates as a result.

VIII. Japan

Japan's tax system is very much like that of the United States. Revenues are derived primarily from the individual and corporation income taxes. Consumption taxes are confined to selected excises, and there is no general sales or value-added tax. Income tax rates are high in Japan, but effective tax rates are relatively low because the tax base has been eroded by a bewildering variety of deductions and tax preferences. The big issue in Japan today is whether to add a value-added tax to the system in order to reduce the budget deficit.

1. Indexation

Japan has never explicitly adjusted its income tax rates and personal exemptions for inflation. Instead, it has relied on discretionary reductions in tax rates and increases in exemptions to offset the effect of economic growth, as well as inflation, on effective tax rates. During the 1960s and 1970s, these tax cuts were made virtually every year. The annual tax cuts have now been abandoned, but adjustments are made periodically as revenues permit. With inflation under control, the tax authorities are not under any pressure now to index the tax system.

2. Treatment of Earnings and Other Income

The nominal income tax rate schedule starts at 10.5 percent and rises to a maximum of 70 percent (88 percent if prefectural and local taxes are included). However, because of the generous deductions and exemptions which are provided for various taxpayer groups, effective tax rates are not nearly as high as these rates suggest.

Earnings are taxed on an individual basis in Japan, while other income is taxed on a family basis. In practice, other income is either not taxed at all (there are exemptions for interest on modest bank deposits and postal savings) or is taxed at relatively low flat rates. Three-quarters of all wage earners discharge their entire tax liability through withholding and do not file year-end tax returns. The tax authorities resist unification of taxes on earnings and other income, because they do not want to impose the requirement to file tax returns on the mass of wage earners.

A major obstacle to achieving equity among taxpayer groups in Japan is that there are considerable differences in compliance among different taxpayer groups. It is said that wage earners pay 90 percent of their tax, while self-employed businessmen pay about 60 percent and farmers only about 40 percent. To narrow these differences, wage earners are given a special deduction, starting at 40 percent of earnings up to 1.65 million yen and declining to five percent on earnings in excess of 10 million yen. Although the tax authorities agree that a frontal attack on noncompliance would be more appropriate, they believe it would be politically impossible to eliminate the special wage earner deduction.

3. The Corporate Tax

The central government levies a tax of 43.3 percent on undistributed corporate profits and 33.3 percent on distributed profits. Beginning April 1, 1987, the rates are scheduled to drop to 42 percent and 32 percent, respectively. The prefectures and local governments have their own taxes on corporate profits, bringing the maximum corporate rate up to about 53 percent. Small corporations are taxed at reduced rates.

There is further relief for dividends at the individual level, where a tax credit of 10 percent of dividends is allowed. In combination, the tax credit and the reduced corporate rate eliminate the double taxation of dividends. This procedure could be simplified by reducing the corporate tax rate on distributed earnings to zero or by giving a full credit for dividends at the individual level. However, the Japanese do not seem to regard this as a major problem, and there are no plans to revise this structure.

4. Taxation of Income from Capital

Japan is noted for its use of tax incentives to promote economic objectives. In fact, it has codified most of its tax preferences in one statute, called the Special Tax Measures Law, which is modified from time to time as the government's objectives change. The special measures include tax exemption for interest on modest amounts of saving, deductions for savings set aside to purchase homes, and deductions for insurance premiums. In addition, capital gains from security transactions are completely free of tax and, as already noted, taxable interest and dividends are subject to a low, flat rate.

At the corporate level, Japan has the usual gamut of investment incentives, including an investment tax credit, accelerated depreciation, a number of credits for research and development expenditures, and generous tax free-reserves for bad debts, employee bonuses and retirement benefits, and losses on inventories, natural resource development, and other approved activities. The variation in tax rates among different assets and industries must be enormous, but the Japanese have not made calculations to quantify this state of affairs. Nor have the Japanese tax authorities shown any interest in making the tax system more neutral.

In an unpublished paper, John B. Shoven and Toshiaki Tachibanaki have calculated the effective marginal tax rate on income from capital in Japan. They find that there is a low rate of tax on capital income at the individual level and a high rate at the corporate level. In addition, the degree of reliance on debt is much higher in Japan than in other countries, thus reducing the tax on returns to equity capital. In combination, these characteristics add up to a relatively low average effective marginal tax rate on a marginal dollar of investment by international standards.

5. Tax Reform

The Japanese have been talking about tax reform for the last several years because the central government has been running large deficits as compared to earlier years. However, they are proceeding cautiously because of the national fetish to achieve consensus before making major policy changes.

The Ministry of Finance has been promoting the adoption of a value-added tax to raise revenues for budgetary purposes. The government has been reluctant to move on this proposal for political reasons. The most recent Tax Advisory Council, which is very influential in Japan, endorsed the value-added tax, suggesting that the tax will be introduced soon.

The Japanese have been greatly impressed by the progress made in the United States to broaden the income tax bases and lower the tax rates. However, they believe it would be difficult to transfer the U.S. experience to Japan. The special provisions they have adopted are delicately balanced to achieve rough equity among different taxpayer groups, and it would be difficult to make major revisions without upsetting this balance. However, the ruling Liberal-Democratic party has already announced that it will propose taxation of currently tax-free savings accounts at a 20 percent rate. There is also considerable interest in reducing the marginal tax rates, particularly those at the top. The goal seems to be a top rate of 50 percent (not including the local income taxes).

IX. PROSPECTS FOR TAX REVISION

The tax systems of Europe, Canada, and Japan are clearly in need of reform both to improve equity and to eliminate the economic distortions generated by tax preferences. Tax rates in these countries are high, but it is claimed that there is not as much room for base broadening to finance significant rate cuts as there was in the United States. Nevertheless, the U.S. tax reform has greatly impressed politicians and tax experts alike, and much soul-searching is going on about the practicability of the U.S. approach in the various countries.

The skepticism about the potential of base-broadening stems in part from the different perspective of tax officials in other countries. For example, capital gains on financial transactions are, in general, not subject to tax or are taxed at preferential rates, and few people believe that it would be politically feasible to tax them as ordinary income even at much lower rates than those now in effect. Moreover, nobody believes that it is possible to tax capital gains in full and limit the capital loss deduction to anything like the $3,000 limit in the United States. The new U.S. restrictions on deductions for investment interest are also regarded as particularly severe in those countries that allow full deductions. The savings incentives are more vulnerable but the revenue losses from these provisions are said to be relatively small in most of these countries (except of course, for the favorable treatment of pensions, which was virtually untouched in the U.S. tax reform).

Despite the many problems inherent in their income taxes, the European, Canadian, and Japanese governments are not giving serious consideration to a consumption expenditure tax or cash flow tax as a substitute. A few academic experts in Sweden, West Germany, and the United Kingdom are actively supporting such a tax, but they have so far had little influence on government policymakers. Tax officials dismiss an expenditure tax both because consumption is already heavily taxed through the VAT and because the transition to an expenditure tax raises difficult equity and administrative problems.

Europe's heavy reliance on the payroll and value-added taxes is not likely to change in the foreseeable future. It is widely recognized that it is unwise to impose heavy taxes on labor at a time when unemployment rates are high, but payroll tax reductions are not in prospect because the revenues are needed to finance social welfare programs. The VAT is now firmly entrenched, and the only revisions likely to be made are removal of exemptions and multiple rates to simplify compliance and administration.

A number of countries are ahead of the United States in tax simplification in one major respect: elimination of the requirement to file tax returns by the large mass of wage earners. Japan has not required tax returns from the mass of wage earners for many years. Sweden has already decided to calculate taxable income and tax for all taxpayers beginning in 1987. The Dutch are considering the proposal of its tax reform commission to go to a two- or three-bracket income tax system, with the first bracket applying to about 90 percent of all taxpayers. This system would enable the tax collection agency to excuse about a third of their taxpayers from filing annual tax returns. The United Kingdom expects to simplify its withholding and filing procedures at the end of this decade, when a new computer system will be installed in the tax collection agency. In the United States, the Treasury is studying the feasibility of a return-free system, but it has not yet completed its investigation. These developments are being followed carefully in other countries.

Table 1

Tax Revenue as a Percent of Gross Domestic Product in Europe, Canada, Japan, and the United States, by Source, 1984[1]
(Percentages)

Country	Individ- ual Income	Corpo- rate Income	Payroll	Con- sump- tion[2]	Prop- erty	Wealth[3]	Total
Sweden	19.4	1.8	15.7	13.1	0.2	0.3	50.5
Netherlands	9.5	2.6	20.2	12.0	0.8	0.4	45.5
France	6.1	1.9	20.9	15.2	1.1	0.4	45.5
Italy	10.9	4.1	14.0	12.2	[4]	0.1	41.2
United Kingdom	10.5	4.1	7.2	11.6	4.2	0.2	37.8
Germany	10.5	2.0	13.7	10.5	0.4	0.6	37.7
Canada	11.6	3.0	4.3	11.5	3.1	0.2	33.7
United States	10.2	2.1	8.4	5.3	2.7	0.2	29.0
Japan	6.7	5.8	8.1	4.9	1.5	0.3	27.4

Source: Organization for Economic Co-operation and Development, *Revenue Statistics of OECD Member Countries, 1965-84* (Paris: OECD, 1986). Figures are rounded.

[1] Includes national and local taxes.

[2] Includes sales, value-added, and excise taxes, import and export taxes, taxes on transfers of property and securities, other transactions taxes paid by enterprises, and miscellaneous other taxes.

[3] Includes annual net wealth taxes and estate, inheritance, and gift taxes.

[4] Less than 0.05 percent.

Table 2
Top Individual Income Tax Rates in Europe, Canada, Japan, and the United States, 1986[1]
(Percentages)

Country	National	Local	Total
Sweden	50	30	80
Netherlands	72	—	72
France	58	—	58
Italy	62	6[1,2]	68
United Kingdom	60	—	60
Germany	56	—	56
Canada	46	2–8	48–54
United States	50	0–6[1]	50–56
Japan	70	18[1]	88

Source: Brookings Comparative Tax Project. Figures are rounded.
[1]Net tax rate after taking into account deductibility of state and local taxes in computing taxable income for the national government.
[2]Applies only to unearned income.

Table 3
Scheduled Changes in Corporation Income Tax Rates in Europe, Canada, Japan, and the United States, 1984-1989
(Percentages)

Country	1984	1985	1986	1987	1988	1989
Sweden	52	52	52	52	52	52
Netherlands	43	43	42	42	42	42
France[1]	50	50	45	45	42	42
Italy[1]	46	46	46	46	46	46
United Kingdom[1]	50	45	35	35	35	35
Germany[1]	56[2]	56[2]	56[2]	56[2]	56[2]	56[2]
Canada[1]	46[3]	46[3]	46[3]	45[3]	44[3]	43[3]
United States	46	46	46	40	34	34
Japan[1]	43[4]	43[4]	43[4]	42[4]	42[4]	42[4]

Source: Brookings Comparative Tax Project. Figures are rounded.
[1]Credit is provided under the individual income tax for corporate tax paid on dividends.
[2]Rate on distributed earnings is 36 percent.
[3]Rates on manufacturing corporations are three percentage points lower.
[4]Rate on distributed earnings is 33 percent in 1984-1986 and 32 percent thereafter.

CHAPTER 2

Sweden

Krister Andersson

INTRODUCTORY REMARKS

In this paper, I will describe the major features of the Swedish tax system and give measures of the distribution of the tax burden. The paper does not try to cover all details of the system nor does it cite all of the research on the tax system.

Section I deals with the individual income tax. Some of the rules concerning corporations are included in this section as well if they also apply to self-employed businessmen. Section II describes the wealth tax and section III the payroll taxes.

Sweden has a value-added tax and that is the topic of section IV. Other indirect taxes are also treated in that section Special rules for corporations are treated in chapter V and local taxes in section VI.

Some of the effects of the tax system (and to some extent the transfer system) is the topic of the following three sections. In section VII, the treatment of savings and investments in general is handled. There, special rules for financial institutions are pointed out. In 1983, the households and businesses paid SEK 154,000 million in direct taxes but the national government only received SEK 48,000 million of this and the rest went to local governments. The indirect taxes amounted to SEK 110,000 million. The value-added tax contributed towards that by some SEK 50,000 million. Another SEK 96,000 million were paid in social security fees. More details about the taxes and their distribution are given in section VIII. Not all activities in society are taxed. The hidden economy is the topic of section IX. Some estimates of its size are cited.

Finally, in section X, some of the proposals for tax reform are reported.

I. THE INDIVIDUAL INCOME TAX

1. The Basic Structure

There are two individual income taxes in Sweden, one paid to the local government and one to the national government. The local one is proportional for incomes above SEK 7,500 and it yields larger tax revenues than the national one. The government establishes the rules for calculating this tax but each local government sets its own tax rate. The national tax is progressive and allows no basic deduction. The actual tax rules for the local and the national income taxes are largely the same. The differences which do exist will be pointed out in the chapter for local taxes.

The personal income tax is based on realization and it is mainly calculated in nominal terms. An income becomes taxable if it can be assigned to any of the six categories of income mentioned in the tax code. These categories are as follows:

- farm income;
- income from self-employed businesses;
- income from owner-occupied dwellings and houses and rent income;
- wage income;
- capital income for example dividends, received interest payments, assets abroad, etc.;
- capital gains, income from temporary activities.

Within each category of income, there can be several sources of income (*forvarvskallor*). If a person has two discrete sources of income which fall into the same category of income, these sources must be considered separately in tax calculations. They have to be kept apart, primarily for the purpose of the local tax. A deficit in one source of income in one county, although within the same category of income, is not deductible from a surplus in another county when the local tax is calculated. As we will see later on, the payroll tax is based on the net result of a self-employed business and since it is not possible to even out the results when calculating the payroll tax (deficits against surpluses), social security contributions will have to be paid on the business that yields a surplus. Furthermore, a deficit in one source of income, although deductible when the tax is calculated, is limited in value. For a person with a marginal tax rate of say 80 percent, the deficit will not be deductible against his marginal tax rate. The upper limit for the value of deficits is set at 50 percent. In general, each unit (farm, apartment building, etc.) which is independent is considered to be a source of income. If several units are run together, they may be considered as one source of income. All wage income is always considered as one source of income no matter how many employers the person has. The category capital income is divided into two sources of income. The first is dividends, interest payments, etc. and the second is income from self-employed businesses and apartment buildings abroad.

2. Requirements for Filing Tax Returns

For wage earners the tax form must be handed in on February 15 of the year after the income year. Farmers and self-employed businessmen have to file by March 31. Everybody with a taxable income exceeding SEK 6,000 or a wealth exceeding SEK 400,000 or a person who owns a house must file. However, special rules apply to pensioners and to seamen. A person with an income lower than SEK 6,000 but whose spouse files must also file.

The main criterion for judging who is taxable in Sweden and who is not, is the concept of residency. Citizenship has, in principle, no importance. However, Swedes who leave the country may be taxable in Sweden if they still have a strong link to the country. Such links are, among others, family or business or a permanent dwelling (not summer house) in the country. It is presumed that for five years after the departure, the person is taxable in Sweden unless he can show that there is no strong link to Sweden. On the other hand, Swedes who temporarily leave the country for at least six months on a job contract to work abroad will not be taxable in Sweden (some governmental employees are excluded).

3. Which Incomes Are Taxable?

Some incomes are excluded from income taxation. Inheritances and gifts are taxed through a special tax. The rates for taxing these vary according to how close a relative the giver is. Some lottery money and scholarships are also tax-exempt. That is also the case for received life insurance money. In most cases insurance received for damage or fire is tax-exempt. Income from subsidies is also tax-exempt. For instance, all parents with children under the age of 16 receive a child subsidy (SEK 400/month, 800/month for each child if more than three children). Other tax-exempt subsidies are rent subsidies, social welfare, unemployment subsidies from the government, payments to handicapped persons, etc. All other incomes are, in principle, taxable.

4. Which Deductions Are Allowed?

Deductions are allowed for expenses necessary for obtaining income. The Swedish tax code states that the tax authorities should try to treat similar cases similarly in order to make the taxes "fair." Nevertheless, in recent years, there has been a tendency to give general deductions in order to simplify the tax forms. These deductions have been applicable to all except those who claim larger deductions. The simplification has also meant that only expenses over a certain level are deductible for some items. A general deduction of SEK 3,000 (for incomes below 30,000 only 10 percent) has been introduced for 1986 for wage incomes. Dividend incomes are reduced by SEK 1,600 for each person (a general deduction).

Living expenses in general are not deductible. Capital losses (if for example one's house burns down) are also not deductible.

5. How the Taxable Income Is Calculated

Let us turn to the different categories of income and see how net income is calculated in each of them and how they are later added together in order to calculate the tax.

5.1. Wages and Dividends

Wages and dividends are taxed on a cash flow basis. They become taxable the year they are received/become available. Everything received from an employer is, in principle, taxable. Payments in nonmonetary forms are therefore included. Free housing, cars, and other larger benefits are always taxable. Options to buy stocks, etc. for a price less than the market value are also taxable. Despite these rules, there are a growing number of fringe benefits granted to employees.

Deductions from wage income, as mentioned earlier, are allowed for all costs which are necessary to obtain the income. That includes commuting costs and expenses for equipment which the employer does not provide but which is still necessary for the job. Increased living expenses are deductible even if the tax law is rather restrictive on this point. Costs for obtaining a job are not deductible.

Capital income is not only received interest and dividends, but also rent income from condominiums and income from housing/businesses abroad. But the returns on capital on housing in Sweden or on businesses are not considered capital income. They are taxed under separate categories of income.

In order to promote private savings, the government has, since the late 1970s, allowed special savings accounts where the interest received is not taxable. Two types are presently used. In one type, the savings are allocated to a fund which buys stocks. Different funds exist. The value of the shares in the fund will depend on how well the fund did during the year and will not be taxable except under the wealth tax. Another type is a savings account where the interest is nontaxable. For both accounts, the maximum savings amount is SEK 800 each month. A special one-time deposit of 5,000 is being allowed in early 1986. Besides these accounts, which all Swedes over the age of 16 can have, all interest and dividends are taxable.

Deductions are allowed for expenses exceeding SEK 1,000 in order to maintain one's portfolio. All persons are also allowed to deduct SEK 1,600 from their capital incomes. (They may not, however, do so to create a deficit).

5.2. Income from Farms, Self-Employed Businesses, and from Houses

Income from Houses. The tax code distinguishes between owner-occupied houses (including summer cottages) and apartment buildings. For owner-occupied housing an imputed value is calculated. The base for the imputed value is approximately 75 percent of the market value. The value is assessed by the tax authorities on an individual basis and changes about every fifth year. The imputed value follows a progressive scale with two percent added to the taxable income for the assessed value up to SEK 450,000, four percent for the part between 450,000 and 600,000, six percent of the part of the assessed value that is between 600,000 to 750,000, and eight percent for the remaining part of the value.

A special deduction is allowed for the house you actually live in (SEK 1,500) and interest payments on mortgages are fully deductible though their value might be limited (see section II.6 on how to calculate the tax).

For income from apartment buildings, other rules apply. They are taxed on received rent income. It is possible for the taxpayer to choose to be taxed either on a cash-flow basis or on value according to the bookkeeping (accounting method) for this kind of income. In both cases, necessary expenses like maintenance, heating, and depreciation are deductible.

A new tax on houses, both private dwellings and apartment buildings, is being introduced gradually from 1985 to 1987. In 1985 the tax will be .17 percent of the assessed value of the house. The tax rate increases to .33 percent in 1986 and to .46 percent in 1987. For apartment buldings the rate is .66 percent from the beginning of 1985.

Income from Self-Employed Businesses. For income to be taxable in this category, three requirements have to be met. The business has to be independent, have a profit motive, and have some continuity. If the requirements are not met, the income will be classified as income in another of the six categories of income.

The accounting method is to be used. Only in rare cases is a cash flow method used. Deductions are allowed for all costs which are necessary to obtain the income. Depreciation on machinery and buildings is allowed. Machinery can be written off immediately if it will not last more than three years. If it lasts longer, it may be depreciated by 30 percent of the book value. With this method, the machinery will never be fully depreciated. An alternative rule can therefore be used. It allows depreciation by 20 percent of the purchase value on a yearly basis. This straight-line depreciation may not be used in conjunction with the 30 percent rule. For a single investment, it is profitable to switch to the 20 percent rule after three years. Yet another method is available. A depreciation of 25 percent of the sum of what the machinery was valued at last year on the tax form and the value of newly purchased equipment is allowed. This method has no link to the value of the machinery in the books. It is only a value for tax purposes without any connection to civil laws.

Depreciation for buildings is allowed by 1.5 percent up to five percent a year depending on the building material and how the building is used. Parking lots, etc. are deductible by 75 percent of the purchase value at a rate of five percent every year.

The inventory at the end of the year is added to the taxable income according to the accounting method (last year's inventory is deductible, so only the increase will affect the taxable income). Firms are required to value their inventories according to the FIFO principle. The inventory has to be valued at acquisition cost or market value, whichever is lower. However, write-downs are allowed up to a maximum of 50 percent (before January 1, 1984, it was 60 percent). A couple of supplementary rules are also possible to use. One of them only applies to raw material. The other is general and allows the firm to make write-downs by 50 percent of the average size of inventories over the past two years.

Besides the possibilities mentioned above, a new law was introduced in 1980 which allows firms to defer taxes by making allocations (consolidation measures) to a profit equalization fund. The size of the fund for each business is limited to 20 percent of the total wage costs. For self-employed businesses, an adjusted net income of the firm together with wage costs may be the basis. If the profit equalization fund is used, then the regulatory inventory write-down is limited to 35 percent instead of 50 percent.

The net taxable income of the self-employed business may, under some circumstances, be divided up among family members.

Income from Farming. Income from farming is, in many ways, treated like income from self-employed businesses. Since 1980, all taxes have been based on the accounting method. Cash flow is no longer the basis for taxation. In addition to income from farming, income from forestry and an imputed value of the residential part of the farmhouse are included as farm income. Products for personal consumption are also taxable.

Income from forestry is worth mentioning since its tax treatment is very special. Unlike in some countries the growth of the forest is not taxable. The income first becomes taxable when the trees are sold. Since the tax schedule is progressive (national tax), large quantities would be taxed very heavily. Special accounts called "forest accounts" are therefore allowed. They are held in a bank and the funds themselves plus interest first become taxable when they are withdrawn. This is one case where a sort of expenditure tax is used within the present Swedish income tax system.

Farmhouses are also given an assessed value every fifth year. For farmhouses (residential part) a regressive scale is used to calculate the imputed value. For 1984 the imputed value was 10 percent of the assessed value if this was lower than SEK 100,000. For the part of the value between 100,000 and 200,000, another six percent was added, and for values above 300,000, three percent was added (for example, for a house worth 400,000, the imputed value would be 19,000). The values are considerably higher than for private houses. For farmhouses, repairs are deductible at once and improvements are deductible through depreciation. This is not the case for private houses.

Deductions are, like for other categories of incomes, allowed for all necessary costs. Depreciations and inventory write-down are also allowed in the same way as for small businesses.

5.3. Capital Gains and Temporary Activities

Capital gains are treated differently depending on their source. The tax code distinguishes between three different kinds: capital gains from houses, from stocks, and from other property.

Capital gains from sold houses. The taxable capital gain is calculated in the following way. An indexed purchase value is deducted from the sales value. Improvements are also indexed and deductible. The indexation converts the historical values into present repurchase values. A special index for the housing sector is used. Since 1981 no indexation has been allowed for the first four years of ownership. Otherwise, only increased real, not nominal, values are taxable. In case of inheritance or gift, the previous owner's purchase value is used and the index is applied.

Other calculation methods are prescribed by the law and if they yield lower taxable profit, they can be used instead of the purchase value. One such method is to evaluate the purchase value of the house to 150 percent of the assessed value for the year 1952 or 150 percent of the assessed value 20 years before the sales year.

For those houses where annual depreciation is allowed (apartment buildings, farmhouses, etc.) the depreciations will be indexed as well and added to the sales value.

A special deduction of SEK 3,000 is allowed for residential houses for each year of ownership between the years 1952 and 1980. The indexation and special deductions may never create a deficit. Taxable capital gains can, in some cases, be postponed if a new, more expensive house is bought (capital gain has to exceed SEK 15,000 and owners must have lived in the house three of the last five years). The postponed gain will also be indexed (increases every year).

A loss may be deducted from other capital gains in any of the three categories mentioned above for a six-year period. But a loss can never be deducted from any regular income like wages or dividends and it may never influence earlier profits.

Capital gains on stocks. For long-term capital gains (holding period exceeding two years) only 40 percent of the profit/loss is taxable. There is no correction for inflation. An individual deduction of SEK 2,000 (3,000 and transferable to the spouse prior to January 1, 1986) is allowed. For stocks not owned two years, 100 percent of the profit/loss is taxable, but a deduction of SEK 1,000 from the gain was introduced January 1, 1986.

Capital gains on other properties. Bonds and personal property are among the sources of gain included in this category. The holding period will determine what fraction of the profit/loss will be taxable. If it is less than two years, 100 percent will be taxable, two but not three years, 75 percent, three but not four years, 50 percent, and finally, four but not five years, 25 percent. After five years the profit will be tax-exempt, except for condominiums which can never reach the zero bracket.

5.4. General Deductions

Besides deductions within each category of income, some further deductions are allowed. Among them are insurance payments for retirement. For retirement benefits, a certain deduction which is adjusted according to the inflation every year is established by the government. Therefore, for 1986 a deduction of SEK 23,300 will be allowed. For farmers and self-employed businessmen, a higher limit, depending on the net result in the firm, is applicable. Alimony and child support (maximum of SEK 3,000) are also deductible. It is impossible to deduct property lost due to theft, charitable contributions, or paid taxes.

6. How to Calculate the Taxes

The sum of the six categories of income minus general deductions is the taxable income. For single persons, the tax schedule can be applied to this sum. But for persons who are taxed together, a special division of the income into labor and capital income will have to be made. Labor income for a couple is taxed separately but the capital incomes are, in some cases, added together when the tax is calculated. The tax code does not follow marital status completely. Persons that are living together and have a child together will be taxed jointly. On the other hand, a husband and a wife who are living apart are taxed separately. The question of joint taxation has consequences for the tax rates applicable to capital income. The concept of A versus B income becomes relevant.

6.1. A Versus B Income

Income from labor is A income and capital income is B income. In practice, all wage income and income from farms and businesses where some work effort has been made by the taxed person is denoted A income. Such income is taxed separately. Other income like dividends, capital gains, rents, and income from farms and small businesses where no active work effort has been made is called B income. Every source of income in each category of income is either A or B income. No partial division is made.

The tax code was changed very recently. Both B incomes used to be taxed on top of the highest A income in all cases but since January 1, 1983, this is no longer the case. Now, the B income of the person with the lowest A income is added to the total of A and B incomes of the person with the highest A income and if this sum exceeds SEK 124,800, the tax rate will be based on that sum. If it is less, then each individual is taxed separately. To make it even more complicated the first SEK 5,000 of each person's B income is treated like A income. The system is very complicated and the tax authorities themselves would like to abolish the "extra tax" on capital income.

6.2. The National Tax Schedule

In connection with a reform of the income tax system in 1981, two tax schedules were introduced instead of one. It has become very difficult for the ordinary citizen to calculate his own taxes. The reason behind the introduction of the two schedules was to limit the value of deductions of deficits in one source of income against other sources. Such deficits could earlier be deducted to their full extent against one's marginal tax rate. The maximum value of such deductions was then limited to what a person with 50 percent marginal tax rate would get. Deduction of deficits made by a person with a marginal tax rate exceeding 50 percent will still only be worth 50 percent and a supplementary tax is calculated in order to limit the value. The second tax schedule is used for this purpose and for calculating the tax rate for high incomes (having a marginal tax rate exceeding 50 percent).

There is one important exception to the rule that the value of a deduction should never exceed 50 percent. If there is a deficit in the category income from houses in combination with a surplus in the category capital income (dividends etc.), then, the limitation does not apply. However, only SEK 30,000 may be deducted from the capital surplus at a tax rate above 50 percent. Any further deficit can only be deducted at 50 percent. This attempt to limit the value of large deductions (especially due to deductibility of nominal interest payments) cannot be offset by an even larger income within that source of income. For instance, an income would perhaps otherwise have been taxed at a rate of 80 percent but if deductions are made to lower the net result, the result will diminish and so will the tax rate.

When all of a taxpayer's net incomes are added up, two sums are calculated. One is for the national tax and one for the local tax. For most persons, these sums are almost identical. We will return to why they may differ in the section for local taxes. The local tax is often around 30 percent (in 1985 the average was 30.17 percent). For the national tax, two schedules are used. The first one, the basic schedule, ranges from zero percent up to 24 percent. Together with the local tax the range will go up to 50 percent. In addition, a supplementary schedule is used for some cases (see above).

The national tax schedule was fully indexed in 1979. A tax rate was determined for each bracket. The brackets were made up of "basic units" and they were adjusted every year according to the inflation rate. The law requiring automatic indexation went into effect in 1979 but was abolished in 1985. Despite the law, the tax schedule was actually only indexed in 1979, 1980, and 1982. From now on, the basic units will be decided upon by Parliament every year. The value is the same for 1986 as for 1985 despite Sweden's high inflation rate (in comparison with other OECD countries).

When the tax is calculated according to the tax scheme (and when the special tax treatment of capital income (B income) is taken into consideration), we need to consider some tax credits. A tax credit is given for 40 percent of the amount paid in union fees (maximum SEK 480). Another tax credit (SEK 1,800) is given to a married couple where only one of them is working. The same credit is given to a single parent. This is the only adjustment left from "family taxation." There are no special tax schedules or deductions for the numbers of dependents. As mentioned earlier, a tax-free child support is received from the government and rent subsidies (nontaxable) often depend on the number of children. But within the tax system, there are no special rules.

Further tax deductions are available for old and unhealthy persons with low incomes. The deductions are often small, but almost all medical expenses are paid by the government.

In some cases, a wealth tax will be added to the income tax (see that section for details). For self-employed businessmen and farmers, a social security fee will be added which corresponds to the payroll tax employers pay and is approximately 35 percent of the net result of the business. I will return to those fees later on.

7. Payment of Taxes During the Income Year

The employer withholds taxes for his employees. They have to show him a tax card in the beginning of the year showing that no old taxes remain. If any do remain, the employer will take them out of the worker's January through April salaries. A local tax chart shows the employer what local tax rate to withhold. The taxes and the payroll tax is then paid to the government each month.

Income from other employment or deductions may cause the withheld tax to differ from the final. In that case, it is possible and frequently the case, that the employee may apply during the income year to the IRS and receive a preliminary tax rate which corresponds to the estimated final one. The employer then withholds taxes based on that tax rate.

The tax form is filled out no later than February 15 the following year. In December, the final result is received and preliminary tax exceeding final tax is paid out. Special rules apply to farmers and businessmen. They deliver their taxes themselves every other month to the tax authorities based on a preliminary tax form for the year.

8. The Size of the Different Categories of Income

Table 2 shows the taxable incomes for 1982.

The figures above are the sum of positive net results. If a source of income runs a deficit it will not be included in the figures. Unfortunately, it is not possible to get information about each category of income where both negative and positive results are added together. Deficits are primarily in the categories of housing and capital. In 1982, the sum of the deficits was SEK 28,503 million. Income from capital, capital gains, and housing was some 20,000 million. The sum of the deficits within these categories was probably larger than the incomes. The net income from capital was therefore negative! However, this does not mean that the taxes were not important, rather the contrary. Other deductions, like payments for retirement purposes and others, added up to 5,916 million. The taxable income therefore became 370,604 million.

9. Summary

The six categories of income give the frame for the individual income tax. The tax code specifies when incomes are not taxable and when deductions are not allowed. The tax system is, on the whole, nominal but corrections for inflation are made in one case. That is the case when capital gains from houses are calculated. The imputed value of housing is also calculated in an inflation corrected way. The assessed value of the house is changed every fifth year. The tax schedule is no longer automatically corrected for inflation. All wages are taxable. They are, by far, the largest portion of the individual's taxable income. In fact, some years they represent almost 100 percent of all taxable income.

Dividends and received interest payments are taxed if they exceed SEK 1,600. Special savings accounts where the interest is not taxable are allowed but they cannot exceed SEK 35,000 in total and the monthly savings rate is maximized to SEK 800.

Capital gains are calculated on a realized basis. For long-term capital gains, on shares with a holding period of more than two years, only 40 percent of the profit is taxable.

The basic deduction (for local taxes) is SEK 7,500. After that, the tax rate is about 30 percent (proportional). The national tax is progressive and a total (local plus national) marginal tax rate of 50 percent is reached at an income of SEK 78,000. The highest marginal tax rate is 80 percent.

There is no special tax treatment due to the number of dependents. However, a tax credit of SEK 1,800 is given to a single income family. Capital income is co-taxed if the highest wage income in a couple plus capital incomes are above SEK 124,800.

II. TAXATION OF WEALTH

1. The General Wealth Tax

Sweden has an annual wealth tax. There is a special section on the income tax form for the wealth tax. The value of all assets as of the last of December have to be declared. Exceptions are the value of retirement insurance, furniture and kitchen devices for personal use, art, and stamp and coin collections. That means that the value of houses, cars, stocks, bonds, diamonds, savings accounts, etc. are all subject to the wealth tax. The assessed values of houses (should be 75 percent of the market value) is used.

For wealth in businesses and farms special rules apply. In principle, only 30 percent of the value is taxable by the wealth tax. Wealth of children under the age of 18 is added to their parents' wealth. A progressive schedule is used for the wealth tax.

The wealth tax raised 924 million in the budget year 1983/84.

2. Other Wealth Taxes

Besides the wealth tax described above, there are some other taxes linked to the possession of assets. There is, for example, a special tax on all forests. At the same time as farmhouses are assessed, a value is assessed for all farmland and forests. The tax is proportional and after a dramatic increase during the late 70s and early 80s, is presently .80 percent of the assessed value. The tax is deductible on the next year's tax form (from farm income). For the budget year 1983/84, this tax raised SEK 312 million.

Special fees have to be paid when property is bought or used as collateral. For the same budget year, they amounted to 1,659 million.

3. Inheritance Tax

There is a special inheritance tax in Sweden. It is progressive but a couple of different tax schedules exist. How close a relative one is determines which schedule is used. For the budget year 1983/84, it only raised SEK 757 million. The tax is very similar in its construction to the gift tax. For more information about the gift tax see the section below.

4. Gift Tax

Any gift exceeding SEK 2,000 within a year to the same person is taxable. In the case of furniture and personal belongings this limit is SEK 10,000. The tax is progressive and how closely related the donor and the recipient are will influence the tax rate. The tax raised 153 million in the budget year 1983/84. Houses are valued at the assessed value and stocks are presently valued to their value on the stock exchange that day. A governmental committee is revising the law (which is from 1914) and is proposing that stocks should be valued at 75 percent of the market value. The reason for this lower value is that a latent tax obligation is transferred. The first tax schedule concerns gifts to spouse, children, and grandchildren. Some examples of the rates are given below.

III. PAYROLL TAXES

Since the middle of the 1960s, the rate for social contributions has increased fivefold, from seven percent to 36 percent today and at the same time the base on which the rate is applied has become broader. In addition to those required by law, the unions have negotiated and received additional contributions.

The social security contributions decided by law are expected to yield some SEK 125,000 million for the budget year 1985/86. This figure should be compared to the expected tax revenues on incomes which are SEK 207,000 million and to the expected tax revenues on goods and services of SEK 154,000 million. If the social security contributions are included as tax revenues, they constitute 25 percent of the total tax revenues. The social security contributions apply both to employees and to self-employed businessmen/ farmers. For employees, the base for the fees is the sum of wages plus benefits (like free car, food, and lodging). Very few items are presently left outside the base (after changes in the mid-80s). For self-employed persons, the rules are a little bit different but on the whole equivalent. The base is, in this case, the net result of the income source.

The social security contributions are deductible for the employer as a wage expense and for self-employed persons from the income in that income source.

Through agreements with the unions the employers have agreed to pay another 5.86 percentage units on behalf of blue collar workers and 9.75 percent on behalf of white collar workers towards various benefits.

Soderstrom (1985) has studied the extent to which social security contributions are pure taxes. In order to classify a contribution as a work compensation and not a tax, the employees actually have to receive benefits from the contributions which they otherwise would not have received and the fees should not be "over priced." Following those two requirements, Soderstrom concludes that some 17 out of the 36 percentage units are not taxes. They are marked with a star in table 5. However, only half of the fee for Sickness Insurance should be included. In total, some 19 percentage units are a "pure tax".

White collar workers have often been in favor of increased benefits paid by payroll taxes instead of higher wages. One reason is that since their marginal tax rate is relatively high, the net result of a wage increase would be rather low and it might not be sufficient to finance the same benefits in a private way.

The General Wage Fee was introduced on January 1, 1983 to finance a tax reform which yielded lower marginal tax rates for low- and middle-income earners.

Literature. There are only a few studies made about the influence of increased social security contributions on wages and prices. Normann (1983) studied whether the social security contributions influence the wages. The study covers hourly wages within industry from 1952 to 1978. The results indicate that the evolution of the fees does not help to explain the development of the wages. Another study has been made by Holmlund (1982). It covers the period between 1951 to 1979 and concerns the development of hourly wages for full-time workers in mining and manufacturing industries. The coefficient for the social security fees is statistically significant and approximately equal to -.5. It should be interpreted as the percentage change of the total labor cost when the fees are changed. If the fees are say 40 percent at time t = 0, and if they increase by one percentage units the reduction in wages will be .5 percent of $1/(1 + .4) = .71$, i.e., 35 percent. However, it is difficult to judge how reliable the results are. In Soderstrom (1985), different assumptions are made for the incidence of social security contributions together with a description of the actual Swedish system. Both Normann's and Holmlund's work are mentioned in that paper.

Extensive work on whether the Swedish pension system is a transfer system or insurance has been done by Kruse and Stahlberg (1977). A life cycle perspective is used. In Stahlberg (1985), further research is reported. She concludes that part of the pension system has redistributed income from white collar workers to blue collar workers and from men to women.

IV. THE VALUE-ADDED TAX

1. General Remarks About the Tax

The Swedish value-added tax (called *Mervardeskatt* or MOMS) is of a consumption type and is based on the destination principle. Its predecessor, a retail sales tax, was introduced in 1960 at a rate of 45. It was converted into the present type of value-added tax (VAT) in 1969 with a rate of 10 percent. The percentage rate has increased over the years and since January 1, 1983 it has been 19 percent (tax inclusive). The tax is delivered to the government by the corporations who successively collect the tax through the production cycle. Each company adds the tax onto its price but the part of their purchase price, which was tax, is deductible. The difference between amount of received VAT and paid VAT is the tax liability of that particular firm. The tax covers roughly 70 to 80 percent of private consumption. The tax rate is nominally uniform, but partial or total exemptions cause some differentiation in effective rates.

All exports are excluded from the VAT. The main rule in the tax code is that goods are taxable unless explicitly exempt. The opposite applies to services. Producers within the public sector are excluded from the tax. This naturally influences the possibility of private corporations competing in these areas. The sellers of some commodities are exempt from taxation. They will thereby neither pay nor get any refund on taxes paid by their suppliers. Commodities in this category are housing, energy, newspapers, health care, and entertainment. Among services that are excluded are those provided by cab drivers, doctors, veterinarians, lawyers, child nurses, banking and insurance services, teaching, etc.

In some cases, only 60 percent of the value is subject to tax. That is the case, for example, for work on houses (construction or repair). In other cases, only 20 percent of the value is subject to tax. Exterior work, like creating a parking lot, road work, bridges, harbors, water or sewage pipes, etc., are such examples. This kind of differentiation seems to have worked out rather well. Nevertheless, there are, of course, a number of examples where the tax rules create difficulties. One such example is within the restaurant sector. A pizza served to be eaten at the restaurant is subject to a tax on only 60 percent of its value. The same pizza picked up and eaten outside the restaurant is subject to full tax.

Self-employed businessmen and farmers with an annual sale not exceeding SEK 30,000 do not have to register for the VAT. Paid value-added tax in those cases will be deducted as a business expense and received VAT as business income.

For firms registered for the VAT, the obligation to pay the tax occurs when the business transaction enters the books (accounting method). The cash flow method is basically not allowed any more. Tax returns are submitted every two months unless annual gross sales are less than SEK 200,000. The form is simple to fill out. Administration costs are very small in comparison to the revenues it generates. Some 80 percent of the total resources within the tax administration is spent on controlling the income tax although it yields less than 40 percent of the revenues (Nilsson, 1985). The value-added tax raised SEK 53,000 million in 1984 (Andersson, *et al.*, 1985).

A new retail sales tax on sales/purchases of stocks was introduced on January 1, 1984. The rate is .5 percent for the seller and .5 percent for the buyer. The tax is presently under debate in Sweden. No other country has a similar tax. It raised SEK 823 million in 1984. The tax will be doubled July 1, 1986 but it is still deductible when the capital gains tax is calculated.

1.1 Effects of the Value-Added Tax on the Price Level

An econometric study by Hansson (1980) suggests that the value-added tax is fully translated into higher prices within a quarter of a year. A multiequation econometric model taking into account market interactions, business cycles, and other policy measures developed by the Econometric Research Unit at the Economic Research Institute of the Stockholm School of Economics (1979) examines the tax increase in 1971 (from 15 percent to 20 percent). They conclude that the tax increase resulted in an increase in the implicit consumption deflator of roughly 2.5 percent after two years compared to no tax increase at all. However, the model does not include the institutional frame of labor market negotiations which is very important for Sweden.

1.2 Other Indirect Taxes

Some commodities are excluded from the value-added tax. In some cases, other indirect taxes are levied on such goods. Energy is such an example. Liquor and cars are others. The following table shows the major indirect taxes besides the value-added tax (table 6). They raised some SEK 39,000 million in 1984.

V. THE CORPORATION INCOME TAX

1. Construction and Rates

This section deals with incorporated businesses. It is by far the most important legal form of enterprise in Sweden. Corporations only have to pay national taxes. The rules changed January 1, 1985. Before that, they had to pay both local and national taxes. One year earlier, the national tax rate was lowered from 40 percent to 32 percent. Since the local tax was deductible when calculating the national tax, the nominal tax rate therefore went down from 58 percent to 52 percent (at a local tax rate of 30 percent). At the same time as the rates went down, the possibilities of making write-downs on inventory was reduced from 60 percent to 50 percent. Special deductions for research and development were abolished (see that section).

The national tax rate for corporations is proportional. The present rate is 52 percent. The Swedish corporate tax system has been, and still is, a classical system of company taxation. First, the corporation pays taxes and then, the recipients of dividends do. However, since the early 1960s some mitigation of this double taxation has been offered.

1.1. The 'Annell Legislation'

According to these rules, firms are allowed to deduct dividends on newly issued shares against current profits. Several restrictions apply. The sum of the deductions may not exceed the amount raised by the issue and the annual deduction may not exceed 10 percent of the amount actually paid of the issue during the taxable year. Deductions are allowed up to 20 years after the year when the shares were issued.

For companies not listed on the Stockholm Stock Exchange, there is another option since July 6, 1982. They are allowed a deduction of 70 percent on distributed dividends not exceeding SEK 1,000,000. The maximum amount of the deduction is therefore SEK 700,000. Another limit is that the deductions cannot exceed 15 percent of the equity capital in the company. The purpose was to create the same tax burden for a company whether it distributes its profit as salary or as dividends. If the Annell deductions are made, the deductions according to this law will be diminished by the Annell deduction.

Persons living in Sweden are taxed for dividends on their personal income tax form. Foreigners will have to pay a special tax (*Kupongskatt*) which amounts to 30 percent of the received dividends.

1.2. Effects of Dividend Relief on Equity Financing

The Annell legislation was changed in 1979 and the percentage rate went up from five to 10 percent deduction of issued equity capital during the last 20 years. In a study by Sodersten (1977), calculations are made on the impact on the demanded profitability of an investment with and without Annell deductions. For an investor with 70 percent personal marginal tax rate demanding 10 percent rate of return (this is assumed to be internationally determined) and a company facing a tax rate of 55 percent and only allowed five percent Annell deductions, the demanded profitability of an investment will be lowered by 19 percentage units due to the Annell deductions. The investor will receive the same return (105 percent) whether or not the Annell deductions are allowed on equity financing but the firm is willing to make investments which yield only 81 percent of what the firm would have demanded from an investment without those deductions.

A comparative study of the taxation of income from capital in the United States, the United Kingdom, Sweden, and West Germany was made in King and Fullerton (1984). It compares the effective tax rates levied on capital income. Different sources of financing are considered. The effective marginal tax rate for equity financing (new shares) at an inflation rate of 10 percent is reported to be 93.2 percent. The figure refers to the "Fixed p-Case" in which all assets earn a pre-tax real annual rate of return of 10 percent. The effective marginal tax rates for retained earnings and debt financing are 69.5 percent and 6.4 percent respectively. In the so called "Fixed r-Case," in which the yield to investors before personal taxes is the same for all investments, the effective marginal tax rate at 10 percent inflation is 94.1 percent for equity financing (new shares). Retained earnings and debt financing receive a rate of 91.2 and 13.4 percent respectively. Inflation was shown to reduce the real value of the Annell deductions.

Sodersten and Ysander (1983) show the difference between financing an investment by borrowed means and with equity financing. Requirements for tax neutrality between the two types of financing is explored. Opportunities for the companies to immediately write down and deduct investments would, in some cases, create neutrality.

1.3. Tax Allowances for Depreciation and Inventories

Inventories have to be valued at acquisition cost or market value, whichever is lower. The FIFO-principle has to be used but write-downs are allowed up to a maximum of 50 percent. Additional supplementary rules may be used. They are equivalent to the ones described for self-employed businessmen under the individual income tax. The rules of a "profit equalization fund" are also applicable here. They enable corporations with small inventories to also defer corporate taxes (based on the wage sum). However, the regulatory rules of inventory write-down still seem to be the most common method (Rundfelt, 1982).

Depreciation rules for machinery and buildings are described under the individual income tax. There is another immediate write-off method for incorporated companies. This system is called the investment fund system.

1.4. The Investment Fund System

During years with large profits, part of the profit can be paid into an account at the Central Bank. No taxes will have to be paid on that amount. The company can later, with general permission for all companies or with special permission, use the fund for investments. On the part of the investment which is financed in that way no depreciation will be allowed since an immediate write-down against the fund is made. The system therefore yields a tax deduction for future investments.

There are several investment funds today. The first one was introduced as early as 1938. Some of the funds are rather specialized (for ship building, damage due to fire, etc.). The most common fund is called "General Investment Fund." At most, 50 percent of the profit can be made into an investment fund. Of the reservation to a fund, 75 percent must be paid into a noninterest-making account. Deductions on the tax form are therefore allowed to be four-thirds of the deposit. In order to stimulate companies to use the system, special investment deductions are sometimes allowed (presently only for investments started before 1984). When the central government agrees to let the companies use the fund, such a deduction will be allowed. It amounts to 10 or 20 percent deduction of the means used from the fund.

The investment fund system was used extensively during the 70s and early 80s. The funds could be used for almost any kind of investment and a general permission to use them was often given.

A similar system is available for self-employed businessmen. The maximum deduction is 50 percent of the profit and it must not exceed SEK 10,000. The amount has to be deposited into a special account in a bank, which unlike other investment fund accounts earns interest.

1.5. The 'Profit Sharing Tax'

The "Profit Sharing Tax" is a special tax distinct from the ordinary corporate tax. It was introduced January 1, 1984 and only concerns corporations. It is an inflation-corrected income tax. The taxable income is calculated in three steps. The taxable income from the ordinary income tax form is the starting point.

Step one is to achieve a nominal result. From the taxable income (positive or negative), the income tax is deducted for the current year. Since a number of calculations have been made to obtain the actual declared profit, some corrections will have to be made. The result will have to be increased by:

- losses carried forward from earlier years,
- deductions due to dividends,
- investment subsidies,
- increase of write-down of inventory.

Step two involves a calculation of an inflation corrected result. The depreciations on buildings are based on historical purchase value. In order to evaluate them at repurchase value, a price index is used. No corrections are made for years before 1973 (a change in depreciation rules took place in 1973). For machinery, an infla-tionary deduction is allowed. The value of the inventories at the beginning of the year is multiplied by the inflation rate of the year. The value of the inventory at the beginning of the year is also multiplied by the inflation rate. An inflationary deduction is allowed on monetary means. Both assets and debts are considered and treated in a symmetric way.

Step three concerns a basic deduction. From the inflation corrected result, a deduction of either SEK 500,000 or six percent of the wage costs is made.

The inflation index used expresses the general price increase during that year. It is based on the consumer price index. The applied tax rate is 20 percent. A special form will have to accompany the ordinary tax form. The tax revenues from this new tax is expected to be SEK 1,500 million in 1984. For more details about the tax, see the Appendix.

VI. THE LOCAL TAX SYSTEM

1. Some Basic Facts

When Swedes fill out their tax forms, a taxable income for both the national and the local taxes is calculated. However, the corporations no longer pay any local taxes. The tax rules are to a very large extent the same and taxable income will only differ in some cases. The Parliament and the central government make the tax rules, but the local tax rate is determined by each county (*kommun*). There are 284 *kommuner* in the country. After the zero bracket which goes up to incomes of SEK 7,500, the tax is proportional. Rates from approximately 27 percent up to 34 percent exist. The average rate was just above 30 percent in 1985. It has increased dramatically in the late 70s and early 80s. Some *kommuner* have now started to lower their rates.

2. Primary and Secondary Kommuner

It should be mentioned that there are two types of *kommuner*, primary and secondary, and all Swedes belong to both types. The number of secondary *kommuner* is 23. Their main responsibility is health care. Of the tax rate of 30 percent, 12 to 13 percentage units are directed to the secondary *kommuner*. In 1983, 61 percent of their incomes was raised by taxes. Another 22 percent was financed by fees and different subsidies, and the rest (17 percent) was financed through subsidies from the central government (11 percent of which was in the form of conditional grants). Their budgets amounted to SEK 81,400 million.

Sweden has a state church. Paying taxes to the church is mandatory. Of the 30 percent tax rate, one to two percentage units are allocated to the church. While church membership is not mandatory, a part of the tax has to be paid anyway. The church keeps records on people's residency and handles some other administrative matters.

Let us return to the primary *kommuner*. They provide schools, including nursery schools; social care for the elderly; libraries; housing; maintenance of some infrastructure; etc. The local tax (15 to 17 percent) raises 42 percent of their total budgets. Another 26 percentage units are received from the central government (22 percentage units in the form of conditional grants). The remaining 32 percent comes from fees, business activities (housing, electricity, etc.) and loans. Their budgets in 1983 totaled SEK 160,000 million.

It is important to keep in mind that the local taxes only finance a fraction of what is provided by local authorities. The transfers to the *kommuner* were some SEK 48,000 million in 1983. The total transfers (final subsidies, not loans) grew twice as rapidly as the GNP between the years 1970 to 1983. In 1983, the transfers to households were SEK 192,000 million, to corporations 50,000 million, to organizations 8,000 million, and to foreign aid 5,000 million. Altogether, these transfers were 192,000 million or 27 percent of GNP.

3. Tax Rules

With the size of the transfer system in mind, let us turn to the tax rules for the local tax. There are no property taxes as they are usually defined. However, Sweden has an imputed value of housing and land. From this, mortgage payments are deductible and there are also some other deductions. This often leads to a deficit in this category of income. This deficit is deductible from other incomes. But despite the deficit, there is a special tax for houses at the local level. It is called a "guaranteed amount" and it is added onto the taxable income. The amount is 1.5 percent of the assessed value of the property. But, for persons with no other income, there will be no taxes on the guaranteed amount unless it exceeds SEK 7,500 since that is the basic deduction and no local tax is paid on amounts less than that.

Since the tax reform of 1971, local tax payments are not deductible when calculating the national tax or the next year's local tax.

Residency as of November 1 the year before the income year will determine to which *kommun* local taxes should be paid. A deficit in one source of income, say housing, in one *kommun* cannot be deducted from the income in another *kommun*. The right to use such deficits as deductions is limited to that particular *kommun*. If the person moves to the *kommun* where the house is, he can deduct the deficit, not only for the present year but accumulated over the previous six years.

VII. SAVINGS AND INVESTMENT

1. Tax Treatment of Savings in General and Its Effects on Required Gross Rate of Return

Returns on savings are heavily taxed in the Swedish tax system. Dividends are paid out of after-tax profit (except if Annell deductions are allowed). The personal income tax taxes dividends again. The basic deduction for capital income is SEK 1,600 and after that, nominal incomes are taxed at the personal marginal tax rate. Capital gains are first considered to be long-term after two years. Houses and condominiums are also taxable when sold but an inflation correction is made. Houses can, therefore, often be sold without having to pay any taxes.

The Swedish tax system influences the attractiveness of different assets. The effective tax rates are very different for different investments. Hansson (1978) has made calculations about these differences. Although the tax system has changed in several respects since his study, the basic differences exist today, too. Figure 1 shows the required gross rate of return (nominal) for an investor with a marginal tax rate of 60 percent in order to yield one percent real rate of return after taxes.

Figure 1
Gross Rate Needed To Achieve One Percent Real Rate of
Return at Different Inflation Rates

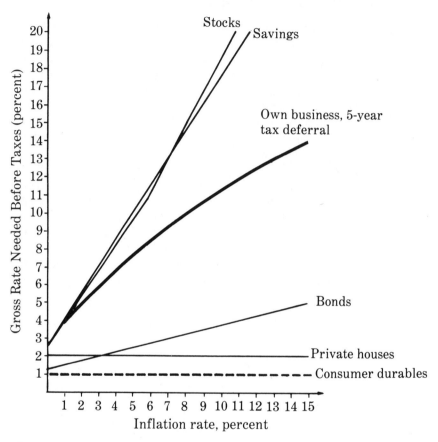

Source: Hansson (1978).

Taking into account the possibility of borrowing funds and full deductibility of nominal interest payments, the required gross rate of return in order to achieve one percent real rate of return after taxes is shown by figure 2. (The deductibility for deficits has been restricted since 1978 to a maximum value of 50 percent even if the marginal tax rate exceeds that.)

Figure 2
Gross Rate Needed To Achieve One Percent Real Rate of
Return at Different Inflation Rates Using Borrowed Funds

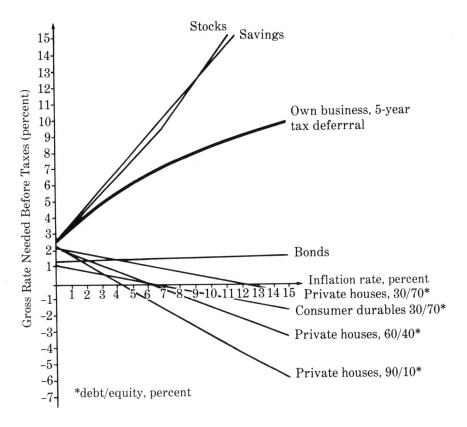

Source: Hansson (1978).

The Swedish tax treatment of capital differs also according to whether the capital is used in Sweden or owned by a Swede. For capital used within Swedish industry, Hansson (in Andersson, *et al.*, 1985) estimates that for the year 1979 the average marginal tax rate was 16 percent. If the capital was also owned by a Swede the rate is 50 percent. For labor income the average marginal tax rate (calculated as an increase of one percent of all labor income) was some 70 percent. For more details see the section about the distribution of the tax burden.

Investment within the household sector is often believed to be favored compared to investment in industry. But at the same time, different investments within the corporate sector receive different tax treatment. According to a study by Sodersten and Lindberg

(1983) which is included in the King and Fullerton report (1983), investments in machinery are favored compared to investments in inventory and buildings. Furthermore, investments in production industries are favored compared to commerce and other industry.

Agell and Sodersten (1982) analyze what the effective tax burden is for different investments. Investments in the corporate sector (machinery), housing, and in consumer durables are considered. Their model assumes one representative household, and a perfect capital market, where the nominal rate of return, i, is calculated according to the formula $i = r + p/(1 - m)$, where r is the real rate of return (assumed constant and set to two percent) and p is the inflation rate. At an inflation rate of 10 percent and with the representative taxpayer having a marginal tax rate of 60 percent, the nominal interest rate on taxable returns will have to be 30 percent in order to yield a real rate of return of two percent. The economy is considered to be closed. Their results indicate that debt financing is the most expensive form of financing (highest effective tax burden). Investments in industry at constant prices are favored by the tax system compared to investments in housing. Even at an inflation rate of 10 percent, investments in industry are favored if financed by undistributed profits compared to equity financed housing but not debt financed housing. This somewhat surprising result has been questioned by Hansson (1983) among others.

The King and Fullerton study (1984) has also made calculations of effective marginal tax rates. Some of their results have been described in the section about the corporate income tax.

The tax system tends to lock in capital in established companies. A concentration tendency, that is, fusions of less profitable companies, creates a few large industries within each sector. Newly started companies often face large difficulties.

Whether high taxes on the rate of return on savings increase or decrease the total level of savings depends on income and substitution elasticities for different groups in society. However, the relative price of consumption in the next period compared to consumption in the present period has gone up compared to what it would be in a neutral nondistorting situation (Andersson and Normann, 1985). The increased governmental pension systems have, according to Stahlberg (1983), resulted in a decreased private savings of 1.3 to four percent.

2. Savings Incentives

In order to increase bank deposits, the government has, since the late 70s, allowed Swedes to open special bank accounts where the earned interest is not taxable. These rules have been described in the section on wages and dividends.

Governmental bonds are issued at the market rate but an additional tax-free "bonus" is given. The number of these that an individual can purchase is limited. The Swedish tax and transfer system is otherwise not favorable to savings. On the contrary, savings often diminish the right to obtain most kinds of transfers like rent subsidies and pensions for the spouses of pensioners. Savings also make it difficult to get educational loans since the loans decrease if net wealth exceeds SEK 139,800 and are unavailable if net wealth is SEK 218,400. Special deductions within the tax system for pensioners are related to income and wealth (the deductions decrease when the individual wealth exceeds SEK 90,000). The transfer and the tax system together sometimes yield marginal effects of more than 100 percent.

3. Investment Subsidies

3.1. Extra Depreciation on Buildings

Besides the rules about depreciation and special investment funds mentioned under the corporate income tax, a couple of allowances should be mentioned.

An extra depreciation, in addition to the annual ordinary depreciation, is allowed on new buildings. It amounts to two percent each year for the first five years and it is called "primary deduction." The total time of depreciation for the building will therefore be shortened.

3.2. Treatment of Research and Development

In 1984, the law concerning a corporation's rights to deduct research costs and subsidies to research was changed. Corporations used to be able to deduct not only research directly linked to their own activities but also subsidies given to some institutions. Such institutions were universities, other public institutions, and private foundations. A special deduction of five percent of all research costs plus 30 percent of the increase of the companies wage costs for research and development was deductible.

On January 1, 1985, "Renewal Funds" were introduced. Corporations with a net (adjusted) profit exceeding SEK 500,000 had to deposit 10 percent of the profit into a noninterest paying account at the Central Bank. The fund has to be used for research and education of employees. The system was used to lower the liquidity of the corporations. The central government has to give its approval to the use of the fund. The labor unions in the company must also approve its use. The deposit is deductible from the corporate income tax. When the fund is used, the deposit is received and it is not taxable income. The expenses covered are, on the other hand, not deductible. Also, investments in machinery and buildings can be written off against the fund. The earliest time money can be withdrawn is in July 1986.

3.3. Governmental Subsidies to Corporations

We know rather little about which companies actually receive subsidies. According to the Central Bureau of Statistics (SCB), the total sum of subsidies (including local ones) in 1983 was almost SEK 50,000 million. Included in that sum are subsidies to farming of SEK 6,200 million, housing subsidies of SEK 9,400 million, subsidies to health care of SEK 5,500 million, and another SEK 6,000 million in support of public transportation.

Subsidies to companies in order to avoid bankruptcy amount to SEK 8,200 million. During the years 1976 to 1982, the shipbuilding industry received substantial amounts (SEK 14,500 million) and other industries 10,000 million.

Another kind of subsidy is used to avoid unemployment or lower the unemployment rate in general. In 1983 SEK 1,800 million was paid to Swedish companies for such purposes.

Investment subsidies and export guarantees amounted to 1,900 and SEK 1,700 million respectively. Another SEK 8,800 million is unclassified.

To add to the confusion, a slightly different view is given by the *Riksrevisionsverket*, (they report the economic outcome of the governmental activities). The central government's subsidies were, according to them, SEK 21,400 for the budget year 83/84 (*Riksrevisionsverket*, 1985). From their specifications, one figure is especially interesting. Subsidies to manufacturing, mining, and construction industries were SEK 2,700 million. To create employment, another SEK 4,400 million was spent.

4. Treatment of Financial Institutions

4.1. Tax Treatment of Received Dividends in General

In order to avoid multiple taxation, Swedish corporations in some cases are exempt from taxation of dividends which they receive. One requirement is that the company have at least 25 percent of the votes in the company that gave them dividends. The stocks must be held in the line of business. On the other hand, if the stock is held for pure dividend reasons without any link to the company's structure and organization the dividends will be taxable. The same rules apply to dividends received from abroad.

4.2. Special Rules for Financial Corporations

Corporations dealing with financial activities, like banking, face rules different from companies in general. They are only exempt from taxation of received dividends from similar companies which are directly linked to their own activities. Holding companies are taxed on all dividends which are not distributed further. Mutual funds are tax-exempt as long as they distribute 80 percent of their received dividends.

VIII. SOME STATISTICS

1. In General

The marginal tax rates in Sweden are high but the tax system allows individuals to deduct nominal interest payments which may be used to finance consumer durables or any private consumption. Although the value of such deductions in some cases may be limited to a value of 50 percent (in case of deficits), they open up possibilities of converting highly taxed labor income into considerably less taxed capital income. The asymmetric taxation of capital income has influenced the effective tax burden. One particularly important area has been capital gains from houses. The combination of interest subsidies from the government, nominal interest deductibility and the fact that taxes are imposed on capital gains after they are adjusted for inflation, all act in one direction. Increased marginal tax rates and rising property prices (partly due to the tax system) meant substantial profits for many during the 1970s. High income earners, especially, borrowed against their homes to finance other private consumption. The adjustment to the tax system resulted in low income earners becoming the ones declaring positive capital incomes while high income earners declared deficits. The value of the deductions exceeded the value of surpluses. The tax revenues could therefore, *cet. par.*, be raised by not taxing capital incomes! This problem will be discussed further in section X. But let us first make a summary of different statistics concerning taxable incomes, marginal tax rates, etc.

2. Aggregate Statistics

The tax share (taxes in relation to GNP) has risen dramatically since the 1950s. Figure 3 shows the development.

Compared to other OECD countries, taxes on personal incomes and payroll taxes are higher in Sweden than average. The tax shares and their distribution are reported in table 7. The figures show the deviation in percentage units from the average.

Figure 3
Tax Revenues in Relation to GNP: 1900 to 1985.

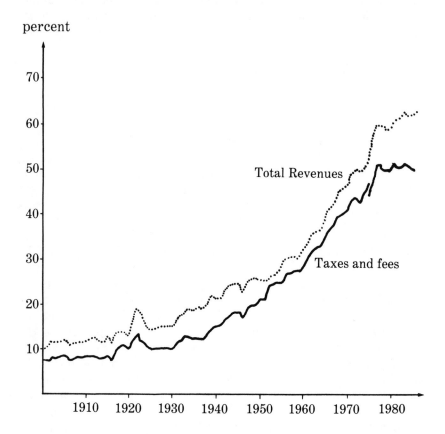

Source: Andersson, et al. (1985).

A classification of taxes on labor and capital for Sweden has been done by Hansson and Normann (in Andersson, *et al.*, 1985). Some 50 percent of the payroll taxes are considered to be pure taxes. Their results are shown in table 8.

Two comments should be made. The taxes total fraction of GNP is 50.7 percent. The difference between this and the figure in table 8 depends on how the payroll taxes are considered. In the table, only part of them have been considered to be taxes. The other comment is that the small share attributed to the corporate tax does not necessarily mean that the tax on equity capital in corporations is low. According to Normann (1985) the production factor capital is more heavily taxed than labor is.

The share of the corporate tax to GNP is low. Sodersten and Ysander (1984) have calculated the return to equity capital before taxes in the industrial sector and compared the nominal tax rate to the effective one for the years 1953 to 1982. No considerations have been taken for capital gains (losses) on financial assets (debts). Their results are shown in figure 4.

The total average marginal effect of an increase of labor income has increased dramatically over the years, even if a reduction has occurred recently. In Andersson, *et al.* (1985), figures are given for the total effect. Income dependent subsidies are taken into account and only the pure tax of the payroll tax is considered as a tax. The results presented in table 9 show the effect when all gross incomes increase by one percent.

Figure 4
Nominal and Effective Tax Rates for Industries 1953-1982

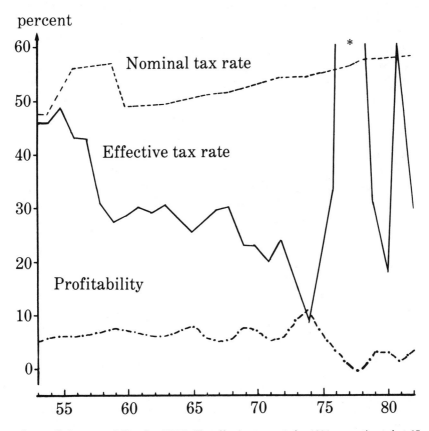

Source: Sodersten and Ysander (1984). The effective tax rate for 1984 was estimated at 15 percent (*Affardsvarlden*, 45/1985).
*Point cannot be plotted because profits were negative.

These high marginal effects are likely to influence the willing-
ness to work. According to a study by Blomquist (1983), the
Swedish income tax yields a 12 percent lower labor supply from
Swedish men as compared to a no-tax situation. Approximately
half of the reduction in labor supply is due to the progressivity.
Other studies within this field have been made by Stuart (1981),
Feige and McGee (1983), Hansson (1984), and Hansson and Stuart
(1985a). Hansson and Stuart show that both the tax that is
increased and the purpose for which it is increased are vital factors
when estimating adverse effects on the economy.

3. Distribution of the Tax Burden

3.1 The Distribution of Positive Net Results and Deficits

Before going into detail with statistics for different income
groups let us study how the sum of positive net results from all
categories of income is distributed. It should be noticed that no
deductions for any kind of deficits are included in table 10.

But deficits in some categories of income will change the result
in table 10. The evolution of such deficits is shown in table 11.

Of the 6.4 million who handed in tax forms, 2.5 million had
deficits in at least one category of income. Two-thirds of the
deductions (value wise) were from the category housing. The
amount of the deficits increase both relatively and absolutely by
income group.

3.2 Tax Shares for Different Income Groups

Within the work of the current Expenditure Tax Committee,
a comprehensive study of the tax burden has been made. A final
report is expected Spring 1986. Hansson and Normann (1985) have
calculated the tax share for different groups expressed as taxes
divided by gross income. The income measure is slightly different
from taxable income. Adjustments have been made so that only
inflation corrected income from capital is included and the imputed
value of housing is calculated as two percent of equity capital in
the house. Transfers are included (on an individual basis). The
number of family members has also been considered. One adult is
equal to .95 consumer units (c.u.) two adults 1.65 c.u., and each
child .4 c.u. The tax shares are measured in three different ways.
The first one is taxes divided by gross income per consumer units,
the second one is taxes divided by taxable income according to the
individual tax files and the third one measures the ratio of taxes to
gross income on the individual level. Table 12 shows these three
measurements.

It is notable how low the tax share is for the lowest decile when
the taxable income is used as the income measure. However, if

gross income per consumer unit represents the income, decile one will have a higher tax share than decile two. The tax share for high income earners is considerably less if gross income is used instead of taxable income. The incomes for each decile are slightly different for different measures of tax shares.

3.3. Distribution Over the Life Cycle

A couple of other studies treating one year in a person's life, one by Franzeen, *et al.* (1976) and one by Gustavsson (1984), showed that the income tax system and the transfer system together made the purchasing power more equal among people. However, if a life cycle perspective is taken, the redistributive element between people will be a lot less obvious. The tax system can, to some extent, be seen as a complement to the transfer system, reallocating resources over the person's lifetime. It can be illustrated as in figure 5.

Figure 5
Redistribution Over the Life Cycle

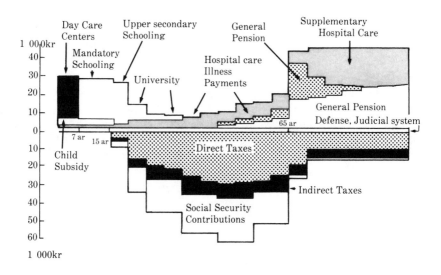

Source: SCB (1985).

As the person becomes older subsidies like free schooling, etc. are replaced by health care and pensions. During the active years, taxes are paid. For each person, the taxes are to some extent payments for previous and later rendered services. An element of insurance is also present since the so-called welfare state guarantees a certain standard of living. Whether the tax system actually redistributes from the "wealthy" to "poor" persons, is still a question (Soderstrom, 1984a, 1984b).

3.4. The Distribution of Wealth and the Influence of Capital Income on Taxes Paid

Only part of a person's wealth is taxable wealth. In Andersson and Normann (1983), the taxable net wealth is reported as SEK 724,000 million for 1979. Nontaxable wealth consists of human capital, pension claims, consumer durables, art, etc. In 1979, the undiscounted value of granted retirement benefits (pensions) was some SEK 1,500,000 to 2,000,000 million. Discounted by a factor of 25, they still amount to some SEK 800 million. The values on the tax form therefore only represent a part of each person's wealth. By studying that part, we can obtain some interesting results.

The influence of capital income on the tax base and thereby the amount of taxes paid has been discussed recently in Sweden (in Andersson, et al., 1985 etc.). As pointed out earlier, high income earners tend to deduct large amounts in interest payments. Yet unpublished material from the Central Bureau of Statistics (SCB) shows that low income earners would have to pay less in taxes if capital incomes were not included as taxable income. Table 13 shows preliminary results on how much less/more different income groups would have to pay in taxes if capital income were tax-exempt. The deciles in the table are arranged according to adjusted taxable income (some transfers and inflation corrections have been made). A positive amount indicates higher taxes.

The tax base is negative for taxation of capital with the present definitions of income. The tax revenues are therefore lower than if capital income were not taxed at all. It is interesting though to notice that low income earners report a positive income from capital while high income earners a deficit. Taxation of capital is therefore contributing in a negative way to the equalization of the after-tax incomes.

4. The Public Sector's Incomes and Expenditures

For the year 1983, the tax revenues on income were some SEK 48,000 million out of a total income of SEK 218,000 million for the national government. They therefore constituted 22 percent of the income. The VAT raised another 22 percent, followed by payroll taxes of 21 percent. Other indirect taxes on goods and services (energy, liquor, etc.) raised 18 percent of the total income. Figure 6 shows the different sources of income for the government.

Figure 6
Sources of Income in the Public Sector

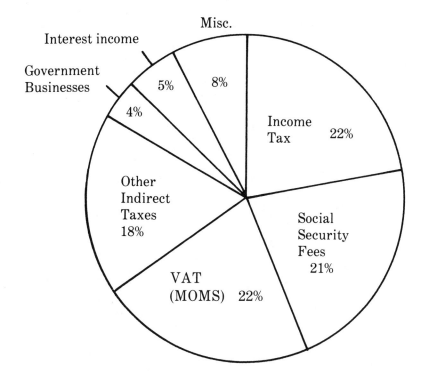

Misc.

Interest income

Government
Businesses

5%   8%

Income
Tax   22%

4%

Other
Indirect
Taxes
18%

Social
Security
Fees
21%

VAT
(MOMS)   22%

Source: *Riksrevisionsverket* (1984).

According to the budget presented in January 1986 for the budget year 1986/87, income taxes will raise 21 percent (SEK 61,400 million out of SEK 286,650 million) of the income. Payroll taxes raise 20 percent, VAT, 23 percent, and other indirect taxes on goods and services, 17 percent of the total income. Compared to 1983, revenues from governmental businesses are increasing (to 11 percent) and the tax on properties (wealth tax, inheritance tax, etc.) an increase of from two to four percent of the total income.

The expenditures (SEK 335,575 million) will exceed the income in the new budget. This will be discussed further.

The total amount of taxes and different fees paid by households and companies in 1983 was SEK 438,000 million. Their distribution is shown in figure 7.

Figure 7
Incomes and Expenditures in the Public Sector, 1983
(SEK billions)

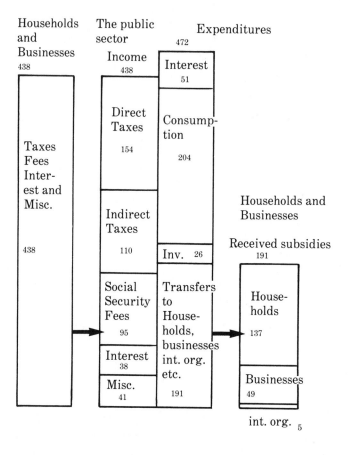

Source: SCB (1985).

The flows within the public sector are shown in figure 8. There are three sectors, the central government, local governments (primary and secondary *kommuner*), and the sector of social insurance. With this overall picture of income and expenditures, let us turn to an issue which has gained considerable attention in Sweden and elsewhere lately, the budget deficit. The local governments are not running a deficit but the central government is.

Figure 8
Transactions Within the Public Sector in 1983
(SEK billions)

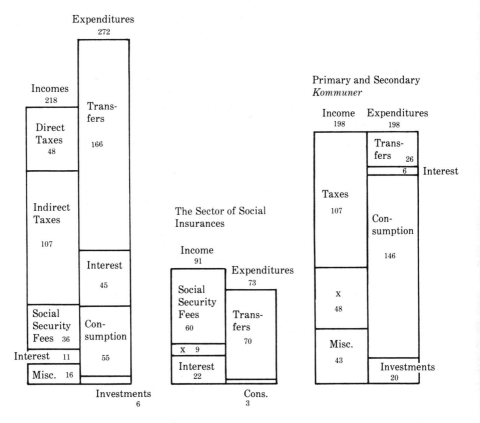

x) Transfers from the
National Government

Source: SCB (1985).

5. The Budget Deficit

When talking about the Swedish tax and transfer systems, it is important to notice the rapid increase of budget deficits since the mid-1970s. Taxes and other income sources are not sufficient to finance the expenditure programs decided by Parliament.

The Swedish budget has been underbalanced, showing deficits, for the last decade. The budget deficit has increased from almost zero percent of the GNP in the early 70s to some 11 percent in 1983. For the budget year 1983/84, 26 percent of the expenditures was financed by loans. Figure 9 shows how the budget deficit developed in relation to GNP since the mid-1970s.

Figure 9
The Budget Deficit and National Debt in
Relation to GNP, 1970-83

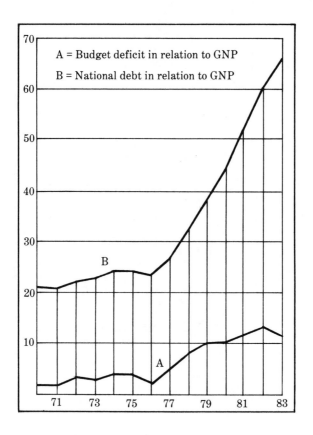

Source:*Riksrevisionsverket* (1985).

According to the budget 1986/87, the debt in relation to GNP will reach 70 percent. The largest part of the debt is financed within the country. Only 21 percent of the debt was financed abroad in 1984. The interest payments on the debt are now by far the largest single item in the budget (SEK 71,000 million out of a total budget of SEK 335,575 million).

IX. THE HIDDEN ECONOMY

1. General Background

Not all activities in society can be reached for taxation. Some are naturally excluded and others are, for some reason, not registered as income. The tax base has become wider and wider as many activities, such as child care, which formerly were done at home are being performed in the market. Nevertheless, some production both of goods and services is not within the taxed sector. Part of the reason is the existence of a hidden economy. Despite massive control, some people do cheat on their tax forms and some are even completely outside the taxed economy.

There is in Sweden, in most cases, no direct link between paid taxes and social security contributions on the one hand and benefits received on the other. The only such links existing are some pension contributions and payments for illness insurance. With very high marginal tax rates, the temptation to stay outside the system increases and a "free rider" problem arises. We will now turn to some estimates of this sector in the economy and we will also study punishments for cheating if caught.

2. The Size of the Hidden Economy

It is a known fact that estimates of the hidden economy are difficult to obtain. Only a few estimates have been done for Sweden. They are all unsatisfactory, especially since between persons or from a company to its employees, goods and services are often exchanged in such a way that taxation is avoided. Hansson (1981) used data from household incomes (taxable and nontaxable) and compared them to consumption data. One low and one high estimate of the hidden economy was made since some assumptions had to be made due to the lack of data. The size of the sector was estimated from 3.8 up to 6.4 percent of GNP during the years 1970 to 1979 (not including drugs, thefts, prostitution, etc.). There does not seem to have been any increase over the years despite a rather large increase in taxes.

A research report made by the Swedish police (*Rikspolisstyrelsen*, 1977) estimated the amount of tax cheating (excluding minor cheating by wage earners) to be from 1.4 to 5.4 percent of GNP.

A large part of the hidden sector of the economy is thought to be private entrepreneurs like painters, construction workers, etc. The accuracy of such accusations is questionable. Myrsten (1980) has made an estimation of the size of the amount of that kind of work. Some six to nine percent of the incomes are found to be "hidden" in the construction sector. Interviews by a research institute (SIFO) indicate that working in the hidden sector within construction was twice as common as in other areas.

So-called monetary methods used to estimate the size of this sector have reached considerably larger estimates. Klovland (1984) estimated it to be from three to 20 percent of GNP in 1982. He concluded, however, that "the uncertainty involved in the currency approach is so great as to make it hazardous to rely on such estimates."

Despite the profitability of cheating on the tax form or working completely outside the taxed sector, the hidden economy seems to be rather small in Sweden. The extensive use of social security number (*personnummer*) in combination with computers is one explanation. The social security number is used in almost all situations in Sweden. In addition to all contacts with authorities, employment, deposits, loans, etc. are registered by this number. The number is also used for purely private matters like subscriptions, library cards, rent contracts, monthly passes for trains, etc.

All tax forms in Sweden are audited. On a large fraction, questions are asked by the tax inspector. Besides, the tax inspector can also bring tax forms with low reported incomes or forms with large deductions to a local tax board (*taxeringsnamnd*). The board is politically chosen and represents the local political situation. In a small town of 20,000 inhabitants there will be at least 10 local tax boards. The members often know the inhabitants individually so it might be difficult to be a big spender with low income.

In a study at Uppsala University (Laurin, 1983), persons were asked about cheating on the tax form. As many as 75 percent said they declared everything, however small. Younger persons cheat more often than older persons and men more than women.

Since the payroll tax is closely linked to the income tax, people who will cheat tend to cheat on it as well. The tax authorities compare income tax forms and the forms for the VAT. Therefore, the rule seems to be, if cheating, you'd better cheat on all taxes. However, special rules within the VAT have encouraged cheating in those cases where it does not influence the income tax. But the VAT is to some extent self-controlling since the taxable amount for one firm is deductible for the next firm. It is a generally held opinion that the VAT is a tax where cheating is rare.

3. Penalties If Caught for Tax Fraud

If fraud is detected, it will be corrected by the tax authorities and special "administrative fees" will have to be paid. Such fees are paid on all discovered cheating (whether or not it's deliberate) exceeding SEK 1,000. The fee is 20 percent or 40 percent of the neglected tax in extra payment. (If an income of SEK 2,000 is forgotten, the fee will be SEK 200 at a marginal tax rate of 50 percent since the lower percentage is used for such cases.) The higher rate is used when the tax authorities normally do not have access to information about the taxpayer from a source other than the taxpayer himself. All employers must provide information about salaries paid to each person employed. The Stock Exchange provides information about dividends and holdings and banks have to report all interest payments exceeding SEK 500 per year (will be SEK 100 in 1988). Reports are made and sent using the social security number.

Besides the fees, the tax authorities may also bring the taxpayer to court if the amount exceeds SEK 15,000. For minor amounts, the court will make the person pay fines, but for major crimes, the person can be imprisoned for up to six years. The period of prosecution is five years for all tax offenses (since July 1985).

X. PROPOSALS FOR TAX REFORM

The present Swedish tax system is complex and considered to be "unfair" by many. The marginal tax rates are high by international standards and adverse effects on the economy are recognized by both economists and politicians. The Social Democratic Minister of Finance, Kjell Olof Feldt, said on the national news on January 9, 1986, that the redistribution of incomes through increased taxes is no longer possible. The increased attractiveness of "unproductive" investments is another problem. Consumer durables, extra houses, stamps, diamonds, etc. are all very attractive items to invest in, partly due to the tax system. The savings rate is very low. The public pension system has changed the need to save for retirement but the high taxes on regular bank accounts together with high taxes on other returns seem to have increased present consumption.

As one would expect, most of the proposals for tax reform concern the taxation of capital income in one way or another.

1. Governmental Initiatives

Simpler tax forms. A simplified personal income tax form was introduced in January 1986. It is more an administrative reform than an actual change in the tax code. The taxpayer will receive the tax form already filled out by the authorities and if he has no further incomes or deductions, he will just sign the form and send it in. The new system requires increased use of computers and information from employers, banks, etc. General deductions are introduced to lower the number of persons actually itemizing. One such deduction is from wage income. It amounts to SEK 3,000. A new deduction for capital gains of short-term stocks is introduced and amounts to SEK 1,000.

An inflation-corrected income tax. A governmental committee was formed in 1978 to investigate an inflation-corrected income tax. The committee studied the definition of the tax base and the use of different indices. The report was presented in 1982 (SOU 1982:1-3). It suggested that both the personal income tax and the corporate tax should be based on inflation-corrected measures. The proposal meant that an introduction of new loans for single-family dwellings would have to be introduced since nominal interest payments no longer would be deductible. The progressive imputed value of housing was proposed to be proportional and set to two percent of the assessed value. The new loans, which the committee considered necessary in order not to force thousands of people from their homes, were a major complication and the tax system has, so far, not been introduced. However, at the corporate level, an inflation-corrected tax has been introduced (January 1984). The new tax became an additional tax, not a replacement. The tax is described in this paper as "The Profit Sharing Tax."

An expenditure tax. The expenditure tax was first examined in 1976 (Lodin, 1976) and then in 1981 a new committee was formed on this issue. It will publish its results during 1986. There seem to be several difficult issues to be solved before an expenditure tax can be introduced. One such problem is that politicians wish to make the tax totally based on individual consumption. This creates some further problems that such a tax opens up for tax planning within the family. Another problem has been the transition problem.

Other committees. One committee is working on the value-added tax. Yet another committee is making a complete revision of the inheritance and gift taxes. A couple of committees are working on issues of capital gains and several are dealing with administrative questions.

The Corporate Tax Committee of 1980 has given reports on the wealth tax on working capital in small corporations, on the right to carry forward losses, and on how to separate labor and capital incomes in small corporations. A new committee has been formed.

2. The Corporate Tax—Views of Business on Tax Reform

The corporate tax affects the growth rate, employment, and the level of welfare in the society. Normann (1985), a researcher at *Industriforbundet* (The Federation of Swedish Industries), which has 3,000 member corporations, argues for a more "neutral" corporate tax. He emphasizes the highly distorting effects of the current system on both investments and finances. He questions the government's intentions to widen the tax base for the corporate tax further (in 1985 inventory write-down was reduced from 60 percent to 50 percent). We have seen earlier that the corporate tax and taxes on capital seem to be relatively low. A common method of calculating the corporate tax burden is to compare taxes paid with profits before consolidation opportunities (which lower the taxable profit) and by that method, a low effective tax share is achieved. However, Normann argues that a better measure is the average tax on corporations' inflation corrected profits. For the years 1978 to 1980, Normann's method gave an average tax share of 29 percent. The payroll taxes were 31 percent at the end of the 70s. Therefore, the tax rate on labor was 24 percent (31/131). Normann concludes that capital was taxed more heavily than labor in the corporations and he is skeptical of an introduction of a general production factor tax (*proms*) meaning an increased taxation of capital in corporations.

Alternatives to the present corporate tax worth considering are, according to Normann (1985), a cash flow tax (CFT) or a neutral income tax on pure profits (NITPP). A CFT allows immediate depreciation of buildings and machinery and full write-downs of inventories. This form of an expenditure tax for the corporate sector would allow deductions for interest payments and for paying the principal, while loans would be taxable income. Losses would be completely written off against profits. A NITPP, on the other hand, would only tax "pure" profits since economically correct depreciations would be used. The value of inventories would be inflation corrected as would interest payments. Normal return to equity capital would be deductible.

A CFT would have a small tax base with large consolidation possibilities and is reminiscent of the old Swedish system with free depreciations. The NITPP has a broad tax base and is reminiscent of the new Swedish "Profit Sharing Tax." Both taxes are neutral for legal corporate forms and for sources of finance.

The corporations are very negative to the combination of nominal and inflation-corrected taxes. They demand that the "Profit Sharing Tax" be eliminated. They also reject proposals for a general production factor tax. The Federation of Swedish Industries is working for a generalized "Annell deduction" for all dividends in order to put Swedish corporations in a situation similar to that of corporations in other countries (Ando, 1984).

Simplified corporate tax. A proposal similar to the NITPP has been made by Sodersten and Ysander (1985). They argue for a "neutral" corporate tax. A NITPP, where "correct" depreciations and inflation adjustments are made, becomes very complicated. They propose a "simplified corporate tax." The main elements are:

1) Free depreciations at the same time as deductions for interest payments are abolished. Inventories can be written off by 100 percent and LIFO is allowed.

2) The connection between taxable net profit and profit according to the civil books is taken away.

3) The right to write off losses against previous net profits for up to three years.

The proposed tax system according to them would "fully tax excess profits" (profits exceeding the cost of financing an investment) but for a marginal investment the effective tax rate would be zero.

Abolished corporate tax. On January 1, 1985, the corporate tax was changed. The local tax was abolished but the nominal tax rate is unchanged (52 percent). The decreasing tax revenues from the corporate sector and the fact that the tax tends to vary inversely with the profitability (due to the consolidation opportunities during "good" years) have led to a debate on whether the tax should remain or not. Figure 4 in the section on statistics shows both nominal and effective tax rates as well as profitability since the early 1950s. Because of consolidation opportunities and the risk of getting other, perhaps higher, taxes, the business sector has pushed only moderately to abolish the corporate tax. There is presently no such proposal.

3. Academic Proposals Which May Influence Tax Reforms

There have been many proposals, both for complete revisions and for changes in some detail of the tax system. A few of them will be mentioned here.

The value-added tax. Soderstrom (1977) argued for an increased use of the VAT. It should replace the income tax but not the payroll taxes for social security. A tax rate of approximately 30 percent (presently 19 percent) would be sufficient in order to yield equal tax revenues. He argues that a VAT as the main source of tax revenues and wealth taxes and subsidies for redistributive purposes, would be a complete and superior tax system.

Labor income tax. Not taxing capital incomes but only taxing returns on human capital, that is wages, has also been proposed. The proposition has risen from elements in expenditure taxes and in inflational corrected income taxes. Capital incomes are sometimes hard to observe, especially in times of inflation, but capital stocks are easier to quantify (Stahl, 1983). He therefore proposed that the ability to pay taxes should be based on the wages for the stock of human capital and on the stock of wealth when it comes to capital incomes. A wealth tax, possibly progressive, could replace the taxes on capital incomes. The abolishing of taxation of capital incomes (deductions) might have to be introduced successively. Andersson (1983) has shown that an expenditure tax and a labor income tax are equivalent under certain circumstances. One difficulty within this tax is that special rules are required on the corporate side in order to distinguish labor (taxable) from capital (not taxable) income. Proposals of how to make such a separation have been made by Jepsen (1985). Since low income earners (incomes below SEK 70,000) report on average a positive capital income, their taxes would decrease by such a proposal. The opposite is the case on average for high income earners.

4. Other Proposals—The View of the Labor Unions

The labor unions (blue collar workers) argued during the 1960s that the corporate tax should be based not only on the net profit but also on the costs for the production factors and bought material. Less efficient corporations would thereby be put out of the market earlier than in the present system. The idea was never transformed into any actual taxes. The governmental committee of 1970 investigating the corporate tax, suggested a continuation of the net profit tax. However, the Social Democratic members of the committee wanted to introduce a tax on the production factors. A general production factor tax, often called *proms* would not influence the choice of production techniques. A system consisting of a production factor tax combined with few consolidation opportunities granted by the tax system has been proposed by Aberg (1983). Free depreciation has also been proposed in conjunction with the proposal.

One of the unions for white collar workers (SACO/SR) demands that personal marginal tax rates be limited to 50 percent, and that the inflation correction which was present in the national tax schedule earlier through the use of "basic units" should be in effect. A deduction of the national tax when calculating the local tax is also demanded in their program.

An organization called The Taxpayer's Union (*Skattebetalarnas forening*) has proposed that a wage earner should be able to keep at least half of any wage increase after taxes. According to the Ministry of Finance (*Finansplanen*, 1986), only 13 percent of all income earners presently have a marginal tax rate exceeding 50 percent (compared to 43 percent in 1982). The Taxpayer's Union estimates that such a reform would only make the tax revenues decrease by some SEK 5,000 million, *cet. par.* but they expect the tax base to increase and fully make up for that loss. There have not been any proposals by any group to lower the marginal tax rate to less than 50 percent.

APPENDIX

1. General Background

After much debate during the late 1960s and the 1970s about economic democracy, the Swedish system of "Wage Earner's Funds" was introduced in 1984. Five separate funds were created and their purpose was, according to the Minister of Finance, to contribute to a growth and stabilization policy which would be compatible with distribution goals. It was thought that the Wage Earner's Funds by extending the labor unions' power would keep wage demands moderate even in high profit industries and during periods of high profits. Wage earners would, through their unions, get increased power over companies and also an increased responsibility over the allocation of capital and its use in the future.

The Wage Earner's Funds are partly financed by a profit sharing tax, partly by an increased general supplementary pension fee of .2 percent. A temporary tax on distributed profits for the year 1983 was also allocated to the funds. The tax rate was 20 percent and the tax was not deductible on any tax form. The annual amount transferred to the Wage Earner's Funds will be between SEK 2,000 and 3,000 million until 1990. Each of the five funds has an upper limit of how much it can receive. The limit was SEK 400 million in 1984 but the amount increases annually by the inflation rate. The limit for 1985 was some SEK 975 million.

Each fund is supposed to invest in stocks in general or lend out money to small corporations. The capital should yield "good" returns, should diversify risks, and should be of some long-term character. "Good" returns is defined as at least three percent of their annual allocation multiplied by the inflation index. This amount must be delivered to a general pension fund. Each fund can hold at most eight percent of the voting power in any company on the Stock Exchange.

2. Actual Rules for the Profit Sharing Tax

As pointed out earlier, the starting point for the calculation of the tax is the taxable income from the ordinary income tax form. The ordinary income tax for the current year is deductible. Consolidation measures which have been made in order to calculate the ordinary taxable income will now have to be taken out so that they do not influence the result. For this reason, losses carried forward from earlier years, special deductions due to dividends, increases in inventory write-offs and investment subsidies are all added back. However, allocations to the investment fund system are not added. In this way, the government recognizes the need to equalize profit over the business cycle. Since the profit sharing tax cannot be deferred, the system of investment funds may be used to achieve some kind of control over when taxes are paid.

The ordinary income tax is based on a nominal result but the profit sharing tax is based on an inflation-corrected result. However, the tax is not based purely on the increased value of equity capital during the period but it is calculated by a practical method of partial adjustments for inflation.

The inflation correction for buildings is made in the following way. The year the building was acquired will determine what index number will be used. The numbers are given by the National Tax Board and start with the year 1973. Older buildings will have to use the value of 1973. The index numbers which reflect the inflation rate for 1985 were:

1973	3.06	1980	1.54
1974	2.78	1981	1.37
1975	2.53	1982	1.26
1976	2.30	1983	1.16
1977	2.06	1984	1.07
1978	1.87	1985	1.00
1979	1.75		

The annual depreciation for each building is multiplied by the respective index. Then, the depreciation from the ordinary income tax form is deducted from this and the result is the inflationary depreciation.

For machinery, another method of depreciation is used. Depreciation is calculated on the sum of the value of old and new machinery. An inflationary deduction is allowed on the booked value of the machinery at the beginning of the year. The inflation rate of the year (last year .07) is multiplied with this value and the deduction is thereby achieved. The value of inventory is also corrected by multiplying the value of the inventory before write-off at the beginning of the year by the inflation rate.

Corrections are also made for monetary assets/debts. The method of dividing all interests into two parts, one inflationary and one real rate of return was rejected. Instead, the stock of each monetary asset/debt is the basis for the inflation correction. All values are taken from the beginning of the taxable year. The monetary debts considered are:
- debts to suppliers, taxes
- advance payments from customers

- reserved for pensions
- reserved for investment funds
- other debts
- repayment of equity capital to owners during the year

The reason why reserved funds for investment funds are included is that the reservation has earlier decreased the nominal result and if it were not included, a use of the fund for investments would be less attractive than other sources of finance.

The following are considered as monetary assets:

- cash and deposits
- bonds, loan claims
- claims on customers
- prepaid costs and accrued interest
- advance payments to deliverers
- nominal positive result (profit)
- payment of equity capital from owners during the year

Bank deposits made due to consolidation measures using the investment fund system should be included in deposits. To help corporations with small equity capital but with high profitability, the entire nominal profit (positive) of the year can be included.

The index used is based on the consumer price index. The same index is used for calculations of capital gains from sold property.

A basic deduction of either SEK 500,000 or six percent of the wage costs is allowed. Proposals for having a deduction based on equity capital were rejected. The corporations will also have to pay the tax on foreign branches unless tax agreements between the countries do not allow this (exempt method). However, foreign corporations will only be hit by the tax if they have a Swedish daughter company. There are no special methods to enable deferral of the profit sharing tax to later years. The tax is deductible in the ordinary income tax calculation for the following year.

REFERENCES

Aaron, H.J. (Ed.) (1981), *The Value Added Tax—Lessons from Europe*. The Brookings Institution, 1981.

Aberg, C.J. (1983), "Behovs en 'stor' reform av foretagsbeskattningen?" is included in *hur klarar vi 1990?*, Riksbankens Jubileumsfond 1983.2.

Agell, J., & J. Sodersten (1982), "Skatteregler och realinvesteringar," *Ekonomisk Debatt* nr 8, 1982.

Ando, S. (1984) "Foretagsbeskattningen i Sverige," *Skattepolitik for framat-skridande*, Federation of Swedish Industries, 1984.

Affarsvarlden (1985), Numbers 45 ("Bolagsskatten konserverar i stallet for att stimulera till fornyelse") and 49 (Bolagsskatten Ger Valfardsforluster "Neutral skatt kravs"), 1985.

Andersson, K. (1983), "The Labour Income Tax—An alternative to the alternative for Sweden?, Seminar paper at Department of Economics, University of California at Berkeley, Nov. 1983.

Andersson, K. et al. (1985), *Finansteoretiska undersokningar, I. Introduktion*, Report by 15 researchers at the Department of Economics at the University of Lund.

Andersson, K., & E. Norrman (1983), "Olika formogenhetstillgangar och deras fordelning." Institutet for ekonomisk forskning.

——— (1985), "The relative price of consumption in different tax systems," Paper presented at the Scandinavian Tax Conference in Lund, December 1985.

Blomquist, S. (1983), "The Effect of Income Taxation on the Labor Supply of Married Men in Sweden," *Journal of Public Economics* 22, pp. 169-197.

Dexe, N., & P-E. Nister (1985), Forenklad sjalvdeklaration, *Skattenytt* nr 10, 1985.

Economic Research Unit at the Economic Research Institute of the Stockholm School of Economics, (1979), "The STEP 1 Quarterly Econometric Model of Sweden," Stockholm School of Economics.

Finansplanen (1986), *Bilaga 1 till budgetpropositionen 1986*. Prop. 1985/86:100.

Franzen, T., et al. (1976), *Skatters och offentliga utgifters effekter pa inkomstfor-delningen. En teoretisk och empirisk studie*. Department of Economics, Stockholm University.

Fredriksson, O., et al. (1983), *Mervardeskatten i Sverige*. TH Forlag, Boras.

Gustavsson, B. (1984), *Transfereringar och inkomstskatt samt hushallens materi-ella standard*. Expertgruppen for studier i offentlig ekonomi.

Hansson, I. (1978), "Skattesystemet, inflationen och investeringarna," *Ekonomisk debatt*, nr. 6, 1978.

——— (1980), "Inflation in Sweden and the Effects of Price Controls," Working paper at Department of Economics, University of Lund.

——— (1981), "Berakningar av skatteundandragaandet i Sverige." *Riksskatte-verket*.

——— (1983), "Skatter, realinvesteringar och verkligheten," *Ekonomsik Debatt* nr 4, 1983.

——— (1984), "Marginal Cost of Public Funds for Different Tax Instruments and Government Expenditures," *Scandinavian Journal of Economics* 86, pp. 115-130.

Hansson, I., & E. Norrman (1985), "Fordelningseffekter av inkomstskatt och utgiftskatt," Department of Economics, University of Lund.

Hansson, I., & C. Stuart (1985a), "Tax Revenue and the Marginal Cost of Public Funds in Sweden," *Journal of Public Economics*.

Holmlund, B. (1982), "Payroll taxes and wage inflation: The Swedish ex-periences," IUI: Working paper 1982:68.

Jepsen, G.T. (1985), "Skattereformen 1985" Paper presented at the Scandinavian Tax Conference held in Lund, December 1985.

Johansson, J., & O. Roos (1984), *Vinsgdelningsskatt. Lontagarfonder.* Tholin/ Larsson/Gruppen.

King, M.A., & D. Fullerton (1984), *The Taxation of Income from Capital*, National Bureau of Economic Research.

Klovland, J.T. (1984), "Tax Evasion and the Demand for Currency in Norway and Sweden. Is there a Hidden Relationship?," *Scandinavian Journal of Economics* 86, pp. 423-439.

Kruse, A., & A. Stahlberg (1977), "Effekter av ATP—en samhallsekonomisk studie," Lund Economic Studies, Lund.

Laurin, U. (1983), "Ett folk av fifflare? En beskrivning av det svenska skattefusket," is included in *Hur klarar vi 1990?*, Riksbankens Jubileumsfond 1983:2.

Lodin, S-O (1976), "Progressiv utgiftsskatt—ett alternativ?" *SOU 1976:62.*

LON (1985), "Gava—en liten hjalpreda for gavodeklaration," *LON* Ser I, Avd D, nr 366.

Myrsten, K. (1980), "Det illegala bygghantverket," Brottsutvecklingen, Brottsfordbyggande Radet, *Rapport* 1980:3.

Nilsson, L. (1985), " Skattefusk och skatteplanering—nagra samhallskonomiska synpunkter" in *Ekonomisk Debatt* 5, 1985.

Normann, G. (1983), "Skatter och inflation, En studie av effekter pa loner och kapitalkostnader," Expert rapport fran bruttoskattekommitten, DsFi 1983:17.

———— (1985), "Bolagsskatten, ger valfardsforluster "Neutral skatt kravs," *Affarsvarlden* nr 49, 1985.

OECD (1984), *Revenue Statistics of OECD Member Countries 1965-1983.*

———— (1984a), *OECD Economic Outlook*, 35.

Rikspolisstyrelsen, (1977), "Organiserad och ekonomisk brottslighet i Sverige— ett atgardsforslag," Rapaport avgiaven av arbetsgruppen mot organiserad brottslighet, AMOB, 1977.

Riksrevisionsverket (1984), *Statens finanser.*

———— (1985), Unpublished survey of estimated tax payments within the corporate sector.

Riksskatteverket (RSV) (1984a), *Handledning for rorelse—och jordbruksbeskattning*, Liber.

———— (1984b), *Forfattningar om punktskatter m m 1984*, Allmanna Forlaget.

———— (1984c), Vinstdelninigsskatten.

———— (1985a), "Fakta om Sveriges punktskatter."

———— (1985b), *Skatte—och taxeringsforfattningarna 1985. Liber.*

———— (1985c), *Handledning for taxering*, Liber.

———— (1985d), *Forfattningar om mervardeskatt.* Allmanna Forlages.

———— (1985e), *Nyheter vid 1985 ars taxering.* Schmidts Boktryckeri AB, Helsingborg 1985.

Rundfelt, R. (1982), "Nagra av bolagsbeskattningens principer." Sveriges Industriforbund. Mimeographed.

SACO/SR, Utrdag ur program, avsnitt "Skatter och bidrag."

SCB (1985), "Offentliga sektorn. Utveckling och nulage.' '

SFS 1985:323 Svensk forfattningssamling.

SIFO (1978, 1979, 1980, 1981), "Den sjunkande deklarationsmoralen," 1978, "En nation av fifflare," 1979, "Svartbetalare och svartjobbare," 1980, "Smaforetagarna," 1980, "Fa uppger for laga inkomster i sjalvdeklarationen," 1981.

Sveriges Industriforbund (1984), Skattepolitik for framatskridande. Tema for Industriforbundets arsmote 1984. Federation of Swedish Industries.

SOU (1982), Realbeskattningsutredningen, *SOU 1982:1-3.*

Stuart, C. (1981), "Swedish tax rates, labor supply, and tax revenues," *Journal of Political Economy*, 89, pp. 1020-1038.

Stahl, I. (1983), "Skattebaser och besakttningstekniker 1990" is included in *Hur klarar vi 1990?*, Riksbankens Jubileumsfond 1983:2.

Stahlberg, A. (1983), "Socialforsakringar i ekonomisk analys." Is included in *"Infor Omprovningen,"* Publica.

_____ (1985), "Transfereringar mellan den forvarvsarbetande och den aldre generationen," Expertgruppen for studier i offentlig ekonomi, DsFi 1985:5.

Sodersten, J. (1977), "Bolagsskattens verkningar" is included in *SOU 1977:87* (Report of a governmental committee on corporate taxes).

Sodersten, J., & T. Lindberg (1983), *Skattpa Bolagskopital* 101 Rapport nr 20.

Sodersten, J., & B-C Ysander (1983), *Bolagsskatt och investeringsvilja.* IUI, Rapport 17, 1983.

_____ (1984), "Bolagsskatten—en politisk och ekonomisk kokkenmodding," *Ekonomisk Debatt* nr 8, 1984.

_____ (1985), "Forenklad Bolagsskatt," *Ekonomisk Debatt* nr 2, 1985.

Soderstrom, L. (1977), "Satsa pa mervardeskatten," *Ekonomisk Debatt* nr 3, 1977.

_____ (1984a), *Ar subventioner effektiva?*, Expertgruppen for studier i offentlig ekonomi, DsFi 1984:8.

_____ (1984b), *The redistributive effects of social protection: Sweden*, European centre for work and society, Maastricht 1984.

_____ (1985), "Arbetsgivaravgifternas incidens m.m.," Mimeographed, Department of Economics, University of Lund.

Table 1
The Individual Income Tax Schedules, 1986

Basic units	Amounts (SEK)	Tax rate (%)
	The Basic Tax Schedule	
0—1	0—7,800	0
1—9	7,800—70,200	4
9—10	70,200—78,000	15
10—18	78,000—140,400	20
18—21	140,400—163,800	24
21—	163,800—	20
	The Supplementary Tax Schedule	
16—19	124,800—148,200	5
19—21	148,200—163,800	10
21—23	163,800—179,400	15
23—26	179,400—202,800	20
26—45	202,800—351,000	25
45—	351,000—	30
	The Total Tax Schedule	
0—1	0—7,800	0
1—9	7,800—70,200	4
9—10	70,200—78,000	15
10—16	78,000—124,800	20
16—18	124,800—140,400	25
18—19	140,400—148,200	29
19—21	148,200—163,800	34
23—26	179,400—202,800	40
26—45	202,800—351,000	45
45—	351,000—	50

Table 2
Taxable Income by Income Categories, 1982
(Million SEK)

Type of Income	Amount
Wage income	370,195
Capital income (dividends, interest, etc.)	14,569
Capital gains	2,860
Income from housing	2,947
Income from farming	4,085
Income from self-employed businesses	10,887
Total	405,543

Source: *Riksrevisionsverket*, (1984)

Table 3
The Wealth Tax, 1986

Wealth (SEK)	Tax rate within bracket (%)
0—400,000	0
400,000—600,000	1.5
600,000—800,000	2.0
800,000—1,800,000	2.5
1,800,000 —	3.0

Source: *Riksrevisionsverket* (1985b).

Table 4
Gift Taxes, 1986

Value of the gift (SEK)	Total amount of taxes (SEK)
Gifts to Spouse, Children, and Grandchildren	
50,000	3,000
200,000	30,000
600,000	177,000
1,200,000	489,000
6,000,000[1]	3,544,000
Gifts to Parents, Brothers, and Sisters	
40,000	6 ,000
90,000	22,400
200,000	78,100
600,000	335,600
1,200,000[2]	755,600

Source: LON (1985).
  [1]The top marginal rate is 70 percent.
  [2]The top marginal rate is 75 percent.

Table 5
Social Security Fees for 1986

Purpose	Rate %
General Supplementary Pension ("ATP")	10.200*
General Pension (*Folkpension*)	9.450
Part-Time Pension Insurance (*Delpensionsforsakring*)	.500*
Sickness Insurance (*Sjukforsakring*)	9.300*
Working Injury Insurance (*Arbetsskadeforsakring*)	.600*
Work Environment Protection (*Arbetarskydd*)	.350*
Wage Guarantee (in case of bankruptcy) (*Lonegaranti*)	.200*
Labor Market Fee (*Arbetsmarknadsavgift*)	1.586
Education for Adults (*Vuxenutbildning*)	.264
Nursery School Fee (*Barnomsorgsavgift*)	2.200
General Wage Fee (*Allman loneavgift*)	2.000
Total	36.650

Source: SFS 1985:323
*See Soderstrom, (1985), section III for explanation.

Table 6
Revenue of Indirect Taxes Levied by the National Tax Board, 1984

Object of Taxation	in 000 Number of Taxpayers	Revenues (M SEK)
Petrol (gasoline)	900	8.976
Spirits for consumption	1	6.093
Fuels	375	5.760
Electric power	540	4.365
Tobacco	16	4.327
Wine	1	1.986
Malt beverages	13	1.083
Shares, stocks	20,587	1.079
Water-power	89	1.030
Motor vehicles	42	892
Confectionery	261	423
General advertising	3,142	405
Gambling	1,295	375
Chemico-technical preparations	162	312
Public permits etc.	—	210
Charter flights	44	141
Carbonated beverages	36	140
Nuclear power	4	87
Video tape recorders	16	62
Beverage packages	1	46
Cassette tapes	117	29
Insecticide	47	2
Total		38.80

Source: *Riksskatteverket* (1985a).

Table 7
Tax Shares in OECD Countries, 1983
Deviations from the Average
(Percentage Points)

Country	Payroll[1]	Personal Income[1]	Corpora-tion[1]	Property/ Wealth[1]	Indirect on Goods/ Services[1]	Tax Share[2]
Sweden	+4	+8	-5	-4	-5	+13
Norway	-5	-8	+9	-3	+6	+11
Belgium	+3	+4	-2	-3	-3	+10
Netherlands	+16	-9	-1	-2	-5	+9
France	+19	-20	-3	-1	+1	+7
Denmark	-23	+21	-5	-1	+8	+7
Austria	+12	-9	-5	-3	+2	+4
Italy	+21	-8	0	-2	-14	+3
Ireland	-10	-3	-1	-3	+17	+3[3]
United Kingdom	-6	-4	+2	+8	0	+3
West Germany	+10	-4	-3	-1	-3	0
Finland	-18	+12	-3	-3	-11	0
New Zealand	-26	+28	0	+2	-5	-3
Australia	-21	+13	+2	+3	+3	-6[3]
United States	+2	+5	-1	+5	-12	-6
Japan	+4	-6	+12	+5	-14	-10
Tax shares, all of OECD	26	33	8	5	29	100

Source: The figures are from Andersson, et al. (1985) but are based on OECD (1984) tables 1, 11, 13, 15, 21, 23, 25, and OECD (1984a) table R8.
[1]Based on the percentage of total taxes.
[2]Based on ratio of tax revenues to GNP.
[3]1981

Table 8
Tax Revenues As Percent of GNP in Sweden, 1984

Taxes on Labor		Taxes on Capital	
Payroll taxes	10.3	Corporate tax	1.3
Income tax on labor	20.0	Income tax on capital	-.6
VAT	6.8	Wealth tax	.2
Other taxes on goods (gas, liquor, etc.)	5.4	Inheritance and gift taxes	.1
		Other taxes on property	.4
Total	42.5		1.4

Source Andersson, et al. (1985).

Table 9
Total Marginal Tax on Labor Income,
Selected Years, 1955-1985

Year	Marginal Effects (percentage)
1955	40.2
1965	55.3
1975	69.6
1982	73.7
1985	71.0

Source: Andersson, et al. (1985).

Table 10
Positive Net Incomes on Tax Returns, 1982

Sum of surpluses (thousands)	Number of people (thousands)	Percent
0-10	366	5.7
10-20	316	4.9
20-30	766	11.9
30-40	673	10.4
40-50	573	8.9
50-60	594	9.2
60-70	604	9.4
70-80	737	11.4
80-90	586	9.1
90-100	416	6.5
100-110	236	3.7
110-150	395	6.1
150-200	116	1.8
200-	63	1.0
Total	6,441	100.0

Source: *Riksrevisionsverket* (1984).

Table 11
Deficits on Tax Returns, 1973-1982

Year	Deficits (SEK million)
1973	4.5
1974	6.0
1975	7.3
1976	9.0
1977	12.2
1978	12.8
1979	15.5
1980	21.1
1981	25.8
1982	28.5

Source: *Riksrevisionsverket* (1984).

Table 12
Tax Shares for Different Income Deciles, 1985

Decile	Gross income per consumer unit	Tax share (Gross income/c.u.)	Tax share (Taxable income, individual level)	Tax share (Gross income, individual level)
1	—31,418	19.0	7.6	2.9
2	31,419—38,197	17.0	12.0	12.2
3	38,198—46,918	22.4	19.9	17.8
4	46,919—54,838	25.1	26.3	24.5
5	54,839—62,856	27.0	29.7	28.2
6	62,857—70,228	28.9	31.3	29.8
7	70,229—77,295	32.1	33.6	31.7
8	77,296—88,383	32.5	35.1	32.3
9	88,384—102,513	32.7	36.7	33.3
10	102,514—and over	38.2	43.6	35.9
Top 2.5%	142,478—and over	43.6	51.7	40.9

Source: Hansson and Norman, (1985).

Table 13
Effect of Abolishing Taxes on Capital Incomes, 1984

Decile	Taxable Income	Difference in Paid Taxes (SEK)
1	—22,300	−75
2	22,300—29,700	−839
3	29,700—37,700	−1,110
4	37,700—47,200	−976
5	47,200—58,700	−458
6	58,700—69,500	−978
7	69,500—79,200	+109
8	79,200—90,200	+1,305
9	90,200—108,800	+3,385
10	108,800—and over	+5,065
Top 2.5%	156,500—and over	+7,617
All		+571

Source: SCB (unpublished).

CHAPTER **3**

Netherlands

Flip de Kam

BASIC STATISTICS OF THE NETHERLANDS

The area of the Netherlands measures 41,500 square kilometers. The country numbers 14.5 million inhabitants. The Netherlands is one of the most densely populated countries in the world (426 inhabitants per square kilometer of land area). Annual population increase over the period 1980-1985 was 70,000 on average.

Employment is 4.5 million man years. Government employees make up 16 percent of total employment. Gross domestic product in 1984 was 123 billion U.S. dollars. The annual growth rate of GDP over the period 1982-1985 amounted to 1.5 percent. Total labor productivity in the market sector of the economy grew at an annual rate of three percent (between 1982 and 1985).

Exports and imports of goods and services were, in 1984, 63 and 58 percent of GDP, respectively. Surplus on the current balance of payments was around five billion U.S. dollars (both in 1984 and 1985).

The national currency is the guilder (Dfl.). In year 1985 one U.S. dollar was equal to Dfl. 3.22 (average of daily figures). As per June 30, 1986; one U.S. dollar equalled Dfl. 2.50.

The most up-to-date information about the Dutch economy is to be found in the OECD Economic Survey 1985/1986 of the Netherlands (OECD 1986a).

I. INTRODUCTION

1. The Public Sector of the Netherlands Economy, 1955-1985

In 1985 public expenditure in the Netherlands amounted to Dfl. 250 billion or 67.6 percent of net national income. During the past thirty years the claim of the public sector on national income nearly doubled. This trend is illustrated in table 1. The growth of public outlays was not primarily caused by increasing exhaustive expenditures. In fact, these have been on a level that is comparable to that in the United States for many years now. The expansion of the public sector in the Netherlands was caused nearly solely by strongly rising transfer payments to families, price subsidies and interest payments on public debt.

Increasing outlays were matched by rising taxes and social insurance contributions. The burden of taxes and contributions went up from 38.6 percent of net national income (NNI) in 1965 to 50.5 percent in 1985. Nontax revenue (2.5 percent of NNI in 1965 and nine percent in 1985) and a growing deficit (four percent of NNI in 1965 and eight percent in 1985) cover the gap between total government expenditures and tax revenue. A more detailed overview of total expenditures and receipts of the public sector in 1985 (in billions of guilders) is in table 2.

In this paper I will describe the major features of the Dutch tax systems. In addition, social insurance contributions will be considered. Social insurance benefits and certain other transfers to households will be mentioned, whenever relevant to our subject. The paper does not try to cover all details of the tax-transfer system in the Netherlands, because this would take a whole series of monographs. As most of the relevant literature is in Dutch, I will mention only a small part of research efforts on the public sector programs under consideration. Unless indicated otherwise, all data and the presentation of existing legislation refer to the situation in 1985.

2. An Overview of the Tax-Transfer System in the Netherlands, 1985

Taxes amounted to Dfl. 102 billion in 1985. The personal income tax is the most important source of revenue (Dfl. 37 billion). The value-added tax is the second most important source of revenue (Dfl. 30 billion). The corporate income tax contributed Dfl. 12.5 billion. All other taxes of the central government—most of them excises—taken together brought in Dfl. 18.5 billion (see table 7). Local taxes are hardly of any importance. Over 90 percent of local government expenditure (except capital investments which are partly loan-financed) is paid through a system of revenue-sharing and grants from the central government. The municipal property tax (Dfl. 2.5 billion) accounts for three-quarters of total tax revenue of the local government. In 1985, social insurance contributions covered Dfl. 84 billion of public outlays (table 9). Other revenues of the public sector amounted to Dfl. 35 billion. The deficit is estimated at Dfl. 29 billion.

Total nonexhaustive public expenditures amounted in 1985 to 47 percent of NNI (Dfl. 175 billion), thus demonstrating the formidable size of the tax-transfer system in the Netherlands. Direct payments to families amounted to Dfl. 115 billion (including social insurance benefits totalling Dfl. 87 billion). The balance between these amounts consists of other government subsidies to families (student grants, rent subsidies and so on). Various price subsidies came to Dfl. 13 billion. Direct payments to business involved up to Dfl. 11 billion. Interest on government debt accounted for Dfl. 26 billion, loans and development aid (seen as transfers to other States) explaining the remainder of total transfers of Dfl. 175 billion.

3. The Distribution Branch of the Public Sector, 1977

There is no (recent) comprehensive picture of the redistribution of personal incomes through the tax-transfer system. Table 3 presents some information for year 1977. The information in table 3 is based on data from several representative national sample surveys.[1]

Factor income, social insurance benefits, and a number of other income components were reported in the surveys used. Income data were weighted to obtain national aggregates. Income tax and social insurance contributions were then calculated for every household, using a microeconomic simulation model. Value-added tax and excises paid were computed using results of regression analysis on microdata from the national consumer survey. Data from other surveys made it possible to impute most other transfer payments and price subsidies to households.

Households have been arranged into five 20 percent-groups (quintiles) on the basis of their net disposable income. Judging

---

[1]The sample surveys used were the Housing Needs Survey 1977 (N = 17,709), the Survey of Living Conditions 1977 (N = 4,159), the Medical Consumption Survey 1979 (N = 7,359), the Survey of Travel Behavior (N = 34,434), and the Supplementary Survey of the Use of Facilities 1979 (N = 17,232). N indicates the number of persons interviewed.

from table 3 the tax-transfer system effectuated in 1977 resulted in a considerable redistribution of personal incomes. The share of the lowest quintile increased from three to 10 percent. This is explained because students of 18 years and over are defined as separate households; they are found in the first quintile and greatly profit from public expenditure on education. The share of the second quintile increased through public sector intervention from eight to 13 percent. The reason being that most pensioners are found in this quintile. This category of households receives generous general old age pensions and, moreover, benefits greatly from public expenditure on health care, homes for the elderly, and heavily subsidized home help services. The share of the top quintile clearly declines, from 45 to 36 percent. Though no research on the personal income distribution in the Netherlands has produced results that contradict the general picture in table 3, some limitations of the presentation should be mentioned here. First, it should be noted that not all (money) flows between households and the public sector could be included in the presentation. Second, the surveys used did not contain much data on most deductions and exemptions in the personal income tax. Third—as will be explained in Chapter II— capital gains in the Netherlands are often not taxed; there was no data on capital gains in the surveys used. On the other hand, the annual wealth tax brings in one percent of total tax revenue (Dfl. 950 million). By definition this tax affects the wealthier people, and it should be noted that the surveys used did not contain data on the wealth tax which households were due either.

4. Organization of the Paper

This paragraph is about the organization of the paper. Section II deals with the personal income tax and the wage withholding tax. Section III describes the corporation income tax. Section IV is about the value added tax. Section V gives an overview of other taxes levied by central government, which bring in less than Dfl. 10 billion. Section VI deals with social insurance contributions. The following sections go into effects of the tax system (and to some extent of the transfer system). In section VII the tax treatment of savings and investments is set out. Section VIII considers the effects on labor supply and gives an estimate of the "hidden economy" in the Netherlands. Then some results on the distribution of the tax burden are presented in section IX. Section X summarizes the recent proposals for tax reform of the Tax Simplification Commission.

II. PERSONAL INCOME TAX

1. Introduction

The personal income tax is levied on the basis of the Income Tax Act of 1964 (ITA 1964). Taxpayers are either resident or non-resident individuals. Residence of an individual is determined "according to the circumstances." In this respect a number of facts may be of relevance, such as whether an individual has (permanent) personal ties with the Netherlands. Resident taxpayers are in principle, subject to income tax on their worldwide income. Non-resident taxpayers are only liable to Dutch income tax for income that is derived from a limited number of domestic sources. To protect its resident taxpayers from double taxation which may result if foreign income is also taxed in another State, the Netherlands has concluded a large number of tax treaties. If no treaty applies, unilateral double taxation relief may be obtained on the basis of national tax law.

The income tax is collected in two ways: either by assessment or by withholding tax at source, the latter method being applied to wages and dividends only. In the case of assessment, the tax inspector issues a tax return form to a person who, in his opinion, is liable to the tax. Taxpayers are obliged to file the completed tax return with the tax inspector. If a qualifying taxpayer does not receive a form he is obliged to ask for one. Generally the tax return has to be filed within three months after expiration of the calendar year. The tax inspector can, at the request of the taxpayer, extend that period and may, when extending the period, require that a provisional return is filed.

The tax inspector makes out the assessment after having received the tax return. In most cases the taxpayer will receive a provisional assessment during the calendar year concerned or immediately after sending in his or her tax return. The final assessment will follow after examination of the tax return by the tax office. It has to be paid within two months after the date of the assessment.

2. Liability to the Tax

Every taxpayer is taxed on his or her own income. There are two exceptions to this rule: certain income of (1) the spouse and (2) minor children.

A spouse will be taxed individually on:
- Profits from her own business.
- A limited part of her husband's business income, that is related to the time she has worked in his business.

- Net income from employment and independently performed services.
- Certain social security benefits.
- Income, other than wages and social security benefits, that is subject to wage withholding tax.
- Periodical payments in respect of study, disability, illness, or an accident.
- Pensions, annuities, and other periodical payments in respect to former business or labor activities.

From this income the following items can then be deducted:

- General social insurance premiums.
- Additions to the "old age reserve" of self-employed.
- Premiums in respect to (taxable) periodical payments. Any other income or deductions are allocated to the partner (husband or spouse) with the highest "personal income." This other income may consist of, for instance, investment income or profits from a "substantial interest." Deductions may include special expenses, charitable contributions, or extraordinary expenses. Hereafter, these income components are dealt with in greater detail.

Minor children are individually taxed if their income consists of:

- Profits from enterprise.
- Profits from a "substantial interest."
- Net income from employment and other economic activities.

Investment income of children under 18 as well as their personal liabilities will always be included in the income of their parents. For children between 18 and 21 this only applies if parents have the right of usufruct.

3. Tax Base

3.1 General Introduction

The ITA 1964 defines "income" as aggregate income from a number of sources. Resident taxpayers are subject to the tax on their worldwide income that has been earned within a given calendar year. Worldwide income from the following five sources is relevant here:

- Business income (subsection 3.2).
- Net income (i.e., after deduction of expenses) from employment or independently performed services. Almost all social security benefits are deemed labor income (subsection 3.3).
- Net income from capital (subsection 3.4).
- Income from periodical payments, for instance certain subsidies, benefits or grants received from the public sector (subsection 3.5).

• Gains from disposing of a "substantial interest" in a company (subsection 3.6). Income from these five sources constitutes aggregate income. Capital gains are not taxed, unless they are realized within an enterprise, qualify as income from independently performed economic activities or are derived from the sale of a "substantial interest."

Income in kind is taken into account at market value. However, in those cases where the item cannot be cashed or where it is unusual to do so, the value will at most be set at the amount that the taxpayer is deemed to have saved through the payment in kind.

Expenses are deductible if the costs are incurred to acquire or to keep the income, including depreciation of goods that produce income. Costs must have been made in relation to income derived from a certain source. Tax authorities may judge whether costs are "reasonable." For instance, according to a decision by the Supreme Court, deductible expenses are those which a taxpayer incurs within reasonable limits in the proper fulfillment of his employment. From subsequent court cases it may be concluded that deduction is allowed if costs have been made for doing a proper job, or if the employee could not in all reasonableness avoid making the expenses involved.

By contrast, in calculating business profits, all expenses incurred in the course of the business are deductible; the tax authorities are not allowed to make a judgement as to whether the expenses involved were reasonable or necessary.

Aggregate income may be decreased with certain deductible items which are not directly related to a specific source of income: a special deduction for self-employed, deduction of special expenses, extraordinary expenses, charitable contributions, and the addition to the old age reserve of self-employed (subsection 3.7). After these deductions, we have income.

Losses from business or a negative income incurred in a given year may—under certain conditions—be compensated with positive income of other years. Losses can be carried forward (eight years) as well as carried back (three years). Subtraction of losses from other years—if any—from income, results in the tax base: taxable income.

3.2 Business Income

Annual business income is calculated in accordance with rules of sound business practice. Various depreciation methods may be followed under sound business practice. Very common is the method of annual depreciation based on a fixed percentage of acquisition cost minus estimated residual value of the asset. For buildings (excluding land) this percentage is between 1.5 and three per annum, for machinery and inventory items it is between 10 and 20 percent.

The ITA 1964 provides for a number of exemptions. Some of them apply to the calculation of taxable profit in general and consequently are also relevant for corporate income taxpayers.

If a self-employed taxpayer ceases his business activities, either through a liquidation or through a transfer of business, the difference between the market value of the enterprise and its book value (on the fiscal balance sheet) will be included in taxable income to the extent that such profit exceeds a termination exemption of Dfl. 20,000. If a taxpayer carries on more than one business, he can apply the exemption for each business.

If a business is sold at a profit and the former owner stipulates that he be fully or partially paid in the form of annuity payments in the future, the system of ITA 1964 implies that both the profit (at the moment the business is sold) and future annuity payments would constitute taxable income. Profit realized from selling a business that is used to buy an annuity is therefore exempted under the annuity exemption, which may vary according to the circumstances and runs from approximately Dfl. 125,000 to 500,000. Annuity payments are taxed when received in later years.

Self-employed may annually set aside a certain amount to add to their old age reserve. The deduction is 11.5 percent of taxable profit for entrepreneurs with a profit below Dfl. 56,900 and 10 percent if profits exceed the latter amount. Moreover, the deduction has a lower and upper limit (Dfl. 1,026 and Dfl. 16,152 respectively). The total amount of the old age reserve may not exceed the net worth of the business, as mentioned in the fiscal balance sheet. The entrepreneur can at any time decide to convert the old age reserve into an annuity right, which is compulsory when he reaches age 65.

The high inflation of the seventies has prompted legislators to introduce two special deductions, which were defended at the time as an instrument to partially protect business against harmful effects of the strong rise of the general price level. Moreover, the introduction of both special deductions has been defended as a way to restore financial viability to large parts of the business community, which had suffered from two oil shocks and large wage increases during the seventies.

The capital deduction (see also section IV, subsection 1) allows the entrepreneur to deduct four percent of his own invested capital at the beginning of a given year, when calculating the annual profit of that year. Inventory for which the inventory deduction has been claimed is excluded when calculating invested capital.

The inventory deduction (see also section III, subsection 4.2) allows the entrepreneur to deduct four percent of the book value of the inventory at the beginning of the year. An inventory which is valued on a last-in first-out (LIFO) basis and goods ordered but not yet delivered are excluded from the basis of this tax facility.

3.3 Income from Labor

Income from labor includes wages of employees and income which is derived from independently performed services. "wage" and "employment" are defined in the Wage Tax Act of 1964 (WTA 1964). Wage tax (see also subsection 6) is withheld at source from wages, salaries, and other benefits in cash or in kind, arising from present or former employment. All social insurance payments are deemed "wages" and are also subject to withholding. Expenses are deductible if the costs are incurred to acquire or to keep income from employment. Employee contributions to social insurances that entitle insured workers to benefits in case of unemployment, illness, and disability (see section IV, subsection 3 for details) constitute the largest deductible item (Dfl. 12.4 billion in 1985) for wage earners. Employee contributions to private pension schemes (that supplement the general old age pension AOW) form another quantitatively important deduction (Dfl. 5.3 billion).

Travelling expenses between home and the place of work are deductible. The amounts are mentioned in the law and are based on the distance the employee has to cover daily. The minimum deduction is Dfl. 200 (corresponding to a distance not exceeding 10 kilometers); the maximum deduction amounts to Dfl. 3,370 (distance over 50 kilometers). The standard deduction for general expenses is four percent of gross income from labor, with a minimum of Dfl. 200 and a maximum of Dfl. 800. If, however, the taxpayer actually incurs higher expenses, those actual expenses may be deducted.

Allowances to compensate employees for costs that come with the job are not taxed (except, of course, to the extent that the tax inspector considers such allowances excessive).

Proceeds from labor activities which do not qualify as employment will be taxed as income from independently performed services. Examples are fees for services, income received from copyrights, and so on.

3.4 Capital Income

Income from capital (investment income) consists of all income from immovable and intangible property, unless such income would also qualify as business income or income from independently performed services. Investment income is taxed on the person who actually has the benefit of the good or right. Income from immovable property includes rent and any other compensation received from the tenants and lessees of land and buildings, less all expenses (local property tax, costs of maintenance, depreciation, etc.). Special rules apply to calculate the imputed rent of owner-occupied property. The law fixes the net imputed rent at 0.6 percent of the market value of the property. Moreover, interest payments are deductible in full. This explains why, in 1985, aggregate negative income from owner-occupied housing amounted to approximately Dfl. 10 billion or 2.5 percent of GNP.

Income from intangible property includes a wide range of investment income, such as interest, dividends, and other distributions of profit. Any distribution of profit by a company, whether or not in the form of dividends, will be considered taxable income derived from the holding of shares. This applies to disguised distributions as well. An example of a disguised distribution is the sale of company assets below market value to a shareholder. A resident taxpayer can be taxed on a deemed annual income, if he owns shares in certain qualifying foreign investment companies. These are companies or other legal entities which mainly own portfolio investments and similar investments. Depending on the nature of the investments, an amount equal to 4.8, six or 10.4 percent will be included in the income of shareholders of qualifying foreign investment companies.

On January 1, 1981 an interest exemption was introduced. Under this exemption the positive balance between interest received and paid is exempt up to Dfl. 700 per year. The interest exemption is doubled to Dfl. 1,400 if the spouse does not file a tax return of her own.

Generally speaking, dividends from Netherlands companies are exempt up to Dfl. 1,000 per year. The dividend exemption is doubled to Dfl. 2,000 if the spouse does not file a tax return of her own. Under Dutch tax laws corporate income is taxed both on the level of the company (corporate income tax) as well as on the level of shareholders (personal income tax). The dividend exemption has been defended as an instrument to limit this "double taxation" of shareholders.

3.5 Income from Periodic Payments

Apart from taxable periodic income which can be claimed on the basis of earlier payment of premiums or a lump sum, such as annuity payments, ITA 1964 recognizes several other taxable payments of a periodical character. Some examples are payments under public law, such as student grants and alimony.

3.6 Gains from a Substantial Interest in a Company

The capital gain realized on the sale of qualifying shares is considered a separate source of income under Dutch income tax law. In fact this provision is an exception to the general rule that capital gains are not taxable (unless qualifying as business income or income derived from independently performed services). A substantial interest in a company exists if a taxpayer owns (or owned during the last five years), either directly or indirectly, alone or with certain relatives at least one-third of the shares of a company and, in addition, together with his spouse owns more than seven percent of the nominal paid-in share capital. Not only gains at the sale of shares will be taxed, but also those realized by disposing of the shares in other ways. The profit is calculated by subtracting the original acquisition price of the shares from the transfer price.

Gains from a substantial interest are taxed at a flat rate of 20 percent. A loss derived from the sale of a substantial interest entitles the taxpayer to a tax credit of 20 percent of that loss.

3.7 Deductions Not Related to Source of Income

The ITA 1964 provides for several deductions of expenses that are not related to a source of income.

Special expenses are deductible from total gross income. In practice the most important deductions under this heading are the following:

• Annuity payments, for instance to former servants, and other periodic payments, such as alimony; also lump sums to replace alimony payments.

• Interest on debts.

• Life annuity premiums paid to an insurance company (with a maximum of Dfl. 16,305 per annum) and premiums for private insurance against the risk of disablement, sickness, or an accident.

• General social insurance premiums paid. This is by far the largest deductible item in ITA 1964 (Dfl. 25.6 billion in 1985).

Extraordinary expenses are intended to take account of ability to pay. These expenses are only deductible if they are borne by the taxpayer (are not reimbursable via private insurance). The law mentions four categories of extraordinary expenses:

• Medical expenses (payments in connection with sickness, disability, childbirth, and death). Expenses are deductible insofar as they exceed 12.2 percent of gross income (for taxpayers with gross income below Dfl. 48,370). The threshold for taxpayers with gross income between Dfl. 48,370 and Dfl. 108,000 is calculated as three percent of gross income plus Dfl. 4,450. The threshold for taxpayers with gross income over Dfl. 108,000 is Dfl. 7,700. The deductible amount (expenses over threshold) may be multiplied by a factor of 1.25 or 1.5, depending on the number of consecutive years that the taxpayer has been claiming the medical expenses deduction.

• Support of certain relatives (payments in excess of Dfl. 800 or—if less—an amount equal to two percent of gross income).

• Training or study costs (insofar as they exceed Dfl. 800 or— if less—an amount equal to two percent of gross income).

• Household help and cost of childcare for one-parent families. These expenses have to exceed 10 percent of gross income (and also a threshold of Dfl. 10,800). The maximum deduction is Dfl. 32,400. This tax expenditure probably constitutes the smallest deductible item in the law, at a cost to the budget of only a few million.

Charitable gifts to qualifying domestic religious, cultural, scientific, and charitable institutions are deductible insofar as they exceed one percent of gross income (and at least Dfl. 120) and do not exceed 10 percent of gross income.

4. Tax Rates

The personal income tax in the Netherlands has steeply progressive rates, that are applied to the taxable sum (that is, taxable income less personal exemptions).

As a rule every taxpayer is entitled to the same personal exemption of Dfl. 7,168. But additional exemptions may be claimed, depending on personal circumstances. The additional exemptions are:

• Single exemption (Dfl. 3,584) for taxpayers 27 years and older that live without a partner.

• One-earner exemption (Dfl. 7,168) for taxpayers with a non-earning partner (marital status not relevant).

• One-parent exemption (Dfl. 5,735) for one-parent families if the household has dependent children under 27 years.

• Additional one-parent exemption if the head of a one-parent family works outside the home and the household has dependent children under 15 years. The additional one-parent exemption is one quarter of earnings, with a maximum of Dfl. 4,333.

Taxpayers working outside the home enjoy a labor exemption of Dfl. 397. There is an additional labor exemption of Dfl. 768 for two-earner families, if the household has dependent children under 12 years.

It may be pointed out that the basic personal exemptions are far below the minimum subsistence level, which in the Netherlands is equal to the net minimum wage for employees 23 years and over. This so-called "social minimum" is about Dfl. 1,550 per month (as per June 30, 1986).

After the relevant personal exemptions have been subtracted from taxable income, the following rate-schedule is applied (onto the taxable sum):

On the first	Dfl. 9,334	16 percent
On the next	Dfl. 7,200	25 percent
On the next	Dfl. 14,319	32 percent
On the next	Dfl. 12,594	42 percent
On the next	Dfl. 19,911	52 percent
On the next	Dfl. 25,558	61 percent
On the next	Dfl. 28,575	67 percent
On the next	Dfl. 105,496	70 percent
On the excess	(over Dfl. 222,987)	72 percent

The personal exemptions, income brackets, and certain other amounts in the law are automatically adjusted for inflation every year, unless Parliament explicitly decides otherwise. This requires a separate bill.

The income tax has two proportional rates which are applied to certain types of income:

• A flat 20 percent rate, which applies for instance to gains from the sale of a substantial interest (section 3.6).

• A flat rate of between 20 and 54 percent; the actual rate percentage depends on the average income of the previous four years as well as the amount of income subject to this special rate. This rate applies, for instance, to profit derived from the sale or termination of business. In general, income subject to this rate is not received annually. The flat rate is intended to smooth the effects of the progressive rates which would otherwise be applicable.

If income from a certain source varies over the years and final assessments have been made, the taxpayer may benefit from the income averaging provision. Under this provision one-third of aggregate source income of three consecutive years will be allocated to each of the tax years concerned. If the recomputed total tax liability (over those three years) is less than that already assessed, the balance will be refunded to the taxpayer.

5. Nonresident Taxpayers

Under Dutch law nonresidents are only subject to personal income tax if they receive domestic income, that is income from certain domestic sources. These sources are enumerated in the ITA 1964:

- Income from a permanent business establishment.
- Income from employment within the Netherlands, including pensions.
- Income from real estate that is located in the Netherlands. As a rule, capital gains will not be taxed.
- Interest on debts that are secured by a mortgage on Dutch real estate.
- Income from shares, bonds issued or debts incurred by a domestic corporation which accrues to a foreign shareholder who owns a substantial interest in that company (subsection 3.6). Capital gains on the sale of such substantial interest will be taxable at the special rate of 20 percent.
- Social insurance benefits and periodical payments under government programs.

Nonresident taxpayers cannot claim deductions for extraordinary expenses or charitable gifts. Their deduction of special expenses is limited to general social insurance contributions and interest on a loan secured by a mortgage on real estate located in the Netherlands.

6. The Wage Withholding Tax

As already mentioned, the wage withholding tax is levied on the basis of the Wage Tax Act of 1965 (WTA 1965). The tax is levied from the employee, that is any individual who is employed by a wages tax withholding agent. Whether there is an employment situation is primarily judged on the basis of civil law. A basic criterion is the required relationship of authority between employer and employee. It should be noted that recipients of private pension income and social insurance benefits are deemed "employees." Likewise, pension funds, insurance companies and institutions which administer and pay social insurance benefits are all deemed "employers."

The wage tax can be credited against personal income tax. If certain conditions are met, the wage withholding tax will function as final tax for the employee. In 1985 over 7.3 million individuals had incomes of their own and were therefore liable for income tax.[2] For over two million taxpayers the wage tax was the final tax, i.e., these taxpayers did not need to file a tax return and did not receive an assessment, because approximately the right amount of (wage) tax had been withheld at source. Slightly over five million taxpayers had to file returns.

The tax base is net wage. Net wage is defined as gross earnings from employment less deductible expenses and relevant personal exemptions. At the request of the employee the tax inspector may license the employer to take into account certain other deductions as well, notably interest on mortgage loans and extraordinary expenses of the employee.

Rates and personal exemptions of the wage withholding tax mirror those of the personal income tax.

The wage withholding tax is levied by self-assessment of the employer. Employers pay the wage tax monthly or quarterly to the tax collector.

7. Quantification of Main Deductions and Exemptions

Table 4 presents a quantification of the most important deductions and exemptions in the personal income tax (including the wage withholding tax). To compute the revenue loss which results from the main existing deductions and exemptions (totalling Dfl. 114.4 billion) it is not sufficient to look only at the income tax foregone. It should be noted that the tax base for the general social insurance contributions closely resembles taxable income (section VI, subsection 2). So most deductions and exemptions also reduce revenue from these contributions. Likewise, the abolition of deductions and exemptions would give rise not only to higher revenue from the personal income tax, but also from general social insurance contributions.

Revenue from the personal income tax and general social insurance contributions amounted to Dfl. 87.3 billion in 1985. The corresponding tax base was approximately Dfl. 210 billion (contributions) and Dfl. 140 billion (income tax, after personal exemptions) respectively. At first sight the elimination of all deductions and exemptions (Dfl. 114.4 billion) could thus broaden the tax base by 50 and 80 percent, respectively. However, tax specialists in this country would not agree.

Some very important deductions in table 4 are general social insurance contributions (Dfl. 25.6 billion), employee social insur-

---

[2]Husband and spouse are counted as one taxpayer.

ance contributions (Dfl. 12.4 billion), and employee contributions to private pension schemes (Dfl. 5.3 billion). The most important exemptions include certain employer contributions to the social insurances (totalling Dfl. 27.6 billion) and to private pension schemes (Dfl. 13.9 billion).[3]

It should be noted that if these deductions and exemptions were repealed, benefits and pensions received—which are now taxed—would, according to conventional tax doctrine, have to be exempted. As contributions to social insurance schemes are equal to benefits from these schemes (on a year-to-year basis) the elimination of the present deduction and exemption of contributions would therefore not result in a broader tax base. Nevertheless, tax revenue might increase quite substantially, as on average the marginal rates of present contributors to the schemes are higher than marginal rates of taxpayers who receive benefits from the schemes.

In the long run the same analysis applies to private pension schemes. However, in 1984 contributions to pension funds and insurance companies exceeded pension benefits paid out by roughly Dfl. seven billion. A reversal of the tax treatment (contributions of employees no longer deductible, contributions of employers no longer tax-exempt and benefits tax-exempt) might increase revenue of the income tax and general social insurance contributions by over Dfl. three billion. In the next century pension benefits will exceed contributions. An alternative tax treatment of pension schemes would then lead to lower revenues than under the present system.

In fact, exempted employers contributions and deductible employee contributions to private pension schemes and employee social insurances do not qualify as suitable items for broadening the tax base. The items mentioned involve over half of the total amount of deductions and exemptions (Dfl. 59.2 billion versus Dfl. 114.4 billion).

Interest deductions are other important items in table 4. As most capital gains go untaxed, the unlimited deduction of interest offers possibilities to reduce one's present tax liability by taking loans, using the proceeds of those loans to buy assets and sell these in due time while realizing a tax free capital gain. One option to counter this type of tax planning might be to limit interest deductions to the amount of positive capital income which a taxpayer includes in his or her tax return. Another option would be to increase the imputed rent of the most important asset, i.e. owner-occupied houses, as the present net rent of 0.6 percent of the freehold value is

---

[3]Data on private pension schemes refer to year 1984.

clearly too low. Opinions may differ as to the correct percentage of net return on this type of investment. Some have defended one percent of freehold value; this result is partly based on a comparison with net return on investment in rented property. However, this is influenced by rent control. It, therefore, does not seem right to use net returns on investment in rented property as a yardstick for rent of owner-occupied dwellings to be imputed. A higher percentage than one would certainly seem defendable.

8. Who Has Deductions and Exemptions?

This paragraph shows the distribution of a number of deductions and exemptions by:

(a) Six socioeconomic groups: (1) self-employed, (2) directors of companies, (3) employees plus unemployed, (4) government personnel, (5) pensioners, and (6) others.

(b) Three income-classes: (1) less than Dfl. 30,000, (2) between Dfl. 30,000 and 80,000 and (3) over Dfl. 80,000. Taxpayers are ranked in these classes on the basis of their taxable income.

All results are based on a 3.3 percent sample survey of all tax returns for tax year 1981. The sample includes 250,000 returns. Data from these returns have been adjusted for changes in the level of prices and incomes between 1981 and 1985. Next, the adjusted survey data have been processed with a microeconomic simulation model which embodies the tax legislation of 1985. All computations have been carried out by the ministry of Finance, at the request of the Tax Simplification Commission (section X, subsection 2).

It should be noted that some (major) exemptions and deductions which are enumerated in table 4 are excluded from the presentation in tables 5 and 6. These are: the exemption of employers' contributions to the social insurances and private pension schemes and the deduction of employees' contributions to the employee social insurances and private pension schemes. Together these programs involve Dfl. 59.2 billion; it follows that the total of deductions and exemptions taken into account in tables 5 and 6 amounts to about Dfl. 55 billion.

In 1985 taxpayers had on average Dfl. 7,480 in deductions and exemptions. Employees (and unemployed) are by far the largest socioeconomic group (3.4 million taxpayers); they had about the average amount in deductions and exemptions (Dfl. 7,460). Directors of companies (0.1 million) had on average the largest amount in deductions and exemptions (Dfl. 27,620) while pensioners (Dfl. 3,000) and taxpayers in the category "others" (Dfl. 1,980) claimed the smallest amounts.

Table 6 shows the distribution of deductions and exemptions by three classes of taxable income.[4] Nearly two-thirds of all taxpayers are ranked as low-income earners (their taxable income being less than Dfl. 30,000). Slightly over one-third of all taxpayers belong to the middle income class (with taxable income between Dfl. 30,000 and 80,000). Two percent of all taxpayers, having a taxable income over Dfl. 80,000, are in the "top class."

On average, taxpayers in the middle class have twice the amount in deductions and exemptions (Dfl. 10,300) of low-income taxpayers (Dfl. 5,260). Deductions and exemptions of high-income taxpayers (Dfl. 26,190) are on average five times those of low-income taxpayers. These results will not come as a surprise, because they are in line with results that have been found for other industrialized countries.

III. CORPORATE INCOME TAX

1. Introduction

The corporate income tax is levied on the basis of the Corporate Income Tax Act of 1969 (CITA 1969). Under Dutch tax laws corporate income is taxed both on the level of the company (corporate income tax) as well as on the level of shareholders (personal income tax).

Taxable entities have to file tax accounts together with their annual tax return. The tax year for domestic taxpayers is the accounting year and not the calendar year, provided regular book-keeping is maintained.

A company that distributes profits has to withhold 25 percent on dividends paid out to its shareholders (dividend withholding tax).

2. Liability to the Tax

The tax is levied on resident and certain nonresident legal entities. Such an entity is considered to be a resident of the Netherlands if it is either incorporated under Dutch law or if it is actually established in the Netherlands. Whether this is, in fact, the case will depend on the specific circumstances. Most important in this connection is the place of central management, but other factors will also be taken into account, for instance the location where the company's books are kept or shareholder meetings are

---

[4]Results in table 6 are estimates, based on published data of the Tax Simplification Commission.

held. The following entities established in the Netherlands are subject to corporate income tax:

- Corporations (limited companies).
- Cooperatives.
- Certain other, less important categories that are enumerated in CITA 1969. The basic idea is that any entity which carries on a business (except individuals and associations of individuals, such as partnerships) should be subject to the tax. Pension funds and hospitals, among other entities, are tax-exempt provided certain conditions are met.

Certain nonresident entities are also subject to Netherlands corporate income tax, provided these entities have domestic income. The most common entities are companies, associations, and limited partnerships with capital divided into shares. Nonresident companies are liable to tax on their income from Dutch sources. In CITA 1969 this is defined by reference to ITA 1964 (see section II, subsection 5).

3. Tax Base

The tax is levied on the basis of taxable profit. The profits should be calculated in accordance with sound business practice, based on consistent principles. Profit consists of all types of income of whatever nature, derived from undertakings carried out in the Netherlands or abroad. No distinction is made between "ordinary" profit and capital gains, which are both taxed on the same basis.

4. Some Important Deductions and Exemptions

4.1 Capital Deduction

The annual capital deduction is four percent of the company's fiscal equity: from taxable profit may be deducted an amount equal to four percent of the equity at the beginning of the year. Some assets, notably participations and inventories for which inventory deduction has been claimed, are for this purpose excluded from fiscal equity.

On October 1, 1986 the deduction was lowered to one percent. Inventories which qualified for the inventory deduction will no longer be excluded from the base on which the capital deduction is determined, the reason being the complete elimination of the inventory deduction (see next paragraph).

4.2 Inventory Deduction

The annual inventory deduction amounts to four percent of the book value of the inventory at the beginning of the year. Inventories to which a last-in first-out system applies are excluded as are goods ordered but not yet delivered. These exceptions may be explained because the deduction originally was mainly intended to limit the effects of inflation on taxable profits. Since October 1, 1986 the inventory deduction has been abolished. The revenue of personal and corporate income tax combined will increase by Dfl. 1.77 billion through the limitation of the capital deduction and the complete disappearance of the inventory deduction.

These measures have a common background. Both tax facilities were intended to protect business against the harmful effects of inflation and to revitalize firms which had severely suffered from "profit squeeze" in the seventies. However, inflation is expected to be practically nil in the next few years and profits have strongly improved since 1983. On the other hand, the fall of oil prices has put government finances under a serious strain. The government's receipts from its share in natural gas profits will tumble from Dfl. 21.3 billion (1986) to nine billion (1987) on a cash basis, because the price of natural gas is linked to international oil prices. The Cabinet has decided upon an austerity plan to curb the threatening rise of the public sector deficit (which already looms large), as well as slashing the inventory deduction and reducing the capital deduction.

4.3 Participation Exemption

The participation exemption has been introduced to avoid double taxation. All proceeds (profits, capital gains) derived from a participation in the share capital of another company, which have been held without interruption since the beginning of the book year, will be excluded from the taxable profit of the "holding" company. The following conditions must be met to qualify for the exemption:

• Capital of the company in which the participation is held must be divided into shares.

• Shareholding of at least five percent. The participation should be equal to at least five percent of the par value of the paid-up capital of the company invested in.

• Uninterrupted shareholding since the beginning of the book year in which the dividend from the participation is received.

To qualify, participants in nonresident companies must meet a few additional conditions:

• Participation must not be a portfolio investment.

- Foreign company is subject to a state tax on profits. The rate of this profit tax is irrelevant. It is not required that the foreign profit tax has actually been imposed or collected.

4.4 Charitable Contributions

Charitable contributions to religious, scientific, cultural, and charitable institutions can be deducted if at least Dfl. 500, up to a maximum of six percent of profit. The contributions concerned may not give rise to rights which can be valued in money terms.

4.5 Quantification of Some Important Deductions and Exemptions

The capital and inventory deduction in the corporate income tax amounted to nearly Dfl. three billion in 1985, which implies a revenue loss of about Dfl. 1.25 billion. No comparable data on the participation exemption and the deduction of charitable contributions is available. The participation exemption no doubt involves tens of billions of guilders a year. So the tax base of the corporate income tax could be substantially broadened by abolishing this exemption. However, most of the extra revenue would drain away because it would be necessary to replace the participation exemption with another device to prevent double taxation of (the same) company profits.

The participation exemption is instrumental in many international tax planning set-ups. If the participation exemption were abolished, revenue from the corporate income tax would no doubt also drop because the attractiveness of the Netherlands as a tax haven would be greatly reduced.

A major facility in the corporate income tax is the Investment Tax Credit (to be dealt with in more detail in section VII, subsection 3.3). Total cost of this program amounts to about Dfl. 5.3 billion. By far the larger part of this amount (Dfl. 4.5 billion) benefits corporations; the remainder (Dfl. 0.75 billion) is credited against income tax obligations of the self-employed.

5. Tax Rate

The rate of the corporate income tax is 43 percent.

IV. VALUE-ADDED TAX

1. Introduction

In 1969 a turnover tax based on the value-added tax system was introduced in the Netherlands. The Value-Added Tax Act of 1968 (VATA 1968) stipulates that the tax is levied on all entrepreneurs, including the retail trade. Every taxpayer is liable for value-added tax (VAT) on his turnover, but he may subtract from the tax due VAT which has been charged to him on his "inputs" (expenses and investments). The VAT which has been charged to an entrepreneur will be referred to hereafter as "pre-paid VAT."

A positive balance between VAT due and prepaid VAT must be paid to the tax collector. A negative balance will be refunded by the tax collector. In this way VAT cannot have cumulative effects. Ultimately the consumer pays the relevant percentage of VAT on his purchasing price. His tax burden equals the aggregate of VAT which was on balance paid by all entrepreneurs that were involved in producing and delivering the goods and services.

VAT is intended to be levied on domestic consumption. For that reason exporters are taxed at a zero rate. Exported goods leave the country untaxed, because prepaid VAT may be claimed by the exporter and will be refunded to him in full. On the other hand, imported goods are subject to VAT.

Under the VAT system all goods and services are taxed at the same relative percentage, regardless of the number of transactions involved (internal neutrality) and regardless of the country of origin of the goods (external neutrality).

It may be noted that some pre-paid VAT is not deductible. VAT on expenses and investments which are attributable to exempt transactions (section 4) is not deductible, nor is there a VAT on meals and drinks consumed in a restaurant, nor for tobacco products.

VAT must be paid on the basis of a return. The period covered by the return is usually one month. VAT which has not been paid to the tax collector can be additionally assessed.

2. Liability for the Tax

Liable for the tax is the entrepreneur who sells goods and renders services. An entrepreneur is anyone who carries on a business independently. Neither nationality nor place of residence are, in principle, relevant.

3. Tax Base

Three types of economic activity give rise to tax liability:
- Deliveries of goods within the Netherlands by entrepreneurs.
- Supply of services within the Netherlands by entrepreneurs.
- Import of goods, regardless of whether the importer is an entrepreneur. VAT is levied on the total amount (excluding the VAT itself) which has been charged for the delivery of goods and services.

4. Exemptions

The import and delivery of a number of goods and services is exempted from VAT. Please note that in these cases the entrepreneur cannot deduct the prepaid VAT that has been charged to him on expenses and investments. Exempt goods and services include, among others:
- Transfer or rental of real estate.
- Medical services.
- Most services provided by banks.
- Postal and telephone services.

5. Tax Rates

Generally speaking VAT has three rates:
- The general rate is 19 percent.
- A lower rate of five percent applies to certain goods and services that are enumerated in VATA 1968, for instance various foodstuffs, works of art, books, medicines, and the provision of lodging and meals by hotels and restaurants.
- The zero rate applies to the export of goods, and the purchase of seagoing vessels and aircraft that are used for international transportation.

On October 1, 1986 both the general rate and the lower rate of VAT were raised by one point, to 20 and six percent respectively. The additional revenue is estimated at Dfl. two billion. This measure forms part of the austerity plan, mentioned earlier in section III, subsection 4.2.

V. OTHER TAXES LEVIED BY CENTRAL GOVERNMENT

1. Introduction

Apart from the three main taxes (personal and corporate income tax and value-added tax) the central government levies a number of less important taxes (in terms of revenue). Table 7 gives an overview of these taxes and their revenue in 1985. Among these taxes, excises are clearly the most important, as they account for almost half of total revenue from the taxes considered here.

In this paper the taxes from table 7 will not be considered in any detail, with two exceptions because the levies concerned are potentially important policy instruments to change the relative wealth and income position of individuals. These levies are:
- The wealth tax.
- The estate tax and the gift tax.

2. Wealth Tax

In the Netherlands only individuals are subject to a wealth tax. It is a tax on net wealth (assets minus liabilities) of residents. Nonresidents are subject to the wealth tax if they own certain assets that are located in the Netherlands. Residence is determined in the same way as for the personal income tax.

Taxable net wealth is calculated on the basis of a tax return that taxpayers have to file with the tax inspector together with their income tax return. In fact, both returns are on one form.

The spouse is subject to the wealth tax herself, but her assets and liabilities are added to those of her husband, regardless of how they have established their matrimonial property rights. Children are taxed separately.

The tax is levied on total net wealth at the beginning of the calendar year. Assets are defined as any assets which have a market value or for which a market value can be estimated. Assets include all sorts of property, tangible or intangible. So, copyrights are an asset, but goodwill and the right to alimony payments are not. Also pension rights and life insurance policies (under certain conditions) have been exempted. Works of art are also exempted and thus offer a "tax shelter" for well-to-do taxpayers who want to evade the wealth tax.

The value to be taken into account is the market value of qualifying assets. There is, however, an important exception for owner-occupied houses: the taxpayer's residence is valued at 60 percent of the (freehold) market value. The reader is reminded in this connection that interest is fully deductible under the personal income tax.

The rate is .8 percent of net wealth, after personal exemptions have been taken into account. The exemption amounts to Dfl. 55,000 (single person under 35 years), Dfl. 89,000 (single person of 35 years and over) and Dfl. 109,000 (one- and two-earner families). There is an additional exemption of Dfl. 6,000 for each child under 18 years and of Dfl. 34,000 per child of 18-27 years who is studying and supported by his or her parents. Self-employed have an extra exemption, which is calculated as 50 percent of the investment in their own business (but at least Dfl. 114,000 and at most Dfl. 317,000).

It should be noted here that wealthy people can use the provision of article 14, paragraph 6 of the Wealth Tax Act 1964 as a device in strategic tax planning. Under this rule no taxpayer has to pay more than 80 percent of his taxable income in income tax and wealth tax together (over the relevant tax year). So any wealthy taxpayer who succeeds in bringing down his taxable income to nil (and there are several ways to do this), does not pay any tax on his wealth either.

3. Estate Tax and Gift Tax

The estate tax and gift tax are levied on the basis of the Estate Tax Act of 1956 (ETA 1956). The estate tax is levied on the (net) value of assets that are acquired through inheritance from a resident of the Netherlands. The gift tax is levied on the (net) value of assets that the donee receives as a gift from a donor who is a resident of the Netherlands. Residence is decided on the basis of actual circumstances. If the donor or the deceased is a Dutch citizen living abroad he is deemed a resident of the Netherlands for 10 years after his or her emigration. The residence of the recipient is of no relevance here. The main exemptions under the estate tax are:
- Benefits from a pension scheme.
- Bequests to the State.
- Acquisitions by husband or spouse, not exceeding Dfl. 444,317. The value of pension rights is subtracted, but the exemption remains at least Dfl. 126,947. There is an additional exemption which—per child—is between Dfl. 146,004 (zero years) and Dfl. 12,695 (22 years), depending on the age of the child(ren).

The main exemptions under the gift tax are:
- Gifts to the State.
- Gifts to children, up to Dfl. 6,348 (per year).

• Gifts which are subject to personal income tax for the receiving party.

The tax rate depends both on the value of the acquired assets (after the relevant exemptions are applied) and the relationship of the heir (or donee) towards the deceased (or donor). The acquisition is valued at market value. The rates of the estate and gift tax are in table 8.

VI. SOCIAL INSURANCE CONTRIBUTIONS

1. Introduction

In Chapter I it was pointed out that about two-thirds of total public outlays consist of income transfers. Apart from transfers out of the government budget, social insurance benefits are an important vehicle for redistributing personal incomes in the Netherlands. In 1985 the latter benefits amounted to Dfl. 87 billion. Benefits are nearly financed in full from contributions (Dfl. 84 billion), the remainder being covered by government grants and interest earned on the financial reserves of the social insurance funds.

Social insurance programs may be divided into two main categories:

• General social insurances; these programs cover all residents and are specified in section 2.

• Employee social insurances; these programs only cover a part of the population, i.e., workers in the market sector and their families, and are dealt with in greater detail in section 3.

Contributions to the general social insurances are paid by households (employees and self-employed) and by employers. Contributions to the employee insurances are paid by employees and employers. Table 9 gives a financial overview of all social insurance programs, in the form of a "balance sheet."

From table 9 it follows that contributions of private households finance about three-fifths of the total cost. Employers finance nearly two-fifths. Government grants are relatively unimportant.

2. General Social Insurance Contributions

All residents are covered by five general social insurances. These programs are:

• General Old Age Pension (residents of 65 years and over are entitled to pension which is equal to net minimum wage) (AOW).

- General Widow and Orphan Pension (AWW).
- General Child Benefit (AKW).
- General Disablement Pension (AAW).
- General Insurance against Exceptional Medical Expenses (covers costs of prolonged stay in hospital, etc.) (AWBZ).

All residents in the age group 15-64 years have to pay premiums for the general social insurances. The contributions for two programs (Old Age Pension and Widow and Orphan Pension) are calculated as 13.1 percent of a taxpayer's premium income. This premium income is defined as taxable income for the personal income tax plus contributions for general insurances which have been deducted as special expenses (section II, subsection 3.7). These contributions rise in proportion to income up to a contribution ceiling Dfl. 63,200).

The contributions for the three other general insurances (known as "supplementary contributions") are then derived from the total amount of AOW and AWW contributions. In 1985 the supplementary contributions were 108.8 percent of the amount of AOW/AWW contributions due (see example 1.)

Example 1
Rates and Contribution Ceiling of the
Five General Social Insurances, 1985

	(percent)		
AOW contribution	11.7		
AWW contribution	1.4		
Total	13.1	of premium income	
		(ceiling Dfl. 63,200)	maximum Dfl. 8,279
Supplementary contributions:			
AKW contribution	32.4		
AAW contribution	30.2		
AWBZ contribution	46.2		
Total	108.8	of AOW and AWW contribution	
		(maximum Dfl. 8,279)	9,007
Maximum of contributions for general insurances			17,286

Both the personal income tax and general insurance contributions are levied in two ways: through (1) assessment and (2) withholding. Self-employed and taxpayers with other income that is not subject to withholding are assessed for their contributions to all five general insurances. If income is subject to withholding of wage tax it is also subject to withholding of AOW and AWW contributions. In practice, such income will consist of wages and social security benefits. In this case the supplementary contributions are paid directly by employers or institutions which provide benefits.

There is no personal exemption, but self-employed and other taxpayers with low incomes who are assessed for their contributions are entitled to reductions. The complicated calculation of these reductions will not be detailed here. On wages, salaries, and social security benefits AOW and AWW contributions are withheld from the first guilder.

Table 10 specifies general insurances by program. The table also indicates, for each program, which part of the contributions involved was paid by employers and which part by households. Table 10 presents the statutory incidence of the contributions under consideration. The economic incidence may of course be quite different, because of the shifting of the burden.

3. Employee Social Insurance Contributions

Participation in the employee social insurances is mandatory for all workers in the market sector. Employee social insurances entitle insured workers to benefits in case of unemployment (for six months), illness (up to a year), and disability (until the disabled person becomes 65 years at which point he or she is entitled to general old age pension). Benefits are equal to 70 percent of the insured wage. The maximum insured wage is Dfl. 68,455 per annum. Civil servants have their own income maintenance programs, which are—generally speaking—substantially more generous than employee insurances. The programs for government personnel are paid out of general revenues. Self-employed people have to rely on private insurance against the risk of income loss through illness and disability.

The contribution is levied on the basis of the gross wage of the individual employee (after deduction of the employee's contribution to his or her private pension scheme). Most contribution rates are proportional; they are due up to a contribution ceiling of Dfl. 68,455 (the maximum insured wage). Disability insurance is the exception. No contribution is due on the first Dfl. 23,750 of wages. The contribution ceiling of Dfl. 68,455 applies.

Table 11 specifies employee insurances by program. The table also indicates, for each program, which part of the contributions involved was paid by employers and which part by employees.

Again, table 11 presents the statutory incidence of the contributions under consideration. The economic incidence may, of course be quite different, because of the shifting of the burden. Indeed there are rather strong indications that an important part of the general rise in employee social insurance contributions and wage withholding tax during the sixties and seventies has been shifted from employees to employers. This process has resulted in a substantial "profit squeeze," which was partially redressed in the first half of the eighties. Very high unemployment may partially explain the modest wage claims of unions at the time.

Employee contributions cover about two-thirds of the cost of employee social insurances. It should be noted that the rates between brackets are in most cases both the marginal and average rate, as contributions are due from the first guilder of wage. However, disability insurance contributions are a notable exception. This program has an exemption of Dfl. 23,750; on wages in excess of this threshold the marginal rate amounts to 16 percent (the average rate is 6.1 percent). This explains why the marginal rate of employee insurance contributions for an average production worker amounts to 24.4 percent instead of the 14.5 percent which is mentioned in the totals row of table 11. See also section IX.

VII. TAXES, SAVING AND INVESTMENT

1. Introduction

The Dutch tax system has a number of provisions that are intended to stimulate saving and investment. Some of the most important are set out in section 2 and section 3 respectively. Paragraph 4 offers some concluding remarks on the effectiveness of tax incentives for investment.

2. Income Tax and Personal Savings

Returns on savings are generally subject to personal income tax. On average they will be rather heavily taxed. However, especially taxpayers with small savings may profit from the dividend exemption (up to Dfl. 1,000 per year) and the interest exemption (up to Dfl. 700 per year). See section II, subsection 3.4.

As has been pointed out in section II, subsection 3.1, most capital gains of individual taxpayers are exempted, with some notable exemptions. It is inherent to the tax system as it stands that the effective tax rate on returns from investment will differ, depending on the assets involved. For instance, investment in owner-occupied housing is heavily subsidized because the net imputed rent is very low (0.6 percent of freehold value) while nominal interest payments are deductible in full. Tax treatment of private pension schemes may lead to rather serious distortions in capital markets. Employer contributions to pension funds are exempt from income tax, while employees may fully deduct their contribution to these funds. The value of pension rights is not taxed under the wealth tax. Pension funds are exempt from tax as they accumulate the returns on assets they hold. As these funds have an investment policy which tries to minimize risks, the tax system discriminates against risk capital for industry and beginning entrepreneurs.

The very lenient tax treatment of pension schemes moreover discriminates against individuals that prefer or have to rely on their own savings for old age. However, self-employed persons may create an "old age reserve"; amounts they add to this reserve are deductible (within rather generous limits, see section II, subsection 3.2). Taxpayers may also deduct annuity premiums up to Dfl. 16,305 per annum, if these are paid to an insurance company. This preferential form of saving, again discriminates against risky investments, such as in high-tech industries or a newly started business.

In fact, the pattern of household savings has fundamentally changed during the past fifteen years, undoubtedly in part under the influence of the different tax treatments of various assets. In 1970 households saved 14 percent of net disposable income, 7.5 percent of which was through pension funds and insurance companies. In 1984 the savings ratio was about the same, but over 11 percent of disposable income was saved through pension funds and insurance companies and only three percent via saving accounts, buying shares, etc.

3. Investment Incentives

3.1 Replacement Reserve

Firms can set aside profits realized on selling old assets, such as buildings, equipment and machinery if these are reinvested within four years (replacement reserve).

3.2 Depreciation Rules

Rules for depreciation and the valuation of inventories are fairly generous in the Netherlands, as it is sufficient that these rules are in accordance with sound business practice.

3.3 Investment Tax Credit (WIR Premiums)

Investments in business assets by firms and self-employed often qualify for Investment Tax Credit (ITC). Business assets not only include buildings and machinery, but also assets such as know-how and patents. Certain assets are excluded from ITC, notably residences, land and building sites, cars, securities, and goodwill.

The basic rate of ITC is 12.5 percent of the amount invested. In addition, taxpayers may, under certain conditions, claim:

• Extra ITC to stimulate small business. The percentage is six (if annual investments are less than Dfl. 47,000) and gradually decreases to nil (if annual investments are over 1.1 million guilders).

• Extra ITC to stimulate investment in assets that limit environmental pollution. The percentage varies from three to 15, depending on the type of investment.

• Extra ITC to stimulate investment in assets that save energy. The percentage varies from four to 25, depending on the type of investment.

ITC may be credited against personal or corporate income tax due. If ITC surpasses the tax due, the balance is paid out to the taxpayer (negative assessment). As this device figured prominently in many (international) tax planning schemes, the possibility of a negative assessment has been repealed by a change of the law as per May 1, 1986.

Tax credits under the ITC-program amounted to Dfl. 5.3 billion (1.4 percent of net national income) in 1985. In view of the large amounts of tax money involved, the relevant question is how effective tax incentives to stimulate investment really are.

4. Are Tax Incentives to Promote Investment Effective?

In this paragraph I will summarize some empirical evidence on the effectiveness of tax incentives in the Netherlands. Analyzing aggregate time-series data, the Central Planning Bureau has made a macroeconomic estimate that one guilder of tax investment credit generates 70 to 80 cents in additional investment (Ministry of Finance 1986). Earlier estimates gave 125 cents in additional investment per guilder of ITC. Assuming that the most recently estimated relationship holds, additional investment (through ITC) in 1985 can be put at Dfl. four billion. This is to be compared to aggregate investments of firms in that year of Dfl. 44 billion. So investment was about 10 percent higher because of the tax investment credit. The question seems warranted whether an alternative use of the tax money involved (Dfl. 5.3 billion) would not be more effective to improve the general investment climate and stimulate economic growth.

Doubts as to the effectiveness of ITC are increased by results of the important microeconomic analysis in the doctoral thesis of Vermeend (1983). The author concludes on the basis of a sample survey of firms that ITC has had limited effects on investment decisions, although this conclusion is somewhat tentative. In general, a number of extra credits—which were intended as instruments to stimulate investment in certain areas and assets— were found to have failed their purpose. Most of these extra credits have been abolished in recent years.

VIII. TAXES, LABOR SUPPLY AND THE HIDDEN ECONOMY

1. Taxes and Labor Supply

Many in the Netherlands believe that the high average and marginal burden of taxes on income plus social insurance contributions reduce labor supply. However, there is no firm empirical evidence in favor of this hypothesis. On the contrary, the participation rate of married women—which is very low by international comparison—greatly went up during the past fifteen years or so, although tax burdens were continuously increasing. Of course, this does not prove anything either, because we lack a counterfactual world with low tax burdens.

2. The Hidden Economy

By its very nature, we do not know much about the size of the "hidden economy." I define the hidden economy as the sum total of income flowing from economic activity that goes untaxed because it is, in violation of the law, not reported to the tax authorities. Such economic activity may consist of both illegal (gambling, prostitution) and legal transactions. Many in the Netherlands believe that the hidden economy has grown in importance because of the heavy burden of taxes and social insurance contributions. For instance, the average production worker is subject to a marginal rate of about 60 percent (table 12) or above. However, there is no firm empirical evidence on the relationship between tax burdens and the amount of unreported income, because data on the past and present size of the hidden economy are not available. In the Netherlands some macroeconomic estimates of the hidden economy have been published. Only those of the Central Bureau of

Statistics (CBS) can be taken seriously. The CBS annually produces the National Accounts (NA). Many human activities that satisfy wants are not quantified in the NA, for example unpaid household labor. As a rule, such activities are not liable to tax either. Other economic activities should—in accordance with international regulations—be included in the NA but are not because of under-reporting or estimation errors. According to estimates of the CBS its NA may underrepresent national income by three to four percent. As most income measured in the Accounts is liable to tax, it might be hypothesized that at least an equal percentage of earned and capital income would not be reported to the tax authorities.

Moreover, it has been estimated by the CBS that five to 10 percent of national income which is registered in the NA is not reported to the tax authorities. Combining the results of such estimates, the hidden economy might amount to something like five to 10 percent of GNP. A similarly sized "hidden economy" has been reported for several other countries that have relevant characteristics in common with the Netherlands.

During the last few years several microeconomic estimates of (parts of) the hidden economy have also been published. One study of the CBS concluded that in 1975 as much as 40 to 50 percent of total interest received by individuals on saving deposits and bank accounts was not reported to the tax authorities. Unreported interest amounted to Dfl. six billion, that is roughly two percent of GNP at the time.

Combining results of various estimates I would venture the following breakdown of the hidden economy (in terms of unreported transactions in billion guilders per year) in 1985:

Unreported income of self-employed	4
Unreported income of employees	4
Unreported capital income (mainly interest)	7
Income from criminal activity	6
Other unreported activity	4
Hidden economy	25

Thus we would have a hidden economy of slightly over six percent of GNP. The reader should be aware that these are not hard numbers, but (very) rough estimates.

Estimates such as these attract a lot of attention in the media. Recently the tax administration has intensified its efforts to combat tax fraud. But several problems have manifested themselves. Both the administration and law enforcement agencies lack sufficient qualified personnel to fight fraud. On the other hand a "tax number" was introduced in 1985 which, in combination with the introduction of data-crunching computers, may greatly improve the efficiency of measures against tax fraud. However, it should be noted that many taxpayers feel uneasy about their privacy, which might be endangered by a free and automated exchange of information between government institutions and market sector organizations, such as banks and insurance companies.

IX. WHO PAYS THE TAXES IN THE NETHERLANDS?

1 Introduction

The concept of "tax burden" may be specified in a number of ways. Usually, the notion relates taxes paid, however defined, to a measure of ability to pay that is usually some variant of income. Several techniques are available to relate income of taxpayers and the taxes they pay.

The simplest technique is standard microeconomic simulation. Essentially it boils down to calculating the tax liability of hypothetical households, using "standard" assumptions about family size, number of income earners, source of income and so on. As a rule it is assumed that households have only "standard" deductions. Then, applying the relevant tax regime and tax rates, taxes due are calculated for a range of income levels. Probably the best internationally known examples of standard simulations are in the regular OECD publications dealing with the tax/benefit position of production workers (OECD 1986b). Paragraph 2 presents results of standard simulations of the tax burden of market sector employees in the Netherlands in 1985.

A technically more complicated technique is empirical micro-economic simulation. Essentially tax liabilities of a sample of households are determined, using data from surveys or tax files on family size, number of income earners, the amount of income from several sources, etc. Also, insofar as this proves possible, empirical data about deductions and taxes actually paid are used. If taxes paid are not known, these may be calculated using other data from the survey or tax files. Paragraph 3 presents results based on surveys and empirical simulations of the tax burden in the Netherlands in 1981. The results of both standard and empirical simulations of tax burdens do not answer the question "who actually pays" these taxes, but rather the less interesting question who is legally liable for payment. Apart from the statutory incidence of taxes (as presented in sections 2 and 3) paragraph 4 presents some data on the economic incidence of several important taxes under various shifting assumptions.

2. Statutory Incidence of Taxes on Income in 1985: Standard Simulation

This paragraph gives results of standard simulations of the tax burden for employees that are employed in the market sector of the economy. Standard family size is in accordance with the usual assumptions of the OECD (1986b): married couple with one earner and two young children. The only income is from labor (plus child benefits). It is assumed that the employee has only standard deductions. Four income levels are considered:

- Gross legal minimum wage (Dfl. 25,600 per year).
- Gross wage of average production worker (APW) (Dfl. 40,000 per year).
- Gross wage two times that of APW (Dfl. 80,000 per year).
- Gross wage three times that of APW (Dfl. 120,000 per year).
year).

At each income level the personal income tax and the employee contributions to the general and employee social insurances are determined. The amounts due are then expressed as a percentage of gross wage (average burden). Moreover, the marginal tax burden is calculated, assuming an increase in gross wage income of Dfl. 1,000. Results are presented in table 12.

As table 12 demonstrates, marginal tax rates do not vary very much between employees who earn the minimum wage level and employees who earn double the wage of an average production worker. In fact, marginal rates fluctuate between 50 and 60 percent for nearly all employees. Marginal rates for lower paid workers may increase to 80 percent or over, in the case that they claim means-tested benefits (such as rent subsidies) or pay means-tested user charges (poverty trap).

The average tax burden gradually rises with income. But the reader may notice that taxes and contributions already eat a quarter out of gross minimum wage.

Table 13 specifies the relation between net wage, gross wage and labor cost for the employer of an average production worker. Total labor cost is defined as gross wage plus the employer's contributions to the social insurances and private pension scheme of the APW.

3. Statutory Incidence of Taxes on Income in 1979/1981: Empirical Simulation

The Income Statistics of the Central Bureau of Statistics allow us to trace the statutory burden of the personal income tax, the wealth tax, and all social insurance contributions (except employee health insurance). The Income Statistics are based on a 3.3 percent sample of all tax returns of a given year. Table 14 gives data on taxes and contributions paid by taxpayers with full-year income in 1979. Taxpayers are ranked into 10 percent-groups (deciles) on the basis of aggregate income. The distribution of the burden of the personal income tax and wealth tax reflects the progressive rates. The average burden of these taxes for all taxpayers together is slightly over 17 percent of aggregate income. Taxpayers in the seventh decile pay the most in social insurance contributions. Low- and high-income earners pay relatively less in contributions. Two factors may explain this pattern: (1) most employees are found in deciles five through nine and (2) no contributions are due insofar as income/wages exceed the relevant contribution ceiling(s). In interpreting the data in table 14 it should be remembered that no data on untaxed capital gains are included (as these are unknown in the sample used).

The distribution of the burden of the personal income tax and social insurance contributions can also be calculated, using data from nationwide representative sample surveys. Table 15 presents some results on the basis of the Housing Needs Survey 1981 (HNS'81) which numbers over 17,000 respondents. The HNS'81 does not contain data on capital gains, whether taxed or not. Neither has the HNS'81 data on most deductions, although the most important items—notably mortgage interest of home-owners and social insurance contributions, cf. table 4—are covered.

Table 15 confirms the general picture in table 14, although the year (1979 versus 1981), income concept (aggregate versus gross income), and income unit (taxpayers versus households as defined by the Social and Cultural Planning Office in both analyses differ.

From table 15 it follows that the average burden of the personal income tax rises rather steeply from 1.7 percent of gross income in the first 10 percent-group to 25.5 percent in the tenth 10 percent-group. This result is in part explained because the dataset used has no information on capital gains and most of the smaller deduction items. Table 15 demonstrates that households in the sixth 10 percent-group pay the most in contributions to both general and employee insurances. The distribution of contributions is regressive as higher-income groups pay a relatively smaller part of gross income to the social insurances.

4. Economic Incidence of the Corporate Income Tax and Social Insurance Contributions, 1973

The presentation of the economic incidence of taxes and contributions heavily depends on the shifting assumptions used. Not very much of this type of work has been done in the Netherlands. Results under various shifting assumptions have been published for the corporate income tax and social insurance contributions for year 1973 (Goudriaan & De Kam 1981a, 1981b). Their main results are in figures 1 and 2.

As the savings ratio goes up with increasing income and in view of the fact that by far most capital and dividend income accrues to high-income earners, the U-shape in figure 1 is no real surprise, incidence assumptions given. That is also true of figure 2.

Figure 1
Economic Incidence of the Corporate Income Tax, 1973

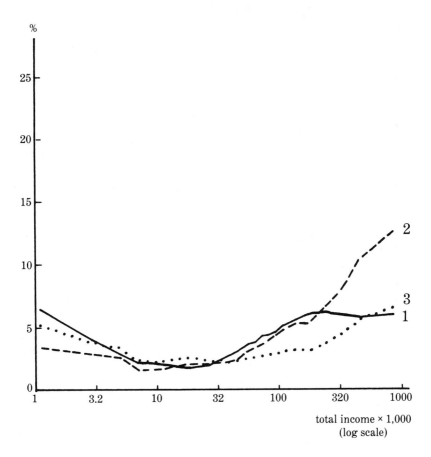

total income × 1,000
(log scale)

Incidence assumptions:
tax is not shifted to taxpayers in other countries
(1) ½ on capital income and ½ on consumption
(2) ½ on dividend income, ¼ on wage income and ½ on consumption
(3) ¼ on dividend income, ¼ on wage income and ½ on consumption
Burden is expressed as a % of "total income", this is defined as taxable income with a few correction which will not be detailed here.

Figure 2
Economic Incidence of All
Social Insurance Contributions, 1973

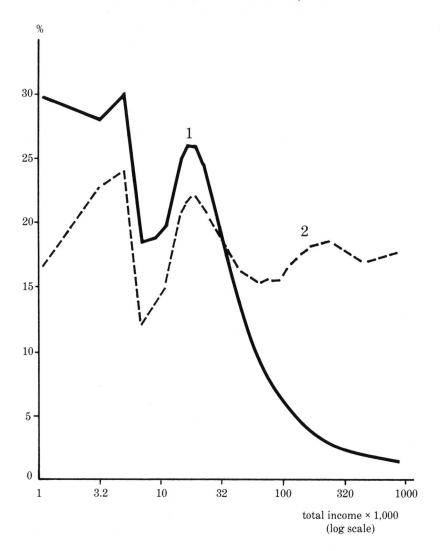

total income × 1,000
(log scale)

Incidence assumptions:
employee and household contributions are not shifted
(1) employer contributions are shifted ½ to wage-earners and ½ to consumers
                        (2) ½ to wage earners and ½ to capital income
All contributions are borne by taxpayers of the Netherlands.
Burden is expressed as a % of "total income"; this is defined as taxable income with a few corrections which will
not be detailed here.

X. REFORM OF THE PERSONAL INCOME TAX

1. Introduction

Since the early seventies regular pleas for tax reform and tax simplification have been voiced by concerned academics, representatives of the Internal Revenue Service, and by professional tax lawyers. The many proposals which were put forward left no trace in the legislation, although politicians paid lip service to the ideal of a more fair and simple tax system that would promote economic growth. In fact, by incorporating more and more complex provisions in the tax law to promote all kinds of policy goals, politicians were instrumental in effectively ruining the tax system. In 1984-1985 this process culminated in the introduction of a very complicated piece of legislation regarding personal exemptions and allowances (as set out in section II, subsection 4). Time then proved to be ripe for a change. The public outcry over the latest additions to an already overburdened tax system moved Parliament to demand of the Secretary of Finance that a Tax Simplification Commission be set up.

2. Tax Simplification Commission

2.1 Four Central Objectives

The Minister of Finance has honored the request of Parliament by forming a commission for the simplification of the wage withholding and income tax in September 1985. This commission reported in May 1986. The commission did not propose to switch to household expenditure as the sole tax base; it assumed the viability of a general tax on personal income. Nor has the concept of taxable income been analyzed in depth. A reasonable analysis of this complex concept would have called for a broader study over a longer period of time than the commission had been granted. Still its report does contain a cohesive package of practical and, in some respects, fundamental proposals, which taken together form many modest steps on the long way to a more comprehensive income tax in the Netherlands.

A major reason for the present complexity of tax laws is the level of the rates: the higher the rates, the greater the need to account for special circumstances. There is no simple solution to this problem. The heavy burden of taxes and social insurance contributions (section IX) is a direct and inseparable consequence of high government spending and an extensive social security system. When the public sector siphons off approximately two-thirds of the national income, as is the case at present in the Netherlands, taxes and contributions must be high. Simplification as such can do little to lower present burdens, as the commission had to work in the context of revenue neutrality; taken together, the proposals were not allowed to produce any appreciable sacrifices from the treasury and the social insurance funds. The four central objectives of the commission were:

• Combining the personal income tax with general social insurance contributions (hereafter, contributions for short); see section 2.2.

• One fixed rate over a broad range of income (section 2.3).

• Wage withholding tax as a final levy as often as possible (no additional assessment); see section 2.4.

• Streamlining deductions and other schemes (section 2.5).

2.2 Combination of Income Tax and Contributions: Income Levy

Practically everyone who pays income tax is also liable for contributions, with the exception of the aged. The tax base is different, but closely related (section VI, subsection 2). Income tax is levied according to a progressive graduated scale with a complicated system of personal exemptions (section IV, subsection 4). Contributions rise in proportion to income up to a contribution ceiling, with special relief provisions for people with the lowest incomes (in particular the self-employed). The commission proposes to combine taxes and contributions into one levy with an identical tax base, while ensuring that the identity and particular purpose of each part is maintained. Under the present system, contributions are deductible for income tax purposes. This is no longer meaningful in the case of a combined levy, because the current deductibility of contributions can be "absorbed" into a lower rate of the combined levy in such a way that the sum of the tax part and the contribution part constitutes the new combined income levy. In practice this need not affect the income position of tax and contribution payers.

Combining taxes and contributions has a series of practical advantages: by far the largest single deduction is eliminated (compare table 4), separate returns, assessments, refunds, and appeal procedures for levying contributions are no longer needed. An even more important advantage arising from combining taxes and contributions is that both together make up an almost constant percentage of income, up to a certain income level. This opens the possibility of having a combined flat rate over a large range of income above the standard deduction (discussed in section X, subsection 2.3 in greater detail).

There is, however, a complication. People receiving a wage or social security benefit currently pay only contributions towards two of the five general insurances (AOW and AWW, see section VI, subsection 2). The other three "supplementary" contributions (AWBZ, AKW, AAW) are paid by the employer or the benefit-paying institution. Economically and financially it makes no difference, of course, whether the employer pays a wage from which he deducts two contributions at source, while he pays the other three directly—which is the current situation—or whether he pays a higher gross wage and withholds all five contributions. Total labor cost for the employer and net income of employees are the same in both cases.

The commission proposes to transfer the payment of supplementary contributions from the employer to the employee, and from the benefit-paying institution to the benefit-receiving party. Employees and those receiving benefits are thus placed in the same position as self-employed, as the latter already pay their own contributions for all five general social insurances.

In order to ensure that nobody suffers a decline in his or her disposable income through the transfer of contributions, gross salaries and benefits must be increased by the amount of the supplementary contributions (a process which is denoted as "grossing up"). Although large sums are involved (Dfl. 20.6 billion or five percent of GNP in 1985), the transfer of the liability for supplementary contributions and the grossing up of wages and benefits is essentially a paper operation: nobody is better or worse off because of it. However, the tax and contribution system becomes simpler and clearer, while the desired flat rate, applicable to as many people as possible, can be achieved only after the transfer of the liability for supplementary contributions. The whole operation requires administrative and technical adjustments of salaries and benefits and of schemes which are linked to gross salary (for example, private pension schemes). The Report demonstrates that and how such problems can be solved.

2.3 Fixed Rate for the Majority of Taxpayers

The proposed income levy has a relatively low individual personal exemption of Dfl. 4,250. This exemption may be transferred between married persons or unmarried persons who are living together. This possibility is, however, limited in various respects. Partial transfer or transfer during the calendar year would not be permitted. A transfer of the exemption is possible only if the income of one of the taxpayers concerned is less than Dfl. 4,250. This last requirement limits the transfer to cases in which the personal exemption would otherwise be lost. Transfer between unmarried partners is possible only if they are both 18 years or over and have been registered at the same address with the local Registrar's Office for at least one year (except in the case of clearly separate dwelling units).

Single taxpayers experience a comparatively large fall in income (though in no case of more than 6.5 percent) because of the abolition of the presently existing extra exemption of Dfl. 3,584 for this category (section II, subsection 4). The commission regards this as the price which has to be paid for the major practical advantages of a system with the same standard personal exemption for everyone. But the abolition of currently existing exemptions for single parents who are raising children under the age of 12 would produce such a drop in income that the commission felt it had to sacrifice some simplicity. These parents under the new system will be entitled to a deduction of Dfl. 3,200. If the parent works away from the home while there are young children in the household, an additional deduction is granted of six percent of net earnings, with a maximum of Dfl. 4,200.

The proposed rate scale has far fewer brackets than the existing one, which consists of nine brackets. The commission presents two options (see table 16). One is a scale with four brackets, on which successive percentages of 40, 55, 65, and 70 are levied. In addition the commission presents an even simpler scale which has only three brackets: in this option the top bracket of 70 percent is eliminated.

The contributions are fully incorporated in the first bracket of the scale. The rate of 40 percent consists of 30 percent contributions and 10 percent tax. The higher brackets consist only of tax. These percentages have been calculated in such a way that the revenue from the contribution part is equal to the revenue from the present contributions.

On the basis of figures for 1985, 88 percent of all levy payers have incomes within the first bracket. This is shown in figure 3. This means in itself an important gain in simplicity and clarity. Besides, the flat marginal rate solves many problems that are connected with the current progressive tax system—for example, the taxation of income from different jobs or pension funds.

Under the present system the aged do not pay any contributions. Special provisions must be made, as the aged would suffer a considerable fall in income if the full proposed levy were applied.

Figure 3
Taxpayers Classified According to Highest
Applicable Rate Scale of the Income Levy, 1985

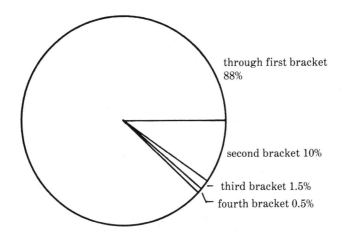

through first bracket 88%

second bracket 10%

third bracket 1.5%

fourth bracket 0.5%

Pension benefits under the AOW scheme will be automatically increased by the amount of the supplementary contributions. The reason is the linking of the net general old age pension to net minimum wage. If the full 40 percent rate were then applied, the aged would also be paying AOW and AWW contributions for which they are not compensated. Consequently, the commission proposes a rate of 23.6 percent for the first bracket, consisting of 10 percent tax and 13.6 percent contributions for the AWBZ, AKW, and AWW. This lower first bracket for the aged gives no rise to complications as far as the implementation is concerned, as the group of the aged is so clearly identifiable.

2.4 Less Assessments, Other Administrative Simplifications

The proposed system results in a substantial simplification not only for taxpayers, but also for employers and the tax authorities.

Many taxpayers currently receive an annual income tax assessment and a contribution assessment. Instead of two notices of assessment, the taxpayer under the simplified system would receive only one income levy assessment. Currently, the employer withholds at source both wage tax and contributions to AOW and AWW, while paying the supplementary contributions himself. In the simplified approach, only one withholding is made, the wage levy, while supplementary contributions are absorbed in the wage levy. The personal exemption which is the same for everyone can only be taken into account by one withholding agent. The employer only needs to withhold according to the 40 percent rate, since every taxpayer who is in a higher bracket receives an assessment anyway. So any shortfall in the wage levy is assessed separately. Because nearly nine out of every ten taxpayers are in the first bracket, the wage levy can in many more cases be the final levy: no additional assessment is needed anymore. In these cases no tax return needs to be filed and no assessment needs to be imposed. Taxpayers and withholding agents will know exactly where they stand: the wage levy is 40 cents of every guilder earned above the standard personal exemption. Since the correct percentage is withheld at source, taxpayers with two or more jobs or the aged with AOW pension benefits and private pension no longer receive an assessment as long as they remain within the first bracket.

In its Report the commission estimates that .6 million taxpayers (eight percent of all taxpayers) need no longer be assessed yearly. By the way, the various proposals permit personnel savings of 1,400 to 1,700 working years for the tax administration (about 10 percent of all personnel that busies itself with personal income tax and general insurance contributions). If other savings at the tax administration are taken into account, there is a potential savings of Dfl. 100 to 110 million a year. These savings are partially realized by other proposals, which aim at some streamlining of deductions.

2.5 Streamlining of Deductions

The current wage withholding and income tax system has a large number of deductions of a widely differing nature, significance, and background. Most of them are derived from the ability-to-pay principle (for example, the deduction of medical expenses); others permit a tax deferral (for example, deduction for pension contributions); and still others can be regarded as an alternative to direct expenditures, in other words as an instrument to promote given social or economic goals of government policy. The Tax Investment Credit (WIR premium) is an example (section VI, subsection 3.3). It is primarily this jungle of deductions and tax preferences which makes the tax system so complicated and incomprehensible to the ordinary taxpayer and gives him the feeling that others pay less than they would under a tax with fewer loopholes.

There are, however, other—at least as important—aspects which are of relevance here. Deductions reduce tax revenues. It has already often been argued that after abolition or a drastic reduction of deductions, income tax rates could be lowered considerably. This is, in itself, desirable, but it also forms an important condition for the simplification itself as a less detailed tax legislation is more readily acceptable at low rather than at high rates. Here it should be pointed out that in an Annex to its Report the commission demonstrates that even a drastic limitation of deductions would only make possible a reduction of rates on the order of a few points in each bracket. Therefore the commission concludes that the feasibility of such an exercise must not be rated very high. Moreover, the commission draws attention to the fact that many deductions are so strongly held to be socially justifiable or are so directly connected with earning personal income that abolition or any substantial reduction thereof would stand no chance of political or social acceptance. In some cases (for example, the deduction of interest) abolition would require such complicated legislation (to counter the use of possible loopholes) that the commission has ruled out such recommendations in its Report, which is aimed primarily at increased simplicity.

What remains is a series of simplifications of existing complicated deductions. These proposals would increase revenue by Dfl. 1.5 billion. The abolition of the largest deduction, i.e., for general insurance contributions, is not included in this figure as it is already absorbed into the basic rate of the income levy. The main proposals are:

• The commission thinks that the deduction of extraordinary expenses (section II, subsection 3.7) can be simplified on a number of points: dispensing with the multiplication factor in the medical expense scheme, a simpler scheme for special dietary expenses, excluding contributions for health insurance schemes, and a reduction and simplification of the present threshold.

• A simplification of standard travel expense deductions is possible by skipping the standardized deduction for the shortest distance (up to 10 kilometers) of Dfl. 200. This enables slight all-over lowering of rates.

Other proposals do not relate to deductions, but do lead to simplification and in most cases to a higher revenue. The commission recommends, *inter alia*, taxing holiday vouchers at their full nominal value, instead of at 60 percent thereof as under the existing legal provisions. Other proposed simplifications concern the abolition of the so-called income averaging scheme and the replacement of the complicated scheme of proportional income tax rates (section II, subsection 4) by a simpler method of calculation.

Self-employed and other taxpayers with low incomes who are assessed can currently avail themselves of special provisions reducing their liability for general social insurance contributions.

The commission has chosen not to do away with this complicated scheme to prevent taxpayers with low incomes from suffering a severe setback. However, the commission urges that a simpler scheme be introduced.

2.6 Income Consequences of the Proposals

The proposals developed by the commission do have consequences for the income position of almost everyone. The commission takes as its basis the distribution of net income existing in 1985 and does not give an opinion on the acceptability or fairness of that distribution. Taxpayers with an income around the social minimum should, in its view, not be affected by the proposals. Disposable income of others should not, in principle, increase or decrease by more than five percent. To avoid any great, abrupt shifts in the personal income distribution through its proposals, the commission designed certain compensatory measures which would harm simplification as little as possible. On the other hand, simplification is impossible if it is required in advance that no one experiences a positive or negative effect on disposable income.

The income consequences of the proposed tax simplification have been traced by means of microeconomic simulations which show the difference in net disposable income before and after the proposals are implemented. These simulations have been done using the 1981 sample of tax returns of a quarter million taxpayers, after adjusting for changes in the level of prices and incomes between 1981 and 1985, and taking into account revisions of the tax legislation during that period (section II, subsection 8).

In table 17, households have been grouped into nine classes, according to their gain or loss of net disposable income as a consequence of the proposals (gain or loss measured in guilders). From table 16 it follows that 48.7 percent of all taxpayers stand to gain from the proposals, whereas 48.2 percent will experience a loss. Only 41,000 out of all 7.3 million taxpayers are going to lose more than Dfl. 2,500 in disposable income. The change in net disposable income lies between plus and minus Dfl. 500 for three-quarters of all taxpayers.

The change in income as a consequence of the proposals may also be expressed as a percentage of net disposable income. From the microsimulations carried out it follows that 11.8 percent of all 7.3 million taxpayers would gain more than five percent in net disposable income. On the other hand 4.4 percent of all taxpayers would lose more than five percent of net income. The conclusion must be that, inevitably, one out of seven taxpayers would experience a change in net disposable income outside the limits which the commission had set beforehand.

Table 18 shows the income effects of the proposals by twenty income classes. Taxpayers have been ranked on the basis of the new tax base (without deduction of contributions and after "grossing up"). On average taxpayers with an income between Dfl. 15,000 and 40,000 experience a slight loss of disposable income. This is also the case for all taxpayers with an income over Dfl. 100,000. Please note that these are averages. Of course, within each class of income many taxpayers will experience gains and many others will experience a loss of net disposable income.

Tables 17 and 18 show an aggregate gain in net disposable income of Dfl. 800 million for all taxpayers taken together, suggesting that as a consequence of the proposals the public sector stands to lose an equal amount. However, this is not the case. The explanation is that a number of proposals, which produce extra revenue of Dfl. 700 million, could not be simulated. In other words, taxpayers as a group will experience an aggregate loss of disposable income of Dfl. 700 million which is not shown in tables 17 and 18. The net gain to the taxpayers does not exceed Dfl. 100 million. In fact, as will be demonstrated in section X, subsection 2.7, the proposals do not harm the public budget at all.

Table 19 shows the income effects for six socioeconomic groups. Self-employed and directors of companies experience on average a loss from implementation of the proposals. On average, households in the other categories gain. Please note that within each socioeconomic group many taxpayers will experience gains and many others will experience losses of income, as table 19 again presents average income changes.

On the whole, the changes in income arising from the proposals remain within reasonable limits, certainly when they are compared to the continuous changes in society and the consequences thereof on a family's disposable income such as, for example, shifts in the labor market (finding another job, becoming unemployed) or changes in personal circumstances (the purchase of a house, growth of the family).

2.7 Check on Revenue Neutrality of the Proposals

The proposals are practically revenue neutral, as follows from table 20. The results in table 20 have been obtained by microeconomic simulation on the sample of a quarter million taxpayers. Some proposals could not be simulated; the budgetary consequences of these proposals (extra revenue of Dfl. .7 billion) have been estimated by separate procedure. Although table 20 suggests that after implementing the proposals revenue falls Dfl. .1 billion short of the amount needed for complete revenue neutrality, it should be pointed out that several proposals which were not quantified will bring in additional revenue. Moreover, operational cost of the IRS might decrease with Dfl. .1 billion per annum (section 2.4). So budget neutrality of the proposals seems guaranteed.

3. Business View on Tax Reform

The confederations of employers have not taken an official position on tax reform. Broadly speaking, employers seem to endorse the recommendations by the Tax Simplification Commission. The confederations have repeatedly asked for lower rates of taxes and social insurance contributions, together with a trimming of the large-sized public sector. Tax preferences for business are seldom mentioned in this connection. On the contrary, recent proposals to limit the capital and inventory deduction (section III, subsection 4.2) and to abolish the negative assessment to refund Investment Tax Credit (section VII, subsection 3.3) have met with opposition from the confederations.

4. Trade Union View on Tax Reform

The two most important confederations of labor unions have no systematically worked out position on the tax system either. The general position is as would be expected: tax preferences to industry and agriculture are generally thought rather too generous. The proposals of the Tax Simplification Commission have been cautiously approved. However, union spokesmen thought negative income effects for certain groups (especially single taxpayers) too large.

5. Prospects for Tax Reform

A substantial revision of the Dutch tax system during the second half of the eighties cannot be ruled out. Tax experts of the three main political parties have reacted positively to most of the proposals which were put forward by the Simplification Commission. The program of the new Cabinet (after the general elections of May 21, 1986) was still under negotiation at the time this report was finished (June 30, 1986). But the Cabinet program is generally expected to contain a separate paragraph on tax reform and tax simplification, along the lines suggested by the commission. Of course, it remains to be seen whether real reform will be possible, since politicians in the Netherlands as elsewhere are sensitive to pleas and pressure exerted by special interest groups. But some hope for a real improvement of the Dutch tax system seems in order. Tax reform will perhaps prove not to be a dream after all.

REFERENCES

Gourdriaan, R. and C.A. de Kam (1981a). De uiteindelijke drukverdeling van de vennootschapsbelasting onder verschillende afwentelingsveronderstellingen, 1973 [The economic incidence of the corporate income tax under various shifting assumptions, 1973]. In: (110) *Weekblad voor fiscaal recht* (5482), pp. 53-68.

Goudriaan, R. and C.A. de Kam (1981b). De druk van de premies voor volksverzekeringen en werknemersverzekeringen, 1973 [The burden of the general and employee social insurance contributions, 1973]. In: (36) *Sociaal Maandblad Arbeid* (1), pp. 51-61.

Ministry of Finance (1985). *Miljoenennota 1986* [Budget memorandum 1986]. The Hague: Staatsuitgeverij (Government Printing Office).

Ministry of Finance (1986). *Wet Investeringsrekening* [Investment Tax Credit]. Heroverweging deelrapport 87. The Hague: April 1986.

Ministry of Social Affairs and Employment (1985). *Financiele nota sociale zekerheid 1986* [Budget memorandum on social security 1986]. The Hague: Staatsuitgeverij (Government Printing Office).

Organization for Economic Cooperation and Development (1986a). *OECD Economic Surveys 1985/1986: Netherlands.* Paris.

Organization for Economic Cooperation and Development (1986b). *The Tax/Benefit Position of Production Workers, 1979-1984.* Paris.

Social and Cultural Planning Office (1985). *Berekend beleid* [Measured policy]. The Hague: Staatsuitgeverij (Government Printing Office).

Tax Simplification Commission (1986). *Ziht op eenvoud* [A Step Towards Simplicity]. The Hague: Staatsuitgeverij (Government Printing Office).

Vermeend, W.A. (1983). *Fiscale investerings faciliteiten* [Tax investment facilities]. Arnhem: Gouda Quint B.V.

Table 1
Public Expenditure, 1955-1985[1]
(Percent)

Year	1955	1960	1965	1970	1975	1980	1985
Central government spending	18.6	13.5	13.1	13.6	14.1	18.2	21.3
Local government spending[2]	13.6	16.1	18.9	18.5	22.0	21.8	22.7
Social insurance payments	5.3	9.1	13.1	15.7	20.9	24.2	23.6
Total of public outlays	37.4	38.7	45.1	47.8	57.7	64.2	67.6
of which:							
Expenditures	18.7	18.4	21.2	21.1	22.7	22.7	20.5
Transfer payments (plus							
interest)	18.7	20.3	23.9	26.7	35.0	41.5	47.1
Memorandum item:							
Net national income							
(billion guilders)	27	38	63	112	200	303	369

Source: Ministry of Finance (1985), p. 159-160.
  [1]As a percentage of net national income.
  [2]Local government spending is financed for over 90 percent by revenue sharing and grants from central government.

Table 2
The Public Sector of the Netherlands Economy, 1985
(billion guilders)

Item		Amounts	
Total public expenditures			250
Taxes		102	
Personal income tax[1]	37.0		
Value-added tax	29.7		
Corporate income tax	12.5		
Other central government taxes (specified in table 7)	18.5		
Local government taxes and other	4.2		
Social insurance contributions (specified in table 9)		84	
Other revenues of central and local government		35	
Total receipts of public sector			221
Deficit			29
Memorandum item:			
Net national income (market prices)			369

Source: Ministry of Finance (1985), p. 127.
  [1]Includes wage withholding tax and dividend withholding tax.

Table 3
Income Redistribution Through the Public Sector, 1977
(Percent)

Type of income	Quintiles (Net Disposable Income)					
	1	2	3	4	5	Total
Factor income (wages, profits, dividends, etc.)	3	8	17	26	46	100
Income after income tax and social security transfers	6	14	19	24	37	100
Income after value-added tax, excises plus imputed grants, subsidies, etc.	10	13	18	24	35	100

Source: Social and Cultural Planning Office (1985), p. 32.

Table 4
Main Deductions and Exemptions, 1985
(millions of guilders)

Deduction or exemption	1985[1]
Capital deduction and inventory deduction[2]	1,450
Special deduction for self-employed	1,965
Deduction of amounts added to old age reserve of self-employed	1,065
Exemption of employer contributions to private pension schemes	13,900
Exemption of employer contributions to employee insurances	7,000
Deduction of employee contributions to private pension schemes	5,300
Deduction of employee contributions to employee insurances	12,400
Standard deduction of travelling expenses of employees	1,620
Standard deduction of other expenses of employees	3,860
Deduction of expenses in excess of standard deduction	1,105
Exemption for dividends received	190
Exemption for interest received	925
Deduction of interest on loans to finance rented property	11,535
Deduction of interest on mortgage loans of home owners	925
Exemption of general insurance contributions paid by employers	20,600
Deduction of general insurance contributions (as special expenses)	25,640
Deduction of interest on debts (as special expenses)	1,750
Deduction of extraordinary expenses	2,250
Deduction of charitable gifts	560
Total	114,440
Investment tax credit (revenue foregone)[2]	820
Memorandum items:	
Revenue from personal income tax plus wage withholding tax	37,000
Revenue from general social insurance contributions	50,300

Source: Report of Tax Simplification Commission (1986), p. 92.
[1]Estimate.
[2]Only self-employed; for corporate income tax, see section III, 4.5.

Table 5
Distribution of Deductions and Exemptions
by Socioeconomic Group, 1985

Socioeconomic Group	Number of Taxpayers (x 1,000)	Amount of Deductions and Exemptions (x Dfl. million)	Average Amount (guilders)
Self-employed	381	8,870	23,280
Directors of companies	94	2,596	27,620
Employees/unemployed	3,417	25,481	7,460
Government personnel	833	10,061	12,080
Pensioners	2,048	6,150	3,000
Others	560	1,308	1,980
Totals	7,331	54,826	7,480

Source: Report of the Tax Simplification Commission (1986), p. 92.

Table 6
Distribution of Deductions and Exemptions
by Taxable Income Class, 1985

Taxable Income Class	Number of Taxpayers (x 1,000)	Amount of Deductions and Exemptions (x Dfl. million)	Average Amount (guilders)
0—30,000	4,670	24,570	5,269
30,000—80,000	2,500	25,750	10,300
80,000 and over	160	4,190	26,190
Totals	7,330	54,510	7,435

Source: Estimates, using data in the Report of the Tax Simplification Commission. (1986), pp. 94-95.

Table 7
Other Taxes Levied by Central Government, 1985
(million guilders)

Tax	Amount
Wealth tax	950
Estate tax, gift tax, and transfer duty	825
Transfer tax, insurance tax, capital tax, stock exchange tax	1,850
Lottery tax	75
Motor vehicle tax	2,680
Import duties	2,050
Special consumption tax on motor vehicles	1,925
Excise taxes	8,170
Total revenue	18,525

Source: Ministry of Finance (1985), p. 127.

Table 8
Rates of Estate Tax and Gift Tax, 1985

Amount of transfer (guilders)		Spouse and Husband, Children, Descendants in Direct Line		Brothers and Sisters, Relatives in Direct Line		Others	
(1)	(2)	(a)	(b)	(a)	(b)	(a)	(b)
0—31,738		0	5	0	26	0	41
31,738—63,476		1,586	8	8,251	30	13,012	45
63,476—126,950		4,125	12	17,773	35	27,294	50
126,950—253,898		11,742	15	39,989	39	59,031	54
253,898—507,792		30,785	19	89,498	44	127,583	59
507,792—1,269,477		79,024	23	201,212	48	277,381	63
1,269,477 and over		254,212	27	566,821	53	757,242	68

(a) Tax due on the amount under (1).
(b) Percentage of tax due on the difference between (1) and (2).

Table 9
Financing Social Insurance, 1985
(billion guilders)

Receipts	Amount	Outlays	Amount
Contributions of households (including employees)	51.2	Benefits under general social insurances	51.5
Contributions of employers	32.7	Benefits under employee social	
Government grants	2.7	insurances	32.4
Interest earned	0.7	Cost of administration	3.3
		Surplus	0.1
Total receipts	87.3	Total outlays (incl. surplus)	87.3

Source: Ministry of Social Affairs and Employment (1985), p. 69.

Table 10
Contributions for General Insurance, 1985[1]

Program	Contribution by Households		Contribution by Employers	
General old age pension	23.0	(11.7)	0.0	(0.0)
General widow and orphan pension	2.8	(1.4)	0.0	(0.0)
General child benefit[2]	1.1	(0.0)	5.7	(4.0)
General disability pension[2]	1.6	(0.0)	8.8	(6.0)
General insurance against exceptional medical expenses[2]	1.2	(0.0)	6.1	(4.3)
Total	29.7	(13.1)	20.6	(14.3)

Source: see table 9.

[1]Contributions in billions of guilders; rates (percentage of premium-income) between brackets.

[2]Employees do not pay premiums for this program, other households do. See text for explanation.

Table 11
Contributions for Employee Insurance Programs, 1985[1]

Program	Contribution by Households		Contribution by Employers	
Unemployment insurance	3.2	(2.8)	1.2	(0.8)
Sickness insurance	1.7	(1.0)	5.7	(5.6)
Disability insurance	7.5	(6.1)	0.1	(0.0)
Early retirement payments[2]	0.2		0.9	
Health cost insurance[3]	9.0	(4.6)	4.2	(4.6)
Total	21.6	(14.5)	12.1	(11.0)

Source: see table 9.

[1]Contributions in billions of guilders: rates (percentage of gross wage less employee contributions to private pension scheme) between brackets.

[2]This program is not really an employee insurance. Whether employees are covered or not depends on the relevant collective labor agreement.

[3]This program also covers nonemployee households; they contributed Dfl. 3.2 of the Dfl. 9.0 billion mentioned.

Table 12
Burden of Personal Income Tax and Social Insurance
Contributions at Selected Income Levels, 1985

Gross Wage Income	Personal Income Tax and Social Insurance Contributions	
	Marginal Tax Burden[1]	Average Tax Burden[1]
25,600 (Minimum wage)	47.3	25.7
40,000 (APW)	58.3	35.7
80,000 (2 x APW)	52.0	40.8
120,000 (3 x APW)	61.0	46.3

Source: Ministry of Social Affairs and Employment (1985), p. 13.

[1]As a percentage of gross income.

Table 13
Labor Cost, Gross and Net Wage of an
Average Production Worker, 1985

Calculation of net wage		Amount (guilders)
Total labor cost		51,380
Employer's contribution to private pension scheme	1,600	
Employer's contribution to employee social insurance	4,630	
Employer's contribution to general social insurance	5,150	
		11,380
Gross wage		40,000
Employee's contribution to private pension scheme	660	
Employee's contribution to employee social insurances	5,870	
Employee's contribution to general social insurances	4,730	
Wage withholding tax	3,320	
		14,580
Net wage		25,420
Plus: tax-exempt child benefit		3,060
Net disposable income		28,480

Source: Central Planning Bureau.

Table 14
Burden of Income Tax and Social Insurance Contributions, 1979[1]

Tax on contributions	Deciles (Aggregate Income)									
	1	2	3	4	5	6	7	8	9	10
Personal income/wealth tax	5.6	8.2	9.9	11.4	12.3	13.0	14.0	15.0	17.0	28.9
Contributions to general social insurances	5.0	5.7	6.9	8.5	9.2	9.7	10.0	9.8	9.1	5.8
Contributions to employee social insurances	0.6	1.2	1.6	2.3	2.8	3.0	3.1	2.9	2.9	1.8
Total burden	11.2	15.1	18.4	22.2	24.3	25.7	27.1	27.7	29.0	36.5

Source: Central Bureau of Statistics.
[1]Percentage of aggregate income.

Table 15
Burden of Income Tax and Social Insurance Contributions, 1981[1]

Tax on contributions	Deciles (Aggregate Income)									
	1	2	3	4	5	6	7	8	9	10
Personal income tax	1.7	4.4	6.4	8.5	10.3	10.9	11.6	12.6	14.7	25.5
Contributions to general social insurances	2.9	3.0	4.9	8.4	9.4	9.7	9.6	9.4	9.1	6.3
Contributions to employee social insurances	0.9	0.8	0.9	2.5	3.8	4.3	4.1	3.9	4.1	2.9
Total burden	5.5	8.2	12.2	19.4	23.5	24.9	25.3	25.9	27.9	34.7

Source: Social and Cultural Planning Office (1985), p. 150.
[1]Percentage of gross income.

Table 16
Rate Scale Options Presented by
Tax Simplification Commission

Tax Rate	Bracket Length	End of Bracket
Four-Bracket Scale:		
40	45,000	49,250
55	35,000	84,250
65	40,000	124,250
70		
Three-Bracket Scale:		
40	45,000	49,250
55	35,000	84,250
65		

Table 17
Frequency Distribution of Change in Disposable Income
Through Proposals of the Tax Simplification Commission

Gain/Loss of Net Disposable Income (Dfl.)	Number of Taxpayers Thousands	Percent	Reduction/Increase of Tax (Dfl. Million)
gain over 10,000	1	0.0	+13
gain between 2,500—10,000	58	0.8	+216
gain between 500— 2,500	1,887	25.7	+1,862
gain between 0— 500	1,630	22.2	+371
no change of income	216	2.9	0
loss between 0— 500	2,576	35.1	−540
loss between 500— 2,500	925	12.6	−870
loss between 2,500—10,000	38	0.5	−143
loss over 10,000	3	0.0	−96
Totals	7,331	100.0	+800

Source: Report of the Tax Simplification Commission (1986), p. 118.

Table 18
Change in Disposable Income Through Proposals of the Tax Simplification Commission, by Income Class

Income Class (guilders)	Number of Taxpayers		Average Reduction/Increase of Tax	
	Thousands	Percent	Total (million guilders)	Per Taxpayer (guilders)
Less than 0	103	1.4	+30	+300
0—5,000	554	7.6	+197	+355
5,000—10,000	245	3.3	+124	+505
10,000—15,000	219	3.0	+22	+100
15,000—20,000	818	11.2	-118	-145
20,000—25,000	757	10.3	-163	-215
25,000—30,000	667	9.1	-208	-310
30,000—35,000	643	8.8	-147	-230
35,000—40,000	662	9.0	-2	-3
40,000—45,000	583	8.0	+127	+220
45,000—50,000	473	6.5	+250	+530
50,000—60,000	618	8.4	+450	+730
60,000—70,000	384	5.2	+240	+625
70,000—80,000	230	3.1	+141	+615
80,000—90,000	130	1.7	+75	+575
90,000—100,000	76	1.0	+16	+210
100,000—125,000	86	1.2	-33	-385
125,000—150,000	35	1.5	-50	-1,430
150,000—200,000	21	0.3	-61	-2,905
200,000 and over	21	0.3	-87	-4,140
Totals	7,331	100.0	+800	+110

Source: Report of the Tax Simplification Commission (1986), p. 120.

Table 19
Change in Disposable Income Through Proposals of the Tax Simplification Commission, by Socioeconomic Group

Socioeconomic	Number of Taxpayers		Average Change of Tax	
	Thousands	Percent	Total (million guilders)	Per Taxpayer (guilders)
Self-employed	381	5.2	-81	-215
Directors of companies	94	0.1	-19	-200
Employees/unemployed	3,417	46.6	+447	+130
Government personnel	833	11.4	+267	+320
Pensioners	2,048	27.9	+49	+25
Others	560	7.6	+140	+250
Totals	7,331	100.0	+800	+110

Source: Report of the Tax Simplification Commission (1986), p. 120.

Table 20
Budgetary Consequences of Proposals of the
Tax Simplification Commission
(millions of guilders)

Proposal	Amount
Introduction of the new rate structure	−1,475
Special relief for one-parent families	−200
Initial deficit through proposals	−1,675
Less refunds of wage withholding tax to holiday workers	+100
Standard deduction for travelling expenses cut by Dfl. 200	+450
Employee overcompensation for travelling expenses taxed	+125
Limitations of extraordinary expenses deduction	+500
Extension imputed income from use of business car to all taxpayers	+150
Full taxation of holiday vouchers	+100
Other way to determine proportional rate of income tax	+50
Abolition of income averaging	+100
Total increase of tax revenue	+1,575

Source: Report of the Tax Simplification Commission (1986), pp. 107-108.

CHAPTER **4**

France

Jean-Louis Lienard, Kenneth C. Messere,
and Jeffrey Owens

AN OVERVIEW

1. Introduction

The French tax systems and revenue sources are very different
from those of other industrialized countries and over the last two
decades they have evolved in very different ways. The following
paragraphs comment first on special features in the systems of
particular taxes and second on relative reliance on different kinds
of revenue sources and trends therein, before making a few
generalizations. A final subsection gives some relevant background
information.

For the most part, the situations described are for the year 1984
or 1985 with some references to development in early years.
Statistics on tax revenues, however, refer to 1983, the latest year
for which firm figures are available.

2. Main Features of French Taxation

Regarding individual income tax, apart from Switzerland,
France is unique among industrialized countries in not using the
withholding collection technique for employed persons, and apart
from Luxembourg, is also unique in using the family quotient
system as a means of giving income tax relief for parents. France
was among the first to apply formal indexation to the tax schedule
(in 1968) and has also been the only country to use formal
indexation (between 1977 and 1981) as a means of increasing the
progressivity of the income tax by overcompensating for inflationary fiscal drag at lower income levels and undercompensating

or not compensating at all at high income levels. Finally, the French income tax system (notwithstanding the family quotient system) is one of the most progressive in industrialized countries and, in contrast to tendencies elsewhere, this progression has been increasing. Because so much of the income tax burden is borne by so few, it is difficult to reduce top rates without sacrificing much revenue. This would help to explain personal income tax revenue trends outlined in subsection 3. (For further details see section I).

Regarding corporate taxation, in 1965 France introduced its imputation system with half-way credit for corporate tax being offset against shareholders' income tax liability. France has since been followed by a number of other European countries (e.g., Denmark, Ireland, Italy, United Kingdom). On the other hand, while the tendency nowadays is towards greater neutrality in the corporation tax by widening the base and reducing rates, France, until very recently, has been moving in the opposite direction (see section II).

On consumption taxes, France had a value-added tax in 1954, thirteen years before any other industrialized country. This was generalized in 1968 to cover services and retail sales. Though value-added taxes now apply in almost all European countries, France differs from other VAT countries in the relatively large share borne by enterprises and in not increasing the tax rate over the last ten years (section V). France is also somewhat unique in its treatment of excises: there are probably more excises than in any other industrialized country including taxes on such products as beetroot and meat, but excises as a whole bring in well under the OECD average because the big money raisers, tobacco, gasoline, and alcoholic beverages, are taxed relatively lightly.

France is the only industrialized country to have introduced a net wealth tax during the last 40 years. (Greece and Spain have also recently done so and Ireland introduced one in the seventies but abolished it soon after.)

3. Revenue Sources and Trends

Table 1 shows that, regarding the main revenue raisers, France presents a very different picture from an average OECD country. On the whole, between 1965 and 1983, this difference has been increasing. Thus, the individual income tax, which on average in the OECD accounted for nearly one-third of total receipts in 1983, provided only 13 percent for France. While the OECD average increased from 26 percent to 32 percent between 1965 and 1983, it increased by only two percent in France. In fact, revenues from the individual income tax as a percentage of GDP are lower in France than in any industrialized country and the intention is to reduce them still further.

At the other extreme, two revenue sources, employers' social security contributions and value-added tax, accounted for over half of France's receipts in 1983 compared to an OECD average of under 30 percent. Social security contributions as a whole represent a higher proportion of GDP in France than in any industrialized country (table 1), more than double the OECD average. Around two-thirds of these taxes are paid by employers. There are a number of taxes on businesses based largely or entirely on payroll, further demonstrating the important role of payroll taxation (see section IV).

Comparing tax revenues to GDP ratios with those of particular tax revenues to total tax revenues, France has, typically, the tax level of a European industrialized country—approaching that of the highest taxed countries of Scandinavia and Northern Europe—and the tax structure of a Mediterranean country in its low reliance on personal income tax and high reliance on payroll and consumption taxes. Some reasons for this are suggested in the following sections.

Table 2 gives a breakdown of French tax revenues for the year 1983.

4. An Overall Impression

France has been a pioneer in European taxation in its adoption of VAT, the imputation system with halfway credit to shareholders on distributed profits, and indexation of the income tax schedule. Otherwise France appears neither to have greatly influenced nor been influenced by tax trends in other industrialized countries. For example, at a time when reform proposals in other countries (United States, Scandinavia, Australia, New Zealand) take the form of widening the base to achieve greater neutrality, France has been increasingly using the individual and corporate income tax system to promote economic and social objectives (see sections I, II, and III). However, as indicated in section X, France may be more likely, in the future, to be influenced by proposals made in other countries (e.g., the United States' tax reform).

With its high payroll taxes and tough rules for claiming VAT credit on imports, together with low personal income taxes and excises, the formal tax burden on enterprises in relation to households is higher than in other industrialized countries. How far this is offset by shifting of the formal tax burden into lower wages and salaries, and higher consumer prices, is not easy to verify. Table 3 provides some relevant background information on recent trends in France.

I. THE INDIVIDUAL INCOME TAX

1. Rates

Since 1982 rates have varied between zero and 65 percent, increasing by five percentage points over 13 or 14 brackets. This kind of range has been in force for a long time, but before 1982 the top rate was 60 percent. In addition, a five percent surcharge for high incomes was introduced in 1984 for 1983 incomes, reduced to three percent for 1984 incomes. It will not apply to 1985 incomes.

Among the more important measures adopted in late 1985 was a general reduction of income tax, applicable to all taxpayers, which would reduce the revenue yield by 61 billion francs from 262 billion francs to 201 billion francs. Table 4 gives the rate schedule for a person without dependents for the year 1986 (in 1985 income) and for 1985 (on 1984) income.

Comparing 1983, 1984, and 1985 incomes:

- A surcharge of five percent was levied on high 1983 incomes (reduced to three percent for 1984 incomes and abolished for 1985 incomes).
- For low incomes (tax liability not exceeding F21,250 and F22,930 respectively for 1984 and 1985 incomes) there was a reduction of five percent of tax in respect of income obtained in 1984. There will be a further three percent reduction for income obtained in 1985.
- For those whose tax liability for 1983 incomes is between F21,250 and F26,900, income tax may be reduced by four times the difference between F1,345 and five percent of the income tax; for the following year the corresponding figures are F22,730 and 34,091 and four times the difference between F1,420 and 4.25 percent of the tax payable.
- Full indexing for inflation of the tax schedule, the ceiling of the family quotient (see section 4) and for professional expenses, for each of these years.

There has been a forced loan of 10 percent for taxpayers whose 1981 income tax assessment exceeded F5,000. Also, taxpayers who are subject to net wealth tax had to subscribe to a forced loan of 10 percent of their 1983 net wealth tax assessment. This loan is being repaid in 1986.

2. Reliefs[1]

There is no basic personal allowance to be deducted from all income, but the zero rate bracket achieves a similar result.

There is a deduction for business or employment expenses which may be actual expenses or, alternatively, 10 percent of wages and salaries with minimum (F1,800) and maximum (F54,770) amounts, plus additional deductions in certain cases up to a maximum of F50,000.

Other major standard reliefs include:

- deductions for social security contributions: 100 percent;
- deductions from retirement and other provisions: 100 percent subject to minimum and maximum liability;
- allowances for old age and disability, with an annual income of less than F43,100 (when they may deduct F6,960—or F13,920 if both spouses are involved) or between F43,100 and F69,600 (when they may deduct F3,480 or F6,960 if both spouses are involved) from taxable income.

There are also nonstandard deductions from the tax base in respect of:

- pension contributions by civil servants to approved salaries: 100 percent;
- whole life insurance premiums: up to F400 plus F100 per dependent child;
- childcare expenses for children under five years: up to F4,310 per child;
- alimony: varies;
- donations to charities: up to three percent of the tax base.

Since 1983 there have been nonstandard credits (i.e., deductions from tax due) for interest paid in acquiring (20 percent) and repairing (25 percent) a principal residence for endowment insurance premiums (20 percent) and for energy savings (100 percent). These are all subject to ceilings as follows:

- interest mortgage for principal residence: F9,000 plus F1,500 per dependent;
- insurance premium: F4,000 plus F1,000 per dependent child;
- energy savings: F8,000 plus F1,000 per dependent.

3. Tax Treatment of Different Kinds of Income

Employment income. As a deliberate reflection of the fewer opportunities of employees (and assimilated persons) to evade or

---

[1]Most of these are described in more detail in section III., Chapter 1. Subsection 2 provides a summary list of those that seem the most important.

postpone payment of tax, they receive a 20 percent deduction from their taxable income. For income earned in 1984 this was subject to a maximum income limit of F495,000 and a maximum deduction of F99,000.

Capital Gains. Capital gains are generally included in the income tax base, but may be subject to separate taxation (usually at 16 percent of gains from sales of shares) or 51 percent on gains derived from taxpayers who improve property with a view to its sale, if they sell completed dwelling houses.

A tax allowance is available to capital gains of five percent for each full year of holding over two years (3.33 percent for building land). This allowance is derived from the exempted treatment of capital gains realized after 22 years (32 years for building land). The tax rate applied to capital gains is the normal marginal tax rate of the taxpayer concerned, but to limit progressivity, taxable gains are divided by five and the tax amount is then multiplied by five.

Dividend income. There is a F3,000 deduction from the tax base for dividend income. This reduced base represents total dividend income plus the related tax credit of 50 percent minus related investment expenses (e.g., management fees), and the tax credit is then subtracted from tax due. Table 5 provides an example confined to shareholder level. (For more complicated examples, taking account also of what happens at company level, see Annex to section 2).

Interest income. There is a F5,000 deduction from the base irrespective of the taxpayer's income.

Net taxable income from French sources may be either included in a personal tax return with other investment income or, for certain types of securities, the taxpayer may elect to have interest income taxed at flat and final rates, which vary from 12 percent (bonds) to 50 percent, (e.g., savings from bank accounts) depending on the nature of the underlying investment.

For interest paid by a foreign resident company to a person having his tax domicile in France, the individual must add the interest paid by the foreign-established company to taxable income. France grants the individual a foreign tax credit only for interest received from a tax treaty country (standard rate—10 percent).

Income from immovable property. Income from rural property qualifies (1983) for a 10 percent allowance (15 percent for certain types of property). Income from urban property qualifies (1983) for a 15 percent allowance. These allowances are intended to cover various overheads (e.g., management changes and amortization).

For 1975 incomes they were 20 percent and 25 percent respectively. For 1978 incomes they were reduced to 15 percent and 20 percent, and for 1981 and subsequent incomes they were reduced to their current sizes.

4. The Treatment of the Family

The income of husband, wife and unmarried children under 18 is aggregated. The income must be divided by a certain coefficient (depending on marital status, number of dependents, etc.). The income tax table is then applied to the result and the income tax thus computed is subsequently multiplied by the same coefficient (see table 6).[2] However, the benefit of this relief is limited to F9,960 for each time a taxpayer is entitled to a coefficient of .5 in excess of one if he is either single, divorced or a widower; or in excess of two if he is married.

Unmarried children of 18 years or older are taxed separately. However, they may elect to be taxed under the above coefficient system (their income being added to that of their parents), provided that such children are:

- less than 21 years of age; or
- studying and are less than 25 years of age; or
- fulfilling their military obligations; or
- invalids.

Married children (regardless of their age) are also taxed separately. However, if they fall under one of the above categories they may elect to have their income added to that of either of their parents, in which case the latter benefits from an additional deduction (from taxable income) of F15,330 per person (i.e., F30,660 if the married couple has no children, F45,990 if there is one child, etc.).

This system has been criticized as providing disproportionate relief to higher income parents and defended as reflecting horizontal equity between parents, couples, and single people at various income levels. Since 1981 a ceiling was put on this relief, which has been increased in line with inflation each year since then.

5. Current Payment System

There is no withholding system as in nearly all other industrialized countries, under which employers withhold tax due from

---

[2]This is the family quotient system which is applied only in France and Luxembourg (see OECD 1986).

employees, though around 30 percent of taxpayers have taken the option of paying their tax on a monthly basis by automatic deductions from their bank accounts. The standard system is that all taxpayers declare the income they have received during year n-1 by the end of February in year n. On February 15th and May 15th in year n, they pay two *acomptes provisionnels* (installments on provisional assessment) equivalent to one-third of the tax paid in year n-1 (and therefore relating to income in year n-2). The taxpayer is notified of the amount of tax to be paid, as calculated by the tax authorities. The taxpayer must pay the "balance" of the tax (i.e., the difference between the amount of income tax for year n-1 and the amount of the two installments already paid) within two months of receiving notice or be penalized by a 10 percent increase. In most cases, payment of the balance is on September 15th.

There are two main exceptions:
- Where a taxpayer received income from bonds and certain other types of securities, he may opt for the *prelevement libaratoire* (deduction at source), which dispenses him from declaring this income on his tax return. This procedure is more advantageous when the rate of tax, which is fixed, is lower than the marginal rate of tax which the taxpayer pays on his total income. The financial institution or the firm pays the tax and the tax-paid income at the same time.
- Payment of tax on certain exceptional income (especially certain categories of capital gains) may be spread over three or five years.

One consequence of this method of collection is that whereas in most industrialized countries some three-quarters of income tax revenues are collected in the same year that income is earned, in France the figure is around 10 percent, (over three-quarters of revenues relating to income earned in the previous year), as indicated by table 7. It would also seem likely that tax from some of these back earnings may never be collected, as people change their addresses.

6. Requirements for Filing Tax Returns

Each year, taxpayers must file a return for all income received during the preceding calendar year and claim deductible allowances. This return must be sent to the local tax inspector by February 28. (As of 1986, a large number of taxpayers only have to fill in a simplified two-page tax return.) The tax inspector reviews the return, calculates the liability, and forwards the assessment to the tax collector. In general, tax notices are received between July and

December. Since 1984, the tax bill issued by the inspector and the statement of the amount outstanding issued by the collector have been combined in one communication.

Payment and collection. All persons taxed in the previous year must pay in the current year two provisional installments and a final payment; each installment payment is equal to one-third of the tax bill issued in the previous year. The dates of the installment payments are February 15 and May 15. The balance is due not later than the date specified in the notice sent by the tax authorities.

For employees tax domiciled in France, there is no system whereby the French employer is required to withhold from the taxpayer's salary a sum representing a portion of the estimated tax liability. The taxpayer is responsible for declaring and paying the tax due. Personal income tax is paid in arrears.

Foreigners working in France for the first time will normally pay their prior year's tax liability in the September following the year of arrival.

Penalties and tax audits. A 10 percent penalty based on the tax liability is levied if there is late payment of tax or filing of the return. Penalties for understated income range from 25 percent (unintentional errors) to 150 percent (fraud).

Individuals are seldom audited. Tax inspectors are entitled to verify the employer's books to ensure that all taxable income has been reported. Taxpayers may be required to furnish foreign tax returns, bank account information, and employer statements concerning the amount of compensation paid.

Special features. Reference to "exterior signs of wealth" (*signes exterieur de richesse*) may be made by the tax inspector for contesting an individual tax return or requesting additional information (e.g., possession of yachts or real estate).

A special *forfaitaire* system is applicable to small farmers and some traders and liberal professions, the amount of taxable income being negotiated with the tax inspector. The taxpayer may opt for assessment on the basis of actual earnings and expenses. The forfeits are adjusted on a yearly basis, but the administration's policy has been to not adjust them fully for inflation, so that traders gradually get into the "normal" income tax assessment system.

"Tax management centers" (*Centre de Gestion agrees*) have been set up by the administration to assist small traders and professions in keeping their accounts and improving compliance. If they have recourse to such centers, these self-employed become entitled to the 20 percent special reduction allowed to earners of wages and salaries.

7. Adjustment for Inflation

On January 1, 1968, French law provided that if there were an annual increase of more than five percent in the price index of the "259 items" as calculated by the National Institute for Statistics and Economic Studies, Parliament could modify the income tax scales.

Over the last decade indexation has occurred every year and, recently, across every income tax bracket. Between 1977 and 1981, however, the tax schedule was made more progressive by indexing at a higher rate for lower income groups than higher income groups. Since 1981 greater progressivity has been achieved by an increase in higher rates (see section 1) and a ceiling on the family quotient (section 3). Details of adjustments to schedules over recent years are as indicated in table 8.

Apart from the allowance for the aged and disabled, tax reliefs are not formally indexed, but have generally been adjusted more or less in line with inflation.

There is no adjustment for inflation of interest income or capital gains for inflation.

8. An Overall View

An overall critical view of the French individual income tax is provided by the 1984 Seventh Report to the President of the Republic by the Tax Council (*Conseil des Impots*). Noting that the yield of the tax is lower than in any other industrialized country whether as a percentage of GDP or total tax receipts, it makes, among others, the following points:

- The system is extremely complex and difficult for the tax-payer to understand, and so he perceives the system to be unjust.
- The base is narrower than in other industrialized countries because of: i) the numerous reliefs; ii) the numerous methods for arriving at the tax base; iii) the prevalence of *forfaitaire* assessments (i.e., income presumed to be the taxable amount after negotiations between the tax inspector and taxpayer, which apply especially to the self-employed (farmers, artisans, liberal professions), whom, it is considered, often hide their real income from tax inspectors; iv) these complexities induce taxpayers (whether voluntarily or involuntarily) often to underdeclare their income.
- This narrow base combined with the high progressivity of the system (around 10 percent of taxpayers pay 64 percent of the tax, around one percent pay 30 percent), and because of the quotient system, there are fewer taxpayers compared with

other countries. Over one-third of households do not pay tax in France compared with 25 percent in the United Kingdom, 20 percent in the United States, and 16 percent in Germany.

- The progressivity of the system has increased in recent years in contrast to Germany, where it has remained constant, and, the United Kingdom and the United States, where it has diminished.

The report also evaluates studies[3] on the economic effect of individual income tax, concluding that because of the importance of so many other factors, it is difficult to evaluate its effect, if any, on growth, work supply, and savings levels. There is some indication (as in other countries) that income taxes may have a negative effect on the participation of married women in the work force, though even here it is suggested that these studies underestimate the importance of the participation of secondary earners in the hidden economy.

II. THE CORPORATION INCOME TAX
(*impot sur les societes*)

1. Introduction

The French corporation income tax has two main characteristics; it is based on the territoriality principle and it provides for partial imputation (the *avoir fiscal* tax credit system) for dividends. Corporation tax receipts in 1984 represented about four percent of total tax receipts and two percent of GDP (table 2). Corporate income tax is payable by corporations (*societes a responsabilite limitee*), limited partnerships with shares (*societes en commandite par actions*), silent partners of limited partnerships, and permanent establishments of foreign corporations.

2. Territoriality

The French corporate tax system, based on the principle of territoriality, net profits earned by foreign-based subsidiaries, and permanent establishments of French companies is not subject to French tax until these profits have been actually paid to France and distributed by the French company to its shareholders. Losses

---

[3]Those quoted are: K. Marsden, "Links Between Taxation and Economic Growth: Some Empirical Evidence" (World Bank Staff Working Paper. No 605); M. Brown, *Taxation and Labour Supply*, (London Alan and Vicon 1981); and a study by Kessler and Straus-Kahn in *Prevision et Analyse Economique Cahiers du Gema*, April/June 1981.

incurred in foreign operations (permanent establishments, subsidiaries, joint ventures) are excluded from the calculation of French taxable income. The main exceptions to this principle are: 1) tax consolidation (see subsection 6 below) and 2) rules applicable to subsidiaries established in tax havens (a subpart F-type legislation).

3. Rate of Tax

The standard rate of corporate income tax for a company established in France is 50 percent of net taxable income. From 1986 a special rate of 45 percent is applicable to reinvested profits. Reduced rates of 25 percent (developed land) or 15 percent (other assets) are applicable to long-term capital gains, i.e., gains on assets held more than two years (see subsection 4 below). By virtue of the territoriality principle, foreign source income is tax-exempt. Therefore, any income tax paid abroad is not creditable in France. Foreign income subject to withholding tax in the source country benefits from a tax credit in France only if the withholding tax was levied by a country with which France has concluded an income tax treaty.

4. The Tax Base

Net profits, including capital gains of taxable entities, are subject to tax. There are relatively few categories of nontaxable income, the major categories being dividends received by parent companies (only a five percent charge applies), income from establishments abroad, and interest from certain French government bonds.

Business operating profits are defined as gross trading profits less operating costs, including administrative and selling expenses. Inventories must be valued at the lower of historic cost or market value. Nevertheless, on the balance sheet, inventories must be shown at historic cost. If market value is lower, a reserve for depreciation of inventories must be disclosed separately as a deduction from cost. Cost is defined as the actual purchase price or actual production cost (excluding financial charges and research expenses) incurred. The market value is defined as the value at which the goods may be sold. FIFO or the average-cost method must be applied; LIFO is prohibited.

All expenses incurred in the conduct of a business are deductible if they are directly related to achieving its corporate purpose and are not specifically nondeductible. Payments to affiliates are allowed, provided they meet the "arm's length" test.

For tax purposes, operating losses may be carried forward to offset profits earned in the five succeeding years. Carried-forward operating losses may not be transferred to another company. Operating losses resulting from depreciation may be carried forward indefinitely if the depreciation was reported in the annual corporate income tax return as deferred for tax purposes.

For fiscal years which closed on or after December 31, 1984, the taxpayer may elect a form of carryback. Losses of a given fiscal year may be offset against undistributed taxable profits of the three preceding years (five years for losses reported on December 31, 1984). The lower amount of either 50 percent of these profits or of the tax loss of the year is a tax credit that may be discounted with a bank. This tax credit may be offset against corporate income tax during the following 10 years and, thereafter, any excess credit may be reimbursed in cash.

The valuation of capital gains differs depending upon the period the asset has been held for:
- Short-term gains (24 months) are taxable at 50 percent. The taxpayer can generally spread them in equal parts over the year in which they are made, and the two following years. Short-term losses can be offset against short-term gains.
- Long-term gains are taxable at the rate of 25 percent for developed land and 15 percent for other assets, provided the remaining 75 or 85 percent is credited in a special reserve account. If these gains are added back to profits, then the normal corporate income tax rate (50 percent) is levied minus the capital gains tax. Long-term gains can be offset against long-term losses and can be carried forward 10 years. A company is allowed to record nonrealized capital gains. This might be advantageous to firms that have carried losses forward for five years. Gains made on the sale of a patent held for two years, or created by the firm, are under certain conditions taxed at 15 percent. (For depreciation rules and investment incentives, see section III below).

5. Dividends

General. Cash dividends paid by French companies to resident and certain categories of nonresident shareholders (see below) entitle the shareholder to a tax credit (*avoir fiscal*) of 50 percent. This tax credit represents one-half of the corporate income tax that was levied on the company paying the dividend. (For examples of the computations see the Annex.) If the profits distributed as dividends did not bear corporate income tax at 50 percent, the dividends are subject to an equalization tax (see below). Dividends paid to nonresidents are subject to a withholding tax of 25 percent or the reduced tax treaty rate.

An equalization tax (*precompte*) is imposed on distributions that have not borne French corporate income tax at 50 percent (e.g., foreign-based income, long-term capital gains, or dividend income), or are made out of profits earned more than five years before that distribution. The equalization tax is equal to 50 percent of the net cash dividend or 33.3 percent of the gross amount. The tax credit attached to dividends received from French companies (50 percent) or foreign companies (foreign withholding tax credit) may be offset against the equalization tax if redistribution is made by the French parent company within five years.

Taxation of Resident Shareholders. Gross dividends received by individuals, including French and foreign tax credits, are added to taxable income. If the French tax payable is less than the French tax credit, the difference is refundable. If the foreign tax credit exceeds the French tax due, there is no refund. French corporate shareholders that do not qualify as French parent companies (see below) include the entire cash dividend received from French companies as well as the related tax credit in taxable income, but one-half of the tax credit attached to the dividend may be deducted from the corporate income tax liability. If such total corporate income tax is less than the available tax credit, the difference is lost, and may not be refunded or carried forward.

The gross amount of cash dividends paid by foreign companies established in tax treaty countries to French nonparent companies is included in income taxable at the rate of 50 percent, with a tax credit recognized for foreign withholding tax actually or constructively (matching credit) levied. If dividends are received from nontreaty countries, only the net amount is taxable at the rate of 50 percent.

French parent companies receiving dividends from their French or foreign subsidiaries benefit from a participation exemption system that avoids double taxation. To qualify as a parent, the recipient company must be incorporated in France and must hold shares representing at least 10 percent of the issued share capital of the subsidiary. The shares must be registered and must have been subscribed at the time of issue, or the parent must promise to hold or have held them for at least two years from the date of purchase.

For qualified parent companies, the cash dividend, i.e., the amount actually received in cash from the subsidiary, less the expense of the parent company relating to such dividend income, is not taxable. The expenses relating to the dividend income, arbitrarily fixed at five percent of the total dividend, (including the 50 percent French or foreign tax credit attached thereto), are included in taxable income. These expenses may not exceed the total of the parent company's actual expenses. This limitation applies in particular if the parent company is a pure holding company with low operating expenses.

The exemption system results in a maximum tax rate of 3.75 percent in the case of a dividend received from another French company, or 2.5 percent of the cash dividend plus foreign withholding tax credit in the case of a dividend received from a foreign company resident in a tax treaty country.

Taxation of Nonresident Shareholders. Dividends and reimbursements of tax credits or equalization tax (see below) are subject to withholding tax at the rate of 25 percent or the reduced tax treaty rate.

For corporate shareholders established in a tax treaty country, the withholding tax rate depends on the percentage of shares, e.g., for a U.S. company holding at least 10 percent of the shares, the rate is five percent. They are entitled to the reimbursement of the equalization tax, but not of the tax credits.

Companies not qualifying as parent companies and individuals are subject to the same rate, e.g., under the France-U.S. Income Tax Treaty, the rate is 15 percent. They are entitled to the reimbursement of the tax credits.

6. Tax Consolidation

French companies must be authorized by the Ministry of Economy, Finance, and of the Budget to use one of the three different group taxation systems. The Ministry has restricted authorization of these group taxation systems to very special cases. Therefore, group taxation is not a widespread French taxing method.

1. Ninety-five-percent-owned subsidiary consolidation: Where one French company holds 95 percent or more of the shares of one or more French companies, either directly or through a 95 percent or more shareholding in another company, such companies may apply to be taxed as a single entity. This means that the subsidiaries are treated as branches of the parent and corporate income tax is paid at the latter's level only.

2. Fifty percent-owned subsidiary taxation: Under this system (*benefice consolide*), the profits and losses of all controlled branches, subsidiaries and partnerships in France and abroad are consolidated. Control is defined at 50 percent of the voting shares (subject to exceptions). Second-tier subsidiary control is determined proportionally. The authorization is for a minimum five-year period.

3. Worldwide taxation: Under this system (*benefice mondial*), income from all domestic and foreign branches, factories, offices, agencies, and all permanent establishments is consolidated. Income from subsidiaries is excluded. The tax rules are virtually the same as those applicable to the 50 percent-owned subsidiary consolidation.

7. Small- and Medium-Size Enterprises ('SME')

No special rate of tax applies. The following specific provisions are applicable:
- Start-up losses may be carried forward to five years;
- If started after January 1, 1982, a "SME" may claim a special 50 percent allowance on profits in the first year and in the four subsequent years, before depreciation allowances are taken. This provision is only available for new SMEs whose assets are depreciable by the declining-balance method amount to not less than two-thirds of their total depreciable fixed assets, whose share capital proportion held by other companies is less than 50 percent, whose turnover is less than F30 million, and whose work force is less than 150.

8. Effects of Dividend Relief on Equity Financing

Literature on the effects of dividend relief available under the imputation system on equity financing is rather scarce. Official sources have indicated that the introduction of the system in the sixties had helped corporations to increase their distributions while keeping for themselves part of the tax benefit thereby contributing also to a recovery in self-financing. Distribution (and retention) policies have to take account of the fact that fiscal shareholders wish to receive dividends every year. The number and variety of tax incentives for savings also have made it difficult to measure the specific impact of the system.

As noted under section X below, discussions have tended to concentrate on the imbalance in the tax treatment of equity and on financing (an obvious issue in times of high inflation) and the possible lack of consistency regarding favoring self-financing (compare the 1985 five percent reduction in tax rate) or distributions (compare the deductibility of dividends of new capital shares).

ANNEX
Tax Treatment of Dividends

I. Dividends received by an individual resident shareholder

Taxable profits of distributing company		100
Corporate income tax (50 percent)		50
Dividend paid to shareholder		50
Avoir fiscal or gross-up (25 percent)		25
Grossed-up dividend over which income tax is due		75
Personal income tax (say 40 percent)	30	
Tax credit (equal to gross-up)	(25)	
	5	
Net tax after tax dividend	45	

II. Dividend received by a French nonparent company

	French Company	Foreign Company No Treaty	Foreign Company Tax Treaty
Gross dividend	100	100	100
Less withholding tax	0	(15)	(15)
Net received	100	85	85
Plus tax credit	50	0	15
Taxable income	150	85	100
Tax at 50 percent	75	42.5	50
Less tax credit	(50)	0	(15)
Net payable	25	42.5	35
Net after-tax dividend	75	42.5	50

III. Dividend received by a French parent company from a foreign company

	French Company	Foreign Company Treaty	Foreign Company No Treaty
Gross dividend	100	100	100
Less withholding tax	0	(5)	(5)
Net received	100	95	95
Amount subject to tax			
150 x 5 percent	7.5		
100 x 5 percent		5	
95 x 5 percent			4.75
Tax at 50 percent	3.75	(2.50)	(2.37)
Net after-tax dividend	96.25	92.50	92.63

III. SAVING AND INVESTMENT

1. Introduction

Unlike many other OECD countries, France has, during the last three years, placed increased reliance on tax expenditures to encourage saving and investment. There are many publicly inspired saving schemes which attract favorable tax treatment. Productive investment is also favored by a variety of tax measures. The general impression, until recently, has been that these schemes have been successful.

2. Saving Incentives Through the Tax System

The main incentives to household saving are provided in the personal income tax system, though relevant provisions can also be found in capital taxes (see section VII). In 1985, these included:

1. Saving for retirement.[4] Contributions to recognized pension schemes are deductible without limit from the taxable income of individuals. The pension is taxed, but the amount is reduced by 10 percent subject to a minimum amount of F2000 and a maximum amount of F24,000. Pension income also carries an allowance equal to 20 percent of the portion of the pension not exceeding F460,000. There are also a number of special allowances for low income pensioners.

2. Life insurance. Premiums paid on life assurance contracts are deductible up to F4,000, increased by F1,000 for each dependent child. Premiums on endowment contracts are deductible up to F3,250 a year, increased by F600 for each dependent child.

3. House purchase. Interest payable on mortgages taken out prior to January 1, 1984 for the purchase of a principal residence in France, limited to F9,000 plus F1,500 per dependent child gives rise to a maximum annual tax credit of 20 percent.[5] Mortgage interest qualifies for this credit for the first 10 years of the loan repayment term.

For mortgages concluded on or after January 1, 1984, the tax credit is increased to 25 percent, with the same limitation of the amount, but the period during which the interest carries entitlement to credit is reduced from 10 years to five years. Interest paid on mortgages for dwellings located outside of France or for

---

[4]Social security contributions to government schemes are fully deductible from taxable income and the pensions paid out by such schemes receive the same tax treatment as those paid by private schemes.

[5]In 1985 the ceilings were increased to F12,000 and F2,000 respectively.

secondary residences in or outside of France is not deductible for French tax purposes.

There is also a homeownership saving scheme (*epargne logement*) which enjoys favorable tax treatment (in most cases the interest paid, which is generally lower than the current market rate, is not subject to tax). This scheme applies to primary and, since 1985, to secondary residences.

4. Equities[6]. French taxpayers who are not subject to the wealth tax (see section VII) are entitled to an annual tax credit equal to 25 percent of the net purchase price of French shares made through a special share savings account. The base of the 25 percent tax credit is limited to F7,000 for a single, widowed, or divorced taxpayer and to F14,000 for a couple.

5. Tax credit for investment in new rental property. Individuals acquiring property for subsequent rental are entitled to a tax credit equal to five percent of the investment up to a ceiling of F20,000 (F10,000 in the case of single people). The credit also applies to purchasing shares in property investment companies.

6. Other. Since April 1984 the government permits:

- Individuals to deduct, up to 50 percent of their salary or F100,000, interest on loans obtained for the equity capitalization of their enterprises.
- Individuals to be exempt from income tax and capital gains taxes on their investments in risk capital investment funds. The stock must be unlisted and held for at least three years.
- Employees' share subscriptions in listed companies to be deducted for 10 percent of their average exchange price, if held for more than three years.
- A tax credit to a holding company, set up to get control over an operating company by employees (50 percent). Interest costs are deductible.
- Special rates to apply to individuals who are partners or shareholders of a partnership or corporation, and who keep a blocked account with their partnership or corporation. If such accounts do not exceed F20,000 they are subject to a final withholding tax of 25 percent (*prelevement*).

3. Treatment of Financial Institutions

Banks, life insurance companies, and other financial institutions are subject to the normal corporate income tax (see section II

---

[6]In addition to the measures described there is an imputation tax credit (*avoir fiscal*) and a F3,000 exception available to shareholders.

above). Banks and financial institutions are also, however, subject to a relatively complex turnover tax system. Their income is divided for tax purposes into three categories:

1. TVA-exempt income, such as interest income.

2. Income subject to TVA (commission for collection of receivables, fees for financial or other advice, lease of equipment, etc).

3. Income exempt from TVA that may, however, be subject upon specific election. This category, in fact, covers the same types of income formerly subject to the tax on financial institutions (*taxe sur les activites financieres*—TAF) applicable prior to January 1, 1979.

In order to compensate for the loss of tax revenues resulting from the elimination of the TAF, a new tax on financial credit was introduced in 1979. It is levied on the total amount of credit recorded as of December 31 of each year. The rate of .165 percent is reduced to .11 percent for banks that have elected to be subject to TVA according to category three mentioned above.

The tax is due not later than July 31 of each year and is deductible for corporate income tax purposes.

Regarding insurance companies, there is a tax on insurance contracts (*taxe unique sur les conventions d'assurances*—TUCA), with rates ranging from .25 percent to 30 percent of the premiums and which are payable by the insurer. For example, the rate of TUCA for certain fire insurance coverage is 30 percent, on life insurance 5.15 percent, and on export credit .25 percent.

There is also a tax on the excess provisions of insurance companies (*taxe sur les excedents des provisions des entreprises d'assurance*), which was established in the 1983 Finance Law and is payable on all kinds of nonlife insurance companies which carry over to a financial year's taxable results the excess provisions created for the settlement of claims arising during previous years. The tax is applied to one-half the excess provisions written back, less an allowance which, for each excess amount, is equal to three percent of that amount and of the payments made in settlement of claims during the financial year by drawing on the corresponding provision, and less any addition to provisions made at the end of the same financial year in order to meet an increase in the estimated cost of claims arising during other previous years.

The tax is calculated by attributing each amount of excess provision (after deduction of the allowance) and each addition to a provision, to the financial year in which the original provision was created. The rate is one percent for each month which has passed since the provision was created. The procedure for assessing, declaring, and collecting it is the same as for the VAT.

4. Investment Incentives at the Corporate Level

1. Depreciation. For tax purposes, land, goodwill, trademarks, and leasehold rights cannot be depreciated. Fixed assets are depreciated according to the declining balance method or the straightline method. However, no declining balance is permitted where accelerated depreciation has been taken or where the useful life of the asset is less than three years. A changeover from declining balance to straight line is allowed when the depreciation allowance computed according to the declining balance method is less than the allowance computed by dividing the net depreciable balance by the remaining number of years. Depreciation allowances can be carried forward indefinitely. The straightline depreciation rates take into account the normal use of an asset. Permitted annual depreciations are for instance:

	Annual Depreciation (Percent)
Factory buildings	5
Office buildings	4
Plant and machinery	10-20

As to the declining balance depreciation, deductions are the result of the multiplication of the usual straightline depreciation rate of the particular asset by a described coefficient. These coefficients are:
- If useful economic life is three or four years.
- If useful economic life is five or six years.
- If useful economic life exceeds six years.

The 1983 Finance Act increased the depreciation rate for the first year, with 40 percent for an asset with a lifetime less than nine years, 42 percent for an asset with a lifetime of 10 years, and four additional percentage points for each additional year up to a maximum of 62 percent for an asset with a lifetime of 15 years or more. This means that an asset, which has a tax life of six years has a declining balance of 2.5 percent and an extra depreciation of 40 percent in the first years, has a declining balance rate of 100/6 x 2.5 x 1.40 = 58.3.

This extra depreciation is determined at December 31, 1985, and has now been replaced by a five percent reduction on the corporate tax rate on reinvested profits (see subsection 2 above). Special accelerated depreciation for buildings has also been available for investment in underdeveloped areas or for declining industries.

Actual deferred depreciation is allowed for loss-making businesses, but only for that portion of the depreciation charge generating the excess of declining balance over straightline. The accumulated excess may be booked and totally deducted during the year when the business returns to a profitable position.

2. Depletion. Depletion reserves may be established in certain branches of the mining, oil and gas industries. The annual depletion deduction is limited to the lower of 50 percent of net income before income tax or 23.5 percent of net sales of the year (reduced to 15 percent for solid mineral extraction). Deductions must be included in a special reserve and are tax-exempt only if an equivalent amount of exploration expenses or capital expenditures for oil exploration are incurred in the subsequent five fiscal years. Moreover, exploration expenses are chargeable against current earnings. Capital expenditures are tax depreciable.

3. Treatment of innovation expenditures. Generally, research and development (R&D) costs must be expensed, but, under certain conditions, they may be capitalized and amortized. Costs to self-develop software must be expensed. The cost of acquiring software from a third party must be capitalized but may be amortized over a twelve-month period. A tax credit of 50 percent is granted for an increase in the research effort from one year to the next, for 1985 (25 percent for 1983-84). The maximum amount is F3 million per year per firm. All expenditures except for buildings can be taken into account. Newly established SMEs (turnover less than F30 million and fewer than 150 employees) may claim 25 percent over their first year research and development. If the profit is not enough to offset the tax credit a cash payment will be made.

Investment in immovable property for the purpose of certain types of research operations may qualify for an exceptional 50 percent write-down allowance.

Patenting expenditure is treated as start-up cost and is written off over the period of legal protection. Royalties or other such costs can be deducted when incurred. Marketing expenditures for the introduction of new technology are treated as ordinary income.

4. Venture capital enterprises. Shares in a *Societe Financiere d'Innovation* (SFI) enjoy an extra 50 percent write-down allowance at the end of the accounting period in which the capital subscription was paid. The capital gains on such shares is tax-exempt if held for three years. The characteristics of a SFI are the following:

- paid in capital at least F10 million in cash;
- no entity or person may own more than 30 percent of the capital of a SFI (49 percent during the first year);
- the fund is committed to having at least 60 percent invested in innovative situations by the end of six years and 80 percent at the end of eight years;

- investment must be made in the form of equity or convertible debentures;
- not more than 25 percent of SFI capital may be invested in a single enterprise;
- after nine years and every three years thereafter, a SFI has to prove to the authorities that it has divested one-third of the capital employed in innovation position;
- in case of nonperformance under the above regulations, 25 percent of the capital otherwise employed must be deposited with the Treasury;
- it may be cancelled by the authorities in case of serious lack of compliance. The SFI is then subject to a penalty of 25 percent of its capital and interest.

5. Assessment of Investment Tax Incentives

It is widely recognized that tax incentives are only some, among many other, factors affecting business decisions, but two rather general statements by official sources are available. The Third Report of the French *Conseil Natural des Impots* concluded in 1977 that the taxation of corporations (including small corporations) was characterized, on the one hand, by a rather tight net of detailed and rather constraining provisions and, on the other hand, by a wide range of special supportive or incentive features.

More recently, when presenting, in 1985, the five percent reduction in the corporate tax rate for reinvested earnings, the Ministry stressed that the various tax incentives to investment taken over the years had not really showed their effectiveness. When they were temporary, they resulted in influencing the timing of the investment but not the overall level of investment; when permanent, they affected the relative costs of labor and capital to the detriment of employment. Also, specific measures often left out many types of investment, whether material (buildings), or nonmaterial (training, marketing, etc.) which are of importance for modernization and job creation.

IV. PAYROLL TAXES

1. Introduction

France relies heavily on payroll taxes and social security contributions to finance public expenditures (approximately 85 percent of the revenues of social security funds is provided by contributions). Table 9 lists the relevant taxes and shows how their yields have changed between 1975 and 1983. In 1983 these taxes accounted for 46 percent of total revenue and 21 percent of GDP.

2. Description of the Main Payroll Taxes

Social Security contributions. The French social security system requires employees, employers, and government to contribute to social funds which are established to provide social benefits, sickness benefits, etc.

The base and the rates for the employee and employer contributions are given in table 10.

As can be seen from table 10, most of these contributions apply to gross earnings (employees) or payroll (employers) up to a specified ceiling. During the last few years the tendency has been to either increase these ceilings or to remove them.

Other payroll taxes. There are four main payroll taxes which are paid by businesses operating in France and which are administered by the Ministry of Finance.

1. Salary tax. Salary tax (taxe sur les salaires) is payable by all employers domiciled or established in France unless at least 90 percent of their sales is subject to TVA, in which case no salary tax is payable. If less than 90 percent of sales is subject to TVA, the salary tax payable is based on the ratio that sales not subject to TVA bears to total sales (pro rata method).

The rate of the salary tax is 4.25 percent on each employee's annual salary or portion thereof not exceeding F32,800, 8.5 percent of the portion between F32,800 and F65,600, and 13.6 percent of the portion above F65,600. This is not a withholding tax and is deductible for corporate income tax purposes.

2. Transport tax. All employers established in one of the following areas and having more than nine employees are required to pay a transport tax. The areas are:

- Paris and the departments Hauts-de-Seine, Seine-Saint-Denis, Val-de-Marne, l'Essonne, les Yvelines, le Val-d'Oise, and la Seine-et-Marne. The rate of the tax is two percent for Paris and the first three of the above-mentioned departments. For the last four, it is 1.2 percent.
- Certain other cities with more than 30,000 inhabitants. The rate of the tax varies from .5 percent to 1.5 percent.

The basis of the tax is the payroll for social security purposes, i.e., the monthly ceiling per employee.

3. Apprenticeship tax. All employers engaged in commercial, industrial, and handicraft activities (with limited exceptions) that are subject to corporate income tax are also subject to a .6 percent apprenticeship tax (taxe d'apprentissage) on total annual gross

wages and salaries. The purpose of the tax is to finance technical and apprenticeship training. The tax is deductible for corporate income tax purposes.

4. Employee training tax. All employers, regardless of their legal form or branch of activity, employing an average of more than nine employees in a given year are obliged to allocate a minimum amount equal to 1.1 percent of total annual wages and salaries (including taxable fringe benefits) to staff training. If qualified training expenses fall below the 1.1 percent minimum, the shortfall becomes the tax payable.

Qualifying expenses include those incurred for in-house training, payments to authorized independent training organizations and financing of authorized training entities (with a percentage limit on total training expenses). The tax is deductible for corporate tax purposes.

3. Effect of Payroll Taxes on Labor Costs

There are various ways to measure the impact of payroll taxes (including social contributions) on labor costs. Table 11 shows the level of these taxes as a percentage of the average earnings of manual workers in the manufacturing sector.

At this level of income, these rates are an accurate guide to the impact of these taxes on labor costs, since the ceilings on the earning base used to calculate social security contributions does not apply (see table 10). At higher income levels, however, the effective average rates will be substantially lower than those shown in table 11.[7]

Another way of measuring the impact of these taxes on labor costs is to measure the contributions as a percentage of the total wage bill. This is done in table 12. The percentages are significantly lower than those in table 11 because (a) unearmarked payroll taxes are excluded (these would add approximately 1.5 percent in 1984) and (b) many social security contributions are subject to an earnings ceiling (see table 10).

Payroll taxes and social security contributions are only two components of nonwage labor costs (NWLC)—albeit the most important components. Other NWLC include: contributions to private pension and sickness schemes (approximately just over five percent of total salaries and wages); cost of holidays (five weeks are

---

[7]For example, in 1984 employees' contributions fell from just under 15 percent of earnings at the average earnings level to under seven percent at four times average earnings. Similarly, employers' contributions fell from just under 45 percent to less than 10 per cent.

compulsory minimum); payments in kind. An international survey by the Swedish Employers Confederation in 1980 found that when all of these NWLC are taken into account the following figures are obtained:

NWLC as percentage of total labor cost (including NWLC) in French industry: 1968 = 40 percent; 1974 = 42 percent; 1980 = 45 percent.

Each of the above comparisons suggest that payroll taxes and other NWLC substantially increase total labor costs in France.[8]

V. VALUE-ADDED TAX

1. Introduction

VAT was introduced in France in 1954, fifteen years before any other industrialized country, although it was not generalized to cover services and retail transactions until 1968. Whereas in 1954 there were fewer than 300,000 entrepreneurs subject to VAT, by 1981 the number had reached nearly two and one-half million. Revenue yields from VAT have remained fairly stable as a percentage of GDP these last twenty years but have declined as a percentage of total tax revenues (see table 13). As with other countries employing VAT, suppliers of goods must add VAT to the net prices of their sales and pay VAT to the government with an entitlement to credit for tax paid on their inputs. In France the credit for tax on inputs is limited in several respects, which generally, do not apply to other countries with VAT systems.

1. Credit is not allowed for tax on certain inputs which could be used for private as well as business purposes, of which motor vehicles and hydrocarbon oils are by far the most important.[9]

2. Tax on purchases of inputs, other than fixed assets may be offset only against tax on sales in the following month and, in any event, refunds of less than F5,000 are not paid (this minimum repayment occurs only in Belgium, Luxembourg, and Germany where it is around half of that in France).

3. A business that has both taxed and exempt supplies, must attribute the amount of each in respect to their sales (which is

---

[8]If the U.S. is compared to France the equivalent figure in Table 12 for the period 1975-80 is just under 15 percent.

[9]Here, however, there has been increasing relaxation in recent years for heavy oils.

administratively expensive) or accept a pro rata formula which may result in lower recovery of tax on inputs.

4. Reimbursements for tax on inputs can be claimed only every third month, whereas in most countries it is every month. Unlike all other countries with VAT except Belgium, the minimum time period for claiming is shorter than that demanded for payments.[10]

Because of this inadequate compensation for VAT on inputs combined with certain derogations from the tax base (see tables 17 and 18), the French VAT is not entirely a neutral tax on consumption. Brookings (1981) reproduces estimates that suggest only 72 percent is paid by households, 17 percent paid by firms, 10 percent by general government and one percent by financial institutions. The French Tax Council Report (1983) notes that noncreditability amounted to 16.5 percent of the VAT yield in 1978, of which around 40 percent was due to the noncreditability of the tax on motor vehicles and oil products, and 60 percent from the noncreditability of the input tax on the supply of exempt goods and services (see table 14), which shows also how this limitation can create significant competitive distortions between various sectors of the economy). In addition, the delay in obtaining refunds on inputs reduces cash resources available to enterprises, which has the effect, especially for small enterprises, of making it difficult to obtain loans.

The main conclusions of the 1983 Tax Council Report is that leaving aside social security contributions, VAT constituted the major budgetary resource (twice as important as the individual income tax and four times more than the corporate income tax). It is well-accepted (tax fraud being relatively low) and is a relatively neutral tax on consumption in terms of its effects on income distribution and different sectors of the economy. Though exportations are treated as favorably, or even more favorably, than is the case in some other countries (in that they are mostly zero-rated rather than tax having been paid and then refunded), limitations on deductibility are generally more severe than those in other countries. These limitations have to remain for budgetary reasons (para. 347), but they do ensure that VAT is initially borne partially by enterprises and that it can create significant distortions between various sectors of the economy (table 14).

2. Tax Rates

Since July 1982, there has been a standard rate of 18.6 percent of the tax exclusive retail selling price. As of January 1, 1986 there

---

[10]For details see paragraph 400, page 86 of the 1985 report of the Tax Council.

is a super-reduced rate (introduced in 1982) of 5.5 percent, another reduced rate of seven percent and a higher rate of 33.33 percent. Table 15, which gives changes in rates since 1968, shows that changes have been relatively slight, although in contrast to all other VAT countries, the standard rate reached its peak in the early seventies and has subsequently declined despite the one percentage point increase in 1982. Table 16 lists the main goods and services subject to higher and reduced rates in 1985.

Around 84 percent of revenues come from goods and services subject to the standard rate. Of the remaining 15 percent, there has been a slight increase in yields from the higher rate of 33.33 percent relative to the lower rate; in 1980 around 10 percent of revenues derived from the higher rate and five percent from the lower rate (table 37 of the 1963 report).

3. Tax Exemptions

Table 17 sets out the main goods and services which are exempt as of January 1, 1986. In addition. exports are zero-rated[11] and certain imports are exempt under the *regime suspensif*, where tax becomes due on the first domestic sale.

Also, certain taxpayers (small traders and farmers) may opt out of the obligation to keep the accounting record required by VAT and thus be treated as consumers who get no tax deduction on their inputs. Others (independent professions such as writers and interpreters) who are, in principle, exempt may opt to pay VAT in order to get credit for tax paid on their inputs.

4. Tax Compliance

Compliance is considered by the Tax Council (1983) to be relatively good, particularly in comparison with that of the personal income tax. Nevertheless, there is a fair amount of evasion, which takes, *inter alia*, the following forms:

1. The production of invoices for fictitious purchases to get refunds of tax on inputs;

2. Concealment by enterprises of transactions through the "black labor" market, e.g., in the construction industry, ready-to-wear textiles, hotel, and restaurant industries;

3. Unreported transactions by employees in the service sector (e.g., plumbing and painting) where payment is made by cash;

---

[11]That is, in contrast to sales of exempt goods, credits for tax on inputs are fully allowed.

4. underestimation of sales of small enterprises;

5. nonreporting of secondary activities of larger enterprises.

"Black labor" market transactions and unreported employee transactions both concern the hidden economy, and are commented on further in section VI (see page 315 of Tax Council Report).

It is invariably difficult to estimate amounts of tax evasion with any degree of accuracy, but the 1983 Report of the Tax Council tried to do so on the basis of adjustments made after tax audits and on the amount of tax which should have been received according to GNP data. Its estimate was that VAT revenue losses amounted to between six and 10 percent of the total yield. It is also believed that the percentage has decreased in recent years.

5. Administrative Costs

The fact that administration of the VAT, the personal and corporate income tax, as well as import duties, is carried out by the same officials makes it difficult to estimate these costs. (We have not found any attempt to do so).

Price Levels. A major concern of most countries with VAT has been the effect on price levels of the move to VAT from pre-existing cascade or single stage sale taxes. This is not the case with France, which has had VAT for three decades. Inquiries have instead questioned what would be the price effects of changing rates or coverage of VAT.

Studies reported in the Tax Council (1983) demonstrate that rate changes have no automatic impact on prices, but depend both on other measures taken by government and the economic situation generally. The Tax Council (1983) indicated that a price reduction represents only a fraction of a rate reduction and is difficult to evaluate after a few months. Rate reductions are considered to be an effective method of reducing prices only if accompanied by other measures such as a temporary price freeze.

The so-called METRIC studies are referred to in both Brookings (1981, pages 27-29) and the 1983 Tax Council Report. They suggest that a reduction of VAT rates by one percent should, other things being equal, reduce consumer prices by .7 percent, though the amount would vary between different goods and services rates. We have not seen estimations of the effects of increases in VAT which, outside France, has been the usual pattern in recent years. However, when the standard rate was increased by one percentage point in June 1982 it was accompanied by a six-month price freeze and it was believed that the increase would have been borne by suppliers during that period.

Effects on Revenues. Brookings (1981) estimated that a decrease of the VAT rate of one percentage point would lead to a fall of 6.6 percent of value-added revenues in 1980, noting that the actual government loss is always smaller than the direct loss because of the increase in economic activity induced.

Effects on Income Distribution (see also section VIII). Studies described by OECD (1981), Brookings (1981), and The French Tax Council (1983) all found VAT proportional or mildly progressive if measured in relation to levels of consumption. If measured in relation to levels of income, Brookings (1981) found it very regressive (table 4, page 26) and the Tax Council (1983) only mildly so.

Table 18 which reflects the 1969 position, shows VAT to be broadly proportional as a percentage of consumption over a wide range of incomes. Since then there has been a greater dispersion of VAT rates (see table 15), so it could be expected that the distribution of the tax has become more progressive.

The studies summarized in table 18 below, by the Tax Council Report[12] of 1983 for the year 1979, showed that in all the selected cases (unmarried, couples without children, couples with two children) VAT paid in relation to gross income declined as income increased, but that in most cases the regressivity was very slight, and even less if measured in relation to disposable income. However, the degree of this regressivity cannot be precisely measured, depending upon a number of assumptions, especially about the rates of savings, since VAT falls on households in an inverse proportion to income saved. However, as the chart shows, VAT is clearly regressive compared to the exceptionally progressive income tax.

---

[12]More complete details are provided in paras. 91-5 and 235-43 of that report. They were based on an analysis of the reduction of the rates of VAT that came into force on January 1, 1973 (See table 15); a six-month exemption for beef on January 1, 1973; a reduction from 20 percent to seven percent on pharmaceutical products in July 1976; the reduction of the standard rate from 20 percent to 17.6 percent on January 1, 1977. A reduction of two percentage points is considered to have the effects on various economic variables over one, three, and five years as reproduced in tables 5 and 6 of Brookings 1981 (pages 28-9) and table IX-A on page 244 of the Tax Council Report.

Figure 1
Proportion of VAT Collected on Households in 1979 of (a) Gross Income, (b) Disposable Income, (c) Individual Income Tax

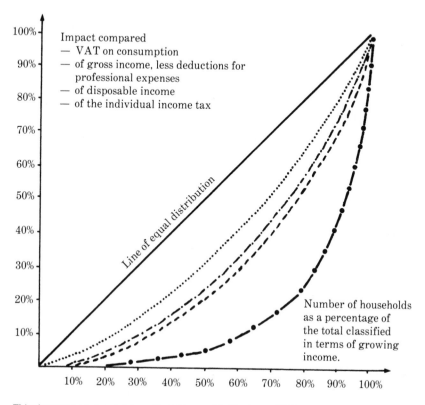

Impact compared
— VAT on consumption
— of gross income, less deductions for professional expenses
— of disposable income
— of the individual income tax

Line of equal distribution

Number of households as a percentage of the total classified in terms of growing income.

This chart was constructed from the table provided in Annex XIII.
Source: "Direction de la Prevision"

These various studies have been constructed by INSEE and the *Direction de la Prevision* in various different ways. Work is underway in the French administration to attempt to synthesize these approaches using the model described in *Les Modeles TVA Economie Prevision*, No. 57. 1983.

VI. THE HIDDEN ECONOMY

1. Introduction

This section examines evidence on the growth of tax evasion and avoidance in France. Most of the statistical evidence comes from work undertaken by the *Centre d'Etude du Couts et Revenue* (CERC), the National Statistical Office (INSEE), and the *Conseil des Impots*.

2. The Impact of Different Taxes

The incentive to evade or avoid taxes on earned income varies at different income levels. At the low to medium income level, social security contributions rather than income taxes provide the largest incentive, whereas at higher income levels the steep progressivity of the income tax is the predominant factor. It is relevant that most employees are not subject to a systematic withholding tax on earned income, though social security contributions are withheld by the employers. Also many liberal professions are subject to a lump-sum regulated taxation. For companies, the incentive to evade is primarily related to employer social security contributions, payroll taxes, and VAT. Because of the cross-checking procedures between these taxes, successful evasion usually requires defrauding on all three taxes.

3. Estimating the Extent of the Evasion

Official studies in France have focused on measuring evasion of specific taxes and of failure to declare income for tax purposes by professionals. No official estimates are available of the overall size of tax evasion or of the hidden economy. Unofficial studies of the overall size of the hidden economy range from six percent (*Nouvel Observateur*) to eight percent of GNP (Frey). In practice, however, these estimates are very high guesses.

National Accounts and VAT Evasion. The 6th Report of the *Conseil des Impots* used national accounts input/output tables to estimate the potential tax yield for VAT assuming there were no errors, evasion under assessment, etc. This was compared to the actual VAT yield and the difference was labelled the "VAT discrepancy." This discrepancy was then adjusted to take account of legal exemption, time lags and other features of the system and the residual factor taken as a first indication of evasion. The results are presented in table 19.

The *Conseil* did, however, qualify the results by noting that the tax base figures used to compile the theoretical tax base already incorporated certain assumptions above the level of evasion; estimating errors could be significant, problems of time lag due to delay of payments/reimbursements can be large. Nevertheless, the trends indicated by the figures may be suggestive (the results are confirmed by studies carried out by the Statistical Institute).

Surveys of Income and Underdeclaration of Income. The *Conseil des Impots* used data produced by INSEE to determine "underassessment ratios." Four sectors were examined:

1. Farm income;
2. Professional income in the nonagriculture sector;
3. Income from property and land; and
4. Wages, salaries, and transfer payments.

The results are reproduced in table 20 and show National Accounts gross income as a percentage of Gross Taxable Income. Some qualifications are:

- Gross taxable income refers to income subject to tax. This is not the same as aggregated economic income.
- A number of statistical adjustments were required to calculate the gross amount of income and dividends.

CERC Study. The aim of the study was to compare the income declared with the relative real income nonwage groups. The results do not refer to the absolute levels of real income.

Methodology. A special survey was carried out in early 1976 among 6,500 nonwage-earning households spread over 66 craft trade and commercial or fee-earning professions, and also on 1,500 wage-earning households, the object being to establish a certain number of consumption indicators for each of these households. The construction of these indicators was based on households' replies to questions as to whether or not they possessed certain consumer durables (car, camper, photographic or cinematographic equipment, hi-fi equipment, television, freezer, dishwasher, second residence) and also concerning the scale of their expenditure on various items (wages of domestic servants, holidays, restaurants, consumption of alcohol and vintage wines). Furthermore, for each family in the survey, the rental value of the main residence was noted, such information being available to the public.

For all these items, the information of a material nature obtained from the survey was converted into value estimates (value of each durable owned, monthly wages of a domestic servant employed so many hours per month, etc.), and then into estimates of the annual expenditure flows that would normally correspond.

2. This information was then compared with the 1974 tax return footnote 3 filed by each household. Such tax data made it possible to calculate three indicators of the presumed level of savings of each of the households of both wage-earners and nonwage-earners in the sample:

- An indicator of the savings probably deriving in 1974, from any purchases or transfers of real estate by members of the household in previous years.
- An indicator of the changes in each household's securities between 1972 and 1974. This indicator was established on the basis of the changes, shown on the tax forms, in each type of investment income received by the household.
- An estimate of the total amount of life insurance premiums paid by members of the household in 1974.

3. These indicators of consumption and savings were calculated for each household. The method used consisted of taking the information for each wage-earning household and looking for a general relationship—a statistical model—between earnings and the various indicators, and then applying this relationship to each of the nonwage-earning households in such a way as to estimate their probable actual income.

The real income of each nonwage-earning household was estimated according to the value of its consumption and savings indicators, by applying a ratio defined beforehand on the basis of observations concerning wage-earning households. In practice, the size of the sample of wage-earners was large enough to allow the constitution of several groups defined on a reasoned basis—this with a view to grouping, as far as possible, households with relatively similar patterns of income utilization. Six groups of households were identified according to the age of the head of household and six ratios were established. Each nonwage-earner was thus assigned the ratio corresponding to his or her age group.

The difference between this total estimated income and the previously calculated reference income should thus be looked upon as an estimate of the gap between outward tax indications and what income really is.

The Findings. For the total number of nonwage-earners involved in the survey, and taking all the craft trades and commercial and fee-earning professions together, the average income estimated by the model represents 1.28 times the average income declared to the tax authorities. The results by professional category are given in table 21. The study emphasized that these ratios did not necessarily provide any indication of tax evasion since not all of the real incomes measured were taxable.

VII. TAXES ON WEALTH

1. The Various Kinds of Tax on Wealth

In 1983 taxes on wealth yielded F65 billion francs, of which around 31 billion derived from taxes on real estate (discussed in section IX); four billion from net wealth taxes, 10 billion from inheritance and gift taxes, and 20 billion from a large number of miscellaneous taxes on capital and financial transactions, of which the most important are a registration tax and an advertising tax for real estate—each of which yielded nearly six billion francs. The discussion in this section is confined to the inheritance and gift tax and the net wealth tax.

2. Inheritance and Gift Taxes

France has an inheritance rather than an estate tax. Thus liability is governed by the relationship of the donee to the donor. The gift tax, with minor variations, follows the rate pattern of the inheritance tax.

Distributions to legal heirs are exempt up to F275,000 in 1985, after which the scale in table 22 applies. Distributions to other donees are exempt up to F10,000 and are charged 35 percent for brothers and sisters for the next F150,000 and thereafter 45 percent; 55 percent for distributions to uncles, aunts, nephews, and nieces; and 60 percent for distributions to others.

There is no inheritance tax on life insurance policies, and certain properties of cultural or historical value donated to the State. There are also certain allowable deductions for debts, medical, and funeral expenses.

At around .5 of total tax receipts and .2 of GDP, receipts from these taxes are slightly below those of most industrialized countries.

3. Net Wealth Tax

A net wealth tax on large properties (*grandes fortunes*) of individuals was introduced in 1981. In 1985 it applied to assets exceeding 3.5 million francs at progressive rates varying from .5 to two percent (table 23). Exemptions are provided for works of art, rural property subject to long term lease, stocks of wine and brandy, and three-quarters of the value of woods. Of most importance is the exemption for "productive assets" (machinery, plant, buildings, etc.) of nonincorporated enterprises.

In 1985 just over 100,000 taxpayers were liable for the net wealth tax and paid 5.3 billion francs or about .25 percent of total tax receipts. Though net wealth taxes are never large revenue raisers, the French yield is particularly low compared with the other countries of North and Central Europe where they have been in existence for many years. Rates and exemptions are broadly in line with those of other countries and so the low yield is probably due to the high threshold—underlined by the fact that the French tax is the only net wealth tax to be qualified by "on large properties"—and its narrow base.

4. Methods of Evasion and Avoidance

This probably takes the same form as in other countries—i.e., the nondeclaration or underdeclaration of value of assets, or by fictitious contracts of purchase to avoid gift taxes.

5. Effects on the Distribution of Wealth

A major survey of wealth taxation in France, including the effects on distribution of wealth was carried out in 1978-79.[13] It concluded that the French succession and gift duty system:

1. Was not sufficiently progressive, since the rate applicable to the last bracket is relatively low, and, because since 1959, insufficient inflation adjustment has been applied to its rate structure or to the exemptions it offers;

2. Because there were numerous statutory and effective exemptions, it was the large estates in particular which could avoid totally or partially the capital transfer tax;

3. Various measures in favor of gifts reduced the progression even further.

Since then, the tax treatment of gifts has been brought into line with those of inheritances and rates for larger bequests to direct heirs, which have doubled (see table 22), though those to brothers and sisters have remained unchanged.

The redistributive effect of the tax on large properties is limited, as was intended, to affect only the very rich, and just one person in 50,000 is paying the tax. However, those who are liable are often having to pay a great deal, since the top rate is over 2.2 percent (see table 23).

---

[13]An English summary by J.L. Haye appeared in the April and May 1979 edition of *European Taxation*, published by the International Bureau of Fiscal Documentation.

VIII. DISTRIBUTION OF THE TAX BURDEN

1. Introduction

There are three main sources of information on the distribution of taxes by income class: the Ministry of Finance MIR models; the National Statistical Office's (INSEE) sample survey of households; the household survey samples carried out by the *Centre d'Etude des revenue et des couts* (CERC). These sources are described in subsection 4 and provide most of the information referred to below.

2. Effective Income Tax Rates by Income Class

Table 24 sets out the average rate of income tax at levels of income that range from the average manufacturing wage to just over 10 times this income level. The rates refer to the amount of income tax that would be paid, after taking into account tax reliefs from family circumstances and other standard reliefs (see section I above). The calculations do not take into account nonstandard tax reliefs (relatively unimportant at the level of average earnings but increasing in importance as income increases) and possibilities for tax evasion at different income levels. Consequently, the average tax rates shown in table 24 probably overstate the effective average tax rates, particularly at higher income levels.

Table 25 overcomes these difficulties by calculating the total amount of tax paid in different income groups as a percentage of the total income in each group. Thus, these rates can be considered as effective tax rates. There is, however, the problem that the income concept used lies somewhere between gross income and taxable income. This may distort the series somewhat, though it is difficult to quantify this distortion.

Table 26 provides an alternative measure of effective tax rates. The data, however, refers to 1970 and during the last 15 years the distribution of the income tax burden has become more progressive.

Each of these tables shows that, although taxpayers begin paying tax only at relatively high income levels (just above average earnings for a two-child couple), the rate of tax increases slowly up to F100,000 and then becomes very progressive. It should also be recalled that a relatively large number of households are not subject to income tax in France (40 percent in 1983) and that a relatively large proportion of the tax is paid by a small number of high income taxpayers (see section I above).

3. Overall Tax Burden by Income Class

There are no official studies on the distribution of the overall tax burden. Nevertheless, information is available on some of the more important taxes paid by households. Section IV provides some information on social security burdens; section V on VAT, and section VIII, subsection 2 on the distribution of income taxes.

Nevertheless, there were some unofficial studies done in 1978 and 1979. The first was a study carried out by R. Bobe which tried to distribute the personal income tax by income class; corporate tax; payroll taxes (but not social security contributions); consumption taxes (mainly VAT); and certain minor direct taxes on households (e.g., transfer taxes, stamp duties). The results are presented in table 27. The methodology used to allocate taxes to households can be briefly summarized:

Consumption taxes. These refer to the VAT and other taxes on consumption (mainly excises). They have been allocated to households on the basis of the family expenditure surveys carried out by INSEE (see sources). It is assumed that consumption taxes are fully shifted into prices.

Direct taxes on companies. These refer to the corporate income tax on resident companies and payroll taxes not earmarked for social security. Three shifting hypotheses are retained:

1. All of these taxes are fully shifted into consumer prices.

2. All of the payroll taxes and half of the corporate tax is shifted into consumer prices and the remaining half of the corporate tax is borne by shareholders.

3. Half of the corporate tax is shifted into consumer prices and half to shareholders. Half of the payroll taxes are shifted in consumer prices and half into wages.

Direct taxes on individuals. These refer to the personal income tax, financed transaction taxes, stamp duties, share-transaction taxes, and some minor taxes on other capital transactions. These are assumed to be fully borne by households.

The conclusion drawn by Bobe was that, in 1965, the French tax system was regressive, no matter which shifting hypothesis was adapted for the direct taxes paid by companies.[14]

A somewhat more recent study was undertaken by Foulon and Hatchuel. The main results are reproduced in table 28, which shows the redistributive impact of taxes and transfers (which include provision of the free education service), between house-

---

[14]A conclusion which was consistent with earlier work carried out by the OECD, see "Income Distribution in OECD Countries," *OECD Economic Outlook*, Occasional Studies, July 1976.

holds, classified according to the occupation of the head of household. About three-quarters of all taxes (including social security contributions) and about 90 percent of cash transfers and current expenditure on education are covered in the analysis. The results presented are sensitive to the assumptions made concerning the incidence of employers' social security contributions, which constitute one-third of total taxes covered. The assumption on which the estimates are based is that employees' contributions are incident on the employee, while employers' contributions and payroll taxes are borne by consumers, being shifted forward into prices. Consumption taxes and personal income taxes are assumed to be borne by households, and companies' taxes by shareholders.

The general picture which emerges is that while cash transfers and education subsidies reduce inequality between occupational groups, the tax system has little or no redistributive impact.

The only other source of information on the distribution of the tax burden is a study undertaken by Balladur and Coutiere which calculated average VAT and income tax rates for 1972. The results are reproduced in table 29.

The conclusion drawn by these authors is that the combination of a regressive VAT and a uniformly progressive income tax produces a "U-shaped distribution of the tax burden, first falling as income rises and then increasing."

4. Basic Sources of Information

The main sources of information on the distribution of income and of taxes are:

1. The General-Directorate of Taxes (*La Direction Generale des Impots*) publishes annual data on pre- and post-tax income. Data refer to tax filers who owe tax. Series are available from 1956. See: Annual Issues of *"Statistiques et etudes Financieres"* Latest edition, *"L'impot sur la revenu" Statistiques et Etudes Financieres"* No. 396, 1985.

2. The National Statistical Office (INSEE) publishes two major sources of statistics:

- An inquiry into the incomes of households (*L'enquete sur les revenus des menages*) based upon a sample of just under 40,000 households and tax returns. Income is determined by a series of adjustments to the tax declarations. The series has been available intermittently since 1956 and the data are published in various issues of *"Les Collections de l'INSEE series Menages."*

- The permanent inquiry into living conditions (*L'enquete permanente sur les conditions de vie des menages*). A sample survey of approximately 11,000 households which provides data on the pre- and post-tax income of households and their expenditure. Most sources of income are covered (wages and salaries, dividends, interest, social benefits, rent, windfall income). Data source: as above.

3. The *Centre d'etude des revenus et des Couts* (CERC) publishes at irregular intervals data on the distribution of income (*Dispersion et disparites de salaires en France*) in France. Source: various CERC documents, e.g., CERC issues No. 25-26 and *Deuxieme Rapport sur les Revenus des Francais*, (CERC No. 51), 1980. The latest available figures on pre-tax income appear in *Constat de L'evolution Recente des Revenus en France 1981-1984*, CERC No. 76, 1985.[15]

IX. THE LOCAL TAX SYSTEM

1. Introduction

France is a unitary country which is divided into 23 administrative regions under which are grouped 95 administrative departments. Within each department there are municipalities. Until very recently, the regions and departments had no major sources of tax revenue. Since 1981 the government has followed a policy of decentralizing revenue and expenditure functions and each level of government now has taxes over which it has a certain fiscal autonomy. In comparison with other OECD countries, lower levels of government obtain a large part of their total revenues from local taxes. Table 30 provides an overview of the sources of finance in 1982—the last year for which definitive figures were available— and shows how they have changed over the last five years.

2. Main Taxes Used by Local and Regional Authorities

There are a variety of taxes in France which operate at lower levels of government. For the most part they apply to the owner-

---

[15]In addition to these official studies a number of academic studies are available.

Bernard Bobe, "La Redistribution des revenus." serie *Sciences Economique* 1978.

Antoine Coutiere, "Augmenter l'impot sur le revenu: des mesures de portee inegale," *Societe*, 1982.

Genevieve Canceill, "L'effet redistributif de l'impot direct et des prestations familiales," *Economie et Statistique*, No 177, May 1985.

A. Foulon and G. Hatchuel, "The Redistribution of Public Funds in France in 1965 and 1970," *Review of Income and Wealth* (September) 1979.

H. Roze, "Impots directs et transferts sociaux," *Economie et Statistique*, September 1984.

ship, occupancy, or transfer of immovable property. The most important of these taxes are described in table 31. There are also a number of minor taxes which are not referred to and which, since 1983, are levied by Regional Councils: motor vehicle licenses tax, driver's license tax, infrastructure tax and real estate tax.

All of the taxes referred to in table 31 have rental value either as the sole determinant of the tax base or as one component of the base. For the most part, the valuation procedure is as follows:

Domestic premises. A distinction is made between domestic premises set aside for professional use other than agricultural, commercial, trade and craft, or industrial uses and those set aside for commercial use. Premises of the former type are valued with reference to a scale which takes account of the average level of rents for property let under market conditions.

Premises for commercial use are valued on the basis of the actual rents where these reflect normal conditions, or otherwise by comparison with "standard" premises or by direct assessment.

Industrial premises. Small businesses of which the premises are valued on the same footing as commercial premises are distinguished from other premises for which the rental value is assessed by applying a rate of return to the cost price.

The last general review was in 1983. Rental values are updated every three years using coefficients determined within each region for each category of buildings or land.

With the exception of the *taxe d'habitation*, the personal circumstances of the taxpayer are not taken into account in the calculation of the tax. Personal circumstances (marital status, children, age), however, play an important role in the determination of the *taxe d'habitation* which, in many respects is very similar to a local income tax (this is how it is classified in table 30). Much of the discussion on the reform of local finance has focused on this tax and the *taxe professionelle*.

3. Grants to Lower Levels of Government

In terms of their contribution to local revenues, grants are roughly equivalent to local taxes. Three types of grants are provided by central government:

- Capital grants. These are intended to finance infrastructure and other types of investment. In 1982 they accounted for approximately seven percent of total revenues of local authorities.
- Current grants. These can be used to finance current expenditures. They are usually determined by taxable capacity or

expenditure needs and, in 1982, accounted for approximately 14 percent of total revenues.

- General purpose grants. Local authorities may use these funds as they wish, though central government does specify whether or not a part of them should be used for capital expenditure and a part for current expenditure. In 1982 they accounted for 25 percent of total revenues.

X. PROSPECTS FOR TAX REFORM

1. Governmental Initiatives

There is a timing problem in discussing these in that the left wing government elected in 1981 has just been replaced (March 1986) by a right wing government. The former government took a number of initiatives, generally in the direction of using the tax system to promote social (especially vertical equity)[16] and economic[17] objectives. Towards the end of its period in power, that government had little to say on tax reform apart from a view that taxation (and especially individual income taxation) should be reduced, as pledged by the President.

The then opposition, however, had a number of specific proposals to reduce the tax burden, especially on higher income groups, and to make the tax system more neutral. Now that the "opposition" has become the government, its main proposals are summarized here, even though they cannot strictly be described as government

---

[16]For example:
- alleviation of taxation of low income (bank allowances; special provisions for particular categories or circumstances) but increasing taxation of high incomes, additional income tax; "compulsory loan" (now repaid) of 10 percent of tax due; creation of a 65 percent marginal tax bracket; ceiling on the *quotient familial*;
- creation of a net wealth tax (not imposed on business capital);
- alleviation of inheritance taxes on small estates but sharp increase of marginal rates (in some cases doubled to 40 percent) (over F11 million);
- creation of a 5.5 percent (instead of seven percent) VAT rate for foodstuffs;
- creation of special levy on banks and insurance companies.

[17]For example:
- creation of tax-favored saving accounts;
- deductibility of dividends paid on new shares;
- reduction to 15 percent of the capital gains tax rate for gains on sale of securities;
- introduction of a number of more specialized incentives for new or small enterprises or research (e.g., see section III above).

initiatives. They include a reduction of the progressivity of the personal income tax with a gradual reduction of the top rate to 50 percent an increase of its threshold in real terms so that fewer people will be paying tax; increasing the tax credit allowed under the imputation system to 100 percent; making simpler and more neutral existing tax incentives for saving (e.g., by extending to other savings the final 25 percent witholding tax now existing for bond interest); abolishing the recently introduced wealth tax, reducing inheritance taxes, and setting a ceiling for total taxes paid by individuals on income and property.

2. Academic Proposals

Some academics (e.g., P. Salin in *L'arbitraire taxe*) have proposed the substitution of an expenditure tax for the income tax, and the total suppression of inheritance taxes, but these have not attracted much attention. Attention has rather focused on the proposals outlined in the last paragraph of subsection 1 above.

3. Views of Business on Tax Reform

Business interests would seek a reduction in reliance on payroll taxes (which, as already noted, is particularly heavy in France), a reduction in the rate of corporation income tax and the suppression or reform of the *taxe professionelle*, described in section IX above.

4. Views of Trade Unions on Tax Reform

Trade union spokesmen find that there is excessive reliance on VAT as a source of revenue and insufficient reliance on income and capital taxation. They favor widening the individual income tax base by moving towards separate taxation, freezing standard allowances and reducing tax expenditures and the deductibility of professional expenses, and also reducing avoidance and evasion by more thorough checks on the income of nonwage and salary earners. They seek also an increase in capital taxation (especially inheritance taxes), a widening of the corporate tax base (e.g., by abolishing certain provisions on reserves), and by reforming the existing social security system by abolishing ceilings and seeking alternative methods to the payroll tax for financing a part of the benefits.

5. Prospects for Tax Reform

There seems to be a general consensus that the total taxation to GDP ratio should be decreased and that more efficiency, transparency, and simplicity could be attained by reducing tax expenditures and, in the case of corporate tax, applying lower rates. In other words, there has been a move away from the interventionist approach to taxation, taken not only by the previous government but also by earlier governments, towards a more neutral market-oriented approach as currently favored in the United States and a number of other industrialized countries within and beyond Europe.[18]

There are constraints on carrying out the kind of proposals outlined here. The desire not to cut back on existing public services limits the amount of revenue that can be foregone and the reluctance of taxpayers (including business) to lose their tax preferences limits the room for rate cutting.[19]

REFERENCES

Doing Business in France, (Price Waterhouse).

European Taxation, Loose leaf volume on Value-Added Taxes, International Bureau of Fiscal Documentation.

J.P. Balladeur and A. Cantiere, *Value-Added Tax Lessons for Europe* (Brookings Institution, 1981).

Income Tax Collection Lags (OECD, 1983).

Revenue Statistics of OECD Member Countries 1965-83 (OECD, 1985).

Sixth Report of the Tax Council to the President of the Republic, (Paris 1983).

"Summary in English of 6th Report," *European Taxation* 1983 No. 9.

The Impact of Consumption Taxes at Different Income Levels (OECD, 1981).

The Report of the Tax Council to the President of the Republic (Paris, 1984).

The Personal Income Tax Systems Under Changing Economic Conditions (OECD 1986).

---

[18]See, for country examples, *Personal Income Tax Systems Under Changing Economic Conditions* (OECD 1986).

[19]This note was written at the end of March 1986. It seems likely that at least some of the proposals summarized under section X above are likely to be put into effect in the near future.

Table 1
Ratio of Tax Receipts to GDP and Total Taxes, France and OECD, 1965 and 1983
(Percent)

	Total Tax		Personal Income Tax		Corporate Income Tax		Employees' Social Security		Employers' Social Security		General Consumption (VAT etc.)		Other Consumption		Other	
	1965	1983	1965	1983	1965	1983	1965	1983	1965	1983	1965	1983	1965	1983	1965	1983
To GDP																
France[1]	35	45	4	6	2	2	2	5	9	13	8	9	5	3	2	2
OECD Average	27	37	7	12	2	3	2	3	3	5	3	5	6	5	2	2
To Total Tax Receipts																
France[1]	—	—	11	13	5	4	7	12	25	29	23	21	14	8	4	4
OECD Average	—	—	26	32	9	7	6	8	10	14	12	14	24	15	8	5

Source: *Revenue Statistics of OECD Member Countries 1965-84* (OECD 1985).

[1] In France, receipts not covered in this table are mainly from social security contributions from the self-employed or unemployed, various earmarked payroll taxes, and miscellaneous local taxes of which the most important is the *tax professionelle* itself, in part, a tax on payroll.

Table 2
Sources of French Tax Revenues, 1983

Tax Source	Amounts (Billions of Francs)	Percent of Total
Total Tax Receipts	1,754	100.0
Income Taxes	312	18.0
On individuals	235	13.0
On corporations	75	4.0
Unallocable between individuals and corporations	2	—
Social Security Contributions	770	43.0
On employees	205	12.0
On employers	511	29.0
On self-employed or unemployed	54	2.0
Unearmarked Payroll Taxes	42	2.5
Taxes on Property and Wealth	65	3.7
On immovable property	65	1.8
On net wealth	31	0.2
Estates and inheritances	10	0.5
Financial and capital transactions	20	1.1
Taxes on Goods and Services	508	29.0
Value-added tax	360	20.5
On specific goods and services	135	7.7
Permission and use taxes	13	0.8
Other Taxes	(56)	3.0
Business tax	50	2.7

Source: Same as table 1.

Table 3
Macroeconomic Indicators and Tax Developments, 1974-83

Indicator	1974	1975	1976	1977	1978	1979	1980	1981	1982	1983
A. OECD Macroeconomic Indicators (Annual Percentage Change, Except Lines 4 and 6)										
1. Nominal GDP growth (percent)	14.7	13.6	15.5	12.3	13.6	14.1	13.4	12.4	14.7	10.9
2. Real GDP growth (at 1975 prices) (percent)	3.2	0.2	5.2	3.1	3.8	3.3	1.1	0.3	1.6	1.0
3. Employment growth (percent)	0.7	-1.1	0.7	0.8	0.4	-0.1	0.0	-0.7	0.1	-0.7
4. Unemployment rate (percent)	2.8	4.1	4.4	4.9	5.3	5.9	6.3	7.4	8.2	8.4
5. Consumer prices (percent change)	12.7	12.4	10.0	9.1	9.2	10.7	13.1	14.0	11.8	9.6
6. General government surplus/deficit (–) as percent of GDP	0.6	-2.2	-0.5	-0.8	-1.9	-0.7	0.2	-1.8	-2.6	-3.2
B. Tax Developments										
7. Total tax yields (billions of national currency)	464.4	543.7	660.5	742.8	845.8	1,003.3	1,177.7	1,331.4	1,561.9	1,754.0
8. Total tax yields as percent of GDP	36.3	37.4	39.4	39.4	39.5	41.1	42.5	42.8	43.8	44.6
9. Personal income tax yields of percent of GDP	4.3	4.6	5.0	5.2	5.2	5.1	5.5	5.7	5.6	6.0
10. Personal income tax yields as percent of total tax revenue	11.7	12.2	12.7	13.2	13.1	12.5	12.9	13.2	12.9	13.4
C. Changes in the Income Tax Base and Tax Liability (1975=100)										
11. Real GDP	100	100	105	100	112	116	117	118	120	121
12. Consumer price index	89	100	110	120	131	145	164	187	209	229
13. Household income	85	100	115	131	150	170	196	226	260	
14. Income subject to tax (before deductions)										
15. Taxable income (after deductions)										
a. Central government income tax	84	100	118	129	148	168	193	222	251	
b. All income taxes	84	100	110	129	148	168	193	222	251	
16. Personal income tax liability										
a. Central government personal income tax	81	100	122	135	158	183	208	243	272	
b. All levels of government	81	100	122	135	158	183	208	243	272	
17. Number of tax units	82	100	92	90	94	97	99	97	99	
Memorandum Item										
18. Number of tax units (million)	12.77	15.49	14.24	14.01	14.56	15.00	15.29	15.06	15.31	

Source: OECD (1986)

Table 4
Tax Rates for Persons Without Dependents, 1985 and 1986[1]

Bracket	Taxable Income (Ffrs) 1985 (on 1984 income)	Rate (percent)	Taxable Income (Ffrs) 1986 (on 1985 income)
1	0—14,820	0	0—15,060
2	14,820—15,490	5	15,650—16,360
3	15,490—18,370	10	16,360—19,400
4	18,370—29,050	15	19,400—30,680
5	29,050—37,340	20	30,680—39,440
6	37,340—46,920	25	39,440—49,550
7	46,920—56,770	30	49,550—59,950
8	56,770—65,500	35	59,950—69,170
9	65,500—109,140	40	69,170—115,250
10	109,140—150,100	45	115,250—158,510
11	150,100—177,550	50	158,510—187,490
12	177,550—201,970	55	187,490—213,280
13	201,970—228,920	60	213,280—271,740
14	Over 228,920	65	Over 271,740

[1]For persons with dependents, see subsection 4. For rates for certain kinds of income, see subsection 3. Liability for tax is with respect to income obtained during the previous year, (see subsection 5).

Table 5
Calculation of Individual Income Tax on Dividend

Cash dividend	200
Tax credit	100
Income subject to tax	300
Tax due (e.g., at 50 percent)	150
Tax credit	100
Net tax due	50

Table 6
Income Splitting Coefficients

Single, divorced or widowed persons without dependents	1
Married persons without children; single or divorced persons with one child	2
Married or widowed persons with one child; single or divorced persons with two children	2.5
Married or widowed persons with two children; single or divorced persons with three children	3.5
Married or widowed persons with three children; single or divorced persons with four children	4
Married or widowed persons with four children; single or divorced persons with five children	4.5
For each additional child the coefficient is increased by 0.5.	

Table 7
Percentage Distribution of 1978 Net Tax Collections
by the Year in Which the Income Was Earned

Country	1978	1977	1976	1975	1974 or earlier
Australia	96	n.a.	n.a.	n.a.	n.a.
Denmark	86	8	6	0	0
France	11	77	9	2	0
Greece[1]	74	26	0	0	0
Ireland[1]	54	36	8	1	1
Netherlands	76	19	5	0	0
Norway	92	6	1	0	0
Sweden	82	14	3	1	0
United Kingdom	76	16	6	2	1
United States	76	23	1	1	0

Source: *Income Tax Collection Lags* (OECD 1983).
   n.a. = not available.
   [1]No account is taken of the distribution of refunds and late payments.

Table 8
Comparison of Inflation Adjustments with the
Consumer Price Index, 1976-85

Year	Indexation Factor	Consumer Price Index
1976	10 percent for all brackets	11.8%
1977	9.5 percent for first four brackets; six percent for next five brackets; three percent for next two brackets; zero percent for last bracket	9.6
1978	7.5 percent for first 10 brackets; six percent for next bracket; five percent for next bracket	9.4
1979	Nine percent for first 10 brackets; five percent for next two brackets	9.1
1980	10 percent for first two brackets; nine percent for next two brackets; eight percent for next four brackets; four percent for next two brackets; zero percent for last two brackets	10.8
1981	13.3 percent for first four brackets; 12 percent for next seven brackets; eight percent for last bracket	13.6
1982	13.5 percent for all brackets	13.4
1983	12.3 percent for all brackets; creation of 65 percent bracket	11.8
1984	9.1 percent for all brackets	9.1
1985	7.6 percent for all brackets	7.6

Table 9
Social Security Contributions and Payroll Taxes,
1975 and 1983
(Billion FF)

Type of tax	1975	1983
Social Security Contributions	222	770
Paid by employees	48	205
Paid by employers	161	511
Paid by self-employed	13	54
Other Payroll Taxes	10	43
Salary tax (*Taxe sur les salaires*)	7	24
Tax for apprenticeship (*Taxe d'apprentissage*)	0	3
Business tax on transport	2	7
Other	1	9

Source: Same as table 1.

Table 10
Rates and Bases of Social Security and
Other Contributions, 1985[1]

Contribution	Annual base (francs)	Employee's percentage contribution	Employer's percentage contribution	Total percentage contribution
I. Social security *(securite sociale)*				
1. Sickness *(maladie)*	Total compensation	5.50	12.60	18.10
2. Old age *(vieillesse)*	0 to 106.74	5.70	8.20	13.90
3. Family allowances *(allocations familiales)*	0 to 106.74	0	9.00	9.00
4. Housing allowances *(allocations logement)*	0 to 106.74	0	0.10	0.10
5. Workmen's compensation *(accidents du travail)*	0 to 106.74	0	Rates depend on activity and number of employees (about 3.00)	about 3.00
6. Widow's allocation *(allocation veuvage)*	Total compensation	0.10	0	0.10
II. Retirement pensions *(retraite complementaire)*	On total salary between			
1. Executives				
Pension				
Obligatory A	0 to 106.74	11.84	2.76	4.60
Obligatory B (minimum)	106.74 to 426.96	4.12	8.24	12.30
Obligatory B Optional[2]				
a	106.74 to 426.96	5.15	9.27	14.42
b	106.74 to 426.96	6.18	10.30	16.48
Voluntary C	above 426.96	Voluntary	Voluntary	Voluntary
Life insurance	0 to 106.74	0	1.50	1.50
2. Nonexecutives	0 to 320.22	1.84	2.76	4.60
III. Unemployment insurance *(chomage)*				
ASSEDIC (Executives and	0 to 106.74	1.92	4.08	6.00
nonexecutives)	106.74 to 426.96	2.42	4.08	6.50
APEC (Executives only)	106.74 to 426.96	0.024	0.036	0.06
IV. National Salary Guarantee Fund *(Fonds national de garantie)*	0 to 426.96	0	0.35	0.35

[1]Excludes private additional benefit coverage.

[2]The enterprise has the choice between three rates: 12.30 percent, 14.42 percent and 16.48 percent. Enterprises created after January 1, 1984 must apply either the 12.30 percent rate or the of 16.48 percent rate.

Table 11
Payroll Taxes as a Percentage of
Average Manufacturing Wage, 1979 and 1984

Type of tax	1979	1984
Employees' type of tax contributions	11.8	14.8
Employers' contributions and payroll taxes	39.0	44.0
Total	50.8	58.8

Source: *Tax/Benefit Position of Production Worker* (OECD, 1986).

Table 12
Payroll Taxes as a Percentage
of Total Wages and Salaries, 1960-1984

	Six-year averages				
Type of tax	1960-1965	1965-1970	1970-1975	1975-1980	1984
Employees' contributions	12.8	14.3	14.4	17.3	18.0
Employers' contributions	22.5	24.7	25.7	29.1	32.3
Total	35.3	39.5	40.1	46.4	50.3

Source: Based on data published in OECD National Accounts; see Jeffrey Owens and Paulo Roberti, "The Financing of Social Security Systems International Comparison; Trends and Policy Issues," *Public Finance and Social Policy Proceedings at 39th Congress of IIPF* (Wayne University Press, 1986).

Table 13
VAT Revenues as a Percentage of GDP and
Total Tax Revenues, Selected Years, 1965-1983

Ratio	1965	1970	1975	1980	1981	1982	1983
Percentage of GDP	8.1	9.1	8.7	8.9	9.0	9.3	9.1
Percentage of total tax revenues	23.3	25.5	23.3	21.0	21.1	21.1	20.5

Table 14
Allocation of the Effect of Noncreditability Over Different Economic Sectors (1978)

Sector	Noncreditability			Percentage of Noncreditability	
	Percentage of All Sectors	Noncreditability of Input Tax on Cars and Oil Products	Noncreditability Due to Other Causes	Value Added	Value of Production
Health	16.0	3.7	12.3	5.3	4.2
Lodging	13.1	0.1	13.0	3.6	3.5
Post and telecommunications	12.8	0.6	12.2	12.6	8.4
Agriculture	9.3	1.8	7.5	3.4	1.8
Commerce	7.7	6.4	1.3	1.3	0.9
Merchant services supplied to enterprises	7.7	3.4	4.3	2.2	1.6
Hotels, cafes, restaurants and canteens	4.3	1.1	3.2	3.3	1.6
Road transport	3.5	3.4	0.1	4.2	2.4
Construction and civil engineering	3.5	3.4	0.1	0.8	0.4
Food and agricultural industries	2.6	1.7	0.9	1.1	0.3
Other	19.5	14.4	5.1	0.6	0.4
Total	100	40.0	60.0	n.a.	n.a.

Source: The 1983 Tax Council Report.
n.a. not available

Table 15
VAT Rates as a Percentage of the Tax-Exclusive
Retail Price Value, 1968-1985

Rate	1968	1969	1970-1972	1973-1976	1977-1981	1982-1985
Standard rate	16.66	19.00	23.00	20.00	17.60	18.60
Higher rate	20.00	25.00	33.33	33.33	33.33	n.a.

n.a. not available

Table 16
Major Goods and Services Subject to Nonstandard VAT Rates
Since July 1, 1982[1]

5.5 Percent	7 Percent	33.3 Percent
Food products (excluding drinks) not expressly subject to other rates	Hotel lodgings, supply of meals for canteens, theaters, concert halls, zoos, transportation of passengers, the supply or drainage of water, medicines, books.	Jewelry, precious metals, cameras, radio and T.V., motor vehicles, record players, tape recorders, caviar, tobacco, pornographic films
Coffee, tea, sugar, jams and jellies, fresh pastry, and chocolate		
Unprocessed, agricultural, seafood, and poultry products		
Dairy products (milk, yogurt, butter, cheese, milk powder, etc.)		

[1]For a more complete list, see The 1983 Tax Council Report, pages 252-254.

Table 17
Exempt Goods and Services Under the VAT

Transactions with social objectives (social and charitable nonprofit activities, activities of qualifying hospitals etc., sales by certain handicapped persons)

Financial transactions (though in principle subject to VAT since 1979 when the separate tax on financial activities was exempt, the majority remain exempt)

Certain transactions subject to other taxes (e.g., auctions of secondhand goods, the entertainment tax on organized betting, entrance fees for sporting events, insurance and reinsurance activities)

Many activities by members of the liberal professions (e.g., medical and legal services (including officially listed tax advisers), education, artists, interpreters, translators, guides)

[1]For a more complete list, see The 1983 Tax Council Report, page 251.

Table 18
VAT Burden by Income Classes (Francs) and by Size of Family, 1969
(Percent)

Size of household	3,000 to 10,000	10,000 to 15,000	15,000 to 20,000	20,000 to 30,000	30,000 to 50,000	Over 50,000	Total
Single person	10.9	11.6	10.7	11.2	11.0	15.0	11.1
Couple with no children	10.6	11.3	11.7	11.8	12.9	11.5	11.6
Couple with one child	11.1	11.4	11.5	11.8	12.1	12.4	11.8
Couple with two children	10.5	11.1	11.1	11.2	11.8	12.0	11.4
Couple with three children	10.1	11.5	10.7	11.1	11.4	10.6	11.1
Other households	10.2	10.9	10.8	11.4	10.7	11.1	10.9
All households	10.7	11.3	11.1	11.4	11.7	11.5	11.3

Source *The Impact of Consumption Taxes at Different Income Levels* (OECD 1981).

Table 19
Discrepancies Recorded Between VAT Collected by the State and Theoretical VAT Due on Uses of Goods and Services Shown in the National Accounts, 1970-81
(billions of francs)

Year	VAT Discrepancy	Portion Attributable to Exemptions, rebates and book differences	Residual Discrepancy	As Percent of VAT Revenue	As Percent of GDP
1970	9.1	1.8	7.3	10.3	0.9
1971	10.3	2.2	8.1	10.2	0.9
1972	10.2	2.2	8	8.9	0.8
1973	10.5	2.0	8.5	8.8	0.8
1974	12.2	2.8	9.4	8.2	0.7
1975-1976[1]	13.2	3.0	10.2	7.5	0.7
1977	19.5	5.7	13.8	8.9	0.7
1978	17.3	4.4	12.9	7.1	0.7
1979[2]	14.5	2.5	12	5.6	0.6
1980[2]	20.3	5.2	15.1	6.2	0.6
1981[2]	24.0	5.9	18.1	6.6	0.7

Source: *Institut National de La Statistique et des Etudes Economiques.*
[1]In view of statistical lag, only the average of the figures for the two years is significant.
[2]Provisional accounts.

Table 20
Underassessment Coefficients[1] for the Major Categories of Income Subject to Income Tax, 1970 and 1975

Source of Income[2]	1970	1975
Income derived from production (farm profits) of sole proprietorships in the agricultural sector	3.31	2.78
Income derived from production (industrial and trading profits and nonprofits trading), of sole proprietors in sectors other than agriculture	1.89	1.31
Wages, salaries and transfer payments (pensions and annuities)	1.08	1.06
Income from property (income from land and buildings and income from investments)	2.07	1.34
Total	1.28	1.17

Source: *Conseil des Impots* and *INSEE.*
[1]For each category of income, the coefficient is equal to the percent of income from national account reported on tax returns.
[2]This is "gross" income in the tax sense of the word, i.e., income calculated before allowances and fixed deductions permitted by tax legislation for each category of income.

Table 21
Income Declared on Tax Returns Compared with
Estimated Average Income by Professional Groups

Profession	Number in the Sample	Average Income Declared	Estimated Average Income	Income Declared as Percent of Estimated Income Average	Median
1 Electrical repairers	101	32,432	50,290	1.57	1.53
2 Various mechanical professions	61	52,059	60,503	1.17	1.24
3 Dental technicians	103	46,662	64,455	1.41	1.34
4 Bakers	99	46,426	64,283	1.40	1.30
5 Pastry chefs	96	42,800	58,756	1.40	1.32
6 Shoe repairers	99	20,904	37,346	1.81	2.07
7 Woodworkers	73	38,474	50,012	1.31	1.63
8 Furniture makers	99	31,245	49,724	1.62	1.67
9 Jewelry makers	66	31,033	60,478	2.00	1.79
10 Building workers	83	49,995	54,912	1.11	1.38
11 Electricians	81	43,525	60,704	1.41	1.31
12 Carpenters	91	35,039	45,790	1.33	1.45
13 Plumbers	77	42,950	53,603	1.27	1.29
14 Painters	85	30,633	46,691	1.54	1.72
15 Agricultural wholesalers	69	68,811	79,446	1.17	1.16
16 Cattle traders	88	47,191	62,871	1.35	1.22
17 Fruit and vegetable wholesalers	77	59,452	77,067	1.32	1.24
18 Soft drinks wholesalers	70	49,052	45,552	0.94	1.26
19 Raw material and machine wholesalers	41	104,248	103,604	1,01	0.85
20 Bicycle and motorbike repairers	69	54,829	71,742	1.12	1.26
21 Grocers	90	34,955	42,385	1.23	1.26
22 Green grocer	79	30,314	49,756	1.68	1.48
23 Milk and cheese retailers	85	38,294	57,711	1.54	1.43
24 Butchers	73	45,811	52,901	1.17	1.40
25 Delicatessen workers	35	54,480	55,517	1.03	1.18
26 Fishmongers	102	38,428	63,516	1.68	1.53
27 Tailors	91	44,795	52,577	1.19	0.95
28 Shoe sellers	93	60,905	63,619	1.06	1.06
29 Furniture sellers	77	85,591	101,634	1.21	1.13
30 Hardware merchants	83	63,349	83,249	1.33	1.39
31 Paint sellers	83	41,762	60,319	1.46	1.44
32 Electrical retailers	89	49,337	67,067	1.38	1.41
33 Pharmacies	110	140,946	162,580	1.17	0.97
34 Book sellers	67	38,273	57,987	1.54	1.45
35 Jewelers	99	50,973	70,653	1.41	1.37
36 Tobacconists	92	35,213	41,488	1.20	1.26
37 Market retailers	67	29,082	45,251	1.60	1.58
38 Service stations	83	53,773	62,475	1.17	1.12
39 Car Salesmen	72	46,166	67,316	1.48	1.35
40 Car repairers	82	45,567	56,610	1.25	1.32
41 Restaurants	80	32,068	49,243	1.58	1.63
42 Cafes	91	29,369	38,366	1.34	1.37
43 Cafe/Tobacconists	86	43,521	61,088	1.42	1.32
44 Cafe/Other activities	79	34,379	47,200	1.40	1.22
45 Hotel and restaurant	103	40,401	58,353	1.47	1.30
46 Hotel	57	37,064	52,645	1.45	1.49
47 Messengers	80	62,419	66,405	1.08	0.98
48 Taxis	94	19,175	39,405	2.12	2.08
49 Cleaners	94	28,898	49,930	1.76	1.66

(Continued on next page)

Table 21 (Continued)
Income Declared on Tax Returns Compared with
Estimated Average Income by Professional Groups

Profession	Number in the Sample	Average Income Declared	Estimated Average Income	Income Declared as Percent of Estimated Income Average	Median
50 Hairdressers	91	23,356	36,352	1.59	1.70
51 General practitioners	88	88,025	114,097	1.30	1.32
53 Radiologists	37	122,297	162,462	1.33	1.24
54 Other medical specialists	85	88,152	113,081	1.28	1.19
55 Dental surgeons	72	110,131	125,532	1.14	1.21
56 Chiropractors	83	59,530	69,916	1.17	1.15
57 Veterinarians	78	81,208	115,016	1.42	1.45
58 Lawyers	73	72,801	110,326	1.52	1.57
60 Consulting engineers	50	80,267	84,593	1.05	1.00
61 CPAs	91	111,693	118,486	1.06	1.07
62 Financial and legal advisors	65	70,277	95,173	1.35	1.25
63 Architects and urban planners	77	99,378	116,819	1.18	1.19
64 Surveyors	80	89.513	95,321	1.06	1.16
65 Driving instructors	78	42,383	56,680	1.34	1.37
All of the professionals here considered, after weighted averaging	5137	50,131	63,154	1.26	1.34

Note: Ratios for professions 1-50 are corrected for non-replies.

Table 22
Inheritance and Gift Tax Rates on Distributions to
Spouses or Other Legal Heirs, 1976 and 1985

	1976[1] (Percent)	1985[2] (Percent)
0—50,000	(5)	5
50,000—75,000	(10)	10
75,000—100,000	(15)	15
100,000—3,400,000	(20)	20
3,400,000—5,600,000	(30)	20
5,600,000—11,200,000	(20)	35
11,200,000—and over	(20)	40

Source: Price Waterhouse (1985) for 1985 rates; OECD (1979) for 1976 rates.

Table 23
Rates of Net Wealth Tax, 1976 and 1985

1976 Wealth Brackets (francs)	1985 Wealth Brackets (francs)	Rate[1] (Percent)
Less than 3,500,000	Less than 3,600,000	0
3,500,000—5,800,000	3,600,000—6,000,000	0.5
5,800,000—11,500,000	6,000,000—11,900,000	1.0
11,500,000—20,000,000	11,900,000—20,600,000	1.5
20,000,000 and over	20,600,000 and over	2

Source: Price Waterhouse (1985) for 1985 rates; OECD (1979) for 1976 rates.
[1]With a surcharge of eight percent of tax payable since 1984.

Table 24
Personal Income Tax Paid and Average Tax Rates, 1983

Size of family	Gross Earning (francs)					
	70,000	100,000	150,000	250,000	500,000	800,000
Income tax paid						
Single person	6,200	15,600	32,700	70,700	180,500	373,600
Two child family	300	4,000	10,900	35,100	112,500	282,000
Average rate of tax						
Single person	8.4	19.6	21.8	28.3	36.1	46.7
Two child family	0.4	4.0	7.3	14.0	22.5	36.4

Source: *The Tax Benefit Position of Production Workers* (OECD 1984), Conseil des Impots *Septieme Rapport au President de la Republique relatif a l'impot sur le revenue* (Paris, 1984).

Table 25
Effective Average Tax Rates on Income for All Taxpayers, 1980, 1981, and 1983

Adjusted Income[1]	Effective Average Rate of Tax[2]		
(francs)	1980	1981	1983
0 - 10,000	0	0	0
10,000 - 25,000[3]	6	6	6
25,000 - 30,000	7	7	6
30,000 - 35,000	8	7	7
35,000 - 40,000	8	8	8
40,000 - 50,000	9	8	8
50,000 - 60,000	10	9	9
60,000 - 70,000	11	10	9
70,000 - 80,000	13	12	11
80,000 - 100,000	16	14	12
100,000 - 200,000	22	20	18
200,000 - 400,000	33	32	30
400,000 and over			
Total all classes	15	16	15

Source: *Statistiques et Etudes Financieres* 1984/85 and authors' estimates 1983.

[1]Total income subject to tax minus losses, childcare expenses, and income-related expenses, (i.e., those directly associated with the cost of earning the income).

[2]Total income tax liabilities (prior to any subsequent adjustment due to tax audits) divided by total income subject to tax in each income class.

[3]For 1980 and 1981 this income class refers to the income class 20,000 to 25,000.

Table 26
Effective Average Income Tax Rates by Decile, 1970

Decile	Net Taxable Income (% of total)	Tax Paid (% of total)	Effective Tax Rate (Percent)
Top decile	33.8	68.1	22.6
2nd decile	16.4	14.9	10.2
3rd decile	12.2	7.7	7.1
4th decile	9.7	4.3	5.0
5th decile	8.0	2.4	3.4
6th decile	6.6	1.6	2.7
7th decile	5.4	0.8	1.7
8th decile	4.1	0.2	0.5
9th decile	2.7	—	—
Bottom decile	1.1	—	—
Total	100.0	100.0	11.2

Source: Based on data published by the Conseil des Impots *Rapport an President de la Republique* (Juillet 1974), tables 14, 19, 24 and 25.

Table 27
First-Round Incidence of Taxes on Household Income, 1965

Net Income (francs)	Hypothesis 1			Hypothesis 2			Hypothesis 3		
	T1[1]	T2[2]	Total	T1[1]	T2[2]	Total	T1[1]	T2[2]	Total
Under 3,000	1.779	0.007	1.786	1.731	0.007	1.738	1.651	0.007	1.058
3,000—6,499	0.680	0.006	0.686	0.669	0.006	0.675	0.469	0.012	0.481
6,500—9,999	0.490	0.012	0.502	0.475	0.012	0.487	0.469	0.012	0.481
10,000—14,999	0.398	0.024	0.422	0.385	0.024	0.409	0.386	0.024	0.410
15,000—19,999	0.343	0.037	0.380	0.336	0.037	0.373	0.340	0.037	0.377
20,000—29,999	0.301	0.055	0.356	0.296	0.055	0.351	0.300	0.055	0.355
30,000—59,999	0.251	0.091	0.342	0.256	0.091	0.347	0.260	0.091	0.351
60,000—99,999	0.243	0.108	0.351	0.269	0.108	0.377	0.271	0.108	0.379
Over 100,000	0.198	0.158	0.356	0.225	0.158	0.383	0.223	0.158	0.381

Source: R. Bobe, *La Redistribution des Revenus*, Economica, Paris, 1978.

[1] All taxes except the personal income tax and related minor direct taxes.

[2] Personal income taxes and related minor direct taxes.

Table 28
The Redistributive Impact of Public Levies and Transfers in France, 1970

Type of Income	Occupation of Head of Household											
	Senior executive grades	Middle executive grades	Em- ployees	Skilled workers	Unskilled and domestic workers	Farm workers	Liberal profes- sions	Indus- trialists and owners of large stores	Crafts- men and small shop owners	Farmers	Non- active	All House- holds
Original income (Y)	73,240 (2.41)	40,392 (1.33)	27,463 (0.91)	24,839 (0.82)	16,919 (0.56)	17,665 (0.58)	156,752 (5.17)	143,945 (4.75)	64,375 (2.12)	41,530 (1.37)	9,645 (0.31)	30,326 (1.00)
Transfers in cash and kind (TP)	8,574	7,715	6,648	8,139	7,473	7,704	10,958	6,732	5,432	6,889	13,242	9,190
Gross income (Y + TP)	81,814 (2.07)	48,107 (1.22)	34,111 (0.86)	32,978 (0.83)	24,392 (0.62)	25,369 (0.64)	167,710 (4.24)	150,677 (3.81)	69,807 (1.77)	48,419 (1.23)	22,707 (0.57)	39,516 (1.00)
Taxes (TX)	29,412	18,055	12,957	12,154	8,399	8,437	47,915	37,115	17,585	10,715	6,899	12,760
Final income (Y + TP - TX)	52,402 (1.96)	30,052 (1.12)	21,154 (0.79)	20,824 (0.78)	15,993 (0.60)	16,932 (0.63)	119,795 (4.48)	113,562 (4.24)	52,222 (1.95)	37,704 (1.41)	15,808 (0.59)	26,756 (1.00)

Source: Foulon and Hatchuel (1979). Appendix 2.
NOTES: The top figure in each category shows the mean amount in French francs per annum. The second figure (in brackets) expresses this as a proportion of the overall mean for all households. Employers' social security contributions and indirect taxes are assumed to be paid by consumers through forward shifting into prices. Employees' social security contributions are assumed to be paid by employees.

Table 29
Value-Added and Income Tax Burdens,
by Income Classes, 1972

Income Class (francs)	Number of house- holds (millions)	Average income (francs)	Average income tax (francs)	Average value- added tax (francs)	Average tax rates (percent)		
					Income	Value- added	Total
Under 10,000	2.8	5,255	12	1,165	0.23	22.17	22.40
10,000—15,000	1.9	12,260	166	1,885	1.35	15.38	16.73
15,000—20,000	2.0	17,108	403	1.986	2.36	11.61	13.97
20,000—30,000	3.6	24.139	850	2,834	3.52	11.74	15.26
30,000—50,000	3.6	37,286	2,353	3,769	6.31	10.11	16.42
50,000—75,000	1.3	58,231	5,780	5,070	9.93	8.71	18.64
75,000—100,000	0.4	83,643	11,287	6,636	13.49	7.93	21.42
Over 100,000	0.3	163,480	34,152	8,886	20.89	5.44	26.33
Total or average	15.9	28,663	2,370	2,893	8.27	10.09	18.36

Source: J.P. Balladeur and A. Cantiere, *VAT: The European Experience* (Brookings Institution, 1983).

Table 30
Finances of Local Governments, 1977 and 1982

Source	1977	1982
Major sources of finance as a percent of total revenue		
Tax revenue	43.0	44.0
Nontax revenue	14.0	14.0
Grants	42.0	42.0
Percent of total tax revenue attributed to each level of government		
Central	51.0	49.8
Local (including regions and departments)	7.3	7.0
Social Security funds	41.8	43.1
Revenues as percent of total tax revenues of local government		
Taxes on income and profit (*Taxe d'habitation*)	20.0	16.0
Taxes on payroll (*Taxe professionelle*)	7.0	6.0
Taxes on property (*Taxe foncier*)	27.0	29.0
Taxes on consumption (Varies)	5.0	6.0
Taxes on a mixed base (*Taxe professionelle*)	42.0	43.0

Source: *Revenue Statistics of OECD Member Countries 1965-1984* (OECD 1985).

Table 31
Annual Local Taxes on Immovable Property and Business, 1986[1]

Type of Tax	Date Introduced	Tax Base	Tax Rate	Major Exemptions	Discretion Over Tax Base	Discretion Over Tax Rate	Collected by	Liability with
Land and building tax	1974	Rental value less 50 percent	Varies, national average 20 percent	Farms, government buildings	Limited	Yes	Central	Owner
Property tax	1974	Rental value	Varies, between communes (5-15 percent in 1984)	Farms, government buildings, and allowances for personal circumstances	None	Yes, within limits	Central	Occupants
Land tax	1974	Rental value minus 20 percent	Varies, national average 70 percent in 1984	Most farm land and public property	Limited	Yes	Central	Owner
Business tax	1976	Rental value of fixed assets and wages	Varies, maximum rate of five percent	Certain professions (farmers, artists, authors, etc.)	Limited	Yes	Central	Business

[1]The beneficiary government of these taxes is the communist.

CHAPTER 5

Italy

Laura Castellucci

INTRODUCTION

Italy enacted basic reforms of its indirect taxes in 1973 and of its direct taxes in 1974. The acts abolished the 18 previously existing *in rem* direct taxes, substituting for them two personal taxes and one *in rem* tax (called IRPEF=*Imposta sul Reddito delle Persone Fisiche*, IRPEG=*Imposta sul Reddito delle Persone Giuridiche;* and ILOR=*Imposta Locale sui Redditi*, respectively).

The tax on gifts and bequests has been maintained, although it too has been reformed. There is presently a new proposal to reduce the burden of the inheritance tax on the vertical line (direct) succession (see section X below).

Indirect taxes have been reduced from 21 to four major taxes, plus some minor ones.

This paper refers mainly to the tax system as enacted in 1973 and 1974. Changes, other than those concerning tax rates and deductions, have been introduced by a very recent act, called the "Visentini Package" (after the Minister of Finance who put the package together), which was enacted in February 1985 (see Appendix A). Despite the great simplification in the number of taxes, the system is still quite complicated and under continuous revision. Considerable expertise is required on the part of taxpayers and experts alike in order to understand the system.

I. THE INDIVIDUAL INCOME TAX

1. Tax Rates

The individual income tax (IRPEF) is, but only in principle a comprehensive income tax. Total taxable income (TTI) is obtained by subtracting from total gross income (a concept approximately equivalent to the U.S. adjusted gross income) a number of income (or nonpersonal) deductions. Tax rates from the rate schedule are then applied to the TTI to get the gross tax liability (GTL). From the GTL a number of tax (or personal) credits are subtracted to get the net tax liability (NTL), which is the amount one has to pay.

Tax rates were revised in 1976, 1983, and 1986 (table 1) and a new proposal is already under discussion. Further adjustments for inflation were introduced by changing, and further complicating, system of tax deductions (see section 6 below).

The Italian system of deductions is peculiar as compared with other European systems, such as the French or the German. Italy has the two types of deductions already mentioned, from taxable income (table 2) and from the tax (table 3). The latter play a particularly important role in the individual income tax,[1] of which there are three kinds (standard exemptions, family-size exemptions, and extra deductions) which differ depending on the sources and level of income. With regard to source of income, the distinction is made between income from employment and pensions on the one hand, and income from self-employment and (unincorporated) business on the other. The underlying idea is to adhere to a principle, called the "qualitative discrimination of incomes," which has a long tradition in the history of the Italian tax system. Although its justifications are now much weaker than they were decades ago, it still retains its influence, as one can infer by comparing the extra deductions of 1985 to those of 1974 (table 3). They have been raised as a way to adjust for the tax rate escalation due to inflation, but the increases have openly favored pension and employment income. This preferential treatment has been more recently justified on the ground that there is much more evasion

---

[1]I personally think that the practical complications caused by the system of "differential" deductions are not worthwhile, but no change in present policies is in sight.

among the self-employed and entrepreneurs than among employees and pensioners.[2]

2. Treatment of Capital Gains

The existence of a speculative motive is a necessary requirement for capital gains to be subject to the individual income tax. The revenue authorities must demonstrate the existence of such a motive, except when it is presumed *de jure* (in which case the taxpayer cannot object). This presumption is based on the length of time elapsed between the acquisition and disposition of the asset enjoying the capital gain. In the case of land and real estate it is five years, for works of art and antiquities it is two years. The tax base is the difference between the sale and purchase prices.

A separate, general local tax is due on the increment of the value of land and real estate (*Imposta sugli incrementi di valore degli immobili*—Tax on the Increments of Value of Real Estate). This tax is subtracted from the capital gains tax liability as determined under the individual income tax.

Capital gains on financial assets are not taxed under the individual income tax, presumably because the speculative motive is considered absent. However, under the Visentini Package, certain transfers were made subject to tax. The existence of a speculative motive is again necessary and is presumed when two conditions are simultaneously met. First, the purchase and sale of the shares must take place within a five year time span; second, the value of the transaction is no less than two, 10, or 25 percent of the entire company's or business' capital, depending on whether the transaction is made, respectively, in the stock market, in the over-the-counter market, or in other settings (as in case of participations in unincorporated businesses). If equities are acquired through gift or inheritance no tax is due. One can see that, as it stands, this new provision is marginal from the point of view of the individual income tax. It could be interpreted as a first step towards extending the tax base to capital gains on financial assets, but there is no evidence that this is likely to occur in the near future.

---

[2]Although this may be the case, I would agree with those who think that such preferential treatment only hurts the honest nonwage income taxpayer, and certainly does not solve the problem of tax evasion. The true reason is more likely to be the government's wish to please the unions, which are opposed to tax benefits for those relying on nonwage income. This same reason lies behind the choice of increases in tax deductions instead of indexing as a way to adjust for inflation. The unions offer self restraint in wage demands in return for tax provisions that favor employment income, while indexing does not provide the same basis for wage bargaining.

3. Tax Treatment of the Family

The taxpaying unit is the individual earner (earner-unit approach). Splitting of an individual's income among family members is not allowed, except in the case of a family business. The profits of a family business can be split among members of the family in proportion to their respective share in them. But even this splitting allowance has been reduced by the Visentini Package, which stipulates that only 49 percent of the income of an unincorporated business can be attributed to the members of the entrepreneur's family.[3] Tax assessment is separate, although separate or joint filing are both possible.[4] In fact, joint filing may be profitable in two instances: first, when tax deductions to which one spouse is entitled exceed his or her tax liability; and second, when one spouse's taxable income turns out to be negative. In the first case, the other spouse may use the excess deductions; in the second, the negative taxable income may be offset against the positive income of the other spouse.

4. Current Payment System

Tax collection is currently through one of two types of withholding. The first type of withholding is a "partial payment" (*acconto*). The second is a final payment. By far the largest part of withholding is of the first type and it applies to all wages and salaries, pensions, and incomes of the self-employed. Since withholding is net of personal deductions and credits, the tax liability of the wage or salary earner or pensioner is completely settled if there is no other income. No return is filed by the taxpayer (see section 5), and only a copy of the employer's withholding certificate must be sent to the Internal Revenue Authority.

---

[3]This may be interpreted as a move that strengthens the nonsplitting ideology followed so far. Proof of this attitude was the attempt to establish the *cumulo* (joint returns of couples), which is the opposite of splitting. The joint returns method was actually introduced in 1974, but it was eliminated in 1977 when excessive tax payments had to be refunded. (Due to the progressivity of tax rates, the *cumulo* produced a joint tax liability higher than that which would be produced under separate assessment. This bracket creep was thought to be unfair: it would have favored families with one income only and discriminated against the working woman.) However, under the above 49 percent rule, and due to the progressivity of tax rates, a large part of a family's business income may escape taxation through the fictitious participation in the business activity by members of the entrepreneur's family not actually contributing to it.

[4]In case husband and wife each earn income, they can either file separate returns or a joint return, but in either case the assessment of the tax is separate. In other words, each calculates his/her tax liability on his/her income and the joint or separate filing is only a question of practical convenience.

The most important withholding of the second type is made by banks and postal authorities on interest paid on deposits to individuals.[5] Such interest receipts are not included with other types of income in the individual income tax base. However, they do enter into the corporate income tax base.

Final payments of all of the most important taxes (IRPEF, IRPEG, ILOR) are due in May (value-added tax is due in March). However, starting in 1978, by November of each year every taxpayer has to pay 90 percent of his or her assessed tax liability for the current year (value-added tax is paid monthly or quarterly, depending on turnover).

5. Requirements for Filing Tax Returns

Except for those who have only one wage or pension income, all citizens must file tax returns by May 31. Self-assessment of one's income tax is indeed a difficult task for many taxpayers, particularly those who are less educated or live in less developed areas. This is especially so because a typical taxpayer has only one wage or pension income, but also owns a small flat with cash or imputed (when owner-occupied) income which is subject to tax.[6]

On filing a return, the taxpayer calculates the tax liability net of all deductions and credits and then subtracts from the tax due the amount which has already been withheld, and that which has already been paid in November as a partial payment. The device of tax collection in November as a partial payment, and in May as the final payment, was motivated by the need to shorten the time elapsing between the production of income and the tax payment and to reduce the discrimination against taxpayers subject to withholding.

6. Adjustment for Inflation

As already mentioned, adjustments for inflation are usually made by increasing the (personal) tax deductions. In 1983, and in

---

[5]In Italy all types of deposits pay interest.

[6]For tax purposes, income from land and real estate is a conventional income established in the Registry of Land and in the Registry of Real Estate, for every physical unit. Since the incomes inscribed in such Registries are those, respectively, of 1939 and 1962, the fiscal authority publishes periodically revaluation coefficients. Such revalued conventional income of an owner-occupied house is then added to the actual taxable income of the taxpayer. It is generally thought that even with the revaluations, the resulting imputed income underestimates true income. This sort of preferential treatment of owner-occupied homes is emphasized by those who favor the introduction of a wealth tax.

1985 for 1986 incomes, tax rates were revised as well (table 1). A new proposal by Finance Minister Visentini for revising the tax rate schedule once more is under discussion.[7]

II. THE CORPORATION INCOME TAX

1. Tax Rates and Tax Base

Since 1984, the standard corporate tax rate has been 36 percent (before that it was 30 percent plus an additional eight percent of the 30 percent tax). Financial corporations are now subject to the same treatment. Until 1977, they were subject to a much more favorable rate of 7.50 percent further reduced to 6.25 percent when the government was the majority owner. Actually, the total tax rate on corporations is more than 36 percent because they are also subject to the local income tax of 16.2 percent (the ILOR, see section IX). The combined rate is 46.368 percent.[8]

The tax base is total net business income as it results from the statutory profit and loss account (economic accounting), adjusted in accordance with the special provisions imposed or allowed by law. The definition of business income, whether corporate or noncorporate, for tax purposes, departs on certain points from the standard, economic, profit and loss definition. Special rules apply among other things to inventory evaluations and depreciation accounting, and in general to the evaluation of outstanding real and financial assets, and to interest charges. To determine the tax base certain extra deductions from general business income are allowed. They concern, in particular, maintenance and preservation expenses for objects of historical and artistic value, charities and gifts to government and nonprofit institutions, and expenses for doing or promoting research. Deductions are also allowed for the ordinary[9] and decennial tax on the Increment of the Value of Land and Real Estate (INVIM) (see section IX), for ILOR, and for losses in previous years up to the last five years.

When the corporation income tax was introduced it was conceived as a tax on a distinct entity, separate from the shareholders (absolutist view). The tax is now regarded as a partial payment of

---

[7]The opposition has a proposal of its own (see tables 13 and 14). They are, of course, against the government's proposal, which is also opposed by the unions.

[8]Since 1977 the local tax is deductible from the national tax. Thus, the actual total tax rate is as follows (where B is the tax base): local tax = .162 B; national tax = .36 (B − .162B) = .3017B; national and local tax = .4636.

[9]According to certain specific rules.

individual income tax and the two taxes are integrated. A description of the integration system is given in section 3.

2. Treatment of Small Firms

Firms with annual turnover of less than 780 million liras are defined as "small firms" and as such are subject to special treatment concerning their accounting for tax purposes. Turnover is the only requirement for belonging in this category (it is adjusted for inflation from time to time). Small firms are allowed to adopt a simplified system of accounting by which taxable income is determined as the difference between all revenues less a specified list of certified expenses, and given percentages of gross revenues for the noncertified ones.

Small firms with a yearly turnover of less than 18 million liras and belonging to particular trading sectors, such as retail trade, handicrafts, grocery stores, and the like, are subject to an even more simplified lump-sum treatment. In such cases, the tax base is determined on a lump-sum basis by applying profitability coefficients to gross receipts. Fiscal experts are generally opposed to such favorable treatment on at least two grounds: first, too many firms claim that they belong to the special category. Lump-sum tax treatment is an incentive to underreport revenues, thereby allowing firms to evade both income tax and VAT (see section V). Second, lump-sum treatment squarely contradicts the principle adopted in 1973-1974 that taxes should be based on actual, analytically assessed income.

3. Treatment of Dividends

Dividends are included by taxpayers in their tax returns. To avoid double taxation, a tax credit is allowed for corporate taxes paid. In outline, the tax credit system (or "dividends-received credit") now works as follows. The tax rate on a company's income is 36 percent. Suppose a shareholder receives a dividend of 64 liras. If there had been no corporate tax, he would have received a dividend of 100 liras. The shareholder calculates his tax credit by multiplying the dividend received by $9/16$ ($.36/.64 = t(1 - t)$). Both the dividend (64) and the tax credit (36) are included in the shareholder's taxable income. Finally, the shareholder calculates his tax liability on his total taxable income and then subtracts the tax credit from the tax liability.

In 1983, a new provision aimed at avoiding a tax subsidy to dividend recipients, was added. Since a tax credit was allowed with respect to all dividends received and since there are numerous corporate tax preferences (such as a reduced rate of taxation on incomes originating in the South and tax-exempt interest on Treasury bonds), the shareholder would receive a tax subsidy to the extent that his dividends originated from such favored sources. As it would be practically impossible to trace the source of dividend income, a new tax on corporations was introduced, called the "balancing tax" (*Imposta di Conguaglio*). This new tax is paid by a company in accordance with the distribution of its income between tax preferences and fully taxed income (see Appendix B).

As a result of integration, the corporation income tax as such is in the end a tax on undistributed profits. However, high-income taxpayers with marginal tax rates higher than the corporate tax rate may partially avoid the individual income tax by transferring their assets to a legal entity especially established for the purpose and kept under the majority control of family members. In this way, part of their income is kept within the corporation, and, by retaining it, the income remains subject only to the proportional IRPEG and not to the progressive (marginal) IRPEF.

4. Effects of Dividend Relief on Equity Financing

There are two types of distorting effects usually attributed to the corporate income tax. The first, concerning a company's dividend policy, has been eliminated through the tax credit system; the second, concerning a company's choice of equity vs. debt financing, is still at work since debt interest on borrowed capital is a cost deductible from taxable income while no deduction of imputed interest on equity capital is permitted. In principle this arrangement should provide an incentive to finance through debt. However this may be, the volume of transactions in the Italian stock exchange has been small and the average citizen does not own shares of stock. In the last few years, there has been a boom in the stock market resulting mainly from an increased flow of private saving into investment funds. The limited size of the Italian stock exchange has always been explained, among other reasons, and apart from our comparatively recent industrialization, by the "unfair" competition of government in absorbing private saving. Interest on government securities is tax free, while dividends are not only liable to progressive taxation, but in addition, stocks are, in theory, registered assets.[10] This latter

---

[10]Stocks are registered assets but only at company level. There exists no "general register," and therefore the fiscal authority would have to check every company's shareholders against individual returns, which is impracticable. It is interesting to note that the announced "general register" of share-owners has never been prepared.

characteristic is greatly feared by the Italian taxpayer. Even the competition from interest-bearing bank deposits is unfair, because interest on such deposits is subject only to a flat withholding tax. Furthermore, bank deposits are protected by bank secrecy (which can only be lifted by a court order).

The recent boom in the stock market through investment funds, which has been accompanied by a reduction in subscriptions for public bonds, can be explained partially by the growing fear that sooner or later interest on public bonds will be taxed. This change has been delayed by the government's fear that it would be required to pay higher interest rates to finance its borrowing.

The unequal taxation of returns on financial assets; the under-capitalization of the corporate sector, with its excessive level of bank indebtedness; and the strong preference of savers for liquid assets, which in turn has boosted the so-called "double inter-mediation,"[11] are widely regarded as responsible for the poor state of the equity market. On the other hand, there is no evidence that dividend relief (which was implemented four months after the enactment of the 1974 Act, and then replaced in 1977 by the tax credit), has induced an increase in equity finance.

III. SAVING AND INVESTMENT

In principle, all income sources are included in the income tax base. The sources are classified as (a) land, (b) capital, (c) labor, (d) unincorporated business, and (e) others (such as speculative capital gains). However, interest on bank and postal deposits, which should enter category (b), is not included in taxable income. Other income from capital, such as interest on private bonds and other private borrowing, and dividends on shares is included in taxable income. (Dividends are eligible for a tax credit, as explained earlier.) Add to the picture that interest on government bonds is tax free for individuals, but not for corporations, and one can appreciate the complexities of taxation of income from financial capital.

Summing up:

1. Dividends and interest on private bonds and other private borrowing are liable to the progressive income tax.

---

[11]Double intermediation refers to the fact that savers don't invest directly in the stock market, but leave to the banks the function of channeling their saving.

2. Interest on bank and postal deposits received by individuals is liable to a flat tax which is withheld by banks and postal authorities and is not included in the taxpayer's return.
3. Interest received by corporations, including interest on bank deposits, is subject to the corporation income tax and the bank's withholding represents a partial payment of that tax.
4. Interest on government bonds is tax free for individuals, but not for corporations.

1. Saving Incentives Through the Tax System

The well-known, exceptionally high saving propensity of households in Italy has been shrinking in recent years. From the early 1960s to the present, total private saving has declined by 10 percentage points, from 27 percent in 1961 to 17 percent in 1983. The main characteristics of monetary and financial markets have remained essentially the same during this period. The Italian money market is characterized by comparatively high liquidity, an almost monopolistic position of the banks in absorbing short-term assets (resulting from the payment of high interest rates on bank deposits), and the dominating position, at least since 1975, of short-term Treasury bonds. The small volume of equity transactions has increased as a result of the entrance of approximately 10 investment funds into the field. The issue of private bonds has been very limited, due to tight legal constraints and tax regulations, while that of public bonds (by Treasury and public corporations and holdings) has greatly increased (see table 4).

Of the two traditional types of saving incentives through the tax system, namely the exemption of saved income (consumption tax base) and reduced and/or nonprogressive taxation of returns to saving, only the second is used in Italy. Nondividend returns on financial assets owned by individuals are subject to a flat withholding tax rate and need not be reported on the tax returns. In the case of corporations, withholding represents only a partial payment. There are different withholding rates for different assets, as summarized in table 5. While the choice of a withholding rate is intended to increase total saving, the different rates, in fact, tend to channel existing saving into tax-preferred assets.

The same rationale lies behind a number of administrative regulations of bank portfolios (these have beeen called a form of "hidden taxation" like inflation). Although they were ostensibly introduced to protect depositors, these regulations ensure that the banking system will subscribe to Treasury bond issues.

The general structure of interest rates also has an important effect on the allocation of saving. Higher interest rates are not necessarily associated with longer asset maturities (see table 6), and assets with longer maturities are not taxed at reduced rates.[12] Such facts may help to explain the Italian savers' strong preference for liquid assets.[13]

2. Treatment of Financial Institutions

No special treatment is given to financial companies except for the provisions for bad debts. Banks are allowed to deduct charges to a reserve for risks on loans, provided such charges are duly registered in their accounts, and do not exceed 0.5 percent of total loans made in each tax period. The limit is reduced to 0.2 percent when the reserve fund reaches two percent of total outstanding loans and no more deductions are allowed when the fund reaches five percent. Losses on loans are deductible, but only when they exceed the reserve set aside for them.

Insurance companies can deduct charges made to set aside, or restore, reserve funds for life and nonlife insurance contracts. Charges to cover payments for accidents that have already occurred but are not yet settled are also deductible.

3. Investment Incentives

General incentives. Government intervention for stimulating investment is pervasive in the Italian economy, but it is also so chaotic that it is hard to get a clear picture of what is going on, let alone to assess the effects. Four points may be singled out. First, a consistently designed and implemented industrial policy does not exist. There are numerous regulations and provisions, enforced

---

[12]A recent recommendation along these lines, put forward by a committee set up by the Ministry of Finance, to make a comprehensive study of the taxation of financial income has not been accepted.

[13]The level and structure of interest rates have long since been the subject of debate in Italy. The main question is whether it is still the official discount rate which performs the pivotal role in determining bank interest rates or whether such a role is now being performed by interest on short-term Treasury bonds. According to the latter view, most common in the banking community, high interest rates on Treasury bonds should be accompanied by high interest rates on deposits and therefore on bank loans as well. The government cannot expect banks to charge a lower interest on their loans, thereby favoring private investment, as long as interest on Treasury bonds remains high. Banks have complained even more about the regulations which set ceilings to certain components of their portfolios, thus curtailing their managerial independence while insuring an almost compulsory source of financing for the government. These regulations were lifted in 1983, but were suddenly reintroduced by the Bank of Italy on January 16, 1986 to be effective until June 1986.

and expiring at different dates, for different periods, and favoring different sectors and subsectors, depending on the type and location of the investment, the year in which it is made, and so on. Second, interventions to promote the economic development of the South are made and administered primarily through a special government agency, called the *Cassa per il Mezzogiorno*.[14] Third, the favored method of intervention is through transfers or grants. Fourth, there is a considerable amount of lending under special terms (*credito agevolato*) to promote small- and medium-size business,[15] exports, and, always, the South. Many regard such transfers and loans as excessive, misdirected, or unnecessary interferences with the credit system. The government acts as a sort of a "hidden banker," who is less efficient than the private banking system in the allocation of credit.

There are three types of tax incentives: (a) repeal of payroll taxes on wages and salaries; (b) tax credits for reinvested profits, and (c) accelerated depreciation.

3.1. Repeal of payroll taxes. The government has at different times temporarily repealed payroll taxes, recovering the revenue through other types of general taxation, or the value-added tax. (The first such repeal was introduced in 1968 in favor of business in the South).[16]

3.2. Tax credit for reinvested profits. Firms can set aside funds, called "funds under tax suspension," which are tax free if reinvested within two years. (A similar mechanism is applied to the local tax on increments in real estate values.) A temporary tax credit for reinvested profits is included in another Visentini bill which is now in the process of receiving approval by Parliament.

3.3. Depreciation. Allowances for depreciation are fairly generous. There are three types of depreciation: standard, financial, and economic.

---

[14]Actually the *Cassa per il Mezzogiorno* was terminated in 1984. In its place and with the same functions a National Fund for the Development of the South was created. The change was only nominal and the name *Cassa per il Mezzogiorno* continues to be in use.

[15]The definition of small business for such loans does not coincide with the definitions for special treatment under the corporation income tax (see section II.2) For purposes of special loans, the basic criterion is the number of employees.

[16]Since 1977 there have been "temporary" national repeals, each lasting generally eight months. Therefore, since that date there have been two repeals a year, from January to June and from June to December. The repeals cover only a part of social security contributions and, although they apply to the whole national territory, they are neither uniform nor equal for every category of worker (they distinguish, for instance, between male and female workers).

Standard depreciation is the economic (physical and techno-
logical) depreciation of real assets used in business, including
structures, plants, and equipment. Charges to reflect economic
depreciation, calculated by applying coefficients listed in the law
to the purchase price plus all supplementary expenses, are deductible as costs from business income, beginning in the year of
purchase. Additional allowances for anticipated depreciation are
allowed, up to a maximum of 15 percent and for the first three
years only. Larger allowances (accelerated depreciation) are also
allowed when the asset is used up more intensively.[17] If an asset is
scrapped before depreciation is fully recovered, the residual value
is deductible (but if sold, the residual value becomes taxable
income).

The crucial question about depreciation concerns the adjustment
of the value of assets for inflation. As mentioned, the asset values
for depreciation purposes are still based on historical cost. The
debate over the proper accounting for inflation has not led to the
adoption of the qualitatively different concepts of replacement
costs or present value in place of the historical cost concept.
Occasionally, particular provisions have been introduced from
time to time, until more general revaluations of listed assets were
allowed in 1975 and 1983.[18] The 1975 Act also allows for the
revaluation of assets already fully amortized, provided they appear
in the accounting statement of the firm. Basically, two types of
revaluations were allowed: a "direct" revaluation, which consists of
the application of given coefficients (20, 30, 40 percent, depending

---

[17]No particular rules hold for anticipated depreciation, and almost the same is
true for the "accelerated" depreciation. The law says that accelerated depreciation
is allowed when the firm "uses more intensively" its assets, but no proof of this fact
is required. The fiscal authority may question this procedure *a posteriori*, but it
does so very rarely, if ever. Depreciation allowances are not only fairly generous but
are also left completely in the firm's discretion, within the established general rules
and magnitude.

[18]When inflation is high, as it was until recently in Italy, depreciation charges
calculated at the purchase price do not enable the firm to replace its real assets at
the end of their lives. The "present value" is the current value faced by the firm
which wants to buy the new asset, while the purchasing price is the "historical
cost," i.e., the price at which the asset was originally acquired. Pressures from the
business sector to have depreciation charges calculated on the basis of the present
value (instead of the historical cost) in order to be able to replace worn out assets
with the charges set aside, have been met by the revaluation provisions allowed in
1975 and 1983. A different provision, with similar aim and results, was introduced
in 1977. This provision, known as *scorporo*, allowed businesses to break up single
chunks of investment. The singled-out capital equipment could then be allocated to
a sort of new branch of the company at its current price. Depreciation charges
would thereafter depend on that price.

on the date of purchase) to the purchase price of each asset, and an "indirect" revaluation, allowed for corporations only (they are free to choose between the two), consisting of a global revaluation of all real assets, up to a maximum of 50 percent of the value of the firm's equity capital.

Financial depreciation. In addition to standard depreciation, so-called "financial depreciation" can be deducted from taxable income when the holder of a temporary (although usually very long) license or concession to utilize a public good or facility for a business purpose, or to organize and run a public service hands over free to the authority issuing the concession (municipality, region or other) the real capital assets acquired for running the business when the concession expires. These supplementary annual financial charges are determined by dividing the original acquisition cost of the real assets by the number of concession years. The rationale would seem to be to exempt from taxation that part of profits which would have to be set aside to repay the value of the assets to be turned over free to the authority at the end of the concession.

Economic depreciation refers to the spreading out of operating losses over a number of years and to depreciation charges for certain intangible expenses, such as those for research and development and those for acquiring patent rights. Expenses for research and development may be amortized over a maximum period of five years. Expenses for patent rights may be amortized over the period of utilization established in the contract at constant annual rates.

Other amortizable expenses are those incurred for the establishment of a new business and for increasing equity capital. Amortization of these expenses is allowed over a maximum period of five years, but the yearly deduction cannot exceed 50 percent of the total expense.

4. Incentives for Particular Industries

Housing. In 1982 an act was passed granting temporary benefits to boost housing. Such benefits have been extended so far to the present. The main provisions are the following: for businesses, capital gains enjoyed by business through the sale of buildings utilized for running the business are exempted from corporate and individual income taxes, provided they are reinvested in the acquisition of other buildings, through the setting aside of a fund tied for that particular purpose. (If they are not so reinvested, a penalty of 75 percent is imposed.) If an individual buys a flat or a house, new or old, to live in or to rent at the legally determined rent ("just" rent or *equo canone*), the limit on the amount of mortgage interest and related expenses deductible from taxable income is raised. (By comparison, tax increases have been introduced for flats or houses held vacant by the owners). Transfers of flats or houses between individuals are, as a rule, heavily burdened by indirect taxation (see section VII). Such taxes have been reduced recently on a temporary basis.

Mining and manufacturing. The buying or importing of new physical capital into mining and manufacturing enjoys favorable tax treatment in the computation of value-added tax (so-called negative VAT).[19] Such tax benefits hold also in the case of leasing.

IV. PAYROLL TAXES

1. Tax Rates

Social security contributions are generally proportional, but sometimes regressive, taxes on wages and salaries. The tax base includes wages and salaries, professional income of the self-employed, and income of unincorporated businessmen (handicraft, trade, and agriculture). Many different rates, whose rationale goes back to the type of risk they were intended to insure against, contribute to make up the final rates. The rates depend on the:
1. type of job and self-employment;
2. sector;
3. blue collar and white collar work;
4. handicraft industry, trade, and agriculture;
5. location in the national territory; and
6. sex.

Table 7 gives the tax rates for several sectors, which range from a low of 47.8 percent for handicrafts to a high of 55.6 percent in industry. Social security contributions are a significant part of total tax revenues and of gross domestic product, as shown in table 8. In 1984, they accounted for about 38 percent of total revenue and 16 percent of GDP.

---

[19]As explained below (section V), the VAT liability is determined not by applying tax rates directly to value-added, but by subtracting the VAT paid on inputs from the VAT received on sales. The favorable treatment enjoyed by manufacturing firms refers to the fact that the VAT to be subtracted can be increased by an extra six percent (four percent until 1982).

2. Use of Payroll Taxes for Social Security and General Revenues

Payroll taxes, or more precisely, social security contributions, are paid directly to the social security agencies (by far the most important is the INPS) so that, strictly, they are not a source of general revenues. However, they fall far short of total social expenditures, and other sources of finance are therefore necessary. In 1982 social expenditures were 25.4 percent of gross domestic product, while social security contributions were 15.7 percent or 14.03 percent of gross domestic product, according, respectively, to the two sources quoted in table 8. In other words, the "insurance approach" and the "budget approach" are both at work simultaneously.

Indeed, the financing of social expenditures comes from two sources: social security contributions and transfers from the government. The second source has become more important over the last 15 years, with the first contributing at present approximately 85 percent of total outlays. Social expenditures have been growing without interruption since World War II, but with peaks in conjunction with the extension of pension payments and medicare to all citizens who had not paid any social contributions (for instance, agricultural workers, in the middle 1960s), with the establishment of the *Cassa Integrazione Gudagni*,[20] and with the increasing shortening of the *contingenza* (sliding scale) time interval.[21] The real problem with social security, in particular with the pension system, which is the most important program, lies not simply in the growth of social expenditures but in the growing difference between expenditures and contributions.

This divergence is not surprising considering the dynamics of payments and revenues in the case of pensions. On the expenditure side, the number of pensioners and the average pension payment are both growing. Contributions depend on the number of working people and the average contribution, which is in turn a function of tax rates and average pay. The number of working people relative to the retired has been declining in Italy as it has in all industrial countries. The aging of the population is a major problem in Italy, and it will become even more so in the future. In addition, when the

---

[20] A public agency which is, broadly speaking, in charge of paying unemployment benefits to workers temporarily unemployed.

[21] The *contingenza* or *scala mobile* is a supplementary payment added to the base wage or salary, which is linked to the cost of living index and intended to adjust wages and salaries for inflation. The adjustment was originally made every six months, then reduced to four months and three months, and it is now back to six months.

economy is growing slowly, as it has been the last few years, the increase in unemployment reduces the payroll tax base.[22]

This well-known dynamic of social security is not reconcilable unless the government decides to reduce pensions or increase payroll tax rates, or to rely more on transfers from general revenues to the social security agencies. Payroll tax rates have been raised on some categories of self-employed, such as craftsmen and trade dealers, leading to some reduction in operating losses, but at the same time there has been a deterioration of social security balances for agriculture workers. All things considered, it is unrealistic to expect either a further increase in payroll tax rates, which are already high compared to other countries, or a reduction in the average pension.

The level of pension payments is not determined on the basis of contributions paid, but as a percentage of the pay received in the three most favorable years of the last ten. This method is not used for the self-employed, whose pensions are based on the contributions paid. For agricultural workers the pay of reference is established by law.

On the whole, pensions have become increasingly less tied to contributions and more tied to the rising pay levels of working people and the rising cost of living. Therefore, the share of government transfers in financing social security is expected to continue to increase in the future.

A look at the composition of social expenditures by agencies and by type of services may also be in order. From table 9 one can verify the divergence between revenues and expenditures of the social security agencies, which have experienced either negative balances or positive balances, as in 1979 and 1978, which were the result of government transfers. While the public social security agencies are in deficit, private social security agencies generate positive balances, reflecting increases in pension reserves set aside by business. As to the type of social security services, the most important are pensions (*previdenze*), social welfare provisions (*assistenza*), and health (*sanita*) (see table 10).

---

[22]Payroll tax revenues also decline when, for a given aggregate level of employment, some workers become self-employed. The reduction in payroll tax revenue is offset, however, by reduced social payments (mainly pensions).

V. VALUE-ADDED TAX

1. Tax Rates and Exemptions

The value-added tax (IVA, *Imposta sul Valore Aggiunto*) is a tax on domestic consumption, but it is paid at every transaction of goods and services. (In other words, it is a multistage, consumption type tax). The IVA is by far the most important indirect tax in Italy. The tax was finally introduced in 1973 after having been delayed beyond the extension granted by the EEC. It was introduced as a substitute for the previous general turnover tax (IGE, *Imposta Generale sull' Entrata*). Multiple rates were adopted to avoid impairing the slight progressivity attributed to the income tax of the time. Empirical evidence shows that the IVA is, in fact, slightly progressive, as a result of the differential tax rates, particularly the first two.

Although progression is a desirable property, the structure of the IVA is excessively cumbersome. First, the definition of "transactions of goods and services" is complicated. Second, a distinction is made among types of transactions, which may be taxable, nontaxable (zero rated), excluded, or exempt.[23] Third, special treatment is allowed for agriculture.[24] Fourth, while the number of taxpayers is large, too many of them are small scale taxpayers. (This is almost exactly the opposite of the French IVA, which is the oldest European tax of this type.)

Tax liability is determined by subtracting the IVA paid on inputs from the IVA received on sales. This method of subtracting "tax from tax" is the standard one, and until January 1985, it was used by every taxpayer.

As one can readily appreciate, differential rates[25] combined with exemptions and exclusions, create a great deal of room for manipulating one's tax liability. However, this is neither the only problem nor the worst. The major problem is the handling of refunds by the revenue authority. When the difference between IVA on sales and

---

[23]Nontaxable transactions include exports, international transportation, necessities. Excluded transactions are those made by subjects who are as such not liable to IVA. These include credit, financial and insurance transactions. Nontaxable transactions are regarded as taxable at zero rate, and enter into the final calculation of IVA; exempted transactions do not. A special mechanism of "tax suspension" on domestic purchases, less than or equal to the amount of firm's exports and other nontaxable transactions, is also allowed.

[24]The agriculture sector was, and still is, subject to an especially favorable method of IVA assessment, called the "agricultural system."

[25]The number of rates was reduced by the Visentini Package to five, i.e., 0, 2, 9, 19, and 38 percent.

IVA on purchases is negative, the revenue authority must refund the difference. Given the structure of the tax, refunds are to be expected, but their volume is huge and very costly. Recently, it has been estimated that about 26 to 30 percent of gross annual IVA revenue gives rise to new "credits" and the total amount of credits is increasing at a faster rate than gross revenue. An important source of the credit is, of course, exports, because in accordance with EEC directives, taxation is based on the principle of the country of destination and not of the country of origin. But the alarming increase in tax credits does not seem to come from these items, which can be checked at customs.

The IVA is generally thought to be evaded to a substantial degree. Indeed, by comparing national income figures with those of IVA returns one can make a fairly good estimate. The degree of evasion turns out to be about 30 percent (there are even more pessimistic estimates). When the tax was introduced, the revenue authorities were confident that compliance would be good because of the conflicting interest of taxpayers, who are simultaneously debtors and creditors of IVA. In other words, taxpayers would cross-check each other to the benefit of the revenue authorities. However, compliance has been very low in practice.

2. Administrative Costs

The administrative and compliance costs of IVA are high both for the taxpayer and for the revenue authority. Since the time of its introduction, the opposition to IVA by business, especially small business, was based on the high costs they would have to face in order to satisfy the demanding bookkeeping requirements of IVA. This consideration may have been responsible for the introduction of a "forfeit system" of assessment for small business. The story of the forfeit system is interesting because it was recently eliminated and then restored, demonstrating the current state of uncertainty on the part of the fiscal authority.

The forfeit system requires only sales records; the deduction of IVA paid on inputs is determined by applying given coefficients to taxable sales. The system came under widespread criticism because it permitted many businesses to evade the tax. The abolition of the system was questioned because, even though additional costs were imposed on the taxpayers, there was no certain benefit for the revenue authorities. Tax consultants would have become the true beneficiaries. Indeed, it is an arduous task for the revenue authorities to administer and check the 4.8 million returns (in

1984).[26] To complicate things further, the number of tax returns has grown by about one-third over the period 1978-84. On top of these already strained administrative conditions, one must add the claims for reimbursement, which were getting out of hand.

In such circumstances the abolition of the forfeit system, although desirable in principle, was really questionable. Nevertheless, it was abolished without properly considering whether the alternative (standard) system was "manageable" by the administration.[27] In February 1985, the forfeit system was reintroduced in the "Visentini Package." The Act provides a new list of the coefficients to be used. Although it is really too early to attach much importance to figures of monthly IVA payments for less than 12 months, the number of new claims for reimbursement seems to have decreased. If this trend persists, the reintroduction of the forfeit system would be warranted.

3. Effects of the VAT on the Price Level

During the late 1970s, several studies on the distributional effects of IVA appeared, but not much research was done on the price effects. Due probably to the fact that there is presently more concern for the administrative problems of IVA, and that the progressivity of the income tax is higher than in the later 1970s (thanks to inflation), there are no theoretical contemporary studies on the effects of IVA on prices and on income distribution.

It is generally thought either that IVA does not raise the price level or, if it does, it raises it only slightly. Pedone[28] reported an average price increase of about two to six percent, assuming an average IVA rate of 10 percent. Ceriani[29] concluded that inflation would be reduced as a consequence of substituting IVA for social security payroll taxes, which occurred in 1977. This conclusion rests on the idea that "the reduction of payroll taxes would cause employers to lower their mark-up amounts, thus cutting inflation."[30] The same position can be found in some studies of the

---

[26]To get an idea of the dimensions of the problem, consider that the number of returns in France is little more than half of those filed in Italy.

[27]The forfeit system in France, while inexpensive for the administration, seems to yield a considerable amount of tax revenues. Thus the problem is more the type of system used rather than the forfeit as such.

[28]A. Pedone, "Italy" in *The Value-Added Tax. Lessons from Europe*, The Brookings Institution.

[29]V. Ceriani, "Gli effetti sui prezzi de manovre del prelievo delle imposte indirette, contributi sociali e tariffe" in *Contributi alla Ricerca*, n. 8, Banca d'Italia, 1981.

[30]A. Pedone, "L'inflazione in Italia: tendenze e previsioni" in "La lotta all'inflazione," Roma, Editori Riuniti, 1977.

Bank of Italy from the same period. The administrative mess and the huge evasion, which go hand in hand, are the truly outstanding and serious problems of the Italian IVA today.

VI. THE HIDDEN ECONOMY

1. The Parallel Economy Explanation

The most credible explanation for the existence of the hidden economy in Italy, given by Contini[31] in the 1970s, known as the "parallel economy" explanation, is still valid today, although the hidden economy of the 1980s is in many respects quite different from that of the 1970s.[32] The parallel economy explanation is that the hidden economy is an anticyclical phenomenon: the "hidden" activity grows when the economy slackens. The hidden economy is the solution to the rigidities of the economy not only in terms of wages but also in terms of all other regulations brought by union power into industrial relations. Such rigidities—the most important being the immobility of labor and the practical impossibility of providing part-time jobs—were overcome by moonlighting jobs which escaped payroll taxation. Of course, moonlighting jobs escaped the income tax as well, but this is not as important a motivation as the payroll taxes. Proof of the decisive role of the payroll taxes is the persistent requests for their "fiscalization" (i.e., contributions' relief at the expense of the budget) on the part of business, and the persistent tendency to switch to more capital intensive techniques as soon as the government allows businesses to release employees.

Other aspects of the social security system are also responsible for the hidden economy. If high payroll taxes are the cause on the employers' (or demand) side, the receipt of social security benefits is an important cause on the workers' (or supply) side. A major part of concealed legal employment comes from pensioners, pre-

---

[31]B. Contini, "Lo sviluppo di uneconomia parallela," Edizioni Comunita, Milano, 1979.

[32]A clear difference appears, for instance, in the sectors which contribute most to it. In the 1970s the most important sector was agriculture, while in the 1980s it was the "professions." Broadly speaking, the main cause for the hidden economy in the 1970s was the reaction to the rigidities in the labor market, whereas in the 1980s this is no longer the case. The causes have become more numerous, and the unions have lost power.

pensioners,[33] recipients of unemployment benefits, and housewives, who don't want to lose their social security benefits.[34] On the labor supply side it is more important not to lose social benefits than to escape income tax.

As far as the IVA is concerned, the level of evasion is high. It is quite common, especially in the small business sector, to under-report revenues by simply not issuing invoices. Very often home repairs, as well as services of physicians, lawyers, and the like, are paid by the client or patient in cash, without a regular invoice. However, this is the common way unincorporated business and professionals avoid both IVA and income tax and not a specific characteristic of the hidden economy.

2. Estimates of Size

A forthcoming paper by OECD[35] contains a complete survey of estimates of the parallel economy by different authorities in Italy, on which this section is based. No accurate micro-level estimates are available except the one produced by the Research Center for Social Investment Studies in Rome, in 1976 (see table 12). Various macro-level estimates are summarized in table 10. The divergence among estimates, which is immediately evident, confirms the difficulties in estimating something that is, by definition, unknown. It also raises the problem of the reliability of the official national accounts. For example, table 12 suggests that the national income accounts underestimate GDP and employment by as much as 20 and 30 percent, respectively, which is probably too high. In fact, if the actual employment rate were so much higher than the official rate, the Italian economy would be in a much healthier state than it actually is. Comparison among the tables shows, as is to be expected, that monetary methods of estimation give the highest figures for the underground economy. Such figures seem to be unrealistically high.

---

[33]Pre-pensioners are people who retire earlier than the compulsory retirement age, after completing a minimum number of working years. Since it is very difficult (impossible in the public sector) to fire workers, a decade or so ago a device was found to reduce employment by encouraging people to anticipate retirement. Essentially, pensions for anticipated retirement were made more generous. Many workers took this opportunity. Once they became pensioners or pre-pensioners, they started a second job: it was quite easy for them to find one in the hidden economy because they were still active and skilled, and most of all their employers did not pay social security contributions on their earnings.

[34]The average consumption level of pensioners is higher than that of blue collar workers in industry and agriculture. This cannot be fully explained by the shorter life expectancy.

[35]Patrizii V., "A Survey of Concealed Legal Employment in Italy," OECD (forthcoming).

VII. TAXATION OF WEALTH

Strictly speaking, there is only one tax on wealth in Italy. It is called the "tax on inheritance and gifts" (*Imposta sulle successioni e donazioni*). This is the only tax whose amount is determined by applying given tax rates to the current value of wealth. But wealth is also burdened by other taxes. The main ones are two local taxes, whose structure we will describe below in section IX—the "tax on the increments of value of land and real estate" (INVIM-*Imposta sugli incrementi di valore degli immobili*) and the "local income tax" (ILOR-*Imposta locale sui redditi*). There is also a special type of indirect tax, called "registration tax" (*Imposta di registro*), which is the oldest Italian tax on transactions *inter vivos*. Its survival in the present tax system, which is currently being modernized, is doubtful.

1. Major Structural Features of Estate and Gift Taxes

Gifts and bequests are subject to the same tax. The tax due at the moment of death cannot be avoided by making gifts during lifetime, because both transfers are taxed equally. The tax is progressive and is determined in two stages. In the first stage progressive rates are applied to the net value of the wealth transferred. Receivables and other rights to wealth are included, while liabilities are deducted. Also included are the goods and rights alienated by the deceased during the last six months of his or her life. In the second stage, progressive rates are applied to the separate amounts received by the different heirs or beneficiaries. The rates in the two stages are different. In the second stage, the rates vary depending on the closeness of kinship[36] but this does not hold for spouses and direct-line kinship.

The assessment of the tax base and tax liability is made by the revenue authority on the basis of the heirs' or beneficiaries' return. In doing so the revenue authority enjoys large discretionary power. This is thought to be responsible for evasion of the tax.

The registration tax generally yields more revenue than the tax on inheritance and gifts (in 1983 it was approximately 2,190 billion liras, against the 411 billion liras of the latter). It is generally considered a bad tax, costly and burdened by legal disputes.[37] It is

---

[36]The tax rates on total net value of wealth now vary from three percent for wealth of 30-50 million liras to 31 percent for wealth exceeding one billion liras. A new bill that is now in the process of approval by the Parliament will reduce rates significantly, both on total wealth and on individual inheritances.

[37]Much more than one-half of all legal disputes come from this tax.

also considered anachronistic and confusing, because its tax base is difficult to define. Three categories of taxable "items" can be singled out: (1) all "written acts," civil and commercial, (2) a large number of transfers of commodities and utilities listed expressly by the law (such as transfers or renting of real estate, takeovers, etc.), and (3) all other oral contracts, when they are required for court decisions. Assessments are based on the market value or selling price. Tax rates can be fixed, progressive or proportional. Economically, it is in essence a wealth tax, paid whenever the required transfers or contracts are made. The tax may be quite heavy, especially on real estate transfers where the seller is not a building firm. In this latter case the tax due is IVA. (The Tax Reform Act of 1973-74 has, in fact, envisaged the registration tax as an alternative and not a complement to IVA).

The registration tax is widely considered to be a major source of immobility in the real estate market, being a strong disincentive to the transfer of non-newly produced real estate.[38]

2. Methods of Avoidance

The general method of avoidance is the underestimation of the value of assets and transactions subject to the wealth taxes. Such values, as reported in the taxpayers' returns, are generally significantly lower than the market value of the assets or the actual value of the taxable transaction. However, even with this allowance, the revenue from the tax on inheritance and gifts is remarkably low, both in absolute value (411 billion liras in 1983) and as a percentage of total direct tax revenues (0.5 percent in 1983) or of GDP (0.1 percent in 1983).[39] The natural explanation for such low revenues is the coexistence of widespread legal and illegal tax avoidance. The most common legal way is to make fictitious sales instead of gifts, the former being less heavily taxed. In such cases great legal expertise and (costly) professional advice may be required, because the revenue authority can presume that certain sales between close relatives are fictitious substitutes for gifts, and the beneficiaries must prove the contrary. As to illegal avoidance, it is generally understood that this is made possible through the exploitation of the large discretionary power of tax assessment of the fiscal

---

[38]There are now temporary provisions to lighten this burden.

[39]The revenue from the local income tax (ILOR), a tax on the income from wealth, is much more significant. In 1983 it was 10.9 percent of total direct tax revenues, and 1.5 percent of GDP. The revenue from the inheritance and gift tax, which is a tax on wealth, appears remarkably low when compared to ILOR's revenue. This fact is widely regarded as indirect evidence of the high evasion of the inheritance tax.

administration, to the advantage of both taxpayers and civil servants themselves.

In Italy, there are no other lawful ways of avoiding inheritance taxation, such as the establishment of controlled nonprofit foundations in the United States or of discretionary trusts in the United Kingdom.

Finally, it must be noted that the actual tax burden for a given amount of wealth depends on its composition, because such assets as money, treasury bonds, jewelry, and antiques can change ownership without registration and therefore without paying any tax, while real estate cannot. But real estate and other registered assets are usually the largest part of inheritance transfers. A further explanation of the low yield of the gift and inheritance tax probably lies with tax on land value increments. This tax is, in fact, deductible from the inheritance and gift taxes, and thus absorbs most of its potential revenue.

3. Effects on the Distribution of Wealth

The philosophy underlying the tax on inheritance and gifts has always been that of redistributing unearned wealth among individuals, and this is the main reason for its high nominal progressivity. As a wealth redistributing tax, it has been widely considered superior to other taxes, on the assumption (which one may question) that it doesn't discourage work and saving. Nevertheless, in view of its very low revenue yield, the actual role played by this tax in the redistribution of wealth seems to have been a minor one so far.

VIII. DISTRIBUTION OF TAX BURDENS

1. Effective Income Tax Rates by Income Classes

The only estimates available so far of effective income tax rates by income classes in Italy are those by Visco, reported here in tables 13 and 14. Table 14 shows the effective national income tax rates by income classes on households, as reported on income tax returns. Table 14 shows the effective rates including the local income tax.

2. Overall Tax Burdens by Income Tax Class

Unfortunately, we do not have published, or even privately circulating, studies showing the distribution of the overall tax burdens by income classes, comparable to the Pechman-Okner estimates for the United States.

The most widely held belief among experts is that the Italian tax system is broadly proportional. The progressive income tax is not a "truly general" income tax, but rather a "special" one on some incomes, with a high level of (illegal) evasion by certain categories of income earners and extensive (legal) erosion of the tax base. Only wages and salaries and pensions are fully taxed; income from self-employment is only partly subject to withholding. It is also generally believed that IVA is slightly progressive, thanks to its multiple rates, but it is known to suffer from extensive evasion. Also the tax on inheritance and gifts is thought to be largely evaded, legally and illegally, because its revenue is unrealistically low.

There is no general agreement regarding the economic incidence of the payroll taxes. Views range from the belief that they are fully shifted onto prices to the assertion, especially by the business community, that they squeeze profits. The persistent request by the business community for fiscal relief from social security contributions (*fiscalizzazione*) is a sign that to some extent this may indeed be the case. With respect to exports, the nonshifting hypothesis seems to be the most likely.

IX. THE LOCAL TAX SYSTEM

Fiscal federalism in Italy is based almost entirely on a system of transfers from the central government to lower jurisdictions. Before the Tax Reform Act of 1973-74, the situation was different, especially for municipalities (*comuni*), whose finances were largely based on their own taxes. Concerning fiscal federalism, the main consequence of the 1973-74 Act was the abolition of local taxes. A new reform of the local tax system is now widely expected, and the present provisions should be regarded as temporary.

The choice of fiscal federalism based primarily on transfers from the central to the lower levels of government was grounded on the "dualistic" structure of the Italian economy. It was thought that, instead of gradually disappearing, dualities would have been accentuated by a territorially decentralized and autonomous local tax system. The rich areas would have become richer, and the poor ones poorer, as a result of the insufficiency of services provided through the limited budget of the poorest local administrations. After the experience of the past years, it is not unlikely that greater autonomy at the local level will be restored because the idea of taxation based on the benefit principle has gained ground.

But the "dualism" argument is still alive. It is likely that a reformed local tax system, based on a compromise between the two schools of thought, will emerge.

1. Major Taxes Used and Relationship to Taxes at the National Level

While abolishing most existing local taxes, the 1973-74 Act introduced what was meant to be the main new local tax, called the "local income tax" (ILOR). Contrary to the national individual and corporation income taxes, which are direct taxes, the local income tax is an *in rem* tax, whose taxable base is essentially all income except labor income[40] and the tax is collected fully through withholding: the local income tax is an *in rem* tax on "unearned income." It has a uniform proportional rate of 16.2 percent with occasional temporary additions. The local income tax is self-assessed according to the same basic rules as the national income tax rules, and it is filed with the same income tax returns.

Although it was originally conceived as a local tax, with the revenues going to the jurisdictions where the income was produced, this never happened. After 12 years, it is now evident that the real purpose of the local income tax has never been, not even marginally, that of financing local governments. Instead, the real purpose has been to impose "qualitative discrimination," that is, a comparatively heavier overall tax burden on nonlabor income. All of the revenues from the local income tax continues to go to the central government, pending the reform of the local tax system.

There are three decreasing levels of territorial decentralization: regions, provinces, and municipalities. Regions are the most recent local government institutions, having been established in the 1970s. Ninety-seven percent of their revenues are transfers from the central government. The rest is supplied by the annual license tax for driving (road fund tax) and other minor levies for the use of public land and goods. Regions in turn transfer 91 percent of their revenues to provinces and municipalities. Thus, the main economic function of the regions is either to "program" the economic activity of lower level jurisdictions, or simply to pass on, passively, any transfers received from the government.

Regions receive transfers from the central government through the formation of funds. One of these, called the "common fund"

---

[40]It is worthwhile noticing that the original 1973-74 Act distinguished between wages and salaries and income from self-employment, with only the former being exempted from the tax. In 1980, the Supreme Court (*Corte Costituzionale*) declared that such discrimination was unconstitutional.

(*Fondo Comune*) is built up from certain indirect tax revenues (such as those on tobacco, spirits, and the production of mineral oil) and other contributions. The fund is allocated among regions by applying certain coefficients to their population, unemployment rate, and tax burden. This fund is intended to finance the normal activities of regions. The other funds are tied to specific purposes. They are the "development fund" (mainly for agriculture), the "national health fund," the "national transportation fund," and others. The total amount of each fund is annually determined in the national budget.

Provinces have been progressively stripped of their original functions. Presently their revenues are less than one percent of GNP, and there are recurrent proposals to abolish them.

Municipalities are the oldest type of local government. Their functions are of two types: (1) their own functions, attributed to them by the national law, and (2) delegated functions, which are attributed by the fundamental law (*Costituzione*) to the regions and are, in turn, delegated by the regions to the municipalities. In practice the functions of the municipalities cover a large area, including metropolitan and rural police, housing and urban planning, health, social welfare and school assistance, trade licenses, control over retail prices, road maintenance, and others. Municipalities provide their services either directly or by establishing "municipal public enterprises."

Municipalities are financed by transfers from central government and regions, supplemented by their own local taxes. Municipalities are the only type of local government whose local tax revenues are not trivial.

Among local taxes, by far the most important is the tax on the increments of value of land and real estate (INVIM) which provides about 15 percent of total municipal revenues. This tax was introduced by the 1973-74 Act, and then extensively revised in 1980. Besides being the main truly local tax, it is also the only other tax on wealth, the more important one being on inheritance and gifts (see section VII). As a general rule, it is due only if, and when, ownership is transferred (by sale, inheritance, or gift). The tax base is the difference between the sale and acquisition price of the asset (standard INVIM). But for corporations the tax is due every 10 years, even if assets do not change hands (decennial INVIM). In this case the tax base is the difference between the current asset value and the value registered the last time the asset was taxed (the initial values were set in 1963). Rates are progressive beginning with five percent for up to a 20 percent increment in value, and rising to over 30 percent for increments of over 200 percent. The tax is assessed and collected by the central government, while the municipalities where the assets are located participate in the assessment and receive the revenue.

There are exemptions both from standard and decennial taxes. Exemptions from the standard tax include transfers between central and local governments, and other public or private non-profit institutions. Exemptions from the decennial tax include real estate owned by political parties represented in the national or regional assemblies, or used for recreation, sports, worship, and other social or cultural purposes. Also, rates are reduced to 25 percent for buildings of historical and archeological value.

Other municipal taxes are directly tied to specific services, such as refuse collection, use of public space for advertising, and the like. In 1983, and only for that year, local governments were allowed to levy a special surtax on real estate (called SOCOF), and 80 percent of the municipalities elected to do so. This was a relatively minor tax, but it is widely regarded as a tentative step towards new forms of local wealth taxation.

X. PROPOSALS FOR TAX REFORM

1. Government Initiatives

Three issues are now the subject of special consideration by the government: the local tax system, taxation of interest income on public bonds, and the annual revision of personal income tax rates.

1.1. The local tax system. Over the last few years there have been great expectations about the reform of the local tax system. Shortly after the tax reform enacted in 1973-74, the difficult financial situation of municipalities became apparent. Their own taxes had been abolished, and in place of these they were entitled to receive transfers from the central government. Since transfers were always made with some delays and were smaller than the foregone revenue, municipalities began stepping up their borrowing from the banking system. The growing interest charges increased expenditures, which were already being pushed upwards by inflation. This established a sort of "vicious circle." In the short run, the way out was to resort to periodic, annual, legislation at the national level, allowing increases in the rates of whatever municipal taxes still existed (such as those on refuse collection, advertising, dogs, etc.), or setting constraints to employment by local authorities to slow down the growth of expenditures. But in the long run a more general reform was needed to provide an appropriate new set of local taxes. As mentioned earlier (section IX), the special surtax on real estate, which was introduced only for the year 1983, was seen as a first step towards such a reform. Unfortunately, the expectations for a true local tax reform have so far been disappointing.

The government has prepared a proposal, soon to be submitted to Parliament, establishing a new local tax, called TASCO (*Tassa sui servizi comunali* Tax on Municipal Services). However, the proposal is so unclear and confused and its expected revenue so difficult to predict, that it hardly deserves to be considered a tax reform. The tax should have gone into effect in January 1986, but it is still under discussion. The tax would be based on the size of rooms, premises, and land situated within the municipal boundaries. Tax rates would be fixed per square meter in seven categories of buildings (houses, hotels, hospitals, etc.) and for four levels of services provided to them by the municipality.[41] The tax would be paid by the owner, or by the occupant of the flat or premises, and payment would be made in two stages, in October and in March. This new local tax would take the place of the two local taxes on refuse collection and on dogs.

Many criticisms have been raised against this new tax. One of them concerns the difficulty of estimating its revenue. Moreover, even allowing for uncertainty, it has been estimated that the revenue would very likely be less than the revenue from the tax on refuse collection, at least for Rome, Milan, and other major cities. It has also been pointed out that the new tax would be "unfair" because it would place a heavier burden on residential space than on office and trade space.

Apparently the benefit principle, recently reintroduced in academic and nonacademic debate, can be applied only in limited circumstances. The four tax rate levels envisaged for the services provided by the municipalities are the only instances where this principle may be applied.

2. Taxation of interest income on public bonds. No actual proposal for the taxation of interest income on public bonds is at present under discussion, but Finance Minister Visentini has publicly declared his agreement with the view that such interest income should be taxed sooner or later. According to the minister this is a large and major loophole in the Italian income tax system, which should be based on the ideal of a "comprehensive income tax."

---

[41]The assessment of the tax would practically follow that of the present refuse collection tax, which is something in between complete self-assessment and assessment by the authority. The taxpayer declares the information required for the computation. This is then performed by the municipality on the basis of the declared facts and the services provided by the municipality.

The unfairness of the exemption of public bond interest from tax is indisputable, but four problems should be borne in mind in this context: First, the whole area of taxation of financial incomes is presently in a messy state, and the problem of public bonds should be tackled within this wider context. Second, the net-of-tax return on government bonds is not completely independent from the real problem of financing a growing public deficit (now well above 15 percent of GNP). Third, if the return on government bonds must be kept high in order to finance the public deficit and if the return on government bonds plays a pivotal role in the determination of the general level of interest rates, elimination of the exemption would have serious consequences for the monetization of public debt, private investment demand, and the supply of saving.

1.3. Annual revision of personal income tax rates. The government will continue to take initiatives to revise, annually, the income tax rates, deductions, and exemptions. No indexing of rates and deductions is in sight. According to the present finance minister the "natural" and "democratic" way to implement tax policy is through annual government initiatives, submitted to Parliament, even given the present comparatively high inflation rate in Italy.

2. Academic Proposals

There are several academic proposals concerning individual aspects of the tax system, but no "systematic" ones concerning the tax system as a whole. The expected local tax reform has roots in the academic profession, which has in recent times rediscovered the benefit principle and, as a result, called for greater fiscal autonomy of local governments. Equally widespread in the academic profession is the view favoring a broadening of the income tax base, and at the same time a reduction of its tax rates. Also an increase of indirect taxation is now widely favored, whereas only 10 years ago the general attitude was negative.

The introduction of a property tax has been vigorously and constantly proposed by Cesare Cosciani over a period of at least 25 years. He has been, in fact, the most authoritative and influential, although not always successful, academic behind various government committees on tax reform. The last reform of 1973-74 disappointed Cosciani by not introducing a property tax. As a sort of substitute, the local income tax was introduced. The main supporters of the property tax are now the Socialist and Communist parties and the trade unions. The advocates of its introduction clearly wish to tie it to a reduction in income tax rates, which are generally regarded as high. Indeed, the reduction in income tax rates supported by these groups exceeds any other proposal.

A major concern in the academic profession has also been the revision of the rates and deductions under the income tax. There are several different proposals (see tables 15 and 16), but no new "ideas" have so far appeared, except for a proposal put forward by Campa.[42] He suggested that a deduction be allowed from the current year's total gross income (TGI-AGI) equal to the income tax paid by the taxpayer during the previous year. The device is equivalent to deducting a certain percentage of the previous year's income, namely the average tax rate on that income. The proposal (which was publicly discussed by the finance minister at a meeting of the European Research Center (CER)[43]) in January 1986, would reduce income tax progressivity in proportion both to the inflation rate and to the "personal" position of the individual taxpayer.

3. Business Views

The Confederation of Italian Industries (*Confindustria*) has never taken an official position on the tax reform, nor has it published or circulated any unofficial reports. One particular view, held by everybody in the business community, is that social security contributions are simply too high, especially if compared with other competing countries. Probably as a result of business lobbying the government has granted another six months of "*fiscalizzazione*" (social security contributions' relief) until June 1986.

4. Trade Union Views

Two major unions have produced their own proposals for revising the income tax schedule (see table 15). Apart from these proposals no general, official position on the tax system has been worked out. It is known that the unions continue to press strongly for the introduction of a property tax and for widening further the (statutory) tax gap between wage and salary income and income from self-employment, on the ground that the latter is subject to more evasion.

---

[42]G. Campa, "L'IVA: situazione attuale e prospettive di riforma" in CER, n. 2., 1984.

[43]The statutory activity of the Center of Economic Research in Rome consists in publishing six bimonthly reports analyzing and forecasting developments in the Italian economy over the medium and long term.

5. Prospects for Tax Reform

Substantial changes of the present tax system are not in sight. As for income tax, a broadening of the tax base to include interest on public bonds may be expected. At the same time, a reduction in individual income tax rates may also be expected, not only in connection with the broadening of the tax base, but also in view of the still high rate of inflation and of the likely introduction of some type of property tax. There will probably be annual revisions of tax rates and of income and tax deductions, since neither the government nor the unions (the opposition) are keen on indexation, which would reduce the basis for bargaining between the government, the unions, and the employers. The property tax, if introduced, is likely to be a local one, because there is now a much wider disposition than in the past in favor of greater financial autonomy of local governments.

APPENDIX A

THE VISENTINI PACKAGE OF 1985 AND THE 1986 BILL

The Visentini Package is a government decree of December 1984 number 853, which was approved with some changes by Parliament on February 17, 1985. The importance of this Act, composed of five articles, is primarily due to the following provisions:

1. After a long debate, the Act reduced the number of value-added tax rates from eight to four (without considering the zero rate, see footnote 18).
2. It reintroduces a "forfeit" system for the assessment of both value-added tax and income tax for small business. In addition, it limited the possibility of splitting income among family members to a maximum of 49 percent of unincorporated business income and introduced limited taxation of financial capital gains (see section I).

Another Visentini bill is in process of gaining approval by Parliament. It contains new revisions of income tax rates and tax deductions, lower gift and inheritance tax rates on direct transmissions, and a temporary tax credit for reinvested profits (see section II).

The problem of the local tax system is at present being dealt with at the proposal level: the proposed new "hybrid" tax, called TASCO (see section X.1), is not yet in the form of a bill.

APPENDIX B
The 'Balancing Tax' for Corporations

The logic, definition and computation of the balancing tax on corporations are illustrated by means of the diagram below. Let t_p be the (proportional) tax rate on corporate profits, and t_p the marginal tax rate on the shareholder. Let P be total profits of a given corporation, and suppose they are divided into a taxable part, P_T, and an exempt part, P_E. Under the tax credit system for the taxation of distributed profits, there are essentially two possible cases.

1. The first case is when the amount of distributed profits D is less than, or equal to, that part of taxable profits which is left after subtracting the tax: $(1 - t_p)P_T$ (the area $P_T - T$ in the diagram). In this case the tax credit system as described in the text needs no correction, because the tax credit $D \dfrac{t_p}{1-t_p}$ to be added to D and then subtracted from the income tax liability of the shareholder will by definition be less than, or equal to, the tax liability T of the corporation. For simplicity it is assumed in the diagram that $D = P_T - T$, i.e., that the amount of distributed profits D is *exactly equal* to the amount of taxable profits left over after deducting the personal income tax liability T, but there is no loss of generality in doing so.

2. The second case is when the amount of distributed profits exceeds, say by ΔD, the amount $P_T = T$. Here if the simple application of the tax credit was applied to total distributed profits, the tax credit would be $(D + \Delta D) \dfrac{t_p}{1-t_p}$. This would amount to extending the tax exemption granted to the P part of the corporate profits to the individual shareholder for whatever part of such exempt profits is distributed, in this case ΔD. In other words, this ΔD part of total distributed profits would remain untaxed under the individual income tax as well as under the corporate tax (except to the extent to which the individual marginal rate t_p differs from the corporate rate t_p). But if the fiscal authority wishes to tax exempt distributed profits under the individual income tax, then, the additional tax credit $\Delta D \dfrac{t_p}{1-t_p} = \Delta T$.

The corporation's total tax liability would become $T + \Delta T$ (one can envisage in the diagram that if $\Delta D = 0$, then also $\Delta T = 0$, while as

Δ D increases also Δ T increases, up to the point where the two areas, meet, and there are no more exempted profits). This is presently the case in Italy, with $\Delta D \dfrac{t_p}{1-t_p} = \Delta T$ being the amount of the *balancing tax* (recall from the text that $t_p = 0.36$, and therefore

$$\frac{t_p}{1-t_p} = \frac{0.36}{1-0.36} = \frac{0.36}{0.64} = \frac{9}{16}.$$

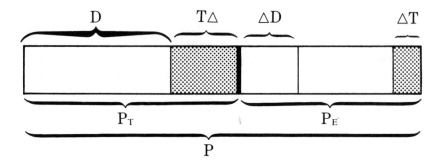

Table 1
Individual Income Tax Rates, 1976, 1983, 1986

1976		1983		1986	
Taxable Income (millions of liras)	Tax Rate (percent)	Taxable Income (millions of liras)	Tax Rate (percent)	Taxable Income (millions of liras)	Tax Rate (percent)
0-3	10	0-11	18	0-6	12
3-4	13	11-24	27	6-12	22
4-5	16	24-30	35	12-30	28
5-6	19	30-38	37	30-50	34
6-7.5	22	38-60	41	50-100	41
7.5-9	25	60-120	47	100-150	48
9-11	27	120-250	56	150-300	53
11-13	29	250-500	62	300-600	58
13-15	31	500 and over	65	600 and over	62
15-17	32				
17-19	33				
19-22	34				
22-25	35				
25-30	36				
30-35	38				
35-40	40				
40-50	42				
50-60	44				
60-80	46				
80-100	48				
100-125	50				
125-150	52				
150-175	54				
175-200	56				
200-250	58				
250-300	60				
300-350	62				
350-400	64				
400-450	66				
450-500	68				
500-550	70				
550 and over	72				

Table 2
Nonpersonal Deductions Under the Income Tax, 1986

1. The local income tax (ILOR)

2. Interest paid on mortgage loans, up to 4 million liras

3. Interest paid on agricultural loans

4. Medical expenses (surgical, dental, and specialist care)[a]

5. Funeral expenses, up to one million liras

6. School and college fees (up to the corresponding fees of state schools and colleges)

7. Compulsory social security contributions

8. Noncompulsory social security contributions and life insurance premiums, up to 2.5 million liras

9. Maintenance and restoration expenses for historical and artistic buildings[b]

10. Alimony

[a]Care by nonspecialists is deductible only in part.

[b]In the 1985 Act, these deductions were made dependent on both the "necessity" of the expenses for the preservation of the estate and the "certification" of such expenses. This clarification was needed to prevent evasion.

Table 3
Personal Tax Credits Under the Income Tax, 1985

Item	Tax Credit (liras)	
Standard Exemptions		
Individual income up to 10 million liras	96,000	(36,000 in 1974)
10 million liras or more	36,000	
Family Size		
Spouse (at home)	282,000	(36,000 in 1974)
Up to four children	21,000	(7,000 in 1974)
Fifth child	36,000	
Sixth and seventh child	49,000	
Eighth child	106,000	
Ninth child or more	134,000	
Other Credits		
Wages and salaries and pensions up to 5,000,000	180,000	(36,000 in 1974)
Wages, salaries, pensions (for the cost of producing income)	296,000	
Lump-sum tax credit in place of income deductions (wages and salaries only)	18,000	(12,000 in 1974)
Extra Deductions		
Wages, salaries, and pensions:		
Up to 10.6 million liras	381,000	
10.6-11.8 million liras	325,000	
11.8-14.0 million liras	183,000	
14.0-17.7 million liras	99,000	
17.7-18.8 million liras	71,000	
Self-employed and noncorporate business:		
Up to 7 million liras	235,000	
7-14 million liras	117,000	

Table 4
Financial Assets of Households, Selected Years, 1965-84
(Billions of Liras)

Asset	1965	1970	1975	1980	1984
Currency	310	423	1,411	2,717	2,647
Bank deposits	1,424	4,011	12,784	20,727	29,623
Postal deposits	351	156	2,056	3,695	5,664
Other deposits	104	172	725	414	4,287
BOT	—	—	55	14,173	19,136
Bonds	687	642	2,429	−1,196	39,174
Shares	−35	230	393	714	1,181
Other financial assets	314	527	1,231	4,386	6,874
Net assets on the rest of the world	189	891	255	273	161
Total	3,344	7,052	21,339	45,903	108,747

Source: Bank of Italy, *Annual Report*, various years.

Table 5
Withholding Tax Rates on Investment Income, 1986

Type of investment	Tax base	Rate of withholding[a] (percent)
Private bonds	Interest, premiums, and purchase discount	12.5[b]
Public bonds	Interest	not taxed
Bank acceptances	All returns	15.0
Deposits and bank and postal current accounts	Interest and premiums due by residents and nonresidents	25.0
	Interest paid by the Bank of Italy to other banks	not taxed
	Interest on interbank current accounts	25.0
Securities	All returns	18.0
Dividends	Dividends paid	10.0[d]
	Other distributions	30.0[e]
Premiums and winnings	Premiums and winnings, except those administered by the State:	
	charity lottery	10.0
	radio and television quizzes	20.0
	others	30.0
Other income from capital	Income from capital other than dividends, and interest on bonds	15.0
	Interest paid by cooperative societies	10.0
Redeemed life insurance[f] during the last five years		10.0

[a]In general, although not always, withholding represents a final payment for individuals and a partial one for corporations.

[b]Nonresidents are subject to a 30 percent withholding rate.

[c]Interest on public bonds is no longer tax free for corporations. They can deduct their interest payments from taxable income when they exceed exempt investment income.

[d]Plus tax credit.

[e]When corporations are exempted from the corporate tax and when the receivers are nonresidents.

[f]Subject to individual income tax, but at a reduced rate.

Table 6
Interest Rates and Rates of Return, Selected Years, 1965-82
(Percent)

Asset	1965	1970	1975	1980	1981	1982
Bank deposits:						
Current accounts	3.45	4.98	7.53	11.50	13.75	14.6
Savings accounts	3.74	4.72	8.20	12.43	14.87	15.4
Postal deposits	2.52	3.60	6.00	8.00	8.00	8.00
Short-term						
Treasury bonds	3.63	6.95	12.04	15.94	20.56	20.90
Long-term						
Treasury bonds	5.40	7.70	10.00	14.20	19.36	20.22
Private bonds	6.70	8.60	10.60	15.40	19.78	20.62
Shares	4.60	4.10	4.90	2.40	1.89	2.24

Sources: Bank of Italy, Economic Bulletin, various years.

Table 7
Rates of Social Security Contributions on Wages and Salaries
in Several Sectors, 1985
(Percent)

| | Industry | | | | |
Payor	Non-building	Building	Handi-craft	Trade	Financial
	Blue Collar Workers				
Rate on employer	45.93	49.28	41.23	39.51	41.45
Rate on employee	8.65	8.65	8.65	8.65	8.65
Total rate	55.58	57.93	49.88	48.16	50.10
	White Collar Workers				
Rate on employer	41.48	41.83	38.98	39.51	39.70
Rate on employee	8.65	8.65	8.65	8.65	8.65
Total rate	50.13	50.48	47.63	48.16	48.35

Source: A. Di Majo, "Struttura tributaria e struttura economica. Il prelievo sulle imprese," Relazione al Convegno di Pavia su "Il sistema tributario oggi e domani," 11-12 ottobre, 1985.

Table 8
Social Security Contributions: Percent of Tax Revenue and of GDP, 1981-84

Ratio	1981	1982	1983	1984
Estimates by A. Di Majo				
Percent of total revenue	39.6	39.3	38.0	37.9
Percent of GDP	14.7	15.7	16.3	16.2
Estimates by OECD				
Percent of total revenue	37.89	37.41	35.87	
Percent of GDP	13.08	14.03	14.56	

Sources: A. Di Majo, (see table 9) 1985, and Revenue Statistics of OECD Member Countries 1965-1984, (Paris, 1985).

Table 9
Economic Accounts of Social Security by Agency, 1978-1982
(Billions of Liras)

Agency	1978	1979	1980	1981	1982
			Revenues		
Total revenue	55,173	69,581	82,587	103,544	123,713
Public Agencies	47,736	60,533	71,474	90,335	108,149
Social con-					
tributions	31,082	39,227	48,860	59,145	71,622
Other					
contributions	15,538	20,093	21,201	29,413	34,615
Private Agencies	7,517	9,158	11,228	13,339	15,712
Social con-					
tributions	7,250	8,833	10,843	12,878	15,166
Other					
contributions	260	317	377	450	533
			Expenditures		
Total expenditures	51,719	62,910	77,220	101,672	119,521
Public Agencies	47,510	58,146	71,566	94,064	110,387
Social services	43,792	51,672	65,027	86,449	102,799
Other					
contributions	671	3,022	2,212	3,163	2,519
Private Agencies	4,289	4,874	5,769	7,738	9,282
Social services	4,199	4,769	5,651	7,597	9,121
Other					
contributions	6	6	8	11	13
			Balances		
Public Agencies	226	2,387	-92	-3,729	-2,238
Private Agencies	3,228	4,284	5,459	5,601	6,430
Total	3,454	6,671	5,367	1,872	4,192

Source: G. Panella, "Il contributo del sistema previdenziale al disavanzo della pubblica amministrazione" in "Il deficit pubblico: origini e problemi," Milano, Angeli, 1984. Figures do not add to totals because some revenues and expenditures are not shown.

Table 10
Economic Accounts of Social Security, By Functions, 1978-1982
(Billions of Liras)

Function	1978	1979	1980	1981	1982
			Health		
Revenue	12,358	18,602	19,625	21,867	21,331
Social con- tributions	6,274	7,557	8,948	9,973	14,244
Other contributions	5,668	10,586	10,383	11,552	6,684
Expenses	12,639	16,335	20,739	23,464	27,621
Services	10,645	13,073	16,552	20,827	25,140
Services less contributions	-4,371	-5,516	-7,604	-10,854	-13,277
Revenue Expenses	-281	2,267	-1,114	-1,597	-6,290
			Pensions		
Revenue	33,495	39,791	51,699	63,908	82,185
Social con- tributions	24,808	31,670	40,012	49,172	57,278
Other contributions	8,018	7,391	10,681	13,335	23,337
Expenses	32,974	39,578	50,579	66,035	78,024
Services	30,133	35,128	44,426	59,989	71,269
Services less contributions	-4,325	-3,458	-4,414	-10,817	-13,991
Revenue Expenses	521	213	-1,120	-2,127	4,161
			Welfare		
Revenue	3,332	3,728	4,388	6,164	6,875
Contributions	3,301	3,758	4,375	6,129	6,836
Expenses	3,346	3,875	4,486	6,169	6,984
Services	3,014	3,471	4,049	5,633	6,390
Revenue Expenses	-14	-93	-98	-5	-109

Source: Same as table 9. Figures do not add to totals because some revenues and expenditures are not shown.

Table 11
Distribution Between Those Working and Not Working,
by the Official Status of Workers, 1976

Type of Worker	Total	Percent Working	Percent Not Working
Employed	18,252	100.0	—
Seeking first occupation	819	13.6	86.4
Unemployed	431	27.8	72.2
Pensioners	6,551	11.5	88.5
Home help	11,029	9.9	90.1
Students	11,873	2.0	98.0
Disabled	529	9.6	90.4
Not declared	823	4.7	95.3

Source: Censis, *L'occupazione occulta*, Roma, 1976

Table 12
Estimates of the Size of the Hidden Economy in Italy

Year	Percent of GDP	Percent of Working Force
Participation Rates Method		
1965	4.2	9.6
1969	6.3	14.0
1973	7.6	17.2
1974	4.9	11.1
1976	13.9	31.3
1977	20.0[a]	31.5[a]
1978	22.0	34.6
1980	10.0-20.0	17.0-30.0
Cash-to-Deposit Ratio		
1968	9.6	14.4
1970	18.0	27.0
1972	22.2	33.3
1974	25.0	37.5
1976	24.6	36.9
1978	30.1	45.1
Other Methods		
1968-73	17.7	26.6
1968-76	15.0	22.5
1960-78	11.4	17.1
1982	20.6	30.9

Sources: B. Contini, "Lo sviluppo di un' economia parallela," Edizioni Comunita, 1979; Censis, *L' occupazione occulta*, 1976; G. Alvaro, "L'Italia sommersa che non paga le tasse," Mondoperaio, n. 2, 1979; L. Frey, "Il lavoro nero nel 77 in Italia," Tendenze dell' occupazione CISL, n. 6, 1978; F. Forte, "I conti dell' economia sommersa," Mondoperaio, n. 2, 1979: D'Aragona; A. Saba, *L'industria sommersa ed il nuovo modello di sviluppo*, Marsilio, 1980; R. Ricci, *Alcune stime dell' evasione statistica nel ramo manifatturiero in Italia, Rivista di Economia e Politica Industriale*, 1978; Frey and Weck, "Estimating a Shadow: A Naive Approach to Hidden Economy Measurement," *Oxford Economic Papers*, n. 1, 1983; M. Deaglio, "Economia sommersa e analisi economica," Giappichelli, 1985; V. Patrizil, *A survey of Concealed Legal Employment in Italy*, OECD, Paris, (forthcoming).

[a]Estimates by Frey. Estimates by Contini for same year are 14-20 percent of GDP and 31-45 percent of working force.

Table 13
Effective National Individual Income Tax Rate on Wages and Salaries and Other Income, By Income Classes, 1977-83
(Percent)

Income Classes (millions of liras)	1977		1979		1981		1983	
	Wages and Salaries	Other Income	Wages and Salaries	Other Income	Wages and Salaries	Other Income	Wages and Salaries	Other Income
0-5	8.56	11.08	9.04	11.08	6.16	11.08	4.20	12.08
5-6	10.30	12.40	10.70	12.4	8.30	12.40	6.50	13.07
6-7	12.31	13.77	12.31	13.77	10.26	13.77	8.14	15.20
7-8	13.71	14.99	13.71	14.99	11.91	14.99	9.38	15.55
8-9	14.97	16.1	14.97	16.1	13.37	16.10	10.33	15.82
9-10	16.17	17.19	16.17	17.19	14.73	17.19	11.58	16.04
10-15	20.58	21.26	20.58	21.26	19.62	21.26	17.80	20.16
15-20	23.63	24.15	23.63	24.15	22.92	24.15	20.52	21.87
20-30	27.52	27.86	27.52	27.86	27.04	27.86	24.28	25.18
30-50	32.71	32.92	32.71	32.92	32.43	32.92	30.33	30.87

Source: V. Visco, "Disfunzioni ed iniquita dell' IRPEF e possibili alternative: una analisi del funzionamento dell' imposta sul reddito in Italia nel periodo 77/83," "La crisi dell' imposizione progressiva sul reddito," *Angeli*, 1984.

Table 14
Effective National and Local Individual Income Tax Rates on Individual Income, by Income Classes, 1980

Income Classes (millions of liras)	Total Income Taxes	National Income Tax	Local Income Tax
0-6	5.67	4.92	0.75
6-11	12.29	12.29	0.0
11-19	19.03	17.7	1.33
19-30	25.12	22.73	2.34
30-50	29.7	26.99	2.71
50-80	34.53	31.55	2.98
80-100	38.08	34.95	3.13
100-150	40.70	37.54	3.16
150-200	43.73	40.76	2.97
200 and up	50.26	47.13	3.13
Total	14.49	13.72	0.77

Source: Same as table 13.

Values of the parameters used in the function: $y_n = ay^b$

National income tax: $a = 1.135$, $b = 0.873$, $r^2 = 0.9997$
National plus local income tax: $a = 1.1523$, $b = 0.8599$, $r^2 = 0.9996$

Table 15
Tax Reform Proposals, 1986
(Liras, except as indicated)

Feature	Visco-PCI[a]	PLI[b]	CGIL[c]	UIL[d]
Minimum rate (percent)	17	25	27	26
Maximum rate (percent)	55	50	65	55
Income Deductions:				
Wages, salaries and pensions	—	4,000 plus percentage of income	6,500	7,200
No dependent income	—	4,000	—	2,400
Family size	—	4,500[e]	—	—
Minimum exempt	6,560	—	—	—
Tax Deductions:				
Wages, salaries and pensions	600[f]	—	24	24
No dependent income	200	—	—	—
Family size	396[g]	—	396	396

[a]Communist Party
[b]Liberal Party
[c]The major trade union
[d]Another important trade union
[e]Splitting is allowed
[f]Plus an extra deduction (125,000 liras) for income less than 11 million liras
[g]Plus an extra deduction (100,000 liras) for stay-at-home spouse older than 60

Table 16
Effective National Individual Income Tax Rates Under Various Tax Reform Proposals, by Income Classes
(Percent)

Income Class (liras)	Visco-PCI[a]	PLI[b]	CGIL[c]	UIL[d]
0-10	9.7	10.0	8.4	7.3
10-20	17.5	15.0	17.7	16.6
20-30	19.7	16.7	20.8	19.8
30-40	23.0	17.5	24.3	23.3

[a]Communist Party
[b]Liberal Party
[c]The major trade union
[d]Another important trade union

CHAPTER 6

Federal Republic of Germany

Annette Dengel
Translated by Birgit Schneider

INTRODUCTION

The German tax system reflects the Federal structure of the Federal Republic of Germany which is subdivided into three levels: the Federal Government, the Lander governments, and the local governments. Under the German Constitution (Fundamental Law), the Federal Government and the Lander independently administer their finances, i.e., they collect and administer their own revenue and spend their own resources. For local governments, "adequate autonomy" is expected. The Federal Government and the Lander are responsible for providing for a certain degree of uniformity of living conditions within the Federal territory.[1]

With a view to its tasks and duties, each government level is entitled to an adequate revenue flow. The distribution of tax sources to the different levels is laid down in the Fundamental Law. After the fiscal reform of 1969, the tax system has developed from a separate system to a tax-sharing system, though some elements of the former system still persist. In accordance with the Fundamental Law, revenue from customs duties—although all such revenue is paid over to the European Economic Community (EEC)—and from taxes on consumption (such as mineral oil,

---

[1]The term "certain degree of uniformity of living conditions" is used in the German Constitution. It means that German citizens should have similar living and working conditions and that there should not be large differences between rich and poor regions.

coffee, tea, and sugar) is reserved for the Federal Government. The Lander governments may, among other things, dispose of yields from the tax on beer, the wealth tax, inheritance taxes, and motor vehicle taxes. Finally, local governments derive revenue from property taxes and the local business taxes (the *Realsteuern*), and from local taxes on consumption, and excise taxes.

The tax sharing structure of the German tax system manifests itself in "joint taxes," the yields of which are allocated according to certain quotas to the Federal, the Lander, and the local.[2] Joint taxes are the individual income tax, the corporation income tax, and the value-added tax. On account of their substantial yields (in 1984 the individual income tax accounted for 41 percent of total tax collection, the corporation income tax six percent, and the value-added tax 27 percent), these taxes form the main pillars of the German tax system.

All three government levels share in the revenue from both individual income tax and the wage tax. A 15 percent share of these taxes is allocated to local governments; the remainder is equally shared by the Federal Government and the Lander governments. One half of the revenue from the capital yields tax and the corporation income tax is allocated to the Federal Government, the other to the Lander governments.

The Federal Government and the Lander share the value-added tax. The allocation quotas are revised at regular intervals; for the years 1986 and 1987 they are 65 percent for the Federal Government and 35 percent for the Lander governments. As this distribution does not meet the fiscal needs of the Lander, a 1.5 percent share of the value-added tax is paid by the Federal Government from its share as a supplementary grant to the financially weak Lander. Moreover, the Federal Government pays a financial contribution to the EEC from its value-added tax share. It follows that the actual share in the value-added tax available to the Federal Government for covering its own fiscal needs is smaller than the share suggested by the allocation quota.

Differences in the financial resources of the Lander governments are offset by a fiscal equalization scheme. Under this scheme, those Lander governments with an above-average fiscal capacity pay an equalization amount to their financially weak counterparts. Here again, the value-added tax is of special importance. Whereas the

---

[2]The quotas for the allocation of the individual income tax and the corporation income tax are set in the German Constitution. The quota of the value-added tax, which changes every two years, is set by discussion between the Federal and Lander governments.

Lander taxes are distributed among the Lander governments according to regional collections, the share in the value-added tax is determined by the number of inhabitants. Earlier, the financially weak Lander received up to 25 percent of the Lander share in the value-added tax in the form of supplementary quotas. In principle, the revenue from the personal income tax and the corporation income tax is distributed according to regional collections. For technical reasons, the distribution of the corporation income tax is determined by the site of production plants, while that of the wage tax is determined by employees' residences.

Special regulations apply to Berlin. Although not differing in its relations with the Federal Government from the other Lander governments, Berlin does not participate in the fiscal equalization scheme between the Lander. Instead, the Federal Government gives financial support by means of subsidies and loans. In addition, with a view to the special status of Berlin, financial grants are, in some instances, paid from the Federal budget for particular purposes (e.g., air travel subsidies, reimbursement of costs arising from the transit agreement, cultural measures, etc.).[3] The yields of the major government revenue sources in 1970, 1975, 1980, and 1985 are given in table 1.

I. THE INDIVIDUAL INCOME TAX

The base of the individual income tax, which is the largest single tax, basically includes the total income of the taxpayer. Any individual who has a residence or a normal place of domicile within the country is fully subject to taxation. Individuals who are not residents, or ordinarily domiciled within the country, are liable to the individual income tax only on their domestic revenue. The income tax law lists seven forms of revenue: farming and forestry; business; professional activities; wages and salaries; returns on capital, leasing and letting, and other sources (e.g., speculative gains.).

As a rule, only monetary income is subject to tax. However, some payments in kind (e.g., in agriculture) are also required to be included in taxable income; in practice they are either left out of account or considered negligible. Imputed income is hardly considered under the tax law. Only in the case of owner-occupied dwellings is a utilization value included in the tax base as revenue from letting or leasing.

---

[3]Financial grants are paid for special purposes; subsidies can be used for any governmental purpose.

As a matter of principle, capital gains are taxed when realized, but the taxation of gains is not uniform. The tax law differentiates between individual and business capital gains. Individual capital gains are tax free unless they derive from speculative transactions or from the sales of substantial holdings. Business capital gains as a rule are fully included in the tax base and are subject to the ordinary income tax rates. Here again there are exceptions. Business capital gains are tax free if earmarked to cover the purchase or production costs of newly acquired assets. Realized capital gains from the sales of certain production plants or parts of production plants, of business shares in the form of substantial holdings, or of assets that serve professional activities, carry tax privileges such as high limits of tax exemption, high free allowances, or the application of only half of the tax rates.

All expenditures to acquire, secure, and/or maintain revenue (so-called operational expenses and costs incurred in earning income) can be fully deducted from income. There are also deductions for old age relief, expenses for special items, and extraordinary expenses. The income tax rate scale is applied to this "taxable income" or the tax base (table 2). For 1986, it is divided into four sections:

- Up to 4,536 DM of the taxable income of an unmarried person (9,072 DM of a married couple) is exempt from tax;
- Taxable income from 4,557 DM to 18,000 DM is subject to a flat (marginal) tax rate of 22 percent if the taxpayer is unmarried (9,072 to 36,000 DM for married couples);
- Marginal tax rates ranging from 22 to 56 percent are applied to taxable incomes between 18,001 and 130,000 DM (36,001 to 260,000 DM for married couples);
- Taxable income above 130,000 DM and 260,000 DM, respectively, is subject to a flat marginal rate of 56 percent.

The individual income tax is collected in two ways: either by self-assessment or by withholding tax at source. The latter method is applied to wages and investment incomes. In the case of self-assessment, the taxpayer sends his return to the tax office. He or she is then notified by a notice of assessment to pay taxes. The tax table used for withholding taxes on wages is derived from the income tax rates, after allowing for the tax free amounts for employees and their families and a "standard deduction" for costs incurred in earning income. Therefore, the same tax table is applied to the income of the self-assessed taxpayer and to wages and salaries.

The tax due is withheld by the employer from the gross wage and paid to the tax office. Whereas advance payments on incomes not subject to withholding are due every three months, taxes on wages are paid every month by virtue of the deduction-at-source approach. Unlike assessment on the basis of filed returns, withholding at source in the case of wages entails low costs of collection and administration for the tax office, as the bulk of such costs is shifted to the business enterprises.

Investment incomes are also taxed at source. The withholding tax applies to certain kinds of domestic investment incomes (such as dividends and interest); it is collected by the payor and is paid directly to the tax office. The withholding rate is 25 percent, with no deductions. When filing a tax return, the taxpayer credits the withholding tax on investment income against the individual income tax. If they are not taxed at source, investment incomes must be declared by the taxpayer on his or her income tax return. The taxpayer is entitled to an exemption on income from savings of 300 DM if unmarried (600 DM in the case of married couples).

The share of each of these three methods of collection in the overall income tax yield is very different. For 1984 the figures are as follows: the tax on wages 81 percent; investment income tax three percent; and tax on the income of the self-assessed taxpayer 16 percent.

Separate or joint assessment is optional for married couples. In the case of separate assessment, each spouse is taxed on the basis of his/her own income. When the couple is assessed jointly, taxation follows the splitting method. In this case, the incomes earned by both spouses are added together and divided by two. The tax rate is then applied to the resulting half. The computed tax is multiplied by two to obtain the tax to be paid by the married couple. Under the progressive tax scale, the splitting method usually results in lower taxes than separate assessment.

Apart from income splitting for married couples, the income tax law provides tax relief for families with children, among which the most important is the children's allowance. It is granted for each child of the taxpayer and, as of 1986, amounts to 2,484 DM. In addition, education expenses on behalf of children and, in the case of unmarried persons, the costs of the care of children if they represent an extraordinary expense, can be deducted up to a certain maximum. Single persons with children are entitled to a household exemption.

The individual income tax does not provide for automatic inflation adjustments. As a consequence, during periods of inflation a growing number of taxpayers move upward in the progressive tax scale. This "bracket creep" has so far been moderated only with half-hearted measures, e.g., by raising basic personal exemptions and by broadening the tax brackets. The proposed tax reform of

1986-88 will bring about a change in the tax rates which will alleviate this problem (see section X).

A major criticism of the income tax is that the basic personal exemptions are hardly sufficient to cover minimum subsistence levels. However, a tax scale which would exempt such amounts is impracticable for fiscal reasons. Another criticism of the income tax is that the initial tax rate of 22 percent is too high and that progression within the range of the first zone of progression rises too fast.

II. THE CORPORATION INCOME TAX

The corporation income tax is paid on the income of nonnatural (i.e., juridical) persons, groups of persons, and funds. Companies having their management or registered site within the country are liable to tax on their entire income, including income from abroad. Companies which do not have management or their registered site within the country pay the West German corporation income tax only on their income in Germany. The tax base is similar to the taxable income as defined for the individual income tax law, but there are significant special provisions in the corporation income tax. The tax rates are (see table 2):

- Fifty-six percent of taxable income of joint stock companies, cooperatives, and private endowments, when the imputation method is applied;
- Fifty percent of the taxable income of mutual insurance companies, nonprofit associations, private law institutions and special purpose funds and of the domestic production plants of foreign corporations when they do not pay dividends or when their payees do not use the imputation method for their dividends;
- Thirty-six percent of distributed profits.

It is clear from the above that the German corporation income tax consists of a split rate for retained and distributed profits. For the 36 percent tax on distributed profits, a tax credit is granted to the shareholder which he can deduct from his individual income tax. Under the imputation method, the shareholder in the end pays only the individual income tax. In the event that the shareholder does not owe individual income tax or that his individual income tax is lower than the imputable corporation income tax, he receives a refund. The purpose of the imputation method is to avoid double taxation of distributed profits at the corporate and shareholder levels. Thus, the corporation tax on distributed earnings is, in effect, a withholding tax.

Corporations file their tax returns at the end of the business year, but they make tax payments every three months during the year. In the case of corporation income tax, an exemption of 5,000 DM is granted. If the income of the corporation exceeds 10,000 DM, the allowance is cut by half of the excess amount. Farming and forestry undertakings are granted a free allowance of 30,000 DM. The German Railways, the Federal Postal Administration—being the two largest state-owned enterprises—the *Bundesbank*, nonprofit housing companies, political parties, and professional organizations, are exempt from corporation income tax.

In the discussion of corporation taxation, the following criticisms are often expressed:

1. Corporations, unlike unincorporated firms, are subject to the wealth tax (see section VII), which is not deductible from the assessed profits on which corporation income tax is levied. This discriminatory treatment of corporations could be remedied were the wealth tax considered deductible in the assessment of taxable profits. This appears all the more desirable as the wealth tax must be paid even in the absence of profits. Therefore, in years marked by losses, corporations are hit harder than unincorporated firms.

2. Corporation income tax strongly influences corporations' choice between equity and borrowed capital financing. Being deductible, interest on borrowed capital reduces taxable profits and as such is not subject to corporation income tax. Corporations' equity is subject to a wealth tax which cannot be deducted from assessed profits and, as a consequence, is also subject to corporation income tax. Borrowed capital, on the other hand, is deductible from the wealth tax base, i.e., is exempt from the wealth tax. Despite the tax imputation method, equity financing is, as a result of the nondeductibility of the wealth tax from the tax base, more expensive than borrowed capital (by roughly 25 percent).

3. Equity financing through retained earnings often proves to be more difficult for corporations than for unincorporated firms. Although the corporation income tax rate and the top marginal income tax rate are identical, that is, 56 percent, corporate equity financing is at a disadvantage. This is the case when the individual income tax rates of the partners of unincorporated firms are lower than the corporation income tax rate, which is rather likely for small- or medium-sized firms. Theoretically, corporations can adjust the tax on equity financing to that of unincorporated firms by distributing all of their profits at the reduced corporate rate and then accepting reinvestment of the funds required for new investment ("distribute-and-call-back-policy").

The corporation income tax on distributed profits is offset either by the tax credit or by the tax refund. In practice, however, the offset is not complete; profits are as a rule liable to church tax (approximately nine percent), and their reinvestment is subject to a tax of one percent (*Gesellschaft-Steuer*). Furthermore, profit distribution and reinvestment are practical only when the shareholder is not anonymous and agrees to the reinvestment. But his consent will depend on the size of the shareholder's total income and on his ability to reinvest his distributed share in light of the fact that he does not actually realize the tax credit until he is assessed for income tax.

4. Finally, the imputation method, the identity of the corporation income tax rate, and the top individual income tax rate have contributed to the alleviation of the conflict of interest between controlling and small shareholders, but have not entirely eliminated it.

III. SAVING AND INVESTMENT INCENTIVES IN THE TAX SYSTEM

The Federal Republic has a double track system of saving incentives: first, there are tax preferences for certain forms of saving; and second, there is a bonus for saving (see table 3).

Compulsory social security contributions (see section IV) are not subject to tax. In addition, premiums paid to life insurance companies and building and loan associations are to a limited extent deductible. Such "providence expenses" are deductible up to 2,340 DM for a single taxpayer and up to 4,680 for jointly filing spouses. Provident outlays in excess of these amounts are also deductible, but only at 50 percent.

In addition, a "before hand" allowance of 3,000 DM (6,000 DM for married couples) is granted for providence expenses other than premiums to building and loan associations. Contributions to pension insurance schemes paid by employers must be subtracted from this allowance. In most cases taxpayers' social security contributions equal or exceed the maximum deductible amounts, so that there is little left for saving incentive purposes.

Another, though quantitatively minor, saving incentive consists of the deduction of up to 300 DM (600 for married couples) from investment income.

The saving tax incentives are generally considered to be inefficient. In particular, the substitution effects in favor of tax-privileged saving are criticized; moreover, there are undesirable side effects on the distribution of income. The savings bonuses of employees are generally considered more efficient. For capital-forming payments to employees, bonuses of 23 percent or 16 percent are paid, depending on the type of investment, up to 624

DM and 936 DM respectively per year. Only single persons with a taxable income lower than 24,000 DM (married couples 48,000 DM) are entitled to these bonuses.

Taxpayers who are entitled to bonuses under the dwelling construction law may opt either for the dwelling bonus or for the deduction of their premiums to the building and loan association from the individual income tax.

No tax preferences are granted to financial institutions. The income of insurance companies is fully subject to the corporation income tax. Banks are also fully taxed, except those which are mainly working in the public interest (e.g., the Bank for Reconstruction, the Equalization of War Burdens Bank, and the German *Bundesbank*).

The turnover of financial institutions and insurance companies is exempt from the value-added tax; however, a special insurance tax is levied on certain transactions of insurance companies. As banks and insurance companies do not receive any preferential tax treatment, they cannot be expected to provide any saving or investment incentives.

The tax system contains quite a few investment incentives. For the most part, tax advantages are granted through accelerated depreciation, but there are also a series of free allowances for specific groups of taxpayers. From among the large number of special provisions, a few may be mentioned here:

- Small- and medium-size enterprises are allowed an additional 10 percent depreciation of the cost of acquisition and production of new fixed assets in the first year following acquisition.
- Fixed assets of a value lower than 800 DM can be written off immediately.
- For fixed assets, more than 70 percent of which are designed for the protection of the environment, depreciation amounts to 60 percent during the first year; subsequently, up to 10 percent per year is allowed until they are written off completely.
- Investments in research and development receive accelerated depreciation of up to 40 percent for fixed assets and 15 percent for buildings. Moreover, gifts for scientific purposes of up to 10 percent of total income can be deducted from taxable income.
- Losses can, within certain limits, be carried forward to subsequent years or back to previous years.

The special status of Berlin calls for support from the Federal Government. These financial aids are granted by way of tax preferences. They are designed to promote the economy of Berlin and trade between Berlin and the rest of the country. The following measures are applied:

- Taxpayers providing a loan of at least eight years for financing business investments in Berlin receive an income tax credit of 12 percent of the loan in the year in which the loan is made. If loans are provided for financing construction in Berlin for a period of 10 years, the tax credit amounts to 20 percent of the loan.
- Enterprises producing commodities in West Berlin and selling them in the rest of the Federal Republic may avail themselves of a three percent reduction of their value-added tax due.
- West German enterprises receive a 4.2 percent reduction on their value-added tax due when they purchase goods from enterprises in West Berlin.
- Assets of a production plant in Berlin are allowed accelerated depreciation of up to 75 percent over the four years following their acquisition.
- Building owners resident in Berlin are entitled to accelerated depreciation of buildings and houses.

Despite the large number of tax preferences, the German tax system is criticized for giving insufficient investment incentives. Existing depreciation provisions are rated unfavorably by comparison with other countries. The criticism refers less to the individual income tax provisions than to the investment-adverse pattern of the whole tax system. Government assumes only limited business risks through the tax system. Private risk-taking and innovation are discouraged.

Criticism is centered on the taxes that are not levied on profits, among which the tax on business property is the most important (see section IX). As a result of this tax, investments are taxed during start-up periods when no profits accrue as yet. The introduction of a tax system which gives more investment incentives through greater governmental risk sharing is called for. This should be brought about mainly by means of improved write-offs for losses (carrying losses forward or backward), by reductions in the individual and corporation income tax rates, and by cutting down the share of non-profit-related taxes. Changes in the tax rates would benefit all sectors of the economy, irrespective of their factor input structure (capital-intensive or labor-intensive) or size. Such changes would be conducive to the establishment of new enterprises.

IV. THE SOCIAL SECURITY SYSTEM

Social security for workers and their families is provided by a system of transfer payments. These are not financed through the tax system, but from employers' and employees' contributions to the compulsory insurance systems. By paying compulsory contributions, employees have a right to social security benefits.

The German social security system is rather complicated. There are numerous requirements before a claim for social security benefits may be submitted. The range of benefits also depends on a number of prerequisites. Therefore, in what follows, only the major features of the social security system will be described.

Social security includes pension insurance, health insurance, unemployment insurance, and accident insurance.

The pension, health and unemployment insurance programs are characterized by some common technical features which will be dealt with first. All three programs are compulsory for workers up to a certain income level, which is the so-called contribution base limit. Contributions are a certain percentage of the gross wage or salary; employees and employers each pay one-half of the contributions. Contributions are withheld monthly by the employer from the wage or salary and paid together with the employer's share to the relevant health insurance organization.

In case of old age, death (benefits for surviving dependents), and temporary or permanent disability, the national pension insurance scheme pays a monthly pension which is related to the contributions paid and the number of years of employment. Old age pensions are regularly adjusted to the growth of the income of the gainfully employed. At the present time the contribution rate is 19.2 percent and applies to gross wages and salaries up to 5,600 DM per month. Every year this contribution base limit is raised by the increase of average wages and salaries.

The pension insurance program is a pay-as-you-go scheme, i.e., the contributions of the insured are not invested, but are earmarked for the pension payments in the same period to retirees. This means that, apart from a certain liquidity reserve, no assets are accumulated. The pay-as-you-go method has, in recent years, raised serious financing problems for the pension insurance system. Owing to decreasing birth rates over the past 20 years, the gainfully employed have faced a growing burden of taxes, for an ever-diminishing number of employed must finance the pensions of those who retire or become disabled. Shortfalls of financing are compensated for by government grants. This cannot be a lasting solution, as this procedure is inconsistent with the insurance principle.

A reform of the pension insurance system is probably unavoidable, for the population is expected to continue to decline. One suggestion is to pay only a basic pension which guarantees a subsistence minimum to the recipients. Larger pensions would be financed by individual saving. Although the burden on the employed would be relieved or at least stop growing, this suggestion has met with strong disapproval. Contributions paid by many employees now in the system would be higher than the pension they would receive at retirement. Moreover, transition problems are to be expected. For this reason, the concept of a basic pension encounters considerable skepticism.

The main objective of health insurance is to protect the insured against an unacceptable decline of income as a result of illness. Health insurance defrays the costs of medical care and services in case of sickness. It also pays sickness benefits, maternity allowances, and death grants. Members of large families of insured workers are covered by the health insurance system (family equalization of burdens) without paying their own contributions. In this way, roughly 93 percent of the population is protected against the cost of illness. Health insurance is compulsory for workers, employees (except civil servants) and farmers with an income of up to 4,200 DM per month. It also covers pensioners, persons undergoing military or civilian service, the unemployed, and students.

Health insurance is entrusted to a number of self-governing bodies. Each health insurance organization independently fixes the contribution rate in accordance with the provisions of the law. For the time being, contributions range from nine to 13 percent; for pensioners, a uniform rate of 4.5 percent is applied at the present time.

Health insurance is also increasingly facing financing problems as the expenses of medical care and services have skyrocketed, the number of aged people has increased, and health consciousness has grown.

Despite repeated small increases of contribution rates, the problems of financing health insurance have not been resolved. If an employee's income rises beyond the contribution base limit, he or she can join a private health insurance plan. The plans relate their premiums to the age, the individual sickness risk of the insured person, and the extent of medical care and services desired. Private health insurance is widely available, but low- and middle-income recipients generally use the government system.

The health insurance organizations are attempting to combat the health cost explosion by so-called "concerted action." This means that doctors' remuneration and prices of drugs are negotiated between the health insurance organizations, the doctors' organizations and the pharmaceutical industry. In addition, the health insurance organizations urge the insured to economize on health services.

The unemployment insurance program is compulsory for all employed and for persons undergoing the military or civilian service; civil servants are not included. The rate of contribution is 4.1 percent up to the contribution base limit of 5,600 DM per month. Responsibility for unemployment insurance rests with the Federal Labor Office, which pays unemployment benefits and vocational retraining costs.

Accident insurance is unlike the three major insurance programs that have so far been discussed because it is organized differently. Accident insurance is compulsory for all employed persons, all children in daycare centers, and all students. Contributions, which are paid exclusively by the employers, are differentiated according to the enterprises' risk categories. Benefits are provided in case of occupational accidents, accidents on the way to work, and occupational diseases. If injured, the insured person is entitled to coverage of the costs of the treatment and vocational rehabilitation, and to a disability pension; in case of death, there is a death grant as well as pensions to surviving dependents.

The social security system provides comprehensive economic protection for private households against the general risks of life, but the costs are heavy. Unlike income taxes, social security contributions are not progressively differentiated according to ability to pay; they are levied at a proportional rate up to the contribution base limit. The burden is, therefore, regressive above the contribution base limit.

Social security contributions impose a greater burden on labor than on capital. The tax burden on labor is often cited as a reason for the substitution of capital for labor. This is particularly significant at the international level where German enterprises must compete against firms from other countries with lower tax rates on labor. High unemployment and changes in demography, which may require an increase in contributions, have led to suggestions on how to counter the substitution process. One idea is to supplement the wage-related contributions with a levy on employers for capital input, the so-called "machine contribution." However, this suggestion raises other difficulties, both of an insurance and economic nature.

V. THE VALUE-ADDED TAX

The value-added tax is the third major tax in the German tax system. It is levied on sales within the country, including imports. The value-added tax is levied at a number of different rates (table 2). The ordinary rate is 14 percent and applies to the bulk of taxable sales. A reduced rate of seven percent is allowed for food (except beverages), books, journals, newspapers, and works of art. The most important exemptions from the value-added tax are the services of medical doctors, hospitals, homes for the aged, private schools, theaters, orchestras, and museums; leasing of land, administration of loans and services of insurance agents and brokers; and all exports.

Taxes are due from the enterprises which carry out the taxable sales. The value-added tax base is the agreed price (taxation of amounts due), but in application, the amounts actually paid (taxation of actual amounts) are taxed. Within 10 days after the end of each month, the enterprise prepares a preliminary statement of the tax due for that month and pays that amount to the tax office. Smaller enterprises may make their preliminary statements every three months or once per year. At the end of each calendar year the enterprise files a final return and calculates the total tax. Thus, enterprises bear the bulk of the administration and compliance costs of the value-added tax.

The German value-added tax is a tax on the net value added of the consumption type, i.e., it is levied only on consumption and exempts savings. In practice, it is a levy on the gross value added at every stage of production with a deduction for taxes paid on purchases by each firm. In other words, sales at each production stage are taxed, but enterprises may deduct from their tax due the amounts charged by other firms on their taxable sales to them, irrespective of the number of production stages. The deduction for taxes paid at the previous stage ensures that the final tax on a product is the tax rate multiplied by the price of the product; pyramiding of taxes is prevented in this way.

From the legal point of view, the value-added tax is an excise tax which is related to the turnover of firms at all stages of production and distribution. In economic terms, it is a general consumption tax because it is ultimately paid by the consumer, as intended by law. The intended shift of the tax burden to the consumer may be expected to work out as a rule: since value-added tax is levied on practically all commodities, substitution of untaxed for taxed commodities is precluded. It is possible, however, that the decline of real incomes as a result of the value-added tax leads to demand shifts in favor of goods which are either tax-exempt or subject to a reduced tax rate. However, such reactions are considered significant only if the tax rates are high.

In the recent past the growing fiscal needs of the government were met mainly by raising the rates of the value-added tax for two reasons: first, further increases of income tax rates were no longer possible politically; and second, the value-added tax is still regarded as being a hidden tax. Since investment is not taxed under a consumption-type value-added tax, the tax promotes growth. In the past, however, it has turned out that the price level rose by more than the tax increase in the wake of increases in the value-added tax rate. This suggests that enterprises use value-added tax increases as an opportunity to raise their own prices.

As was mentioned earlier, some transactions are exempt from the value-added tax. The effect of the exemption depends on the production stage of the tax-exempt enterprise and on its share in the gross value added of the product. When the tax-exempt product or service enters the taxed sector, there is a backlog and cumulative effect: the enterprise at the stage which follows the tax-exempt one is taxable on the value added by the tax-exempt enterprise (backlog effect). The major cumulative effect occurs as a result of the taxation of gross value added at each stage of production and distribution thereafter (i.e., including the value added at earlier stages). Another less significant cumulative effect results from the fact that the value-added tax levied at preceding stages is itself also taxed (tax on tax).

Finally, attention should be drawn to some further tax preferences under the value-added tax:

- Enterprises whose annual returns are lower than 20,000 DM are exempt from the value-added tax. They are not granted a deduction for taxes paid on their own purchases (the pre-tax either), nor are they allowed to make out bills with an open tax statement.
- Enterprises with annual returns of up to 60,000 DM are granted a regressively designed tax reduction which, depending on total sales, can equal 80 percent of the tax due. Firms with this form of tax privilege continue to deduct taxes paid at prior stages in full.
- Farming and forestry enterprises pay tax at an eight percent tax rate. However, they are allowed an eight percent global deduction for taxes previously paid, so that they do not pay any value-added tax.

VI. THE HIDDEN ECONOMY

As in almost any other country, a great deal of business is transacted in Germany for cash without a bill. This is called the shadow, secondary, hidden, or underground economy, illicit work, or moonlighting. Though the phenomenon of the hidden economy has been observed in Germany for more than 20 years now, it has only recently been openly discussed and subject to research. It is obviously difficult to obtain facts about the size of the hidden economy.

Two criteria characterize the activities in the hidden economy: they have counterparts similar in substance and form in the regular economy, and they are carried out in evasion of legal regulations and requirements and are, therefore, illegal.

The work of craftsmen accounts for a substantial part of this hidden economy. It is common practice for such work to be performed without payment of the taxes prescribed by law, in particular the income tax, social security contributions, and the value-added tax. Both parties involved in such transactions gain. The worker is paid a cash wage which may be higher than his regular net wage, but lower than his gross wage, and the customer "saves" the value-added tax and pays a lower wage than in the regular sector.

The main reason for the emergence of hidden economy is the heavy burden of taxes and contributions. Craftsmen and other workers drift into the hidden economy to avoid paying taxes. A typical employee is subject to a marginal tax rate of roughly 40 percent. Under these circumstances, it is tempting to work for cash in the hidden economy. The particular taxes which are important in the decision are not known. However, there is no evidence that social security contributions, which give employers rights to old-age pensions, medical care, etc., are regarded as less onerous than income or value-added taxes. Moreover, illicit work is appealing to the customer because he can evade the 14 percent value-added tax.

A precise estimate of the size of the hidden economy in the Federal Republic of Germany is not available. All attempts have so far met with methodological difficulties, and no exact empirical study has as yet been undertaken. According to estimates which are based on the quantity of money in circulation, the hidden economy may be as large as two to 10 percent of the GNP. For craftsmen, the unreported income in 1978 is estimated at roughly 60 billion DM, and the tax loss is estimated at 20 billion DM, which is more than six percent of the total tax yield. It should be noted, however, that these estimates are treated with considerable skepticism.

There are few proposals that would make a dent in the hidden economy. Illicit work is looked upon as a natural reaction to the generous social policy and high tax rates. Penalties, fines, and similar measures are considered to have little or no effect. A substantial reduction in the tax burden, therefore, is generally considered to be the only efficient measure to reduce the size of the hidden economy.

VII. WEALTH TAX AND INHERITANCE AND GIFT TAX

The wealth tax is levied on the total property of individuals, corporations, funds, and associations. Individuals resident or permanently domiciled within the country, domestic corporations, associations, and funds are subject to taxation on their internal wealth as well as their wealth abroad. Individuals not resident or permanently domiciled within the country, foreign corporations, associations, and funds are liable to wealth tax only on their domestic wealth.

The wealth tax is levied on farming and forestry wealth, real estate, business assets, and other property (e.g., savings and bank deposits, securities, precious metals, jewelry). The wealth tax is levied at a uniform rate throughout the country; its yield (1.08 percent of the total tax yield in 1984) belongs to the Lander governments. The tax rate is 0.5 percent for individuals and 0.6 percent for juridical persons. The tax base is obtained by summing up all types of wealth (gross wealth) and then subtracting liabilities. Personal and specific property-related allowances are deducted from net wealth in arriving at the tax base to which the tax rates are applied.

The property-related allowances are:
- 1,000 DM for savings or bank deposits;
- 10,000 DM for assets exceeding 1,000 DM, for capital claims and shares in corporations;
- 10,000 DM for life, capital and property insurance;
- 4,800 DM for pension claims.

The personal allowances are:
- 70,000 DM per person, jointly assessed under the family tax scheme;
- An additional 10,000 DM if the taxpayer is older than 60 years;
- 50,000 DM in addition if he is older than 65 years.

Corporations, associations and funds are not taxed until their total wealth is 20,000 DM. In addition, a great many organizations that serve the public interest are exempt.

The main problem with the wealth tax is the assessment of individual property items. Assessments are based on current value, with the following exceptions:

- Farming and forestry enterprises and buildings are assessed on the basis of the value of the estimated yield of the property;
- The value of a business is the sum of the amounts which would be paid for individual items in the business by a party acquiring the whole enterprise and assuming the enterprise is carried on.

Tax assessments are quite unsatisfactory. In some instances, the assessment dates back to 1964, so that the assessed property value is far below the current value. In particular, substantial value differences are observed in assessments of real estate because current assessments are obtained by applying uniform percentage increases from the base year. A new assessment for the purpose of eliminating such distortions would, however, involve considerable administrative expenses. The differences in taxation of alternative types of property should be removed.

More problems arise with respect to the wealth tax liability of juridical persons. In economic terms, the wealth of juridical persons belongs to individuals. Yet this same wealth is subject to the wealth tax at the shareholder level. Since their shares are merely claims to a share of the net wealth of the corporation, the same economic value is actually taxed twice.

The inheritance and gift tax is levied on acquisitions caused by death (*mortis causa*), gifts among living persons, purposeful grants, and the wealth of trust funds every 30 years. The tax is payable by the acquirer, the tax base being the total acquisitions from within the country and outside. This tax is uniform throughout the country, but the yields belong to the Lander governments. In 1984, the revenue from the inheritance and gift tax amounted to 1.56 billion DM.

All liabilities and charges related to an acquisition may be deducted from its total value. Personal exemptions are differentiated according to the degree of relationship between the decedent or the donor and the recipient. The tax scale is also differentiated according to the degree of relationship. It is subdivided into four classes with progressively graduated rates. It starts at three percent for acquisitions of up to 50,000 DM in tax class I and ends in class IV at 70 percent for acquisitions of more than one million DM. The personal exemptions are summarized in table 3.

To prevent double exemptions, acquisitions by the same person over the preceding 10 years are aggregated. The tax due for the total amount is reduced by the tax levied on earlier acquisitions.

Assessment of acquired property for inheritance tax purposes raises the same problems as the wealth tax. One criticism of the inheritance tax is that it is levied on unincorporated firms, but not on corporations. As a result, unincorporated firms may face serious liquidity problems. To equalize the tax burden on incorporated and unincorporated firms, it has been suggested that a special equalization levy be imposed on corporations. Other proposals are to reduce the tax rates for unincorporated firms that are carried on by the heirs, permit the heirs to pay tax over a period of years, and raise the wealth tax rate on corporations.

The wealth tax and the inheritance and gift taxes are charges on wealth. The wealth tax is regarded as a prior charge on unearned income, with tax to be paid from the returns of wealth. The wealth itself should not be affected by the wealth tax. In this respect, the wealth tax is a supplement to the individual income tax.

The comparatively low rate of the wealth tax and the high exemptions account for the relatively small yield, so that the wealth tax has very little redistributive effect. A four-person family, for example, with a taxpayer aged 60 years is liable to wealth tax only when the wealth exceeds 290,000 DM. Moreover, wealth is, as a rule, undervalued, and a considerable amount of wealth is concealed from the tax authorities. Savings deposits are particularly easy to conceal because banks do not provide information on deposits of living persons to the tax authorities. Finally, gold, jewelry, and works of art easily escape taxation.

In contrast to the wealth tax, the inheritance and gift taxes affect the wealth itself and reduce the amount acquired by the recipient. Avoidance of the inheritance tax is difficult because banks are obliged to report deposits of the decedent to the tax authorities. As a consequence, all property, including property that was originally concealed, is disclosed to the tax authorities and subject to taxation. Moreover, the heirs must provide information to the tax office on all objects possessed by the decedent. Avoidance of the gift tax, on the other hand, is much easier, particularly in the case of gifts of cash and movable property.

The redistributive potential of the inheritance and gift taxes must be rated as poor, again as a result of high exemptions and low rates in the first tax classes which account for most of the acquisitions *mortis causa*. Furthermore, assessments for inheritance and gift tax purposes are inadequate. Altogether, neither the inheritance and gift taxes nor the wealth tax has a significant effect on the distribution of wealth.

In conclusion, attention may be drawn to a proposed reform of the wealth and inheritance taxes. Since tax avoidance is greater in the case of the wealth tax and since the inheritance tax affects wealth itself, consideration might be given to the elimination of the wealth tax and an increase in the inheritance tax rates. The redistributive effects of such a system would probably be greater than the present dual tax system. This proposal is opposed by those who believe in the fundamental right of individuals to private property and in the right of inheritance of that property. Moreover, such a reform may reduce saving and, therefore, economic growth.

VIII. THE DISTRIBUTION OF TAX BURDENS

There exist no statistical records in the Federal Republic on the distribution of tax burdens by income classes. However, section X provides data on the average and marginal income tax rates at diferent income levels.

IX. LOCAL TAXES

Local governments, which constitute the lowest level of the Federal state structure, are guaranteed their autonomy by the constitution. As a consequence they can, within the limits of the law, decide on all local matters. The proviso "within the limits of the law" was made to ensure that legal and economic unity in the Federal Republic is preserved and that, in particular, uniformity of living conditions is promoted. Local governments enact their own legislation (the municipal statute), are responsible for their own administration, control their own budgets, and have the right to impose certain fees and excises. As a result of the tension between the uniformity-of-living-conditions requirement and the guarantee of municipal autonomy, local governments are not authorized to levy their own taxes. The yields from certain tax sources, however, accrue to them for their exclusive use, but legislative control of these taxes remains vested in the Federal or Lander governments. Local governments derive approximately one-third of their revenue from local taxes, one-third from Lander grants, and one-third from fees, contributions, and credits.

1. Local Taxes

Local governments are entitled to receipts from the following taxes: a) property tax: levied on real estate of farming and forestry enterprises as well as on land and buildings; b) business tax: levied on business enterprises; business capital and profits (the tax base is nearly the same as the base of the wealth tax); c) local consumption and excise taxes: these include entertainment tax, beverage tax, dog tax, ice cream tax, and hunting and fishery tax; and d) a 15 percent share of the yield of the wage and the income taxes.

In 1984, the real estate tax yielded 7.1 billion DM and the business tax 28.32 billion DM. These two taxes are of great importance to local governments not only on account of the revenues they bring in, but also because local governments control the disposition of these revenues. The tax offices, which are Lander authorities, fix the basic assessment and rate for these taxes, while the local governments add their own surtax. However, the local surtax cannot exceed the limits fixed by the Lander government. In 1983, the average local surtax for the business tax was fixed at 349 percent, for tax A on land and buildings (agricultural and forestry undertakings) at 256 percent, and for tax B on land and buildings at 291 percent. The right to set the surtax is an important method of protecting the fiscal autonomy of local governments. There are significant disparities in the tax rates among municipalities, so that regional differences are large.

The business tax is strongly criticized as being unsuitable for a municipal tax. Business profits are cyclically very sensitive and there are large disparities in the per capita yields of these taxes among the municipalities. Therefore municipal revenues are highly variable over time and there are great disparities in the fiscal capacity of the various municipalities. To remedy this disadvantage, in 1970 governments were granted a share in the yield of the wage and income taxes. In turn, they are required to transfer a portion of their business tax collections to the Federal and Lander governments. In 1984, this transfer amounted to 15 percent of the business tax yield.

The local share of the income tax exceeds the local contribution from the business tax to the Federal and the Lander governments. In 1983 the business tax apportioned by local governments was 70.87 DM per inhabitant, while the average yield of the municipalities' share in the income tax was 383.83 DM per inhabitant.

Municipal consumption and excise taxes apply only to the local areas. In 1984, yields from these taxes amounted to 1.53 billion DM.

2. Lander Grants to Local Governments

Local governments are entitled to a certain portion of the Lander governments' collection from joint taxes. The proportion is fixed by the Lander legislatures. In addition, the Lander governments provide the following general and functional grants to local governments.

General grants. These are designed to improve the revenue capacity of municipalities. The proceeds are available to the local governments without any strings attached (see table 4). General grants are subdivided as follows:

- **Balancing grants** are determined on the basis of needs and taxable capacity. The needs measure is related mainly to the size of the population and is, as a rule, weighted in accordance with a municipality's size. Other criteria, such as the proximity to the German Democratic Republic (GDR) border, are also considered. Taxable capacity is based on the revenue from municipal taxes and from the municipalities' share in the income tax. For the *Realsteuern* a uniform tax factor is applied.
- **Financial Grants** are payments for costs incurred by the local governments for services provided at the request of the Lander government. Since these costs are related to the size of a municipality's population, the grants are distributed on a per capita basis.
- **Grants based on need** are distributed, upon application of the municipality, to cover their extraordinary needs. The allocation is based on the municipality's overall fiscal situation, and not on the particular need to be financed by the grant.
- **Functional grants** are allocated to special municipal administrative authorities responsible for such things as schools, road construction, and social matters. These grants are provided with strings attached. Roughly one-half of all grants going to municipalities are for these purposes; local governments complain that, as a consequence, their autonomy is compromised.

X. THE 1986-88 TAX REFORM AND OTHER PROPOSALS

In the summer of 1985, the "law on incentive-stimulating tax reductions and on the relief of families" was passed. It will bring about in two stages (on January 1, 1986 and January 1, 1988) a major reduction in income taxes. The essentials of the legislation are an increase in the children's free allowances and the basic personal exemption, and a flattening of the tax rates. The tax relief will total 19.4 billion DM, or roughly eight percent of the yield from the wage and income taxes. The Federal Government will bear 8.2 billion DM of these costs, the Lander governments 11.2 billion DM.

The revision of the tax scale is designed to reduce the adverse incentive effects of the progressive tax rates. Taxpayers will be relieved of an average of eight percent of their present tax liabilities, and the marginal tax rates will be reduced by up to 5.5 percentage points and by another 0.5 percentage point for each child. The increase of the basic personal exemption will provide relief of 72 DM to unmarried persons (144 DM for married couples).

The following changes will be made in the first stage of the tax reform:

- an increase in the children's free allowance from 432 to 2,484 DM;
- an increase in the basic personal exemption from 4,212 to 4,536 DM for single persons and from 8,424 to 9,072 DM for married couples;
- a reduction of the tax rates mainly for taxpayers with low incomes and large families.

In the second stage, the marginal tax rates in the progressive zone will be cut. Figure 1 shows the average and marginal tax rates under the 1981 and 1988 laws.

**Figure 1. Comparison of Marginal and
Average Individual Income Tax Rates, 1981 and 1988**

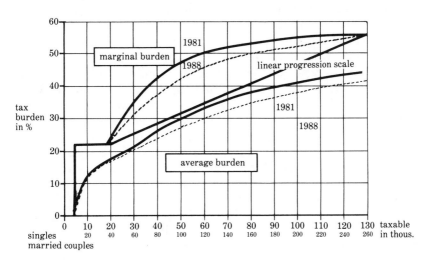

The main problem with the 1981 tax schedule was that the marginal tax rates rose too quickly in the lower part of the progressive zone (up to taxable incomes of about 60,000 DM for single persons, and 120,000 DM for married couples), where the majority of recipients of medium and high incomes is concentrated. For incomes ranging from 18,000 to 60,000 DM for single persons (36,000 to 120,000 DM for married couples), the marginal rate rose

28 percentage points (from 22 percent to 50 percent), while in the range of incomes between 60,000 and 130,000 DM (120,000 to 260,000 DM for married couples) it rose only six percentage points (from 50 to 56 percent). Under the 1988 schedule, the marginal tax rate in the lower part of the progressive zone will rise from 22 to 46 percent, an increase of only 24 percentage points. In the upper part of the progressive zone, the marginal tax rate will rise linearly from 50 to 56 percent (see table 5). When this revision of the tax schedule is completed in 1988, the average effective tax rate will be reduced to 23.67 percent. The share of direct taxes in aggregate tax yields will decline by 1.5 percentage points (from 60 to 58.5 percent).

The Federal Government has announced its intention to flatten the progressive tax rates further in several steps so as to come closer to a linear schedule. The plan is equally welcome among academicians and politicians. This change cannot be made in a single step because of the large revenue implications.

A proposal to broaden the lower proportional tax zone was considered but rejected by the government on the ground that it would require even more progression in that zone. However, after a relatively brief period, the additional progressivity would have to be moderated. Inflation-caused income increases would aggrevate this problem. The government has, therefore, decided in favor of the concept of a linear tax scale, with an understanding that the flattened schedule would be accepted over the long run.

In relative terms, the new tax scale implies greater relief for taxpayers with higher incomes. This appears appropriate as these taxpayers were subject to excessive marginal tax rates under the former tax scale. A comparison of absolute amounts of relief for lower and higher incomes would be misleading.

Trade unions sharply criticize and partially reject the tax reform undertaken by the present government. In their view, the reduction of the top tax rates represents a redistribution "from the bottom to the top." According to them, the tax reform brings the highest relief in absolute figures not for the zone with the steepest progression, but to the top zone in which the rate is flat. In absolute figures and in percent of tax due, the average tax relief is smaller in the lower part of the progressive zone than at the top of that zone.

Trade unions also oppose the rise of children's free tax allowances from 432 to 2,484 DM per child, arguing that taxpayers with higher incomes derive a larger tax advantage from these allowances. Instead, the trade unions demand payment of equal amounts for all children, without, however, precluding the possibility of varying this amount according to individual incomes.

In the opinion of the trade unions, reduction of mass unemployment is much more important than general tax reduction. They criticize the government's tax reform on the ground that it does not have sufficient impact on employment. The stimulating effect of tax reform on demand is considered to be very low, as taxpayers with high incomes, who receive the largest tax cuts, will save a large portion of their cuts and will use this savings to increase their wealth.

The trade unions call for:

- using all available financial resources for a medium-term investment program;
- increasing the direct grant to children and removing their tax-free allowances;
- distinctly higher tax relief for those with low incomes:
  - a larger increase in the basic personal exemption;
  - an extension of the lower proportional zone, eventually to taxable incomes of 24,000 DM for single people (48,000 DM for married couples);
  - a lesser degree of progression in the lower part of the progressive zone, i.e., up to annual taxable incomes of 60,000 DM for single people (120,000 for married couples);
  - A higher degree of progression in the top brackets to avoid cutting average effective tax rates in that part of the distribution;
- more efficient tax collection and control by hiring a larger number of tax inspectors and tax investigators.

So far, the trade unions have not demonstrated how these proposals would be financed.

The National Association of German Industry, although welcoming the income tax reform, argues that it does not solve the problems of business taxation. It believes that the tax system adversely affects the propensity to take risks, violates the neutrality principle with respect to the legal form of firms, and impairs the competitiveness of German industry in world markets. It believes that tax relief for business enterprises would stimulate economic activity and increase the national product. The result would be higher tax collections, which could then be used to finance further tax cuts. The tax relief of the 1986-88 reform is not satisfactory for the following reasons:

- The maintenance of the top individual income tax rate and of the corporation income tax rate at 56 percent does not provide any relief for large business enterprises. Only small-scale unincorporated enterprises will obtain relief.
- There will be continued discrimination against retained profits of corporations. Distributed profits will be taxed at

lower rates at the individual level, but no change will be made in the high tax rate on retained profits.

The agenda of the National Association consists of the following tax proposals:

- Reform of the business tax and abolition of the business capital tax.
- Abolition of the wealth tax on business assets which would improve the neutrality of business taxation on different legal forms of firms and simplify the tax law as a result of the elimination of the need to assess business assets. As an alternative, the wealth tax might be allowed as a deduction from the tax base on computing the income taxes.
- Reduction of the tax burden on earnings by reducing the top individual income tax rate and the corporation income tax on retained profits.

All the changes are to be financed by raising the value-added tax.

Table 1
Amounts and Distribution of Government Revenue by Major Revenue Sources, 1970, 1975, 1980, 1985
(Millions of DM)

Year	Federal	Lander	Local	Total
Individual Income Tax[1]				
1970	22,978	22,977	7,152	53,107
1975	43,775	43,776	13,887	101,438
1980	65,138	65,139	22,253	152,530
1985	77,580	78,394	26,430	182,404
Corporation Income Tax				
1970	4,358	4,359	—	8,717
1975	5,027	10,027	—	10,054
1980	10,661	10,661	—	21,322
1985	15,918	15,918	—	31,836
Value-Added Tax[2]				
1970	26,689	11,436	—	38,125
1975	36,911	17,171	—	54,082
1980	63,078	30,370	—	93,448
1985	71,936	37,889	—	109,825
Wealth Tax				
1970	—	2,877	—	2,877
1975	—	2,229	—	3,339
1980	—	4,664	—	4,664
1985	—	4,287	—	4,287

(Continued on next page)

Table 1 (Continued)
Amounts and Distribution of Government Revenue
by Major Revenue Sources, 1970, 1975, 1980, 1985
(Millions of DM)

Year	Federal	Lander	Local	Total
Local Business Tax				
1970	2,177	2,177	6,373	10,727
1975	3,444	3,444	11,010	17,898
1980	3,232	3,232	20,625	27,089
1985	2,205	2,205	25,190	29,600
Property Tax				
1970	—	—	2,683	2,683
1975	—	—	4,150	4,150
1980	—	—	5,804	5,804
1985	—	—	7,103	7,103
Inheritance and Gift Tax				
1970	—	523	—	523
1975	—	530	—	530
1980	—	1,017	—	1,017
1985	—	1,511	—	1,511

[1]Includes withholding tax on wages, the self-assessed income tax, and the capital yields tax. Revenues of the income tax were distributed in the ratio of 43:43:14 in 1970-79, and in the ratio of 42.5:42.5:15 since 1980, among the Federal, Lander and local governments. Revenues of the capital yields tax has been divided since 1970 in the ratio of 50:50 between the Federal and Lander governments.

[2]The yield of the value-added tax has been divided between the Federal and Lander governments in the following ratios:

1970	70:30
1975	68.25:31.75
1976/77	69:31
1978-82	67.5:32.5
1983	66.5:33.5
1984/85	65.5:34.5
1986/87	65:35

Table 2
Tax Rates of the Major Taxes 1986-88

Individual income tax:
   1. Tax exemption of 4,536 DM/9,072 DM for singles/married couples.
   2. Taxable income from 4,537 DM/9,073 DM to 18,000 DM/36,000 DM is subject to a flat tax rate of 22 percent.
   3. Taxable income from 18,001 DM/36,001 DM to 130,000 DM/260,000 DM is subject to a tax rate ranging from 22 to 56 percent.
   4. Taxable income above 130,000 DM/260,000 DM is subject to a flat marginal tax rate of 56 percent.

Corporation income tax:
   1. Non-distributed profits are taxed at a rate of 56 percent.
   2. Distributed profits are taxed at a rate of 36 percent.

Wealth tax:
   1. For individuals, the tax rate is 0.5 percent.
   2. For juridical persons, the tax rate is 0.6 percent.

Value-added tax:
   1. The ordinary tax rate is 14 percent.
   2. Food, books, journals, newspapers and works of art are taxed with a reduced rate of seven percent.
   3. The services of medical doctors, hospitals, homes for the aged, private schools, theaters, orchestras and museums, the leasing of land, administration of loans and services of insurance agents and brokers and all exports are exempted from the value-added tax.

Inheritance and gift tax:
The tax rate depends on the amount of the acquisition and the tax class of the recipient.
   I: from 3 to 35 percent
   II: from 6 to 50 percent
   III: from 11 to 65 percent
   IV: from 20 to 70 percent

Local business tax:
The tax offices fix the basic assessment, which comes to five percent of business profits and 0.2 percent of the business capital. The local governments add a surtax, which averaged 349 percent in 1983.

Property tax:
The tax offices fix the basic assessment for agricultural and forestry undertakings (property tax A) and for land and buildings (property tax B). On this the local governments add a surtax, which averaged 256 percent for property tax A and 291 percent for property tax B in 1983.

Table 3
Tax Allowances and Tax Preferences
of the Major Taxes, 1986

Individual income tax

1. Children's allowance, which amounts to 2,484 DM, is granted for each child of the taxpayer.

2. Education expenses on behalf of children can be deducted up to 1,200 DM if the child lives at home and up to 2,100 DM if the child lives away from home.

3. Unmarried persons are allowed to deduct a household exemption of 4,000 DM for the first child and an additional 2,000 DM for each additional child.

4. Orphans and people with a physical impediment have a special allowance; for orphans it amounts to 720 DM; the amount for people with a physical impediment depends on the degree of their impediment (from 600 up to 2,760 DM).

5. Providence expenses (premiums paid to life insurance companies and building and loan associations) are deductible up to 2,340 DM for a single taxpayer and up to 4,680 DM for a married couple.

6. Providence expenses other than premiums to building and loan associations are deductible up to 3,000 DM for single persons and 6,000 DM for a married couple.

7. A deduction from investment income of up to 300 DM for single persons and 600 DM for married couples is allowed.

8. Compulsory social security contributions are not subject to tax.

9. Bonuses to employees for capital-forming purposes up to 623 DM for single persons and 936 DM for married couples are not taxable.

Corporation income tax

1. An exemption of 5,000 DM is granted. If the income of the corporation exceeds 10,000 DM, the allowance is cut by half the excess amount.

2. Farming and forestry undertakings are granted a free allowance of 30,000 DM.

3. Numerous investment incentives (see section III).

Wealth tax

1. The following property-related allowances are granted:

   1,000 DM for savings or bank deposits

   10,000 DM for money assets exceeding 1,000 DM, for capital claims and share in corporations

   10,000 DM for life, capital and property insurance

   4,800 DM for pension claims.

2. The personal allowances are:

   70,000 DM per person, jointly assessed under the family tax scheme

   An additional 10,000 DM if the taxpayer is older than 60 years

   50,000 DM in addition if the taxpayer is older than 65 years.

   Corporations, associations and funds are not taxed until their total wealth is 20,000 DM.

(Continued on next page)

Table 3 (Continued)
Tax Allowances and Tax Preferences
of the Major Taxes, 1986

Inheritance and gift tax
1. The personal exemptions are:

250,000 DM for spouses
90,000 DM for children and children of deceased children
50,000 DM for parents and grandparents
10,000 DM for brothers and sisters and their descendents, parents-in-law,
children-in-law, divorced spouses
3,000 DM all other heirs or donees.

Property tax
The real estate of the following institutions is not subject to the property tax:
churches, public corporations, burial grounds, airports. There are no personal
exemptions.

Local business tax
The following enterprises are not subject to the local business tax: *Deutsche
Bundespost, Deutsche Bundesbank*, agricultural and forestry undertakings, homes
for the aged, schools and hospitals. There are no exemptions.

Table 4
Lander General Grants to Local Governments, 1983
(Thousands of DM)

Lander	General grants, (total)	Grants Balancing grants	based on need	Financial grants
Total	20,480	16,909	281	3,290
Schleswig-Holstein	860	626	1	233
Niedersachsen	2,390	1,945	30	955
Nordrhein-Westfalen	6,764	6,514	165	85
Hessen	1,744	1,595	10	139
Rheinland-Pfalz	1,166	894	12	260
Baden-Wurttemberg	3,399	2,848	38	513
Bayern	3,223	2,109	22	1,092
Saarland	384	375	0.617	9

Table 5
Reduction of Marginal Tax Burden under the 1988 Law

Taxable income in	Marginal tax burden (percentage points)				Reduction of marginal burden (percentage points)	
	1981 tax scale		1988 tax scale			
	Basic scale	Split scale	Basic scale	Split scale	Basic scale	Split scale
20,000	24.7	22.0	23.8	22.0	0.9	—
30,000	35.7	22.0	31.6	22.0	4.1	—
40,000	43.2	24.7	37.7	23.8	5.5	0.9
50,000	47.8	30.6	42.5	27.9	5.3	2.7
60,000	50.4	35.7	46.0	31.6	4.4	4.1
70,000	52.0	39.8	48.5	34.9	3.5	4.9
80,000	53.3	43.2	50.0	37.7	3.3	5.5
100,000	55.1	47.8	52.4	42.5	2.7	5.3
150,000	56.0	52.7	56.0	49.3	—	3.4
200,000	56.0	55.1	56.0	52.4	—	2.7

CHAPTER 7

United Kingdom

Nick Morris

INTRODUCTION

1. Purpose

This paper presents the main features of the United Kingdom tax system. Although the discussion is intended, for brevity, to be fairly general, figures are presented for many of the major rates and levels in the tax system. These figures refer to financial year 1986. Where the 1986/87 levels are already known they are added.

The paper begins with a treatment of the income tax as it affects individuals and companies, then considers the effects of this system on savings and investment. Payroll taxes (National Insurance contributions) are then considered, followed by value-added tax and excise duties. In section VI, known facts about the hidden economy are summarized. This is followed by a description of the (low level in the UK) taxation of wealth, and some discussion of the overall distribution of tax burdens. The local tax system, including the equalization procedure known in the UK as block grant, is then briefly described. A final section summarizes some of the recent debate on tax reform.

2. Revenue Raised by United Kingdom Taxes

In total, direct and indirect taxes in the United Kingdom raised some £140 billion in 1985/86, or four percent of UK GDP of £320 billion. Table 1 shows the breakdown of these taxes. This £140 billion contributes to the UK government's total receipts of £155 billion, the remaining £15 billion being provided by the trading surplus of public corporations, rent, and interest and dividend receipts of the government.

Some £79 billion is raised from taxes on income, of which £39 billion comes from income tax and ACT (a tax on dividends of which £1.2 billion is from North Sea oil) and £24 billion from National Insurance contributions. Corporation tax contributes some £6.6 billion of which £1.6 billion is levied on North Sea activity. The remaining £8.7 billion in 1985/86 results from direct taxes—petroleum revenue tax and royalties—on North Sea production.

Taxes on expenditure raise some £57 billion with VAT raising £19 billion and local rates £14 billion. The remainder is provided by excise duties on petrol, drink, and tobacco (£15 billion), vehicle duty and licenses (£3.2 billion), stamp duty (£1.2 billion) and a number of smaller items. Taxes on capital raise only £2 billion, with about £800 million coming from each of capital gains tax and capital transfer tax.

I. THE INDIVIDUAL INCOME TAX

1. Allowances, Rates and the Schedular System

Income tax in the United Kingdom is charged according to a number of different schedules. The most important is schedule E income, which covers income from wages and salaries. Individuals may deduct from their schedule E income a personal allowance at levels summarized in table 2 (for comparison, average earnings in 1985/86 were around £9,000). Previously allowances were granted for dependent children, but these were phased out between 1979/80 and 1982/83. The higher allowances granted to persons over 65 are subject to a taper. Where total income exceeds £8,800, the additional part of the allowance is reduced by two-thirds of excess income until the allowance is reduced to the standard level.

After all deductions, taxable income is taxed according to the rates shown in table 3. The UK is unusual in that it has a very wide basic rate band, and some 95 percent of all taxpayers pay tax at a marginal rate of 30 percent. Above £16,200 rates rise fairly steeply to a top rate of 60 percent. The top rate for earned income used to be as high as 83 percent until 1979, and before 1984 a surcharge of 15 percent was charged on investment incomes above £7,100.

Pensions and, from 1982, sickness and unemployment benefits are treated, for the purposes of income tax, as if they were earned income as are some other benefits, including a proportion of the supplementary benefit paid to the unemployed, and the invalidity benefit. Anyone who becomes unemployed during the year and ends up having total income less than his or her personal allowance plus reliefs, can claim a tax refund.

Income tax is withheld from earned income by employers under a system of pay-as-you-earn (PAYE). This is organized on a cumulative basis; at any point in the year, income tax paid is intended to reflect the balance of allowances and income so far accumulated. This results in fairly complex administration when, for example, employees move from one job to another.

Some 77 percent of the total income tax revenue collected in 1985/86 of £41 billion (before repayments) is collected under Schedule E. The other schedules are:

Schedule

A	Property income
B	Woodlands
C	Paying agents
D	Profits of trades, professions, self-employed, etc.
F	Dividends, etc.

Schedule A covers income from rents of land, but not of furnished lettings, which are treated under schedule D, as is income from lodgers and boarding houses. Deductions are allowed for maintenance and repairs, for services the landlord is obliged to provide and for other expenses such as rates which the landlord has to defray. Assessments are made primarily on the basis of the previous tax year but with some adjustment to allow for changes in the present year.

Schedule B applies to the occupation of "woodlands in the UK managed on a commercial basis and with a view to the realization of profit." For these, the "annual value" is determined as if the land were not woodlands but were left in its "natural and unimproved state." Tax is then charged (at standard rates) on an "assessable value" equal to one-third of this annual value. Woodlands thus face a very preferential tax regime. The occupier of woodlands may elect to be treated under schedule D instead if this is to his advantage. Tax under schedule B is payable in one installment on 1 January in the year of assessment.

Schedule C applies to paying agents who are entrusted with the payment in the UK of "interest, public annuities or shares of annuities" out of the public revenue of any government or the revenue of any public authority or institution outside the UK. Such agents must deduct tax at the basic rate (30 percent) and pay the net amount to individuals entitled to receive it.

Schedule D, the main method of taxing the self-employed, trades and professions, is divided into a number of different cases. These are Trades (I), Professions (II), Interest Receivable (III), Overseas Income (IV and V), and Miscellaneous Income (VI). Assessments for schedule D are made on a preceding year basis, with special rules for starting and finishing years. Schedule D assessments require a statement of profit and allowable expenses incurred by the individual or business. A much wider range of expenditures can be deducted under schedule D than under schedule E; under D any expenses incurred in earning the income can be allowed, while only those necessarily incurred (e.g., for essential protective clothing, but not for travel to work) are allowed under schedule E. Tax under schedule D is paid in two lump sums, on 1 January and 1 July in the year following the beginning of the relevant tax year.

Schedule F is concerned with the taxation of dividends. The system is that the company providing the dividend is responsible to the Revenue for Advance Corporation Tax on payment of the dividend and the recipient gets an equivalent "tax credit." This is set at three-sevenths of the net dividend, which is equal to 30 percent of the total gross dividend. If the individual is a basic rate taxpayer there is no extra liability; a further adjustment occurs for higher-rate taxpayers.

2. The Treatment of Capital Gains

Capital gains are subject to a rather lighter tax regime than income tax. The first £5,900 of the capital gains an individual makes in any one year are exempt from tax, as are the first £2,950 of the capital gains made by most trusts. Capital gains above this amount are charged a flat 30 percent. This exemption is considerably larger in real terms than it has been in the past. When the tax was first introduced in 1965, there was no exemption, but in order to make the tax cost-effective, a small exemption of £50 was introduced in 1968. In 1971, this was replaced by an exemption for any gains on asset disposals up to £500 per year. In 1977, an exemption of the first £1,000 of gains was introduced, and this was increased to £3,000 in 1980 and to £5,000 in 1982, being indexed to inflation since then. Today, most ordinary individuals do not incur a capital gains tax charge (owner-occupied houses and pension funds are exempt). Corporation tax is charged on the realized capital gains of companies. Table 4 gives rates of capital gains tax from 1977/78 to 1985/86.

The most complicated part of the UK capital gains tax is the provisions for indexation. Clearly, with high inflation, charging tax where there may have been no real gain, as using an historic cost base would do, is somewhat inequitable. Capital gains (or losses) are generally calculated as the difference between the consideration received on the disposal of an asset (the sale price or, in certain circumstances, the market value of the asset at the time of disposal) and the aggregate of the cost of acquiring the asset (expenditure incurred on the asset to enhance its value and certain costs incidental to the disposal of the asset).

The Finance Act 1982 included a provision that, in calculating chargeable gains, all the allowable costs should be indexed from March 1982 or from 12 months after acquisition of the asset (whichever is later), using the Retail Prices Index. These indexation provisions were extended by the Finance Act 1985 (effective, broadly, for disposals from April 1985): (i) to base the relief on the March 1982 market value of assets acquired before 1 April 1982 (for companies) or 6 April 1982 (for individuals and trusts); (ii) to extend (in lieu of the 12 month proviso in the previous sentence) the indexation allowance from the date on which the asset is acquired or from March 1982; if later, and (iii) to allow indexation to create or augment a loss.

3. Tax Treatment of the Family

The UK income tax treatment of married couples dates back to Victorian times when the husband was almost always the sole breadwinner and owner of all the couple's assets. All income is, therefore, aggregated for tax purposes and treated as the husband's. There are two exceptions to this basic rule: first, the husband is allocated a separate allowance for use against his wife's income—the wife's earned income allowance; and second, a couple can opt for separate assessment on earned income if both so desire. However, because the higher allowance granted to married men (known as the married man's allowance) would not then be available, the option for separate treatment is only beneficial to couples with joint incomes which take them well into higher rate bands in 1985/86 with incomes above £25,000.

The existence of a special allowance for married men, around 1.6 times the single allowance, and the wife's earned income allowance means that two-earner couples receive the equivalent of 2.6 single allowances. Further, aggregation of incomes also means that the wife pays tax on income above her earned income allowance at her husband's marginal rate.

Finally, the aggregation of incomes requires that all investment income belonging to the woman is treated as her husband's, so that women with only this source of income pay tax on the whole income at their husband's marginal rate and are not permitted to avoid providing their husband with full details about this income.

4. Payment Systems

Most tax on earned income is collected under the PAYE system, whereby employers withhold the correct amount of tax from employees' remuneration. The tax they should deduct is calculated on the basis of a single number "tax code" supplied by the Inland Revenue, which also provides tax tables for those employers whose payment systems are not yet computerized. The tax code contains the personal allowances to which the individual is entitled, plus any tax relief, less any adjustment including unpaid tax from a previous period or small amounts of additional income. Where the employee's income falls sufficiently over the year for a refund to be payable, this is also paid by the employer. The employer is then responsible for paying the full amount of tax withheld, less any refund paid, to Inland Revenue.

Where an employer has not received a tax code for any individual, the tax is calculated on an "emergency code" where the individual is treated as a single person with a full income record in the tax year. So those just starting work have to pay tax on their earnings and will only receive a refund (because they have had no earnings previously) when their case has been processed by Inland Revenue (which at present can take many months).

Many tax reliefs are not included in the tax code, but are allowed at source. This is the case for life insurance policies—although this relief was abolished for new policies in 1984—and for mortgages, where most people pay a net amount under a scheme called MIRAS (mortgage interest relief at source). Building society interest is paid net-of-tax, with the building societies being responsible for payment of tax on behalf of their customers calculated at a "composite rate" which is supposed to be the average of the tax individuals would otherwise have paid. There is thus a redistribution towards those who should have paid tax on their building society income (the working population) and away from those who would not (typically pensioners).

Schedule D payment systems are somewhat complicated, and the following is only a very brief overview. The basic idea is that the individual or partnership has to supply records and background documentation showing all expenses incurred and income earned from the schedule D activity. This trading account does not have to coincide with the tax year, but if it does not, an apportionment will be made in some cases. For businesses which have been going for some time and are not about to close, the account on which tax is deemed to be due is that ending in the preceding tax year. If the account ends at the beginning of that tax year (say on April 10th) then tax will be paid on activities which took place as much as two years previously. In the case of new businesses, and for those which are about to close, the rules are as follows:

OPENING YEARS

Year 1	Actual profits apportioned
Year 2	First 12 months of trading
Year 3	Preceding year basis

CLOSING YEARS

Last year but 2	Preceding year basis, but actual profits if these exceed profits
Last year but 1	On a preceding year basis
Last year	Actual profits

The assessment is, in principle, made by a tax inspector on the basis of records supplied, but in most cases the taxpayer's computations, particularly if professionally advised, will be accepted on the approval of the inspector. However, a number of schedule D cases are selected for a more in-depth examination. There are special rules for the treatment of many expenses, and where these expenses are claimed the inspector will wish to satisfy himself that the rules have been observed.

Once assessed, tax is payable in two installments on 1 January and 1 July of the relevant year. When assessment is made after 1 July, the payment is due within 30 days. Interest is currently payable on unpaid tax at a rate of 11 percent from its due date, although interest of £30 or less is normally overlooked.

Tax payable in respect of capital gains is due on 1 December following the year for which they were assessed, or within 30 days of the notice of assessment, if later. All payments other than schedule E are paid directly to Inland Revenue by post, bank giro, or personal payment.

5. Tax Returns

The basic principle employed is that individuals must fill in a tax return if requested to do so by Inland Revenue. In practice, only a minority of taxpayers receive tax returns, with tax inspectors selecting those with abnormal circumstances, or whose details they expect to have changed, on a rather ad hoc basis. An individual may request a tax return—this may be to his benefit if, for example, he has recently married and wishes to claim the higher allowance, or if he has been taxed on an income which is higher than the amount he has, in fact, received. Husbands submit tax returns on the behalf of both themselves and their wives.

6. Inflation Adjustment

Very little of the tax system is, in fact, adjusted for inflation by law, but a general practice has emerged that many of the allowances and levels in the income tax system are revalued in line with prices, although there are also many that are not. The main allowances and reliefs are, however, covered by provisions enacted in the Finance Act 1980.

These provisions specify that, unless Parliament otherwise determines, the basic rate band, the higher rate bands, and certain personal reliefs, such as the single person allowance, married man's allowance, age allowance, and the wife's earned income allowance are increased each year by the same percentage as the percentage increase (if any) in the Retail Price Index for the preceding December. The resulting figure in the case of tax bands and income limits is rounded up to the nearest £100, and in the case of the personal reliefs to the nearest £10.

There are no provisions for the revaluation of preceding year assessments under schedule D to allow for inflation. There are, however, indexation provisions built into the capital gains tax; these are described in section 2 above.

II. CORPORATE TAXES

1. Corporation Tax

The main tax on companies is the corporation tax. In 1986 this tax will raise some £6.6 billion, of which £1.6 billion will be from North Sea operations. Companies resident in the United Kingdom are liable to corporation tax on worldwide income and capital gains. They are regarded as resident if their central management and control is situated in the UK, which includes designated areas of the UK Continental Shelf. Nonresident companies are liable to a corporation tax on trading profits, capital gains, and other income attributable to a UK branch. Any other income arising in the UK is subject to income tax and not to the corporation tax. Moreover this liability is often reduced under double taxation agreements.

The corporation tax is normally payable nine months after the end of the company's accounting period and is based on taxable profits for that period. This tax follows the imputation system; retained and distributed profits are charged at the same rate. When a dividend is paid, Advance Corporation Tax (ACT) is payable at the rate of three-sevenths of the dividend. Quarterly returns must be made for dividends paid and received. The net payment is subject to ACT and the relevant ACT is payable 14 days after the end of the quarter.

ACT can be offset, up to a maximum of 30 percent of taxable income, against the corporation tax charged on profits of the period in which the dividend is paid. ACT which is unused in the period can be carried forward or back and set against other years' profits (up to six years back). ACT is not payable by nonresident companies.

Until 1984, corporation tax contained generous provisions for allowances to be set against taxable income. For example 100 percent of plant and machinery and a smaller proportion of buildings could be allowed against tax in the first year. The 1984 Budget, however, contained provisions which phased out these allowances and at the same time reduced the rate at which the corporation tax was charged. Table 5 summarizes the rate structure, which falls to 35 percent by 1987 for most companies, with small companies charged at 30 percent throughout the period. These rates are set for one year periods ending on 31 March. Where a company's accounting period ends on a different date, the taxable profits are apportioned and charged at the appropriate rates. Capital gains are charged to corporation tax at normal rates (for all companies) but the amount of the gain is reduced by whatever fraction (e.g., three-quarters for the year to 31 March 1986) brings the effective rate of charge to 30 percent.

The small companies' rate applies only to a UK resident company whose profits do not exceed £100,000, with intermediate rates for those up to £500,000. These limits are reduced if there is more than one company under common control.

The profit charged to corporation tax is calculated by adding together the various sources of income (e.g. trading profit, rents, investment income, deposit interest) and the chargeable proportion of capital gains. Reliefs available against income generally (e.g. interest and royalties paid) are deducted.

Dividends from nonresident companies are subject to corporation tax, but credit is given for foreign tax paid on the dividend. Measures have been introduced from 6 April 1984 to tax UK corporate shareholders in respect to profits made by companies established in low-tax territories. Only UK resident companies can be taxed and then only if they have 10 percent or more of the controlled foreign corporations (CFC) profits allocated to them. A CFC is a nonresident company, controlled by UK residents, which does not pay tax in its country of residence at 50 percent or more of the corresponding UK rate. There is a list of excluded countries where the provisions are most unlikely to be applicable and there are other exclusions (e.g., where there is an acceptable distribution policy). In order for corporation tax liability to arise the tax authorities must give specific notice that the above legislation applies to a given situation.

As part of the reform of the tax system in the 1984 Budget, capital allowances have been revised. Initial and first year allowances are to be phased out and, when the process is complete, only annual and writing-down allowances will be available.

A first year allowance (FYA) is given for plant and machinery in the accounting period of expenditure by reference to the date on which it is incurred. The rates are summarized in table 6.

An annual 25 percent writing-down allowance (on a reducing balance basis after deducting any FYA) is given. However, this cannot normally be claimed on any asset in the same accounting period as FYA. FYA at 100 percent continues to be available for scientific research expenditure, and expenditure in development areas. On disposal of plant and machinery, proceeds (limited to original cost) are deducted from the pool of expenditure subject to writing-down allowances. Any excess is treated as a balancing charge subject to tax. Any amount by which proceeds exceed original cost is treated as a capital gain.

On new industrial buildings (but not shops or offices) the cost of construction (excluding land) qualifies for an initial allowance in any accounting period by reference to the date on which expenditure is incurred. These allowances are also summarized in table 6. Any annual four-percent writing-down allowance (straight line basis on cost) is given and may be claimed in the same accounting period as an initial allowance.

On second-hand buildings no less than 25 years old, purchase cost (or original construction cost if less) is allowed over the balance of the 25 year period. Industrial and commercial buildings in specially designated areas (where development is encouraged) continue to qualify for 100 percent first year allowance on cost of construction. The similar allowance for small workshops (wherever situated) ceased on 27 March 1985. All or part of the initial allowance may be disclaimed.

On the disposal of a building less than 25 years old a further allowance or charge may be used to ensure that the total net allowances equal the difference between price paid and price realized. The charge cannot exceed allowances received. Any balance is treated as a capital gain. Hotels are treated similarly to industrial buildings, except that the initial allowance is 20 percent and will be reduced to nil for expenditure after 31 March 1986. Writing-down allowance at four percent continues.

On agricultural buildings an allowance is granted and thereafter a 10 percent straight line rule applies. The initial allowance is to be reduced to nil for expenditure after 31 March 1986. Similarly the writing-down allowance will be reduced to four percent straight-line. There are special rules for allowances on capital expenditure on films, patent rights, dredging, mines and oil wells, and some know-how costs.

Trading losses can be set off against general income and capital gains for the year of loss or the preceding year. Unused trading losses can be carried forward indefinitely but can only be set against profits of the trade in which the losses were incurred. There are anti-avoidance provisions governing the carry-forward of losses where the ownership of a company changes. The utilization of other losses (e.g., loss rental) is more restricted.

Each company within a group of companies is taxed separately but there are provisions permitting a trading loss (and some other deficits but not capital losses) in one resident company to be offset against profits earned (including chargeable capital gains) in the period of loss in another resident group company with at least 75 percent common ownership with the UK parent company. A specific claim must be made on each occasion. Similar rules apply to consortium companies.

Dividends can be paid from one member of a UK group (at least 51 percent owned) to another member without ACT being payable. Similarly, interest may be paid to another group company without deduction of tax. In both cases, appropriate notification must be given to the tax authorities and these remain in force until cancelled. Unused ACT can be surrendered down to a 51 percent subsidiary.

2. North Sea Taxes

The North Sea tax system at present consists of three taxes. The first is license royalties, which are levied at 12.5 percent of total revenue from each field. In the earlier fields, licensed in rounds one through four, a deduction is allowed for shipment costs, worth between one and four percent of revenue, depending on the field. A full description of the development of the system and its effects is given in Devereux and Morris (1983).

The mainstay of the system is petroleum revenue tax (PRT). Unlike royalties, and not as its name suggests, PRT is a tax on profits and not on revenue. It is levied on revenue from oil production, less exploration, operating costs, and capital expenditure. "Losses," inevitable in an activity which involves such long time lags, may be carried forward (though only at historic cost) and charged against future liability. Properly scrutinized "abortive exploration expenditure" and losses on failed fields elsewhere in the North Sea may also be fully offset by any company involved in the field. There are also a number of other deductions before the final tax is calculated. An "oil allowance" of 500,000 tonnes (1 tonne equals 1,000 kilogrammes which is approximately 7.5 barrels) per annum, up to a cumulative total of five million tonnes, is allowed free of tax. "Uplift" means that an additional deduction of 35 percent of capital expenditure is permitted. PRT is then levied at 75 percent of any remaining profit.

PRT contains a number of other complications. A "safeguard" provision was introduced in 1975 to give help to the less profitable fields. This means that if gross profits in any chargeable period are less than 15 percent of cumulative "upliftable" expenditure, the whole of PRT liability is cancelled. A further "tapering" provision ensures that the PRT liability in any chargeable period (of six months) cannot exceed 80 percent of the excess of gross profits above 15 percent of capital expenditure to date. Safeguard and uplift were limited from 1981 by introduction of "payback." This means that uplift is only allowed until "payback"—when the field first starts making a profit after allowing royalty, SPD and APRT, but not PRT—is reached, and that safeguard is only allowed for a period of one and one-half times as long as it takes to reach payback.

PRT between 1980 and 1983 was due two months after the end of each chargeable period and an advance payment of 15 percent of previous liability was also levied at that time. The timing of advance payments was changed in 1983 so that the tax is now collected in six equal monthly installments, based on 75 percent of the previous period's liability. The remaining 25 percent of liability, adjusted as necessary to account for any fluctuations from one period to the next, is collected two months after the end of the chargeable period.

The third tax, and the one on which the rules are least well defined, is corporation tax. For the purposes of this tax a "ring fence" is drawn around the North Sea profits, so that losses made onshore may not be offset against North Sea profits. Corporation tax, unlike the other taxes, is levied on a company and not a field basis. This means that liability for a particular field depends crucially on what other interests the company has in the North Sea. Corporation tax is charged at 52 percent of ring-fence profits made by the company after other North Sea taxes, capital allowances, and interest payments have been deducted. There is considerable scope for disagreement between the companies and Inland Revenue over such things as what proportion of a company's borrowing are attributable to the North Sea, and where the "ring fence" ends.

3. Dividends and Equity Financing

Under the UK system, it is rarely tax efficient to pay dividends, as these are taxed at the marginal rate of the shareholder in question. This marginal rate is above the effective marginal rate payable by the firm on additional profit, and the shareholder nearly always pays more if he takes his return as income through dividends rather than as a capital gain. In most cases, therefore, if the firm and its shareholders were considered as a single unit always choosing the most efficient route, then no dividends would be paid.

There is a considerable volume of literature on why firms do pay dividends when this is the case. Under the imputation system, it can be to a company's benefit to pay dividends if a significant part of its shares are held by tax-exempt institutions who can benefit from imputation against the distributing firm's tax liability. In some cases, groups of shareholders may emerge who do prefer distributions for tax reasons (see Mayer (1985) for a discussion), and in other cases shareholders may simply prefer cash receipts. The literature also contains a number of models which suggest that dividends can provide a useful signalling function (Ross (1977), Miller and Rock (1985)), although these theories have received considerable criticism. Edwards (1984) notes that dividends do not satisfy the requirements of a signal as often understood, while Stiglitz (1982) suggests that more tax-efficient methods such as equity market purchases, share repurchases or takeovers could be employed instead. A further group of theories emphasizes the certainty of a crash payment instead of a capital gain sometime in the future.

Empirical studies of dividends have not really been able to distinguish between these competing theories. Most studies find that profits or cash flows emerge as the primary determinants of dividend behavior, while some papers have highlighted the importance of relative tax liabilities (Feldstein (1970), King (1974; 1977), Poterba (1983), Poterba and Summers (1984)), but this evidence is at an aggregate level. A recent study by Edwards, Mayer, Pashardes and Poterba (1985) indicates that cross-sectional relationships are weaker. Mayer and Pashardes (1985) investigate the effects of individual controls in this context.

Many firms underwrite new equity issues, thus transferring the downside risk to the underwriter. Several explanations for this behavior have been put forward, although the cost of underwriting seems to be very high relative to its perceived value. Some authors suggest that such behavior may occur because managers may receive benefits (bribes, special deals) which would not otherwise accrue. This is a subject for controversy although Hansen and Pinkerton (1982) question it. It has also been suggested that such issues can be timed to take account of market conditions, at such times, proceeds are received more quickly and there is less uncertainty.

In the case of the UK, new equity issues are usually underwritten, so little empirical and theoretical work comparing direct and underwritten offers exists. Much of the relevant literature concentrates on describing reasons for this behavior, though in the main with little empirical backup to support the theories (see Lamb (1976), Feldstein and Green (1983), for a useful discussion).

III. SAVINGS AND INVESTMENT

1. Saving Incentives and Fiscal Privilege

The United Kingdom tax system contains a very large number of ways in which particular forms of saving are treated preferentially. The two most important are the treatment of pensions and the treatment of owner-occupied housing. Both are very favorably treated, and a high proportion of personal saving in the UK is, in fact, channelled into these two forms.

Pension funds (including the pension business of insurance companies) are exempt from tax as they accumulate the return on assets they hold. When individuals make contributions into pension funds, these contributions are deductible from their income in calculating income tax liability. On the other hand, when a pension is paid, it is treated as part of earned income and is subject to income tax. In addition to the tax-free status of contributions and accumulation, part of an individual's pension rights can be paid out as a tax-free lump sum.

The existence of a tax-free lump sum creates a kind of double exemption for pensions; the lump sum has been accumulated out of tax-free income and is then paid out tax free.

Owner-occupied housing also enjoys considerable fiscal advantage. First, any increase in value of the property, providing it is the individual's main residence, is free from capital gains tax. Second, interest on the first £30,000 of the loan is allowed to be set against taxable income. A married couple may only claim one £30,000 relief (worth about £100 per month to a basic rate taxpayer at current interest rates), but unmarried cohabiting individuals may claim £30,000 each on the same property.

The precise tax advantages to all forms of saving are somewhat complex, but a recent study carried out at the Institute for Fiscal

Studies (IFS) has summarized these by measuring the "degree of fiscal privilege" accorded a large number of different savings vehicles. The results taken from Hills (1984) are summarized in table 7. Fiscal privilege is defined as the percentage of the underlying real rate of return of the asset which is added or taken away by the tax system. A degree of fiscal privilege of 100 means that an amount equal to the underlying rate of return is added by tax advantages, one of 100 means it is taken away. With nonperfect indexation of the tax system and varying real rates, fiscal privilege is variable between time periods, particularly those with different inflation rates; the table shows calculations for the latest period available, 1978/79-1982/83.

There is a wide degree of variation in fiscal privilege for basic rate taxpayers, and an even wider one for higher-rate taxpayers. For those paying tax at a marginal rate of 30 percent, fiscal privilege can vary from over 100 (insurance contract, house with 50 percent mortgage) to less than 100 (interest bearing accounts). The 1984 Budget made some changes to this regime, mainly by abolishing relief on new insurance policies, but the effect on the whole picture of fiscal privilege was fairly small. The effects of the budget, on the assumption of five percent inflation, are shown in table 8.

The 1985 Budget made little difference to the wide variation in fiscal privilege which exists in the UK tax system. Top rate taxpayers could, in the period 1978/79 to 1982/83, choose assets which yielded tax advantages of around four times the underlying real rate of return (a house with a 50 percent mortgage), or others where the tax penalty was three times the underlying return.

2. Treatment of Financial Institutions

In the UK, banks and other financial institutions have generally been treated in the same way as other companies, although there are often exceptions. In 1981 a special 2.5 percent levy on the level of their Sterling noninterest-bearing balances, averaged over the last three months of 1980, was imposed on banks. This additional tax was justified, as have been more recent calls for changes in their treatment, by the observation that although the banks are more profitable than other UK businesses, they pay low amounts of corporation tax. The low levels of their corporation tax payments occur because they have historically taken advantage of various mechanisms to reduce their tax liability (engaging in leasing business, in particular).

For a more complete discussion of the tax treatment of financial institutions and whether their apparent high level of profitability did, in fact, occur, the reader is referred to the IFS Report "Issues in Bank Taxation."

3. Incentives to Save and Invest

The tax system provides individuals with a very wide range of incentives to invest in particular assets, as indicated in section 1 above. As a result of the very generous treatment of owner-occupied housing and of pensions, a very high proportion of personal saving is channelled into each of these. Money thereby saved is then available for investment by large financial institutions. Thus, in the UK, the majority of transactions in equities and in government stock is carried out by large institutions—particularly by pension funds.

An examination carried out at IFS (1983) of the ownership of shares (see *Savings and Fiscal Privilege*, chapter 5), indicated that these large institutions were less likely to hold shares in small companies or companies failing significant degrees of variability or specific risk. On the other hand, they were more likely to choose highly marketable shares. Of course, not all of this is directly due to tax considerations; large institutions may not, for example, find it cost-effective to investigate a small company in order to decide whether to invest in it. But the general pattern of institutional behavior coupled with the channelling of approximately 90 percent of personal saving to these institutions certainly has a large effect on the UK equity market.

Incentives for firms to invest are also highly variable. Following the oil price shock of 1973/74, many companies accumulated large tax losses which they were permitted to carry forward and use against future profits. These firms were then unable to take advantage directly of allowances on plants, machinery, or industrial buildings.

However, firms in this position can lease plants and buildings from companies (e.g., banks) with positive tax liabilities and thus take advantage of some of their unused allowances. There is debate over the relative value to lessee and lessor of such an arrangement, but it is generally agreed that most of the benefit goes to the lessee. The 1984 tax reforms led to a severe reduction in capital allowances (see section II), which will reduce the advantage of leasing, and the transitional arrangements that have led to an acceleration of investment over the last two years. In the long run, incentives to invest are likely to be much less variable as the new system comes into operation.

IV. NATIONAL INSURANCE CONTRIBUTIONS

1. The National Insurance Contribution System

The only payroll tax in the United Kingdom's tax system is National Insurance contributions. These were introduced as a flat-rate tax in 1948, when the National Insurance benefit system was introduced following the Beveridge Report of 1942. In principle, National Insurance contributions are supposed to pay exactly for benefits from the National Insurance Fund, but in fact payments from the fund and receipts from contributions bear little relation to each other. Indeed, governments have often used National Insurance as a means of raising additional taxes which are, in a sense, less visible than the direct income tax. A National Insurance surcharge was introduced in 1978 and gradually phased out until it was abolished in 1984. The standard employees rate of National Insurance contributions has been raised from 6.5 percent to nine percent over the period since 1979.

National Insurance contributions are paid partly by the employee and partly by the employer. Table 9 summarizes the rates which apply in 1985/86 and in 1986/87. Contributions are lower for employees who are "contracted-out" of the State Earnings-Related Pension Scheme (SERPS) and who instead belong to a recognized pension scheme. Employees who earn less than the National Insurance "floor" (set equal to the state pension for a single person) pay no contributions, and no employee contributions are paid on earnings above the NI ceiling, although since the 1984 budget, employer contributions are paid on all income, however large. Contributions for those with incomes above the "floor" are paid on the whole of income, which leads to a very high marginal rate of tax on an increase in weekly income from £37.99 to £38.01.

The 1985 budget introduced a special regime for low income earners. Under this scheme, summarized in table 10 for 1986/87, a five percent rate is paid on all earnings for those with weekly earnings between £38 and £59.99, seven percent on all earnings for those with incomes in the next tranche and so on. The normal rate of nine percent applies for those with weekly incomes above £140. These changes contribute to making some marginal rates extremely high.

The main class of National Insurance contributions—class 1 contributions-apply to ordinary employees. The self-employed pay contributions according to the rules for class 2 and class 4 contributions. These are summarized in Table 11. All self-employed individuals must pay class 2 contributions, which count towards certain contributory benefits but not unemployment benefit,

SERPS, invalidity pension, or widows benefits, unless they hold a certificate of exemption. People with earnings in the tax year below £1,925 may obtain such certificates.

Self-employed people with taxable profits above £4,150 per annum must also pay class 4 contributions of 6.3 percent of profits for profit levels between £4,150 and £13,780 per annum. These contributions are normally calculated and collected along with schedule D by Inland Revenue.

Individuals may also make voluntary (class 3) contributions of £4.65 per week. These allow those not paying other contributions to qualify for certain contributory benefits; they are paid by means of a special stamp, available from post offices, which is stuck onto a contribution card.

2. National Insurance Contributions and Government Revenue

When National Insurance contributions were first introduced in 1948, the intention was that they would be sufficient to pay for benefits with some help from the Exchequer and that gradually a fund would develop so that there was an actuarial link between contributions and payments made to National Insurance beneficiaries.

Table 12 compares how contributions, government contribution to the fund, and payments from the fund actually developed, all deflated to current prices by movements in average wages. It shows how little relation there was in fact between contributions and the benefits paid by the fund. Contributions have changed from funding 93 percent of payments in 1948, to 73 percent in 1960 to 80 percent in 1980, and the payments contribution has dropped from 30 percent to a low of just over 14 percent.

In 1976 a surcharge was introduced at two percent of earnings, and was increased to 3.5 percent in 1978. It was reduced gradually thereafter and finally withdrawn in 1984.

3. Payments from the National Insurance Fund

Table 13 summarizes expenditures made from the National Insurance Fund in the year 1982/83. It shows that the vast bulk of expenditure was on the state retirement pension, which made up some £1.4 billion of the total payments of £1.7 billion. The most important other benefits in terms of expenditure were unemployment, sickness, invalidity and disability benefits.

V. INDIRECT TAXES

1. Value-Added Tax

Since 1979, value-added tax in the United Kingdom has been levied at a single rate of 15 percent. This replaced an older system in which the basic rate was eight percent and there was a higher rate of 12.5 percent on "luxury" items. Value-added tax will raise nearly £19 billion in 1985/86, around half the amount raised by income tax and ACT.

Various categories of goods are either "zero-rated" or "exempt." Zero-rated goods are charged no VAT, but inputs used in their creation can be reclaimed and set against other VAT. An exempt trader is not charged tax, but neither may he reclaim the cost of any inputs. So it is always better to be zero-rated than exempt, and if the value of goods sold is less than the cost of their inputs, then it may even be better to be standard-rated than exempt. Table 14 summarizes the main categories of goods which are zero-rated or exempt, while table 15 shows how consumers' expenditure is split between these items. Those zero-rated cover some 30 percent of all consumers' expenditure, while those which are exempt account for another four percent. Housing is also exempt, so that only some 56 percent of consumer spending is subject to VAT.

Small traders, with turnover in 1985/86 less than £19,500 are also exempt from VAT. Because traders selling goods may be able to reclaim all or only part of the cost of inputs, (because the goods require labor or the output of exempt traders) effective rates of VAT are highly variable between goods.

Compliance with VAT is generally felt to be high and administrative costs fairly low. The exemption of small traders means that only quite sizable companies have to administer the tax.

2. Excise Duties

As well as VAT, the United Kingdom tax system contains a number of "excise duties." These are flat-rate taxes (per pint, packet, or gallon) levied on alcoholic drink, tobacco, and petrol and its derivatives. Table 16 summarizes the rates at which these taxes are levied and provides estimates of the effects of duties on prices.

The structure of excise duties has been changed somewhat in recent years. Pressure from the European Community to harmonize has meant that duty on wine has been reduced in real terms while that on beer has been increased. The flat-rate duties are usually increased in line with inflation at each annual budget.

3. Licenses and Other Taxes

As well as VAT and excise duties, revenue is raised through a system of licenses. The most important of these are vehicle excise duties (£100 per car and more for goods vehicles) which raise some £2.5 billion per year. Other licenses, including broadcast receiving licenses raise £800 million.

There are also duties on betting, gaming, and stamp duty on financial transactions; these combined raise around £2 billion. Finally, new cars are subject to a purchase tax which yields around £770 million per year.

VI. THE HIDDEN ECONOMY

1. Income Unreported for Tax Purposes

The "hidden or black economy" is used to denote all activity which goes unmeasured in official statistics (including, for example, housewives' time) or merely to indicate the amount of income which remains undeclared for tax or benefit purposes. In this paper, hidden economy refers only to income which remains unreported for tax purposes and which, therefore, causes a reduction in overall tax revenue.

The last "official" estimate of the size of the black economy was made by Sir William Pile in 1977, when he was chairman of the board of Inland Revenue. He stated then that it was "not implausible" that the amount of unreported income amounted to some 7.5 percent of the national income. The background to this figure was never published, nor was any justification, so it cannot be regarded as definitive.

Incentives to evade taxes of various kinds are quite variable throughout the tax and benefit system. The greatest incentive occurs for benefit recipients, where earning an additional pound can cause an equal reduction in benefit. Higher rate taxpayers also face a large incentive to evade income tax. It is generally agreed that evasion of VAT is less important, partly because the smallest traders are already exempt.

Income tax for most employees is administered pay-as-you-earn (PAYE) and therefore, unless the employer cooperates in evasion, it is difficult for an employee to pay less tax than he should. However, evasion on secondary earnings is much more common; in the UK only a minority of taxpayers receives tax returns, and there is a general ethos that secondary earnings are somehow less subject to tax than primary earnings.

The incentive to evade tax on particular income varies among taxpayers. Most individuals in the UK—because of the very wide basic rate band for income tax—stand to gain 39 percent of the undeclared income, while their employers would gain 10.45 percent by not having to pay employers' National Insurance contributions. Higher rate taxpayers would gain 60 percent (the highest rate of income tax), but at these levels of income employee National Insurance contributions are not paid—although employers still pay 10.45 percent.

Incentives to avoid declaring income for benefit purposes are much larger. After an initial earnings disregard, recipients of supplementary benefit lose income pound for pound, and may lose entitlement altogether, while recipients of family income supplement face a tax rate of 50 percent and recipients of housing benefit between five and 33 percent. There is a band of income, popularly known as the "poverty trap," in which combined tax, NI, and lost benefits can cost the individual more than 100 percent of his additional earnings.

Balanced against the incentive to evade is the probability of being caught and the penalties involved. Although the revenue departments chase large evaders quite vigorously, their scrutiny of ordinary individuals' behavior is patchy. This was the conclusion of a recent enquiry carried out by a committee under Lord Keith, and many enforcement powers are being increased. In the period from 1980/81 to 1984, only 344 convictions for evasion of income tax were made each year, and some 188 of these were for straight-forward theft of giro cheques and payable orders (Inland Revenue Annual Reports). In the period from 1980/81 to 1982, only 99 prosecutions per year for VAT fraud were carried through, involving a total of £2.5 million in penalties and the recovery of £2.1 million in arrears.

The Keith Committee report contains an analysis of traders' accounts which is reproduced in table 17. It shows that of a total of 1.63 million schedule D returns, only 49,000 were examined in depth, while of 530,000 company returns only 3,000 received detailed scrutiny. The report also presents results from a pilot compliance study carried out in 1981: some 20 percent of the sample "probably," and 40 percent "possibly" understated their income.

2. Estimates of the Size of the Hidden Economy in the UK

The size of the black economy in the UK is the subject of continuing speculation, but of little serious research. Apart from the Inland Revenue's estimate of 7.5 percent, various claims as to the size of a rather ill-defined black economy have been made. Perhaps the most spectacular is Feige's 33 percent (Feige (1979)), which was derived from an attempt to model the demand for notes and coin by the normal economy and attribute any unexplained part to the hidden economy. Guttman (1977) pursues the same approach more systematically. A more modest version of this kind of work was carried out by Matthews (1984) who puts the extent at 15 percent although he believes that 1.3 million of the three million UK unemployed are engaged in black economy activities. MacAfee (1980) attempted to estimate its size from the residual between the expenditure and income measures of GDP and came up with a figure of three percent.

Evasion estimates are regularly included in the national accounts and these are reproduced in table 19. Recorded employment income is boosted by one percent, self-employment income by 21 percent, and company profits by 0.1 percent to allow for evasion.

A rather different approach has been adopted by some authors, notably O'Higgins (1980) and Dilnot and Morris (1981), which compares expenditure with income in a large and representative sample of households. Dilnot and Morris produce an estimate of unreported income of between two and three percent of GDP.

Although the literature in this area is somewhat limited, a major study of the question has been carried out over the last two years at IFS and will be published during 1986.

VII. CAPITAL TAXES

1. Introduction

Taxes on capital in the United Kingdom have been steadily diminishing in importance throughout the post-war period. In 1985/86 the total raised from such taxes will be £1.9 billion, or only 1.4 percent of all tax revenue. Of this £1.9 billion, £800 million is raised by capital gains tax (see above), £800 million from transfer tax and £350 million from other taxes on capital which are gradually being phased out. There is no wealth tax in the United Kingdom. Some £1.2 billion is raised from stamp duty on financial transactions. In this section, we concentrate on the structures of capital transfer tax and the stamp duty.

2. Capital Transfer Tax

The capital transfer tax (CTT) was imposed by the Finance Act (1975) as a successor to estate duty, which has been charged since 1984 on estates passing at the time of death. CTT is levied on the value of assets transferred by gift, assets of deceased persons passing on death, assets held under a settlement where there is a change of interest or a distribution, and (every tenth year) on assets held in, for example, a discretionary trust. Assets are valued for CTT purposes at the price they might reasonably be expected to yield on the open market.

The rates of CTT are shown in table 20. There is no charge on transfers below £67,000 and there are then rising schedules for lifetime rates up to 30 percent and on death up to 60 percent for estates over £300,000.

The rates for transfers on death also apply to transfers made within three years of death. Overdue CTT is charged interest at eight percent per annum for tax on lifetime transfers and six percent for transfers on death. CTT attributable to land, buildings, shares, securities, and the net value of businesses may be paid by installments over a period of up to 10 years.

There are a number of transfers of assets which are exempt from CTT. These include transfers between husband and wife, transfers to national bodies for the public benefit, to charities, to political parties (subject to a limit of £100,000 if made within one year of death), and some wedding gifts.

Relief is allowed for agricultural property and other business assets, including unlisted securities, which can reduce the tax by up to half. Tax payments may also be deferred in the case of timber and National Heritage properties.

3. Stamp Duty

Stamp duty is payable upon various documents, including many used in legal and commercial practice. Payment of the duty is indicated by stamps impressed on the documents themselves following presentation to the Office of the Controller of Stamps or, where composition arrangements operate, through a printed indication on the documents of the amount or payment of the duty.

The main items covered by stamp duty are conveyances and transfers of land, buildings and property other than stocks and shares, which are chargeable to an *ad valorem* duty on the purchase price or the value of the property. The rates of duty and the respective reduced rate bands which have applied since 1958 are set out in table 21.

Transfers of stocks and shares are also chargeable to *ad valorem* duty on the price or value of the shares. From 1974 to 1984 the rate of duty was two percent, except where the purchaser was resident outside the Scheduled Territories where the rate was at one percent. The Finance Act (1984) reduced the duty to a straight one percent for all transfers of stocks and shares on sale or by way of voluntary disposition, but it was abolished in the 1985 Budget.

Grants of new leases of land, buildings, and other property are charged by reference to the elements of rent and premium separately. The duty on the rent depends on the average rent and the term of the lease; the premium is charged with the same duty as a conveyance on sale for the same amount.

There is an *ad valorem* duty of one percent, imposed in accordance with EEC directives, on the raising of capital by companies. Duty is, in general, payable on life insurance policies at the rate of 50p per £1,000 of the sum insured. There is an *ad valorem* duty of .25 percent on the value of property put into a unit trust. Banks in Northern Ireland are enabled to pay by composition stamp duty on bank notes issued by them. Duty is at 50p per £100 of the average value of notes in circulation each half year.

VIII. THE DISTRIBUTION OF INCOME

1. Introduction

There is literature both on UK income distribution and poverty and on the effects of the tax and benefit system on that distribution, which is too extensive to summarize here. The reader is referred to Morris and Preston (1986a, b) and to Dilnot, Kay, and Morris (1984) for a summary of that literature.

Taxes in the United Kingdom are divided into three main groups based on in their impact on households: direct taxes such as income tax and National Insurance paid by employees and payroll taxes (employers NI), indirect taxes directly incident on final expenditure (excise duties, VAT), and those indirectly incident on final expenditure, usually termed intermediate taxes. The measurement of the first, direct taxes, is relatively straightforward, although the precise incidence of tax expenditures (mortgage interest relief, pension relief) is still a matter for debate. Indirect taxes obviously depend on levels of expenditure, while the incidence of intermediate taxes is also subject to a number of interpretations.

The only comprehensive study of the incidence of taxes, benefits, and other government expenditures on the distribution is carried out annually by the Central Statistical Office (CSO). This analysis has been subject to considerable criticism, particularly for its treatment of intermediate taxes (see Kay and Keen (1985) for a summary of the main arguments and the development of an alternative framework).

2. The CSO Analysis

Table 22 is taken from the abbreviated CSO analysis for 1984 (the full analysis will not be published until mid-1986). It gives estimates of original income before all taxes and benefits and the deduction, in order, of direct taxes and indirect taxes and then the addition of benefits in kind from public expenditure.

The lowest quintile of the original income distribution (mostly single female pensioners) has very little original income indeed and receives most of its income from cash benefits. Direct taxes hardly affect this group, while indirect taxes remove about 23 percent of their disposable income. Benefits in kind (e.g., health care) boost their income after all taxes from £2,490 to £3,820, according to the CSO method of allocation.

The pattern for all households is somewhat different from that of this group. Cash benefits make up about 17 percent of gross income, while direct taxes remove an equal amount. Indirect taxes account for some 25 percent proportionate effect.

The highest decile only receives trivial amounts of cash benefits, and pays 23 percent of their gross income in direct taxes. Indirect taxes form 24 percent of their disposable income, while benefits in kind are rather less important.

IX. THE LOCAL TAX SYSTEM

Local authority expenditure is financed partly by "rates" levied on domestic and business property and partly by grants from the central government. Local authorities are responsible for most local items of expenditure including local roads, refuse removal, personal social services, and education. A small proportion of local revenue is raised from fees and charges. Rates are calculated as the product of the "ratable value" of the property and a "rate poundage," which is set by the local authority. In recent years the rates charged by particularly high-spending authorities have been limited, with more or less success. Ratable values are supposed to reflect the market rental value of the property, and are set irregularly—they were last recalculated in 1974. To maintain constant real expenditure, rate poundages rise year by year.

An overall limit is set for aggregate exchequer grant (AEG), and within this limit allocation is set by a complex formula. AEC comprises Rate Support Grant (RSG) and various specific and supplementary grants (SSG). SSG are "matching grants" earmarked for expenditure on specified services such as the police, home improvements, and transport.

Rate support grant is made up of block grant and domestic rate relief grant. The latter is a payment of 18.5p in the pound subsidy to domestic ratepayers so that they pay a lower rate poundage than occupiers of commercial, industrial, and other properties. Block grant is a "non-matching grant" not intended for particular services but determined by a local authority's total planned "expenditure for block grant purposes." Local authorities have discretion as to the purpose to which block grant is applied.

Block grant is used as a method of equalization between authorities: if ratable value is low, the authority will get more than if it is high, all other things being equal. The calculation of block grant is complex, depending on a number of items—of which the most important is grant related expenditure (GRE). This is an assessment of the cost to a local authority of providing a certain standard of service, and depends on factors such as the number of pensioners, schoolchildren, main roads, and housing. When expenditure per head exceeds GRE per head by more than a threshold amount (in theory some 10 percent of national average GRE) block grant begins to be reduced rapidly.

In addition to setting the rules for GRE and for thresholds, the central government sets a target (officially known as expenditure guidance) for each local authority; this varies in fairly arbitrary ways between authorities. There are penalties for authorities spending more than the target which involve reductions to grants known as penalty, holdback, or abatement.

Although the discussion above is far too brief to give a clear picture of the system of local government finance in the UK, it is probably enough to give the (correct) impression of extreme complexity. This complexity has grown over recent years as central government has sought to reduce local autonomy and to exert tighter control over local authority expenditure. At present, these attempts are meeting with resistance from a number of authorities, a notable recent example being Liverpool. Other authorities are protecting their spending levels by running down capital assets when more directly funded spending from rates would lead to a large increase in grant penalty.

In the immediate future the face of local authority finance will be changed in two ways. First, a group of authorities, including the Greater London Council and the Metropolitan Authorities, were abolished as of May 1986, and second, the government has issued proposals for the phasing out of domestic and commercial rates and their replacement by a lump-sum "community charge." Business rates, which are at present highly variable among authorities, are to become directly related to the number of people living in a particular authority. A description of their charges and their effects is given in Smith and Squire (1986).

Table 23 presents estimates of the amount raised from domestic rates in 1986. Of the total of some £13 billion, about half comes from domestic and half from business rates. In London, separate rates are levied for education and for the police, and these are shown separately in the table, as are figures for the Greater London Council (abolished in May 1986) and the London boroughs.

X. PROPOSALS FOR TAX REFORM

1. Income Tax

Over the last thirty years there has been a lively debate in the UK about the possibility of moving the tax base from income consumption. Proponents of this view, including Kaldor (1955) and the Meade Committee (IFS, 1977), argue that the present attempt to distinguish between income and capital leads to many of the avoidance possibilities inherent in the present system, contributes to much of its administrative complexity, and leads to severe distortions in the savings market. The proposed expenditure tax would allow deductions for investment in "registered assets" but would tax their realization. Although an expenditure tax is unlikely to be introduced in one step, the UK system has been moving towards it gradually by extending reliefs to more and more assets, though as we saw in section III, the rather piecemeal movement which has occurred has led to an extremely patchy structure of savings incentives. However, extension of reliefs to equities and to bank deposits would leave the UK with something (nearly) approaching an expenditure base.

There is, however, an opposite school of thought which believes that the solution to the widely-perceived distortions in the UK system lies in a move towards a comprehensive income basis for taxation, to which the present government subscribes. This was the reason, for example, for the abolition of reliefs on life insurance policies. However, it is now generally recognized that progress by this route is unlikely because of the political impossibility of abolishing reliefs for pensions and mortgage interest.

Another item which may receive attention in a Green Paper shortly to be published is the structure of tax for the self-employed under schedule D. At present this is calculated on a preceding year basis, and there is some pressure to move this to a current year basis, as with schedule E.

Tax in the UK is collected on a cumulative basis, so that the Revenue attempts to ensure that payments at any point in the year are correct. A move to end-year assessment is possible. Also, the responsibility for provision of information may be shifted more towards the individual.

As noted in section 1, proposals are about to be brought forward to reform the treatment of husband and wife, which is widely seen as discriminatory against wives. The government proposal is likely to be a system of transferable allowances, where each spouse gets a single person's allowance but can transfer all or part of it to the other partner. There is likely to be considerable resistance to this from women's groups concerned over the dampening effect on women's labor supply. There are also some questions over how severe the administrative problems are under the present PAYE system.

2. Corporation Tax

As noted in section II, corporation taxes were "reformed" in 1984, when the previous system of allowances was phased out and a lower rate applied. This system is subject to considerable scrutiny at present, particularly as it is seen as reducing investment. The new structure is quite sensitive to inflation. It is similar to the 1965 system which led to severe problems following the inflationary stimulus of 1973/74. If severe inflation were to re-emerge, further changes would inevitably follow.

3. National Insurance Contributions

It is possible that the National Insurance system may be integrated with income tax and a more coherent structure applied. The most probable form this could take would be to raise an additional amount on the income tax base and predicate it for use for social security benefits.

4. Local Rates

Reform of the local rating system was one of the promises made by the Conservative government both in the 1979 and the 1983 elections. As noted in section IX, the Government has now published a Green Paper ("Paying for Local Government" CMND 9714) which recommends the phased abolition of domestic rates and their replacement by a poll tax to be called community charge. Business rates are to be replaced by a tax related to the number of adults in a particular area levied on businesses. These proposals have large distributional consequences both for individuals—the poor pay more—and for companies—businesses in high-rate areas pay less and those in low-rate areas more. The interauthority transfers, although large, are very complex and have as yet been inadequately analyzed inside or outside government. An IFS Report on the subject will be published in March 1986.

These proposals for reform follow several decades of debate and a Royal Commission (the Layfield Commission) on the subject. The latter body recommended the imposition of a local income tax, but this proposal was never implemented because the administration of such a tax was felt to be too complicated under existing UK income tax practices. Other proposals have included a revised capital base for taxation, possibly using capital values or even site values as the basis, and the possibility of a local sales tax.

5. Benefits

The UK benefit system, not covered in this paper, has undergone significant reform and the results of recent government reviews are about to be implemented. These include some limited moves towards integration with the tax system for administrative purposes.

6. Capital Taxes

Although the present government has steadily reduced the level and scope of capital taxes, the opposition (Labor) is committed to increasing them, either by significantly increasing tax rates or by the introduction of a wealth tax, a possibility which has been discussed over a long period.

REFERENCES

Central Statistical Office "The Effects of Taxes and Benefits on Household Income 1984," *Economic Trends*, December 1985.

Devereux M.P. & Morris C.M., *North Sea Oil Taxation*, IFS Report Series 6.

Dilnot, A.W. and C.N. Morris "What Do We Know About the Black Economy," *Fiscal Studies*, Vol. 2, No. 1, March 1981.

Dilnot A.W., J.A. Kay, and C.N. Morris, "The UK Tax System, Structure and Progressivity 1948-1982" *Scandinavian Journal of Economics*, November 1984.

Edwards, J.S.S. and C.P. Mayer, Issues in Bank Taxation IFS Report Series 1 (1982).

Edwards, J.S.S, C.P. Mayer, P. Pashardes, and J.M. Poterba "The Effects of Taxation," Corporate Dividend Policy IFS Discussion.

Feige, E. (1979), "How Big Is the Irregular Economy?," *Challenge*, November/December 1979.

Feldstein M. and J. Green, "Why Do Companies Pay Dividends?" Paper (1985), *American Economic Review* 73 (1983).

Feldstein, M. (1970), "Corporate Taxation and Dividend Behaviour," *Review of Economic Studies,"* (37), 57-72.

Guttman, P. (1977). "The Subterranean Economy," *Financial Analysts Journal*, November/December 1979.

Hills, J. *Savings and Fiscal Privilege*, IFS Report Series 9 (1984).

Kay, J.A. and M. Keen, "Measuring Tax Burdens," IFS Working Paper 64, April 1985.

Kemsley, W.F.F. (1975), "Family Expenditure Survey." A study of differential response based on a comparison of the 1971 sample with the census, *Statistical News*, November 1975.

King, M.A. (1974), "Taxation and the Cost of Capital," *Review of Economic Studies* (41), 21-35.

King, M.A. (1977), *Public Policy and the Corporation* (London: Chapman and Hall).

King, M.A. and D. Fullerton (1984); *The Taxation of Income from Capital* (Chicago: University of Chicago Press).

Kwan, C.Y. (1981), "Efficient Market Tests of the Informational Content of Dividends Announcements," *Journal of Financial and Quantitative Analysis* (16). 193-205.

Lamb, P. (1976), "On the Informational Content of Dividends," *Journal of Business* (49), 73-80.

MacAfee, K. (1980). "A Glimpse of the Hidden Economy in the National Accounts," *Economic Trends* (February).

Mayer, C.P. (1985), "Corporation Tax, Finance and the Cost of Capital," mimeo, Oxford.

Mayer, C.P. and P. Pashardes (1985), "Dividend Setting in the Presence of Controls," mimeo, IFS.

Morris, C.N. and I. Preston, "The Effect of Direct Taxes and Cash Benefits on the United Kingdom Income Distribution 1968-1983," IFS Working Paper 74 (1986).

O'Higgins, M. (1980). "Measuring the Hidden Economy: A Review of Evidence and Methodology, Outer Circle Policy Unit, 1980.

Poterba, J.M. (1983), "Public Policy and Corporate Dividend Behaviour: the Postwar British Experience," mimeo, MIT.

Poterba, J.M. and L.H. Summers (1985), "The Economic Effects of Dividend Taxation," in E. Altman and M. Subrahmanyam, *Recent Developments in Corporate Finance* (Homewood, Illinois: Dow-Jones Irwin).

Ross, S. (1977), "The Determination of Financial Structure: An Incentive Signalling Approach," *The Bell Journal of Economics* (8), 23-40.

Stiglitz, J. (1982), "The Inefficiency of Stock Market Equilibrium," unpublished paper.

Smith, S. and D.L Squire, "Who Will Be Paying for Local Government", IFS Commentary 1986.

Table 1
Revenue from Taxes in the United Kingdom, 1985/86

Tax	£Billion
Taxes on Income	
Income tax	35,700
ACT	3,650
Corporation tax	6,595
North Sea oil taxes including royalties	8,700
National Insurance contributions	24,700
Adjustment	−600
Total	78,745
Taxes on Expenditure	
VAT	18,700
Local rates	13,771
Petrol and derivate duty	6,609
Tobacco duty	4,377
Alcohol duty	4,345
Betting and gaming duty	720
Car tax	770
Vehicle excise duty	2,450
Licenses	790
Stamp duty	1,232
Other taxes in expenditure	3,100
Total	56,864
Taxes on Capital	
Capital gains tax	806
Capital transfer tax	790
Other taxes on capital	350
Total	1,946
Total, All Above Taxes	13,555

Source: Estimates based on Financial Statement and Budget Report 1985/86, HM Treasury, 1985.

Table 2
Income Tax Personal Allowances, 1985/86

	Standard	Aged Over 65
Single	£2,205	£2,690
Married man	3,455	4,255
Wife's earned income	2,205	—
One parent family	3,455	—
Dependent relative/housekeeper	100	—
Blind person	360	—
Widows Bereavement	1,250	—

Table 3
Income Tax Rate Bands, 1985/86

Taxable Income	Tax Rate (Percent)
0-16,200	30
16,201-19,200	40
19,201-24,400	45
24,401-32,300	50
32,301-40,200	55
Above 40,200	60

Table 4
Rates of Capital Gains Tax, 1978/79-1985/86

1977/78 to 1979/80	Total Net Gains for Year of Assessment (£)	Tax Chargeable (Percent)
Individuals	Not exceeding £1,000 pounds	Nil
	£1,001 to £5,000	Excess gains over £1,000 at 15%
	£5,001 to £9,499	£600 plus excess gains over £5,000 at 50%
	£9,500 or more	All gains at 30%
Trusts	Not exceeding £500	Nil
	£501 to 1,249	Excess gains over £500 at 50%
	£1,250 or more	All gains at 30%

1980/81 to 1985/86	Tax Chargeable at 30 Percent on Excess of Gains (£) Over					
	1980/81	1981/82	1982/83	1983/84	1984/85	1985/86
Individuals	3,000	3,000	5,000	5,300	5,600	5,900
Trusts	1,500	1,500	2,500	2,650	2,800	2,950

Source: *Inland Revenue Statistics,* 1985, Appendix A.J

Table 5
Rates of Corporation Tax, 1984-87

Year Ending	Normal Rates
31 March 1984	50%
31 March 1985	
31 March 1986	
31 March 1987	
Small companies' rate	30

Table 6
Corporation Tax Allowances, 1984-87

Date of Expenditure	First Year Allowance for Plant and Machinery	Industrial Building Allowance
Prior to 14 March 1984	100%	75%
14 March 1984-31 March 1985	75	50
1 April 1985-31 March 1986	50	25
Thereafter	None	None

Table 7
Fiscal Privilege, 1978/79-1982/83

Asset	Degree of Fiscal Privilege		
	Basic rate Taxpayers	Zero rate Taxpayers	Top rate Taxpayers
Five-year insurance contract	132	60	10
House with 50 percent mortgage	104	124	386
Pension contributions (10 years)	56	-6	172
Pension contributions (25 years)	37	-6	112
Consumer durables (50 percent loan)	31	0	80
National savings accounts	31	0	80
Ten-year insurance contract	28	-23	77
Unit-linked insurance	13	-38	77
House owned outright	0	-10	42
Twenty-year insurance contract	-27	-67	21
Shares (3 percent dividend)	-42	-6	-60
Gilts (3 percent coupon)	-47	0	-122
Ten-year insurance (Interest-bearing)	-48	-99	0
ITC (10 percent gearing)	-57	-6	-124
Shares (5.5 percent dividend)	-60	-6	-118
ITC (no gearing)	-72	-28	—
Building society accounts	-78	-109	-291
Unit trust	-81	-38	-132
ITC (Retentions)	-84	-78	-53
Interest-bearing accounts and par gilts	-116	0	-301
ITC (Interest-bearing assets; no gearing)	-226	-154	-339

Source: J. Hills, *Savings and Fiscal Privilege*, IFS Report Series 9.

Table 8
Changes in Fiscal Privileges in the 1984 Budget

Fiscal Privilege for Basic
Rate Taxpayers at Five Percent Inflation

	Before 1984 Budget (Percent)	After 1984 Budget (Percent)
Business expansion scheme	+270	+276
SAYE share options	+129	+134
Ten-year life insurance contract	+61	-31
Ten-year pension contract	+55	+58
House with 50 percent mortgage	+28	+28
Direct share ownership	-32	-28
Gilts	-50	-50
Unit trusts	-52	-39

Source: V.C. Fry, E.M. Hammond, and J.A. Kay, *Taxing Pensions*, IFS Report Series 14.

Table 9
National Insurance Contributions, Class 1, 1985/86 and 1986/87

	Class 1 Rate (percent)			
	In SERPS		Contracted Out	
Year	Employee	Employer	Employee	Employer
1985/86	9.0	10.45	6.85	6.35
1986/87	9.0	10.45	n.a.	n.a.

	Class 1 Rate (percent)	
Year	Lower Earning Limit	Upper Earning Limit
1985/86	£35.50	£265.00
1986/87	38.00	285.00

n.a. not available

Table 10
National Insurance Contributions of Low-Income Earners, 1985/86

	Percentage NIC Rate on All Earnings	
Weekly Earnings	Employees	Employees
Below £38	0	0
£38–59.9	5	5
£60–94.99	7	7
£95–139.99	9	9
£140–285	9	10.45
Above £285	a	b

a. Amount payable is £25.65 (.09 × 285).
b. Amount payable is £29.78 (.1045 × 285).

Table 11
Self-Employed Contributions, 1985/86

Class 2 Contribution per week	£4.75[1]
Class 4 Contribution	6.3%[2]

[1] Not paid or earning below £1,925.
[2] Rates on taxable profits between £4,150 and £13,780 per annum.

Table 12
National Insurance Contributions and Payments, 1948-80[1]

	Amounts (£thousands)						Percent			
Year	Contributions	Receipts from Government	Other Income	Total Receipts	Payments	Reserves	Contributions/ Payments	Receipts/ Payments	Contributions and other Payments	Government Payments
1948	3,699,835	1,205,236	281,564	5,186,643	3,952,446	1,234,195	93.6	131.2	100.7	30.5
1949	5,051,884	1,711,662	402,726	7,166,278	5,423,204	2,946,305	93.2	132.1	100.6	31.6
1950	4,963,588	1,731,126	451,948	7,146,666	5,340,236	4,700,864	92.9	133.8	101.4	32.4
1951	4,764,571	1,193,605	409,410	6,367,591	5,255,331	5,446,821	90.7	121.2	98.5	22.7
1952	4,645,045	677,924	428,092	5,751,067	5,510,816	5,188,986	84.3	104.4	92.1	12.3
1953	4,843,830	705,614	446,661	5,996,112	5,631,933	5,404,482	86.0	106.5	93.9	12.5
1954	4,729,234	686,203	499,534	5,914,973	5,480,810	5,615,935	86.3	107.9	95.4	12.5
1955	5,157,531	832,020	436,771	6,426,327	6,095,364	5,585,977	84.6	105.4	91.8	13.7
1956	4,924,654	806,626	411,947	6,143,231	5,860,726	5,456,182	84.0	104.8	91.1	13.8
1957	4,695,005	804,752	417,937	5,917,698	5,898,345	5,215,717	79.6	100.3	86.7	13.6
1958	5,345,226	1,256,101	403,203	7,004,536	7,125,811	4,911,835	75.0	98.3	80.7	17.6
1959	5,314,054	1,263,927	403,854	6,981,841	7,226,083	4,451,916	73.5	96.6	79.1	17.5
1960	5,214,867	1,243,366	394,884	6,853,121	7,154,265	4,127,462	72.9	95.8	78.4	17.4
1961	6,425,149	1,315,780	326,286	8,067,223	7,975,621	4,054,294	80.6	101.1	84.7	16.5
1962	6,445,507	1,278,681	374,192	8,098,387	8,184,540	3,827,528	78.8	98.9	83.3	15.6
1963	7,227,086	1,386,273	324,698	8,938,066	9,256,222	3,374,199	78.1	96.6	81.6	15.0
1964	7,470,444	1,366,030	233,488	9,069,970	9,199,406	3,089,214	81.2	98.6	83.7	14.8
1965	8,827,406	1,685,934	352,503	10,865,850	10,715,977	3,112,998	82.4	101.4	85.7	15.7
1966	8,710,068	1,641,733	308,162	10,659,968	10,733,348	2,902,949	81.1	99.3	84.0	15.3
1967	9,137,894	1,651,641	344,578	11,134,121	11,637,575	2,290,464	78.5	95.7	81.5	14.2
1968	9,502,833	1,768,097	290,710	11,561,645	11,934,062	1,776,785	79.6	96.9	82.1	14.8
1969	9,604,024	1,734,574	264,642	11,603,246	12,464,440	1,244,379	79.7	96.3	81.9	14.4
1970	10,039,029	1,794,621	217,907	12,051,564	11,794,982	1,388,840	85.1	102.2	87.0	15.2
1971	10,039,365	1,944,781	196,531	12,180,682	12,232,242	1,178,109	82.1	99.6	83.7	15.9
1972	10,507,662	1,930,905	181,908	12,620,481	12,146,530	1,509,012	86.5	103.9	88.0	15.9
1973	11,040,849	1,823,129	209,082	13,073,067	12,341,748	2,058,255	89.5	105.9	91.2	14.8
1974	12,411,681	2,082,757	281,019	14,775,463	13,205,773	3,287,886	94.0	111.9	96.1	15.8
1975	12,173,603	2,230,494	379,665	14,783,765	14,155,891	3,166,923	86.0	104.4	88.7	15.8
1976	12,754,277	2,288,679	463,988	15,506,947	13,975,641	4,185,757	91.3	111.0	94.6	16.4
1977	13,247,328	2,378,867	599,747	16,225,946	15,175,856	4,976,194	87.3	106.9	91.2	15.7
1978	12,197,771	2,680,897	601,111	15,479,781	15,119,686	4,722,180	80.7	102.4	84.7	17.7
1979	12,406,343	2,765,069	639,462	15,692,863	15,061,131	4,739,284	82.4	104.2	86.6	18.4
1980	12,553,224	2,848,000	608,056	16,009,010	15,597,312	4,427,562	80.5	102.6	84.4	18.3

[1] 1980 prices, deflated by movements in average earnings.

Table 13
Payments from the National Insurance Fund, 1982/83

Benefits and other items	Amount (£thousand)
(1) Unemployment	1,499,648
(2) Sickness	494,456
(3) Invalidity	1,593,181
(4) Maternity	153,000
(5) Widows	725,000
(6) Guardian's allowance and child's special allowance	2,100
(7) Retirement pension	13,548,856
(8) Death grant	16,935
(9) Injury	46,469
(10) Disability	343,535
(11) Death	51,000
(12) Allowances and benefits under schemes made under the Industrial Injuries (Old Cases) Act 1967 (or under corresponding earlier schemes)	5,400
(13) Pensioner's lump-sum payments	102,000
Total Benefits	18,581,580
Administration expenses	720,187
Transfers to Northern Ireland National Insurance Fund	84,770
Payments to Post Office, Consolidated Fund and Trading Funds	29,189
Other payments	287
Total Payments	19,416,013

Table 14
Rates of VAT, 1985/86

Zero	15 Percent	Exempt
Food	All other commodities	Land
Water		Insurance
Books		Postal services
Fuel and power		Betting
Construction		Finance
Exports		Education
Transport		Health services
Children's clothing		Burial and cremation
Protective clothing		
Large caravans		

Table 15
Average Household Consumer Spending, 1984

	Percentage of Consumer Spending	Pounds per Week
Zero-rated items	29.6	44.87
Food	17.8	27.03
Fuel, light, power	6.5	9.89
Children's clothes	1.9	2.85
Books and newspapers	1.6	2.41
Public transport	1.8	2.70
Exempt items	3.5	5.30
Housing	11.1	16.79
Standard-rated items	55.9	84.72
Food (ice cream, meals out, etc.)	4.6	6.95
Adult clothing	6.4	9.74
Alcohol and tobacco	4.8	7.27
Durable goods	7.6	11.46
Others	32.5	49.30
Total	100.0	151.67

Source: IFS estimates based on 1982 Family Expenditure Survey and taken from Davis E.H., and J.A. Kay, "Extending the VAT Base: Problems and Possibilities," *Fiscal Studies* Vol. 6, No. 1, February 1985

Table 16
Selected Excise Duty Rates, 1985/86

Item	Rate		Approximate Excise Duty	Approximate Excise Duty as Percent of Price
Spirits	£15.77 per litre of alcohol		£4.73 (per bottle of whiskey)	43–63
Beer	£25.80 per hectolitre plus £0.86 per degree of original gravity above 1030 degrees		18p per pint	20
Sparkling Wine	less than 15% over 15%		£161.80 as still wine	
Petrol	Light hydro-carbon oil	£0.1794 per litre	17.9p per litre	43
Derivates	Heavy hydro-carbon oil	£0.1515 per litre	15.2p per litre	40
Tobacco	26.95 per 1,000 cigarettes, plus ad valorem amount c. 20% of price		80p per packet	65 (king size)

Table 17
Inland Revenue Treatment of Traders' Accounts, 1980/81

| | Schedule D Accounts | | Companies | |
	(£000s)	(percent)	(£000s)	(percent)
Accepted after brief scrutiny	1,482	90.9	352	66.4
Reviewed for technical points	99	6.1	175	33.0
Examined in depth	49	3.0	3	0.6
Total	1,630	100.0	530	100.0

Source: Keith Committee Report (1983), table 19.

Table 18
Inland Revenue Pilot Compliance Study, 1981

Predicted Result of Investigation	Percentage of Sample
"Probably understatement of income"	20
"Possible understatement of income"	40
"Probably no understatement of any consequence"	40
Total	100

Source: Keith Committee Report (1983), table 20.

Table 19
Evasion Adjustments to Income Items in the
UK National Accounts, 1978

	Evasion Adjustment	Published Item	Adjustment as Percentage of Published Item
Income from employment	850		1.0
Income from self-employment	2,760		21.0
Company profits	25		0.1
All income	2,640	140,930	2.6

Sources: MacAfee (1980), and 1979 Blue Book.

Table 20
Capital Transfer Tax Rates, 1985/86

Chargeable Value (£000)	Rate on Death (percent)	Lifetime Rate (percent)
0–67	nil	nil
67–89	30	15
89–122	35	17.5
122–155	40	20
155–194	45	22.5
194–243	50	25
243–299	55	27.5
Over 299	60	30

Table 21
Stamp Duties on Transfers of Land, Buildings, and Property Other than Stocks and Shares, 1985/86

Commencing date	Thresholds and Rates of Stamp Duty				
	Nil up to (£)	0.5 percent (£)	1 percent (£)	1.5 percent (£)	2 percent (£)
		Considerations Exceeding			
1 August 1958	3,500	3,500	4,500	5,250	6,000
1 August 1963	4,500	4,500	6,000	—	—
1 August 1967	5,500	5,500	7,000	—	—
1 August 1972	10,000	10,000	15,000	—	—
1 May 1974[1]	15,000	15,000	20,000	25,000	30,000
6 April 1980	20,000	20,000	25,000	30,000	35,000
22 March 1982	25,000	25,000	30,000	35,000	40,000
13 March 1984	30,000	—	30,000	—	—

[1]Northern Ireland 1 August 1974.

Table 22
Summary of the Effects of Taxes and Benefits, 1984

Type of Household and Income	Quintile Groups of Households Ranked by Original Income					Average Overall House-holds
	Bottom	2nd	3rd	4th	Top	
Average per household (pounds per year)						
Original income	110	2,480	7,130	11,200	19,750	8,130
plus cash benefits	3,130	2,400	1,140	810	600	1,620
Gross income	3,240	4,880	8,260	12,010	20,350	9,750
less income tax and employees' NIC	−10	330	1,380	2,430	4,740	1,770
Disposable income	3,250	4,550	6,880	9,580	15,610	7,980
less indirect taxes	760	1,300	1,890	2,490	3,700	2,030
Income after cash benefits and all taxes	2,490	3,250	4,990	7,090	11,920	5,950
plus benefits in kind	1,330	1,340	1,370	1,520	1,560	1,430
Final income	3,820	4,600	6,370	8,610	13,480	7,370
Percent that are public sector rentals	59	35	27	15	8	29
Average per household (number)						
Children (i.e., aged under 16)	0.4	0.4	0.8	0.9	0.7	0.6
Adults	1.5	1.7	2.0	2.2	2.7	2.0
People in full-time education	0.3	0.3	0.6	0.8	0.7	0.5
Economically active people	—	0.6	1.3	1.7	2.3	1.2
Retired people	0.8	0.7	0.2	0.1	0.1	0.4

Source: "The Effects of Taxes and Benefits on Household Income 1984," *Economic Trends,* December 1984, HMSO.

Table 23
Revenue from Local Rates, 1985/86
(£millions)

Local Government	Business Rates	Domestic Rates (incl. Down Rate Relief Grant)	Down Rate Relief Grant
Inner London Boroughs	343	195	54
Outer London Boroughs	494	600	84
Inner London Education Authority	650	227	—
Greater London Council	376	232	—
Metropolitan Police	141	87	—
City of London	102	1	—
Metropolitan Districts	1,190	1,157	128
Metropolitan Councils	344	336	
Non-Metropolitan Districts	420	487	388
Non-Metropolitan Councils	2,806	3,259	
Total	6,864	6,581	

Source: IFS Analysis of Local Government Finance.

CHAPTER 8

Canada

Harry M. Kitchen

INTRODUCTION

Before launching into a review of the major taxes in Canada, some indication of the relative growth in tax revenues at each level (Federal, provincial, and local) and some evidence on the relative importance of selected taxes may be useful.

Table 1 displays the absolute levels of taxes collected by each level of government and as a percent of gross national product (GNP) for selected years. Of interest here is the fact that total taxes have increased by almost $145 million from 1926 to 1984, or to place the rate of growth in a better perspective, from almost 14 percent of GNP in 1926 to almost 35 percent in 1984. Over this same time, local taxes decreased in terms of their relative importance (from 4.9 percent of GNP in 1926 to 3.8 percent in 1984), although notable variation exists from year to year. Provincial taxes, on the other hand, have exhibited a relatively stable increase rising from 2.1 percent of GNP in 1926 to 12.2 percent in 1984. Federal taxes have also grown in relative importance from a low of slightly less than seven percent of GNP in 1926 to 18.5 percent of GNP in 1981 and 1984.

While table 1 displays the relative importance of all taxes for selected years, table 2 records the relative importance of the major taxes used by the Federal, provincial, and local governments in 1970 and 1980. In terms of the total revenues obtained by all levels of government, taxes accounted for 82.6 percent in 1970 and 75.5 percent in 1980. This decline of seven percentage points consisted of a four percent decline in Federal taxes and a three percent decline in provincial/local taxes.

The personal income tax continues to be the most important source of tax revenue for both Federal and provincial governments.

In each year, it accounted for approximately 28.5 percent of all revenues, although its relative importance declined from 20 percent to 17.6 percent for the Federal government and correspondingly increased from 8.4 to 11 percent for the provincial governments (table 2).

General sales taxes, in total, generated the second largest sum of revenue, although the relative importance of this revenue source declined from 1970 to 1980. Corporate income taxes provided a sizable sum of tax dollars for both Federal and provincial governments while the property taxes were the major tax generator for local governments. The relative importance of the other tax sources is noted in table 2.

I. PERSONAL INCOME TAX

1. Introduction

The personal income tax in Canada is imposed under the provisions of the Income Tax Act. It regards the individual rather than the family as the taxpaying unit. Both residents and non-residents earning income in Canada are taxed, but a careful distinction is made between these individuals. Nonresidents pay Canadian income tax solely on their Canadian income. Residents of Canada, however, must pay Canadian taxes on their world income with appropriate credits applied against Canadian income taxes for all income taxes paid to foreign treasuries. In arriving at taxable income, there are two major concepts of income appearing on the individual tax return. These are total income and taxable income.

2. Total Income

Total income includes most forms of money income received from employment (wages and salaries), self-employment (business, professional, farming, fishing, and commission income), pensions (old age security, Canada or Quebec pensions, private pensions and superannuation), and other sources (taxable family allowance payments, unemployment insurance benefits, taxable dividends, interest and other investment income, rental income, taxable capital gains, etc.). While the tax reform legislation of 1971 narrowed the gap between the economic definition of comprehensive income and actual income for tax purposes, a number of exclusions still exist. For example, not all money income is included. The most notable exclusion is that of a substantial amount of capital gains. In fact, the Federal budget of 1985 stipulated that from 1985 onwards, realized capital gains will be exempt from taxation up to a lifetime limit of $500,000, subject to a phase-in over six years. The limit was $20,000 of actual capital gains in 1985. It is $50,000 in 1986; $100,000 in 1987; $200,000 in 1988; and $500,000 in 1989 and thereafter. Once capital gains exceed these limits, one-half of the excess must be included in income and taxed at the normal rates. However, if losses are incurred, one-half of these losses can be deducted from capital gains. Any unused loss may be carried backward for three years or forward indefinitely and offset against past or future capital gains until the losses are completely absorbed. Other exclusions include income on savings through private pensions and life insurance, fringe benefits received by employees from employers (for example, contributions to pension plans), workmen's compensation payments, war disability pensions, blind persons' allowances, guaranteed income supplement, spouses' allowance, mothers' allowance, gifts and inheritances (except for Quebec where the province imposes a provincial tax), $500 of scholarship income, and lottery winnings.

3. Taxable Income

Taxable income is the figure obtained after a number of exemptions and personal deductions have been subtracted from total income.

3.1 Exemptions

Exemptions may be claimed by the taxpayer for himself and his dependents. Additional exemptions are also permitted for the blind, the aged, and the disabled.

Table 3 records the Federal personal exemptions for selected years from 1973 to 1986. Since 1974, the increase in exemption levels (education excluded) has risen to offset some, if not all, of the inflation increases (see discussion on indexation below).

While an evaluation of the current exemptions suggests that more relief is provided to higher income taxpayers vis-a-vis lower income taxpayers, it is highly unlikely that any changes, such as replacing exemptions with tax credits, will arise in the foreseeable future. The only serious attempt to replace exemptions with an alternative means of tax relief failed. For instance, The Report of the Royal Commissioner on Taxation (1966) recommended a tax rate schedule that would yield effects similar to those of a tax credit system. They set up two separate tax schedules, one for single taxpayers and one for married taxpayers. Both schedules were designed so that the first few hundred dollars escaped tax.

This implied that all taxpaying units of the same size (tax credits were recommended for additional dependents) would receive the same dollar value of tax relief. This plan, however, was never implemented and has not resurfaced in any recent discussion of tax reform.

3.2 Deductions

Personal deductions can be separated into two general categories. The first includes expenses incurred in earning employment income. This allows workers to deduct 20 percent of their employment income to a maximum of $500 per year. Deductions are also allowed for moving expenses, union and professional dues, tuition fees, and childcare expenses (children under 14) up to $2,000 per child with a limit of $8,000 per family. The second category includes a number of deductions not tied directly to employment income and, in most cases, limited in the amount that is allowed to be claimed. This category includes four subgroups. First, taxpayers are entitled to deduct only those medical expenses for themselves and their dependents which exceed three percent of net income. The rationale for this is straightforward. It is designed to relieve hardships that would arise if a number of nondiscretionary or involuntary expenses were not deductible. Second, on the assumption that it is important to allow deductions for voluntary support of socially desirable activities, deductions for charitable donations are allowed as long as the total is less than 20 percent of the taxpayer's net income (total income minus contributions to pension plans, unemployment insurance premiums, tuition fees, union or professional dues, and childcare expenses. Deductions not allowed in calculating net income include medical expenses, interest and dividend income deductions, pension income deductions, education deductions, deductions transferred from a spouse, and a number of other miscellaneous items).

Third, to encourage savings for various purposes, there are a number of allowable pension and savings deductions. Registered pension plans (RPPs) and registered retirement savings plans (RRSPs)[1] have similar features and are designed to meet a number

---

[1]Registered pension plans (RPPs) are employer or union sponsored retirement arrangements of either the defined benefit (the sponsor of the plan promises a certain level of pension benefits upon retirement) or money purchase type (provides whatever benefits the accumulated contribution and return on investment will buy), or a combination of the two.

of social goals as well as economic objectives. The arguments for tax assistance for retirement savings include: encouraging individuals to save for their own retirement to counter the "moral hazard" problem that people may not save enough if they expect society will provide for them anyway; the ability to average one's income over a lifetime especially through the use of RRSPs; and to move the tax system towards an expenditure tax basis. Unlimited use of RRSPs would, for example, produce a tax system which is equivalent to expenditure taxation.

Annual contributions to RPPs by an employer may not exceed $3,500 annually. Annual contributions to RRSPs will vary depending on the circumstances surrounding the employee. If the employee is contributing to an RPP, his/her contributions are limited to the lesser of 20 percent of earned income or $3,500 minus his/her contributions to RPPs. If the employee is not a member of an RPP, his/her contributions are limited to the lesser of 20 percent of earned income or $7,500.

A further deduction introduced in 1974 and extended in 1975 allows for the exclusion from taxable income of $1,000 per year of interest and grossed-up dividend (see discussion under corporate income taxation) from Canadian sources. In addition, any unused portion of this deduction can be transferred to the taxpayer's spouse in the same year.

Finally, in an attempt to preserve the spending power of pension income received by the elderly or retired, the Canadian government introduced legislation in 1974 allowing for the deduction of $1,000 of pension income received from private pension plans. As well, any unused portion may be transferred to the taxpayer's spouse in the same tax year.

Fourth, deductions are allowed for contributions to the Canada or Quebec Pension Plan (the maximum limit for Canada Pension Plan Contribution is $419.80 in 1986) and for contributions to the unemployment insurance fund (the maximum per person is $604.89 in 1986). These contributions are defended on the premise that they protect the income of individuals in specific circumstances, that is, retired or unemployed.

Table 4 records total deductions as a percent of total income assessed for selected years from 1961 to 1983. Total deductions have grown from 6.8 percent of total income in 1961 to 14.1 percent in 1983 (the latest year for which data are available). This increase has been attributed to the introduction of a series of new deductions over the 23-year period. The footnotes in table 4 record the year in which these new deduction programs were introduced. As of 1986, however, the standard deduction of $100 has been dropped. This deduction allowed taxpayers to claim a flat deduction of $100 in lieu of itemizing charitable donations and medical expenses. As well, contributions to registered home ownership savings plans are no longer allowed.

4. Federal Tax Rates

Federal tax rates are graduated by a bracket system. Under this system, the income tax is divided into brackets and marginal rates are applied to the income in each bracket. Table 5 provides information on the effect of indexing the tax brackets since 1982. Effective from July 1, 1986, a three percent surtax is imposed on Federal personal incomes.

5. Provincial Income Tax

Under the Federal-Provincial Fiscal Arrangements and Established Programs Financing Act, 1982, the Federal government collects income tax revenue for the provinces as long as the provinces accept the same tax base. Specifically, the provinces must include the same items in income and accept the same deductions, exemptions, and rate structure established by the federal government. Each province may specify its own income tax rate as a percentage of federal tax payable. In addition, the Federal government will administer provincial tax credits that are judged not to disrupt the harmony of the personal tax system. All provinces, except Quebec, follow this procedure. Quebec continues to levy and collect its own personal income tax revenue.[2]

Table 6 illustrates the variation in the provincial income tax rates in 1986. Alberta has the lowest at 43.5 percent of Federal tax payable while Newfoundland has the highest at 60 percent. A number of provinces have introduced various schemes for removing part of the income tax burden from low income earners. For a listing of the various schemes, see the footnotes to table 6.

Once the provincial tax rate has been added to the Federal marginal rates, the combined effect, depending on the provinces, is

---

[2]The most significant differences between the Federal system and Quebec's system are: (1) different dollar values on personal exemptions; (2) a different system of indexation of personal exemptions; (3) no personal exemptions allowed for dependent children on whose behalf family allowances are received; (4) availability allowances in lieu of childcare deductions for children under six delivered as a refundable tax credit against personal income tax; and (5) different tax rate structures. For a discussion of the differences between the Federal personal income tax and trust levied by Quebec, see *The National Finances*, 1984-85, pp. 90-92.

to establish top rates of between fifty and sixty percent of taxable income.[3]

6. Miscellaneous Issues

There are a few additional features of personal income taxation which ought to be discussed. These include the averaging scheme, tax indexation, tax credits, and the minimum tax.

6.1 Averaging

In principle, the introduction of an averaging scheme leads to a fairer distribution of one's tax burden over time. While income averaging of one form or other has existed in Canada for some time, changes in the early eighties left Canadians with two averaging schemes. First, farmers and fisherman have the opportunity of using block averaging. This method uses a block of five consecutive years in which the farmer or fisherman pays income tax in the first four years on his/her unaveraged annual income. At the end of the fifth year, he/she has the option of averaging his/her income over the preceding five years and recalculating taxes payable based on equal annual allocations of income. One criticism of this scheme is that the blocks cannot overlap. This means that taxpayers must play a guessing game to select the years in which it would be optimal for them to select this scheme.

Second, a forward averaging scheme, applicable to everyone, was implemented in 1982. This scheme states that the amount of income (regardless of source) eligible for forward averaging in a given year is equal to the excess of the income in that year over a threshold level of income which is equal to 110 percent of the average inflation-adjusted income in the preceding three years (the minimum income that can be averaged is $1,000). Individuals choosing this scheme are required to pay a refundable tax at the marginal rate of approximately 50 percent (combined Federal and provincial) on the amounts being carried forward. When these amounts are brought back into the tax base, the taxpayer will pay taxes at the appropriate marginal rates for that year and correspondingly will be able to claim a tax credit equal to the amount of tax originally paid.

While these averaging schemes are better than no schemes at all, they are still deficient. The forward averaging scheme has been

---

[3]For a detailed listing of the combined Federal-provincial marginal tax rates for 1984, see table 16 below.

used by very few taxpayers, primarily those who received capital gains when capital gains were partially taxable. Now that almost all forms of windfall income (capital gains, lottery winnings, gifts and inheritances) escape tax, the use of this scheme is likely to be minimal. Furthermore, this averaging scheme is beyond the grasp of the majority of citizens who are wage earners and equally deserving of the benefits of an income averaging plan.

6.2 Tax Indexation

In the Canadian tax system some measures have been introduced to cope with the taxation of inflationary (illusory) gains. As far as capital income is concerned, the taxation of inflationary gains is mitigated considerably by the fact that a substantial amount of capital income goes untaxed. The first $1,000 of capital income (interest and dividends from Canadian sources) is exempt for all persons. An additional $1,000 of pension income is exempt for pensioners. In addition, capital income accumulating in RRSPs and RPPs is not taxable so indexation is not a problem. The remainder of capital income is taxed at normal rates.

Problems with so-called "bracket creep" have been handled largely by indexation of income brackets (see table 5 for an illustration of the inflation adjusted brackets) and personal exemptions (see table 3 for an indication of changes in exemption levels reflecting changes in inflationary increases). Since 1974, the year when indexation was introduced, the indexed values have increased by an amount equal to the increase in the consumer price index.[4] However, for 1986 and beyond, only partial indexation of brackets and exemptions will prevail (a 1985 budgetary change). This percentage increase will amount to the excess of the consumer price index over three percent.

While indexation has improved the tax system, some problems still exist. The government has backed away significantly from the indexation system in existence prior to 1986. As well, the value of the $1,000 capital income has gradually eroded over time as have the limits on RRSPs and RPPs. Extensions of these limits would be desirable, for they would improve the economic efficiency of our tax system; however, they would lead to a further revenue loss for the government.

---

[4]For example, the consumer price increase (CPI) which was used for indexation purposes in 1985 was equal to the 12-month increase in the CPI running from October 1, 1983, to September 30, 1984.

6.3 Tax Credits

Believing that the current tax system was too harsh in its current treatment of certain groups of taxpayers or recognizing the political popularity of providing relief at the provincial level, a few governments have introduced a number of tax credits designed to remove part of the tax burden on individuals primarily at the lower end of the income scale. (A discussion of these schemes is presented under property taxes in the section on the local system).

Most of the Federal tax credits, available to individuals, businesses or corporations are designed to encourage private investment and hence, to accelerate economic growth. One which is not is the child tax credit. This is designed to reduce taxes payable for all families whose income (the sum of the incomes of both parents or of one parent plus any individual who claims a tax exemption for the child) is less than a stipulated amount. Furthermore, this credit is indexed at the same rate as the income brackets and personal exemptions.

6.4 Minimum Tax

The 1985 Federal budget announced that the government would be implementing a minimum tax on personal incomes, effective January 1, 1986. The intent is to increase the tax liability of those high income individuals who use the tax incentives and deductions provided by the current tax system so as to pay little or no tax.

The minimum level of income above which this tax may apply will depend on the taxpayers allowable exemptions and deductions, but will generally be in the range of $45,000 to $50,000. Individuals with income above this level will only pay tax at the established minimum rate if this calculated tax liability exceeds the taxpayers regular income tax liability. The calculation of the income level subject to the minimum tax differs from the calculation for regular taxes in the following way; contributions to RPPs, RRSPs, $1,000 of interest and dividend income, $1,000 of pension income, and interpersonal transfers, and a few other minor deductions cannot be made under the minimum tax. As well, the excluded one-half of capital gains less the lifetime capital gains exemptions must be included in income. Allowable deductions include a $40,000 minimum tax deduction plus medical expenses, charitable donations, disability and education deductions, capital and non-capital losses of other years, unemployment insurance benefit repayment, and a new minor deduction. Depending on the province of residence, the combined Federal/provincial minimum tax rate will range from 24 to 27 percent of the calculated (for minimum income tax purposes) taxable income (the Federal rate is 17 percent).

7. Administration of the Tax

The personal income tax system in Canada is a self-assessment system, one which encounters a relatively insignificant delinquency rate. Over the past few years, however, higher tax rates have had a tendency to foster an ever growing underground economy.

The Income Tax Act stipulates that all employers must deduct, at source, income taxes payable on all wages and salaries paid to employees. These taxes must be remitted by the employer to Revenue Canada on a monthly basis. Taxpayers who are self-employed are required to pay taxes on a quarterly basis. The final tax adjustment, whether a refund to the taxpayer or an additional payment by the taxpayer, without the incurrence of a financial penalty, must be made by April 30 of the following year.

The requirement for filing returns is very simple—any individual with taxable income is required to file a return. Withholding taxes on virtually all income paid to nonresidents is taxed at a nominal rate of 25 percent unless the country in which the nonresident resides has a tax treaty with Canada. If a tax treaty exists, the stipulated rate is less than 25 percent.

II. THE CORPORATE INCOME TAX

1. Introduction

The corporate income tax represents the second largest source of revenue (personal income tax is greater) for the Federal government and the fourth largest for the provinces (personal income tax, motor fuel tax, and fuel oil taxes are first, second, and third respectively). The Federal corporation income tax the retail sales tax, like the personal income tax, is imposed under the Income Tax Act. All provinces also levy corporation taxes although the Federal government collects the tax for seven of them (Alberta, Ontario, and Quebec collect their own corporate tax). Since the structure of provincial corporation taxes, except for the rates (see table below), corresponds closely to the Federal system, much of this discussion will center on the latter. The Federal tax is imposed on the taxable income of all corporations resident in Canada and nonresident corporations carrying on business in Canada. The taxable income of resident corporations includes that earned both inside and outside Canada. For nonresident corporations, only income earned inside Canada is taxable.

2. Calculation of Taxable Income

The calculation of corporate income taxes payable proceeds in much the same way as the calculation of personal income taxes payable. Put simply, taxable income is defined as total revenue minus total costs.

2.1 Revenue

The total revenue of a corporation is the accrued value of its sales during its taxpaying year. Note that total revenue is not the same thing as the total value of production. The difference arises in the accumulation/decumulation of inventories.

2.2 Costs

Calculation of costs tends to be somewhat more complex than revenue. The general criterion is that the costs (calculated on an accrual basis) must be made for the purpose of gaining or producing income, and that the expenses must be reasonable. Costs are typically divided into two basic areas—current and capital. Current expenses (wages, salaries, rent, utility costs, etc.) are those costs incurred in the current period for the purpose of earning income in that period.

Capital expenditures cover the purchases of assets which are expected to produce income over a number of years. They may be classified into four general categories for which different costing techniques exist: depreciable assets (e.g., buildings and machinery), depletable assets (e.g., resource properties), nondepreciable assets (land), and inventories.

The corporate tax system in Canada allows two types of deductions for capital purchases. The first of these is the interest costs incurred on debt issued to purchase the capital (if debt is issued to nonresidents, there is a limit on the interest which can be deducted). The second is the imputed cost of "using up" the asset through use (i.e., depreciation). This depreciation is commonly referred to as capital consumption allowance (CCA). The capital consumption allowances and other allowances or credits are incentives that have been provided to limit taxes payable and hence, foster investment. These schemes will be discussed in the section on savings and investment.

The cost of inventories, for tax purposes, is deducted on an accrual basis; that is, the cost of inventories is deducted when they are actually used as opposed to when they are actually produced. Further deductions are allowed for scientific research and development (R and D) expenses (see the savings and investment section).

3. Special Provisions for Selected Oganizations

The corporate tax laws provide special provisions or treatment for a number of organizations including charities, cooperatives, financial institutions, and resource producers.

3.1 Charities

Registered charitable institutions are exempt from income taxation and may issue receipts to taxpayers who make donations to them. There are two different types of charities for which the rules differ. These are charitable organizations and charitable foundations.

Charitable organizations are organizations that devote all of their resources to charitable activities. In the current year, they are obliged to spend 80 percent of the receipted donations from the previous year.

Charitable foundations are corporations or trusts operated solely for charitable purposes, with the intent of making donations to other charities. These are further broken down into two subcategories of public and private for which different rules apply. Public foundations exist when 50 percent of the directors and trustees deal at arm's length, and if no more than 75 percent of their capital is obtained from a single source. Furthermore, they must expend the larger of 80 percent of the receipted donations received in the previous tax year or 90 percent of the income (net of capital gains and losses) during the current year. Private foundations are defined as all nonpublic ones. The disbursement quota on qualified investments (those used in the work of the foundation) is 90 percent of the income earned in the current year. For nonqualified investments (all the rest), it is the greater of five percent of their market value at the beginning of the tax year or 90 percent of income earned from them during the tax year.

3.2 Cooperatives

Cooperatives are also entitled to special provisions under the Income Tax Act. Some producers' marketing cooperatives are simply agents of the producer and are seen as nonincome earning by law. In addition, some cooperatives are exempt from taxation by virtue of being charitable or nonprofit organizations. Income earning cooperatives have the ability to deduct patronage dividends distributed (that is, dividends paid to patrons on the basis of their volume of business with the firm) within legislated limits. The benefits from the small business tax (discussed below) also apply to cooperatives.

3.3 Financial Institutions

Several types of financial institutions, however, are public corporations and are taxed accordingly (for example, chartered banks, credit unions, and insurance companies). All the rules applicable to the taxation of corporate income apply to them; however, there are some special provisions which are applicable to the calculation of taxable income.

Two special provisions affect the treatment of chartered banks. First, they may deduct from income a reserve to cover losses on loans and bad debts up to a reasonable amount. Second, they need not withhold tax on interest payments to nonresident currency depositors. This differs from other financial corporations.

Like chartered banks, credit unions, caisses populaires, and savings and credit unions are allowed to deduct a reserve to cover bad debts (the rate, currently, is 1.5 percent of the asset value of certain assets). Second, they may deduct all payments allocated to members in proportion to their borrowing during the year. Third, in order to provide these institutions with the advantages arising from the small business tax rate without actually allowing them to use this rate, these institutions are allowed an additional deduction which is related in a specified manner to excesses in taxable income on cumulative reserves.

Special provisions applying to life insurance corporations are as follows. First, dividends received from taxable Canadian corporations are deductible except for those on term-preferred shares acquired in the ordinary course of business. Second, capital gains may be allocated to particular policyholders who are deemed to have realized the gain. Third, resident life insurance companies are taxed only on business income arising in Canada and no foreign tax payment is allowed as credit. Fourth, a tax deduction is allowed for reasonable reserves in respect of anticipated policy claims where death occurs in the taxation year but is not reported to the insurance company until after year end. Lastly, insurance companies may deduct refunds of premiums and an investment reserve of up to 1.5 percent of assets up to $2 billion and one percent on the excess. In addition, nonlife insurance corporations that receive all their premiums from charitable organizations, churches, and schools or one-half of their premium income from farmers and fisherman are tax exempt.

Investment and mutual fund corporations are considered to be financial institutions for tax purposes if they are Canadian public corporations and meet certain specified conditions regarding the source of their income. Investment corporations may deduct from tax 16-2/3 percent of taxable income less any taxed capital gains. As with other public corporations, dividends are tax free. In addition, mutual fund corporations may distribute capital gains by special gains dividends and through redemption of their shares. Share redemptions and capital gains dividends are treated as capital transactions and are, therefore, treated as capital gains in the hands of shareholders.

3.4 Resource Producers

Corporations involved in the production of minerals, oil, and gas are liable for corporation income tax at the usual rates on their taxable income. Taxable income is calculated in much the same way as for other corporations except for a number of special provisions affecting their deductions for capital costs and other types of taxes paid.

Resource companies obtain generous write-offs under the corporation income tax for capital costs on the basis of three special provisions. First, mining companies obtain accelerated depreciation on capital involved in new or expanding mines. Second, the costs of exploration and development of resource properties are written off very rapidly. Third, an additional deduction known as a depletion allowance is permitted against resource profits in certain circumstances. Finally, resource producers are able to deduct a special resource allowance from their resource income.

Corporations who are involved in resource production are allowed to write off all exploration expenses in Canada when they are incurred. Canadian mineral and resource properties may be written off at a declining balance rate of 30 percent. The development expenses of oil and gas wells on already known deposits and the costs of acquiring oil and gas leases and wells may be written off at 10 percent. The limit on such deductions in any one year is the income earned before depletion allowances and loss carry-forward deductions, and after the deduction of dividends received from taxable Canadian corporations. There is also a partial deduction for foreign exploration and development expenses.

Mineral producing firms may claim up to 33-1/3 percent of "eligible expenditures" incurred. Eligible expenditures include Canadian exploration and development expenses, the purchase of processing machinery and equipment used to process Canadian ore in Canada, and townsites and social assets required for new mines. The cost of acquiring resource properties is not included. This system of earned depletion has some built-in incentive to encourage firms to undertake exploration expenditures in Canada. Depletion earned by mining exploration expenditures can be deducted from any source (up to 25 percent of income) and not just from resource profits.

Due to the National Energy Program (NEP) in 1981, oil and gas expenditures are not eligible for depletion allowances. In addition, oil and gas exploration expenditures outside Canadian land no longer exist. Depletion may still be earned at a rate of 33-1/3 percent of exploration and development expenditures on synthetic oil production, prescribed enhanced recovery projects, tertiary recovery projects, enhanced crude oil upgraders, and exploration on Canadian lands.

As a brief note, the NEP also introduced a new set of taxes in addition to the corporation tax. These taxes are the natural gas and liquid tax, the petroleum and gas revenue tax, and the incremental oil revenues tax. These rates, which are designed to obtain some of the rents from oil and gas production for the public sector, are explained in greater detail later in this paper under the discussion of tax rates.

To compensate for these additional taxes, the Petroleum Incentives Program (PIP) was introduced. These incentives fulfill two objectives that the system of earned depletion was deemed not to have fulfilled. First, the new incentives are specifically designed to favor-Canadian owned and controlled firms. Second, since the incentives are in the form of grants rather than tax deductions, they are available to all firms in the year of eligibility and not just those currently in a taxpaying position.

4. Tax Rates

Under the Federal-Provincial Fiscal Arrangement Act of 1982, the Federal government has undertaken to collect both the provincial and Federal corporate income taxes provided the provinces agree to the same tax base. Alberta, Ontario, and Quebec have opted out of this agreement and currently collect their own corporate taxes.

Corporations are subject to provincial corporate taxes if they have a permanent establishment in that province. If they have business income from permanent establishments in more than one province, this income is allocated by means of a formula that is standard for all provinces.

From table 7, one notes i) the differential rates as they apply to manufacturing and processing profits versus nonmanufacturing and nonprocessing profits; ii) the small business rate versus the rate on larger corporations; and iii) the differential rates for similar corporations across provinces.[5]

---

[5]Ten percentage points of all Federal corporate tax rates are abated to the province; therefore, the Federal rate minus the abatement provides the tax base to which the provincial rates are added in order to get the combined Federal/provincial rates.

Manufacturing and processing profits are taxed quite favorably. The rate of Federal income tax imposed on these profits is 40 percent (this will fall to 36 percent by 1989) while the rate on nonmanufacturing and nonprocessing profits is 46 percent (this rate will be reduced over a three year period beginning July 1, 1987 from 46 percent to 43 percent of taxable income). For small businesses (see below), the rates are 20 and 25 percent respectively (on July 1, 1987, these will fall to 18 and 23 percent respectively). When combined with the accelerated depreciation provisions and tariff protection of manufacturing industries, a strong incentive is provided for the growth of these industries relative to others.

The Federal small business tax rate of 25 percent on the first $200,000 of taxable income of nonmanufacturing and nonprocessing firms applies to Canadian-controlled private corporations (CCPC) regardless of their size or accumulation of past incomes (public corporations or foreign-controlled corporations are excluded). For manufacturing and processing profits of CCPCs the Federal rate is 20 percent.

Differentials in the provincial rates for similar corporations create differences in the combined Federal/provincial rates. For example, the provincial rates on CCPCs engaged in manufacturing and processing range from zero (Saskatchewan and Alberta) to 10 percent (Newfoundland, Prince Edward Island, Nova Scotia, Ontario, and Manitoba) for a combined Federal provincial rate ranging from 10 to 20 percent of taxable income. A similar range exists for CCPCs involved in nonmanufacturing and nonprocessing activities (from 18 percent to 25 percent of taxable income). For corporations which do not qualify as CCPCs, the combined Federal/provincial differentials range from 46 to 52 percent of taxable income earned from nonmanufacturing and nonprocessing activities and from 41 to 52 percent of taxable income earned from manufacturing and processing activities. Finally, all provinces except for Prince Edward Island impose differential tax rates on CCPCs versus non-CCPCs (see table 7 for an indication of these differentials).

The tax rates listed in table 7 may not reflect effective tax rates on the respective corporations. Effective tax rates will differ from listed tax rates through the use of investment tax credits and tax exemptions.

Investment tax credits on new production facilities subject to certain limitations (defined as a specific percentage of new investment expenditures) are allowed in geographically depressed areas (Atlantic Canada, Gaspe, and selected regions in other provinces) and in specific corporate activities (transportation equipment, and scientific research and development expenditures, for example).

These deductions from taxable income are designed to promote investment and hence employment in selected areas.

Provincial tax exemptions such as Ontario's three-year provincial income tax exemption on the first $200,000 of active business income of new CCPCs will change the tax rate on corporations qualifying for this exemption. These CCPCs must have been incorporated after May 13, 1982.

In addition to provincial and Federal corporation taxes and municipal property taxes, the Federal government levies various sorts of taxes on the oil and gas industry. Provinces also levy an assortment of taxes and royalties to capture part of the value or rent of resources in their jurisdictions. These taxes vary from province to province and from resource to resource. In addition, the tax bases vary from income to value of production to quantity produced, even to value held. The complete outline of these various taxes applied on resources at the Federal and provincial levels is too lengthy to pursue here (see Boadway and Kitchen, 1984, ch. 3). Instead, this brief paragraph has been included to indicate to the reader that such taxes and levies actually exist in the natural resource sector in Canada.

Finally, effective tax rates on large corporations have been altered by the imposition of a temporary five percent Federal surtax (from July 1, 1985 to June 30, 1986) on incomes not qualifying for the small business tax rate. This surtax, however, will be replaced by a three percent surtax on all corporations effective January 1, 1987.

5. Treatment of Dividends

There are two types of dividends which are affected by corporate taxation: first, intercorporate dividends and second, dividends to individual shareholders.

5.1 Intercorporate Dividends

All dividends received by Canadian public corporations are exempt from taxable income. This avoids the double taxation that would arise from the taxation of income which had been taxed previously at the corporate level.

Dividends received by private corporations are subject to a 25 percent refundable tax at the time of receipt. When these dividends are paid out, the firm receives a tax credit of $1 for every $4 of dividends paid. Therefore, it is just as if the firm paid no tax on dividends received. This provision discourages the use by individuals of private corporations from holding dividends in order to defer personal tax payments.

Dividends received from foreign affiliates carrying on an active business in a tax treaty country are also tax free. This is based on the premise that foreign taxes have already been withheld against them.

5.2 Dividends Paid to Individuals

One of the most controversial issues that arises with the corporation tax is the alleged double taxation of shareholders to whom after-tax corporate income ultimately accrues. The gross income of a corporation is first taxed by the corporation income tax and then again by the personal income tax when dividends are distributed. To the extent that the corporation tax has not been shifted to purchasers of the corporation's output through higher prices or to suppliers of inputs by lower prices, the shareholder's return on capital is being taxed twice.

Relief from the double taxation of corporate source income is provided in three forms. First, the shareholder is entitled to claim $1,000 of interest and dividend income (from Canadian sources) as a deduction in calculating taxable income. Second, capital gains, subject to exemption limits, are excluded from the personal income tax base. Third, further relief is provided for Canadian recipients of dividends from Canadian corporations through the dividend tax credit.

The actual method of calculating the dividend tax credit is as follows. Dividends received are grossed up by 50 percent (that is, the grossed-up dividend value is obtained by multiplying the actual dividend value by 1.5). (Effective on January 1, 1987, the dividend tax credit will be reduced from one-half to one-third of the cash dividends received by individuals from tax-paying Canadian companies). Federal taxes are calculated on this grossed-up dividend and a tax credit of 34 percent of the actual dividend paid (or 22.67 percent of the grossed-up dividend) is applied against Federal taxes. Provincial taxes are then calculated as a percentage of Federal taxes, thus compounding the tax credit. For example, the Ontario statutory rate in 1986 is 49.2 percent (table 6 in personal income tax discussion) of Federal taxes. Thus the dividend tax credit will be 22.6 percent + (.492) (22.67 percent) = 33.82 percent of grossed-up dividends. This is roughly equivalent to a system that gives a tax credit equal to the amount of grossing up of dividends. The magnitude of the difference varies from province to province. In further discussions of this scheme here, it will be assumed (for the sake of simplicity) that the credit is the same as the amount that is added to dividends when they are grossed up. In fact, the following numerical example will illustrate the characteristics of this method.

Table 8 shows the effect of the existing 50 percent dividend tax credit on taxpayers with different marginal tax rates under the assumption that all corporate profits of public corporations are paid out as dividends.[6] The dividend received of $500 is grossed up by the tax credit rate of 50 percent to give ($500 x 1.5) = $750. This is added to taxable income, tax payable is calculated—column (d)—and a credit is given of $250 (0.5 × $500)—column (e). Table 8 assumes that full credit is given even for people in low tax brackets, which is not the case in practice if they do not have sufficient other income. The total tax burden—column (f)—is then $500 (assuming a 50 percent corporate tax rate) plus personal tax net of tax credit (e). The additional tax burden (g) is column (f) less what would have been paid in the absence of the corporate tax— that is, under full integration (such as the partnership method). Finally, column (h) calculates the proportion of additional tax burden removed (see the footnote to table 8 for a calculation of the percent of the burden removed under this method). The reduction is the same proportion for all income groups, (this is identical to the deduction under a dividend-paid deduction scheme). If the dividend tax credit had been 100 percent, all the additional burden would have been removed.

Recall that the 50 percent dividend tax credit is given regardless of the amount of corporate tax paid. In cases in which the corporation paid relatively little tax (for example, because of the depletion allowance or accelerated depreciation) shareholders might be "overcompensated" for corporate taxes paid. If we review table 9, we observe the effect of giving the full dividend tax credit on income that had only been taxed at 25 percent, for whatever reason. Column (b) records the actual dividend received from $1,000 of corporate source income. Column (c) records the grossed-up dividend, while column (d) lists personal income tax payable before the tax credit of $375. Column (e) indicates the level of personal income tax payable after deducting the credit of $375. Column (f) records the total tax burden (corporate tax of $250 plus the personal income tax after the deduction of the tax credit). The figures in column (g) indicate the additional tax burden under this integration scheme compared with the taxes which would be payable under the partnership method (full integration). In every

---

[6]Recall from the earlier discussion that the tax credit given is not exactly 50 percent of dividends owing to the fact that the tax credit is divided between Federal and provincial levels of government and varies with provincial tax rates. However, this complication has been ignored for illustrative purposes.

instance, the tax burden in table 9 is less than would exist under a fully integrated system. Column (h) records the percentage of the tax burden removed in this case. This is calculated to be 125 percent, that is, more than full credit is given. This may not be undesirable since presumably the tax incentives were put in place to encourage the activity in the first place. To offset the benefits partially by not allowing the full dividend tax credit would detract from the usefulness of the original incentive, despite the apparent inequities involved.

This illustration ignores the fact that corporate profits are partly retained and partly distributed. To see what this means, assume that one-half of profits after tax are distributed and one-half are retained. Furthermore, assume that the half retained shows up as capital gains to the shareholder and is realized. Table 10 indicates the effect of the tax system on individuals of various tax brackets from $1,000 of corporate profits before tax (assume a 50 percent corporate tax rate). The combined system of a 50 percent dividend tax credit and exclusion of capital gains from taxable income yields an additional tax burden given by column (h) over and above the tax burden in the absence of the corporate tax (or a fully integrated system). Column (i) shows the percentage of tax burden removed from the unintegrated system. As shown, except for the highest tax brackets, the tax removed is less than that in the case where all profits were distributed (because of the inclusion of taxable capital gains in this calculation). In this example, the pattern of reduction of the tax burden is much more regressive than many of the other methods. Higher income groups have a higher percentage removed. Thus, on equity grounds, the current system comes out worse than most of the alternatives considered.

For private corporations subject to the higher tax rate (46 percent), the integration effects are identical to those discussed in the preceding few paragraphs for public corporations. For private corporations subject to the small business tax rate (25 percent), however, a special 12.5 percent tax is imposed on the dividends distributed by the corporation to prevent the shareholder from gaining credit for more tax. This is designed to ensure approximately full integration. To illustrate this point, assume $1,000 of corporate income is taxed at the small business rate of 25 percent leaving after-tax income of $750. If this is distributed to shareholders, the distribution tax of 12.5 percent leaves net dividends of $666.67. Grossed-up dividends are 1.5 x $666.67 = $1,000 and a dividend tax credit of .5 x $666.67 = $333.33 is given. This is exactly the amount of tax that was paid by the corporation, so the taxpayer is in the same position as if the dividend had been received directly as personal income. As a parallel measure to the reduction in the dividend tax credit beginning in 1987, however, this 12.5 percent dividend distribution tax will be repealed.

6. Effects of Corporate Taxation on the Choice of Financing Instrument

Basically, there are three choices of financing for corporate investment decisions. (A lengthier discussion of this topic is covered in Boadway and Kitchen, 1984, ch. 3.) The first is the issuing of debt instruments (bonds) on which interest must be paid; the second is retained earnings from current or past profits; and the third is new equity issues.

If the corporate tax is completely neutral, it will not provide an incentive for the firm to choose one financial instrument over another. However, in Canada, interest payable on debt instruments is deductible from income before corporate tax liability is established while dividends paid and earnings retained are not deductible prior to the determination of corporate tax liability. Thus, an incentive for debt financing is provided. Of course there will be a limit to the extent to which firms will issue debt over equity instruments. Eventually, the increased leverage (debt-to-equity ratio) will create greater risks for shareholders and creditors, primarily because the firm has relatively more contractually fixed obligations to meet, thus increasing the relative variability of the residual rate of return to shareholders and the probability of bankruptcy. Ultimately, this will lead to higher rates of return to compensate both bond-holders and equity-holders. This increase in the cost of finance, at some point, will offset the tax advantage of increased leverage.

Personal taxes can also offset the cost of finance and the choice between debt and equity. Once the taxpayer has exceeded the $1,000 deduction for interest and dividend income from Canadian sources, the treatment of income from debt instruments differs from the treatment from equity instruments. For example, interest income is taxed at the taxpayer's marginal tax rate while the tax on dividend income is reduced by the dividend tax credit and capital gains (subject to certain limits) are exempt from personal taxes. Under this system, personal income taxes alone will favor equity financing.

When incorporating the effects of both corporate and personal income taxes, however, the overall system in Canada tends to favor debt financing. For example, referring back to tables 7, 9, and 10, complete integration of the corporate and personal income tax would remove 100 percent of the additional burden (last column of each table) and put the taxation of dividend and capital gains income on the same basis as the taxation of interest income. Since the proportion of the additional burden actually removed by the dividend tax credit and the exclusion of capital gains is less than 100 percent in almost every case (table 9 records one exception), the tax treatment favors debt financing. Indeed, most of the financing for new investment expenditures in Canada, over the past five years, has come from the issuance of debt.

III. SAVINGS AND INVESTMENT

The Canadian personal and corporate income tax system provides a number of incentives to promote the level of savings in Canada and to increase the volume of investment.

1. Savings by Individuals

The savings incentives provided under the personal income tax system in Canada are designed to both encourage and protect one's savings (registered pension plan contributions; registered retirement savings plan contributions; $1,000 of interest and dividend income from Canadian sources;[7] and the pension income deduction of $1,000). The rationale underlying these various schemes was provided in the section on personal income taxation (under deductions).

While these deductions provide an incentive for individuals to save, particularly for high income taxpayers because of the greater tax savings, the extent to which they are actually used is an empirical question. For these specific deductions, the distribution of claims varies across income groups (see table 11). In all but the pension income deduction plans, the percentage of tax returns claiming these deductions is skewed towards the upper end of the income scale with the RRSP showing the greatest degree of variation. For example, less than one percent of all taxpayers reporting total income of less than $5,000 took advantage of this program while more than 60 percent in the $100,000 took advantage. In fact, a number of additional taxpayers earning more

---

[7] In 1983, taxpayers were allowed to lump one-half of all net capital gains (i.e., after deduction of capital losses) with interest and dividends in this deduction. However, the Federal budget in May 1985 changed the rule with respect to taxing capital gains so that capital gains are no longer included in this deduction limit.

than $100,000 were ineligible because their limit had already been reached under contributions to an RPP.

The distribution of taxpayers claiming the pension income deduction tends to be bimodal with the percentage of taxpayers claiming this deduction being highest in both the $10,000 to $20,000 range and then, again, in the $100,000 and over group. Perhaps this result is not surprising, since a large number of pension income recipients tend to be either in the lower income groups and in receipt of little other income or extremely wealthy, where pension income may be very high yet the amount that can be claimed for deduction is still limited by the ceiling of $1,000.

The variation in the average claim per tax return was greatest under the RPP, although the average absolute value of the claim for each income group was less than it was under the RRSP, a result that is not surprising in view of the higher limits and more voluntary nature of the latter program (the former is frequently a condition of employment).

Under both the interest and dividend deduction (for Canadian-source income) and the pension income deduction plan, the average claim rose as incomes increased, then fell slightly and rose again, suggesting that taxpayers at the lowest end of the income scale were generally young, in school, and/or unemployed and in receipt of little if any income in this form. On the other hand, taxpayers in slightly higher income groups tended to be older, possibly retired, and living off income from past savings or various pensions. When compared with this income range, middle income taxpayers (on average) claimed lower deductions under these two plans, implying that this group generally consisted of wage and salary earners who had not had time to accumulate savings from which they could earn substantial sums of dividend and interest income. Finally, in the upper income range, the average claims under both plans increased.

1.1 Composition of Personal Savings

Changes in allowable savings deductions may alter the composition of personal savings. Table 12 provides some modest evidence on changing the composition of savings, along with the relative increase in the importance of overall personal savings from 1971 to 1983. While personal savings as a percent of personal disposable income increased by a factor of 2.2 from 1971 to 1983, the relative importance of RRSP contributions increased by a factor of 3.8, rising from .5 percent of disposable income in 1971 to 1.9 percent in 1980 and 1983. Registered home ownership savings plans which did not exist in 1971 and do not exist any longer, absorbed .2 percent of disposable income in 1983. While there is neither a complete nor obvious explanation for the rapid increase in savings or for the change in the composition of savings over the last few years, it does appear as if many individuals or families have adjusted their savings pattern to take advantage of the available tax savings. However, the reason why these savings instruments have not absorbed a higher percentage of personal disposable income over the 1980 to 1983 period can be attributed largely to the fixed limits on allowable contributions to these plans rather than a lack of desire to utilize them so as to save taxes.

2. Investment Incentives

In addition to the existence of differential corporate tax rates and special provisions for calculating corporate taxable income of selected organizations (see the section on corporate taxation), the government provides a number of other investment incentives. These include the use of capital cost allowances (depreciation), investment tax credits, and the special treatment of research and development expenses. Each of these will be considered in turn.

2.1 Capital Cost Allowance (CCA)

The actual capital cost allowance (that is, the tax depreciation) is established by a set of rates in the Income Tax Act. The procedure for calculating the allowance relies on the two accounting concepts of declining balance (this involves the application of a specified rate of depreciation to the undepreciated original cost of the asset) and straight-line depreciation (a given rate of depreciation is applied to the original cost of the asset until it is fully depreciated). Under the former method, the actual capital cost allowance declines in each subsequent year, whereas it is constant under the latter method.

Each type of asset is assigned to one of 37 different classes for the purpose of calculating the CCA. The proper procedure for dealing with each of these assets is outlined in detail in the Income Tax Act. The act allows a maximum of one-half of the CCA to be written off in the year in which the asset is acquired, the remainder being depreciated over subsequent years. This provision applies to all classes of assets. Specific rules as they apply to eligibility, service lives, patents and licenses, rental and leasing properties, and the recapture of depreciation are spelled out in the Income Tax Act.

In addition to the normal calculation of CCA as outlined above, the complexity of this allowance begins to emerge once one encounters its variation in different sectors. For example, manufacturing and processing firms are allowed to write off 50 percent of machinery and equipment expenditure used in Canada per year. Special provisions also exist for the mining industry. All new buildings, machinery, and equipment may be written off at a straight-line rate of 30 percent. In addition, the full undepreciated capital cost may be written off as profits are realized. Equipment that conserves energy may be written off using a 50 percent straight-line method. Assets whose primary purpose is to prevent, eliminate, or reduce water and air pollution may be written off at 50 percent over two years. Investment in films with prescribed amounts of Canadian content may be written off immediately as may films that are commercial messages and Canadian videotapes. Accelerated depreciation is allowed on certain investments in areas classified as depressed.

While the evidence on the extent to which accelerated depreciation is effective in increasing investment is not entirely conclusive, at least three Canadian studies[8] have suggested that the government can influence the decision of firms to invest by changing the corporate tax rates or by providing tax incentives (including accelerated depreciation). In fact, one of these studies (McFetridge and May, 1976) indicated that the accelerated depreciation provision introduced in May 1972 caused net investment to rise by 3.55 percent in 1973, 6.42 percent in 1974 and 7.15 percent in 1975. Typically, a tax incentive, it was concluded, has its initial impact one year after it is introduced and its modal impact in the third year.

A second study (Harman and Johnson, 1978) found similar results for expanded investment but at significant costs in terms of tax revenue lost; for example, the increase in investment induced by the 1972 accelerated depreciation allowance was $313.3 million compared to the loss in tax revenue of $568.2 million. The results cast doubt on the efficacy of these tax incentives as an investment-inducing measure given the costs involved in foregone revenue.

---

[8]G.O. Gaudet, J.D. May and D.G. McFetridge, "Optimal Capital Accumulation: The Neo-Classical Framework in a Canadian Context" (August 1976), 58, *Review of Economics and Statistics*, pp. 269-73. D.G. McFetridge and J.D. May, "The Effects of Capital Cost Allowance Measures on Capital Accumulation in the Canadian Manufacturing Sector" (July 1976), 4, *Public Finance Quarterly*, 307-322. F.J. Harman and J.A. Johnson, "An Examination of Government Tax Incentives for Business Investment in Canada" (November-December 1978), 26 *Canadian Tax Journal*, pp. 691-704.

2.2 Investment Tax Credit

An investment tax credit is designed so that a specific percentage of investment in new productive facilities (buildings, machinery, and equipment) can be deducted from taxes payable. In turn, the base for the capital consumption allowance is reduced by the amount of the investment tax credit claimed. At the moment, the basic percentage deduction is seven percent; however, the rate applicable to the Federal government's designated slow growth areas is 10 percent except for the Atlantic provinces and the Gaspe where the allowable rate is 20 percent. Beginning in 1987, the general investment tax credit will be phased out but the 20 percent rate in Atlantic Canada and the Gaspe Peninsula will be retained and extended to include investments in adjacent offshore areas. Further investment tax credits are awarded to selected industries—50 percent for certain manufacturing industries in designated geographically depressed areas, falling to 40 percent in 1987; 10 percent for research and development (R and D) generally but 20 percent in the Atlantic and Gaspe regions; and 25 percent for R and D expenditures by corporations receiving the small business tax rate. Unused investment tax credits can be carried back three years and forward seven years.

Without any empirical tests of the effectiveness of this instrument alone, it is likely that its effectiveness in expanding the level of investment will be similar to that of accelerated depreciation with one exception, and that is the investment tax credit will be more beneficial than accelerated depreciation in providing an incentive for short run projects.

2.3 Research and Development Expenditures

The corporation tax treats research and development (R and D) expenditures liberally by means of three special provisions. First, 150 percent of all current expenditures for R and D on scientific research and experimental development (excludes market research, product testing, etc.) undertaken by the firm or contracted out to another firm, may be deducted fully regardless of where the research is completed (that is, inside or outside Canada). Second, 150 percent of capital expenditures on R and D undertaken in Canada is fully deductible in the year in which it is incurred. Third, both current and capital expenditures are eligible for an investment tax credit. As mentioned above, the applicable rate is generally 10 percent, but it is 20 percent in the Atlantic and Gaspe region and 25 percent for corporations receiving the small business tax rate.

The current policies provide a significant stimulus to increasing the levels of R and D expenditures in Canada. Indeed, in one

Canadian study[9] on the effects of corporate taxation on R and D expenditures, the authors concluded that R and D incentives in Canada were superior to those of all but one of twenty countries examined (Singapore was the exception). When subsidies and R and D contracts were considered jointly, the incentives were among the most generous (if not the most generous) to be found anywhere. Finally, they argued that a case for more generous support for R and D is difficult to make, particularly given the ease with which technology developed in one area can be transported elsewhere.

IV. PAYROLL TAXATION

The payroll tax is not widely used as a means of funding social services in Canada. In fact, a payroll tax, as such, is only used by two provincial governments. On the other hand, a variant of payroll taxation exists through the government's use of compulsory contributions to the Unemployment Insurance Commission (UIC) and the Canada or Quebec Pension Plans.

1. Payroll Taxes

In Canada, the funding of provincial health insurance programs (hospital and medical care) consists of the use of premiums on employees and/or employers, the application of payroll taxes, and funding from general revenues.

Ontario, Alberta, and British Columbia use premiums to offset entirely or partially the cost of health insurance expenses. Quebec uses a payroll tax which, in the fiscal year 1985-86, fully covered the cost of its health insurance program. Manitoba used a combination of payroll taxes and general funding to fund its health insurance program with the payroll tax covering approximately 20 percent of the insurance costs in 1985-86. The remaining provinces (Newfoundland, Prince Edward Island, Nova Scotia,

---

[9]Donald G. McFetridge and Jacek P. Warda, *Canadian R and D Incentives: Their Adequacy and Impact*, Canadian Tax Paper No. 70, Canadian Tax Foundation, Toronto, 1983.

New Brunswick, and Saskatchewan) funded their health insurance programs from general funds.

Quebec levies a payroll tax on employer payrolls at the rate of three percent. The revenue generated is earmarked for the funding of provincial health services. Manitoba also levies a payroll tax at the rate of 1.5 percent on the employer's total compensation paid to employees. The revenue collected is used to finance part of the provincial health costs and part of the education levy.

At the moment, the government of the Northwest Territories (NWT) is contemplating the introduction of a payroll tax on the nonresident labor force. Their argument is that a large proportion of the labor force works in the NWT (hence, consuming a number of government services) for part of the year only, but because these individuals claim residency in another province or the Yukon, they pay their provincial or Territorial personal income taxes to another government. The government of the NWT is hoping that the implementation of a payroll tax on the nonresident labor force will capture some tax revenue which is currently being lost.

2. Unemployment Insurance

Unemployment insurance is financed jointly by the private sector and by the Federal government. The private sector contribution takes the form of an earmarked proportional payroll tax on the employment earnings of each worker up to a maximum. For 1986, the maximum insurable earnings per week is set at $495 and the maximum weekly benefits is set at 60 percent of maximum insurable earnings. Both employees and employers pay premiums, with the employers' share being 1.4 times that of the employee (in 1986, the rate on the employee is 2.35 percent while the rate on the employer is 3.29 percent). For the self-employed, it is not required that unemployment insurance premiums be paid. At the same time, no benefits will be paid. Where unemployment insurance premiums are paid, they may be deducted from income for tax purposes.

The Canadian unemployment insurance scheme differs from that in the U.S. in two significant ways. First, in Canada, contributions are made by both employer and employees, whereas only employers contribute to a similar scheme in the U.S. At the same time, contributions in the U.S. are experience rated, that is, those with higher numbers of layoffs in the past pay higher premiums. This is not true in Canada. Second, all benefits received in Canada are taxable. This is not true in the U.S., where a portion is taxed.

There have been a number of Canadian studies on the effects of unemployment insurance on the unemployment rate.[10] Most of these studies employ regression techniques to find the statistical relationship between the rate of unemployment and a characteristic of the unemployment insurance scheme such as the ratio of unemployment insurance benefits to weekly wages. The published studies have tended to indicate that unemployment insurance increased the unemployment rate in Canada, that the 1971 liberalization of the Act served to increase the unemployment rate beyond what it would otherwise have been, and that the 1979 tightening up had the opposite effect.

As for the effects of unemployment insurance on labor force participation rates, one study on the Maritime provinces concluded that the 1971 amendments to the Unemployment Insurance Act did not decrease participation rates.[11] In fact, in two of the provinces (Prince Edward Island and New Brunswick), there was a positive impact from the 1971 revisions. This indicates, they suggested, that the shortening of the eligibility period of unemployment insurance benefits to eight weeks caused those who would otherwise remain outside the labor force to work at least part of the year. Increases in participation rates by groups such as married women and young people more than offset the decreases in participation rates of others owing to the increase in benefits.

---

[10]Samuel A. Rae, Jr. "Unemployment Insurance and Labour Supply: A Simulation of the 1971 Unemployment Insurance Act" (May 1977), 10 *Canadian Journal of Economics*, 263-278.

Herbert G. Grubel, Dennis Maki, and Shelley Sax, "Real and Insurance-Induced Unemployment in Canada" (May 1975), 8 *Canadian Journal of Economics* 174-91. See also the comment by S. F. Kaliski, "Real and Insurance-Induced Unemployment in Canada" (November 1975), 8 *Canadian Journal of Economics* 600-603.

Christopher Green and Jean-Michel Cousineau, *Unemployment In Canada: The Impact on Unemployment Insurance* (Ottawa: Economic Council of Canada, 1976).

S.F. Kaliski, "Unemployment and Unemployment Insurance: Testing Some Corollaries," (November 1976), 9 *Canadian Journal of Economics*, 705-12.

Fred Lazar, "The Impact of the 1971 Unemployment Insurance Revisions on Unemployment Rates: Another Look" (August 1978), 11 *Canadian Journal of Economics*, 559-70.

Charles M. Beach and Stefan F. Kaliski, "The Impact of the 1979 Unemployment Insurance Amendments" (June 1983) 9 *Canadian Public Policy*, 164-73.

[11]N. Swan, P. MacRae, and C. Steinberg, *Income Maintenance Programs: Their Effect on Labor Supply and Aggregate Demand in the Maritimes; A Joint Report of the Council of Maritime Premiers and the Economic Council of Canada* (Ottawa: Ministry of Supply and Services, 1976).

The lack of experience-rated premiums in Canada can create some distortions; for example, the unstable firms experiencing frequent layoffs are being subsidized by the stable firms with infrequent or very limited layoffs. One analysis, however, indicated that the coexistence of income taxation and unemployment insurance distorts the firms' layoff decisions in such a way that less than complete experience rating may be desirable.[12] Full experience rating might also discourage the hiring of workers needed to meet temporary increases in a firm's production. Also, it might discourage desirable layoffs of probationary workers who are performing unsatisfactorily.[13]

The availability of unemployment insurance benefits financed by uniform taxes reduces a firm's incentive to stabilize its employment. Indeed, most of the problems revolving around the unemployment insurance scheme can be attributed to its current funding method.

2. Canada Pension Plan

The Canada Pension Plan (CPP) is administered by the Federal government and applies to residents in all areas of Canada except for Quebec, where the province has its own pension plan (QPP).

The CPP/QPP is a form of social insurance in which the benefits paid are at least partly related to contributions. It is also, in part, a transfer program since the plan is not actuarially sound (an individual's contributions during working years are not expected to cover exactly the benefits expected to be received upon retirement).

The CPP is financed by what is basically a proportional payroll tax with a fixed exemption level and an upper limit. For employed persons, both the employer and employee pay 1.8 percent of annual gross employment earnings above the exemption level ($2,500 in 1986) and up to the maximum pensionable earnings for the year ($25,800 in 1986). Self-employed persons must pay both shares, or 3.6 percent. Contributions are compulsory for all eligible persons between the ages of 18 and either 70 or retirement, and they may be deducted from income for tax purposes.

---

[12]Robin W. Boadway and Andrew J. Oswald, "Unemployment Insurance and Redistribution Taxation," (March 1983) 20 *Journal of Public Economics*, 193-210.

[13]Jonathan R. Kesselman, *Financing Canadian Unemployment Insurance*, Canadian Tax Paper, No. 73, Canadian Tax Foundation, 1983, p. 27.

Although the existence of a public pension scheme may serve as a substitute for private pensions, there is no empirical evidence to support or reject this point. Published evidence of the effect of public pensions on savings in Canada is sparse. One study generated a wealth series for the CPP/QPP from 1966 onwards.[14] When this independent variable was tested in alternative consumption functions, the authors found no evidence that the CPP/QPP had a negative effect on personal savings. In fact, they argued that many contributors to these public plans would not have saved in the absence of a pension plan. For those who do save for retirement, the relative magnitude of the CPP/QPP is so small as to have very little effect. Further studies have confirmed that the existence of the CPP does not generate a significant effect on aggregate savings.[15]

V. THE PROVINCIAL/LOCAL TAX SYSTEM

1. Introduction

Provincial and local governments in Canada constitute the second and third levels of government. While each of these levels has its own constitutional responsibilities in the tax system, the provincial government has more freedom and fewer restrictions with respect to expenditure and taxation powers. For example, the provincial governments are free to set their own personal and corporate income tax rates (see tables 6 and 7 respectively) and free, if they choose, to administer their own personal and corporate income tax systems. Local governments, by comparison, are creatures of provincial governments and as such, are constitutionally controlled in their tax and expenditure powers; that is, they derive all of their powers from provincial legislation and can only use those taxes specifically allocated to them.

---

[14]J.E. Pesando and S.A. Rae, Jr., *Public and Private Pensions in Canada: An Economic Analysis*, (Toronto, University of Toronto Press of the Ontario Economic Council), 1977.

[15]Phelim Boyle and John Murray, "Social Security Wealth and Private Saving in Canada" (August 1979), 12 *Canadian Journal of Economics*, 456-68.

Peter Wrage, "The Effects of the Growth of Private and Public Pension Plans on Saving and Investment in Canada," Discussion Paper no. 174 (Ottawa: Economic Council of Canada, 1980).

Michael J. Daly and Peter Wrage, "The Impact of Canada's Old Age Security Program on Retirement Savings, Labor Supply and Retirement," Discussion Paper No. 203 (Ottawa: Economic Council of Canada, 1981).

2. Provincial/Local Revenues

While provincial governments generate the largest percentage of tax revenues from personal incomes (21.5 percent in 1980—table 13), they also collect sizable sums of money from retail sales taxes (10 percent in 1980) and from corporate income taxes (5.8 percent in 1980). The remaining tax revenue comes from taxes on motor fuel, tobacco, health insurance premiums, and social insurance levies along with a collection of miscellaneous taxes. Overall, the provinces obtain over half of their total revenue from taxes with an additional 28 percent (approximately) coming from other own-source revenues (natural resource revenue and return on investment account for about 21 of the 28 percentage points). Unconditional and conditional grants account for a further six and 14 percent respectively of all revenues.

Local governments, by comparison, are much more dependent on grants and relatively less dependent on taxes and other own-source revenues. Unconditional grants (from the province only) account for almost five percent of all local revenues while conditional grants total more than 41 percent (almost all of which comes from the province with less than two percent coming from the Federal government) of all local government revenues (see table 13). Local taxes on real property amount to more than 30 percent of local revenues with the business tax generating a further three to four percent. Other locally generated revenues, which account for about 20 percent of all revenues, come from the sales of local services (water, etc.), the issuance of privileges, licenses and permits, and the imposition of fines and penalties, etc.

Earlier in this paper, a discussion of personal and corporation income tax rates was presented. The one remaining provincial tax of significance is the retail sales tax. This tax is employed in every province, except for Alberta, at rates (January 1, 1986) ranging from five percent in Saskatchewan; six percent in Manitoba; seven percent in British Columbia and Ontario; nine percent in Quebec; 10 percent in Prince Edward Island and Nova Scotia; 11 percent in New Brunswick; and 12 percent in Newfoundland. In each of the provinces, there are differences in allowable exemptions and limits on other allowable exemptions. These exemptions are primarily designed to remove some of the tax burden which would otherwise be imposed on low income earners.

The real property tax (table 13) is the primary tax source for local governments. This tax, as it applies to both residential and nonresidential property, displays more variation than any other major tax in Canada. The major explanation for this rests with the level of government responsible for administering the tax. Property taxes are, by and large, administered by local governments while other taxes such as personal and corporate income taxes, taxes on manufacturing, and retail sales taxes are controlled by Federal and provincial governments. Clearly, the level of administration will dictate the degree of uniformity prevalent in establishing the tax base and tax rates. In the case of property taxation, uniformity seldom exists among municipalities within the same region or metropolitan area. Adjacent municipalities frequently tax identical properties at different rates. This is true for both residential and nonresidential property and it is especially noticeable in the larger metropolitan areas and in regional governments with different municipal tax jurisdictions (see Harry Kitchen, 1984).

As distinct from the United States, municipal income and sales taxes are not allowed in Canada.

Although both retail sales taxes and property taxes have been criticized for various reasons, the bulk of the criticism has revolved around the regressive impact which each of these taxes has on taxpayers and the distortions created by their actual imposition.

To overcome part of this alleged regressivity, various relief schemes have been implemented by provincial governments. For example, two of the more popular forms of tax relief which have captured the interest of provincial and municipal politicians and administrators are homeowners grants and tax credits. Homeowners grants, although not as widely used as they once were, still play an important role in Saskatchewan and British Columbia. While these programs differ in specific details they are designed to reduce some of the property tax burden on owner-occupiers with grants that vary depending on the specific circumstances of the recipient. Eligible taxpayers over 65 years of age are generally entitled to larger payments than taxpayers under 65 years of age.

Property tax credits against personal income taxes exist in Quebec, Ontario, and Manitoba. In Quebec, personal income tax liability is reduced or cash refunds are paid to property owners or tenants. For property owners, the credit equals 40 percent of property taxes paid less two percent of the household's taxable income with a maximum credit of $400. For tenants, the same rules apply except that property taxes are limited to the portion of the dwelling occupied. In Ontario, the property tax credit formula is $180 or "occupancy cost" (property taxes or 20 percent of rent), whichever is the lesser amount, plus 10 percent of "occupancy cost" less two percent of taxable income. This is not available to senior citizens; instead, they receive a flat grant of $500 per person. In Manitoba, the credit is the lesser of $375 minus $150 or one percent of taxable income, whichever is lower, or the amount of property taxes or rent paid on the principal residence.

Alberta has implemented a property tax credit scheme just for renters. Renters are allowed to deduct from provincial income taxes payable an amount equal to $80 plus five percent of rent paid, up to a maximum of $250, reduced by one percent of taxable income. The minimum tax credit is $50. Homeowners, on the other hand, are allowed a property tax reduction equal only to the lesser of $200 or total taxes on the owner's principal residence.

Ontario is the only province to have implemented a retail sales tax credit to remove some of the tax burden alleged to exist under the current retail sales tax system. This credit is equal to one percent of personal income tax exemptions. Further regressivity in every province has been removed through the use of exemptions for a number of essential items including prescription drugs, shelter, food, and children's clothing.

Given the relative importance of retail sales and property taxes as revenue generators for provincial and local governments respectively, table 14 measures the burden of each of these taxes as a percent of personal disposable income for selected years. For comparative purposes, it also measures personal income tax as a percent of disposable income. From 1933 to 1981, property tax revenues as a percent of disposable personal income declined, whereas personal income taxes and retail sales taxes both increased in relative importance.

VI. TAXATION OF WEALTH

1. Gifts and Inheritances

Since the Canadian tax system has always excluded gifts and bequests from the income tax base of the recipient and where applicable taxed them separately, it is probably useful to review and assess the current status of these two taxes. At the moment, only one province, Quebec, levies separate gift taxes and succession duties. While this has not always been the case, the situation has evolved since the tax reform of 1972, when the Federal government vacated the gift and estate tax fields and allowed the provinces to decide whether they wanted to impose their own taxes on these two potential sources of revenue. Initially (1972), all provinces except Alberta adopted succession duties and gift taxes; since then, however, all provinces with the exception of Quebec have eliminated them.

Although it is difficult to pinpoint a specific factor as the catalyst leading to the termination of these taxes, most provinces have dispensed with them for a number of reasons, including the fact that they generated small sums of revenue and were, therefore, relatively expensive to collect. When the responsibility for collecting the taxes was shifted to the provincial level, it was frequently too costly to establish the administrative machinery necessary to collect and enforce both taxes. In addition, tax competition undoubtedly had something to do with their elimination; once one province abandoned these taxes, others questioned the value of retaining them and subsequently followed.

1.1 Current Treatment

In Quebec, the gift tax, which is levied on the donor, is applied at a flat rate of 20 percent. Except for interspousal gifts and bequests that are totally exempt, the level of exemptions is a direct function of the relationship between the donor and the recipient. In Quebec, the tax rates applied to inheritances depend solely on the amount received by the beneficiary without regard to the size of the deceased's estate.

While the succession duty, which is a tax on an inheritance, has been levied in an attempt to generate tax revenue, the gift tax has never been designed to raise revenue, even though this may have been an obvious by-product. Instead, the gift tax was introduced to protect the revenues generated by succession duties—that is, the tax on gifts prevents one from avoiding succession duties through the act of transferring one's estate prior to death.

Because these taxes exist only in one province, there is an incentive for taxpayers to relocate so as to avoid gift and inheritance taxes. The extent to which this is done, however, is not thought to be extensive.

The more obvious way in which these taxes are avoided is through the creation of legal trusts. These allow wealth to be passed from one generation to the next without incurring a tax liability on the value of property transferred. Interspousal transfers of gifts and estates are currently exempt from gift taxes and succession duties. The creation of trusts for the purpose of passing property from generation to generation, etc., is eventually limited by specific rules against indefinite continuation.

2. Property Taxation

It has been suggested that the ownership of residential dwellings represents the single most important component of personal wealth in Canada. As well, it has also been suggested that the property tax might be considered as a tax on wealth. Without reviewing the arguments in favor of or against the notion that this tax can be a crude proxy for a wealth tax, table 15 displays information on property taxes as a percent of residential homeowners equity (market value minus outstanding mortgage) across income groups for three provinces in Canada in 1982. One notes that the pattern is not consistent across income groups or across provinces; hence, one cannot suggest that the tax is progressive, regressive, or proportional over any extensive income range or region.

VII. THE HIDDEN ECONOMY

The hidden economy refers to the economic activity that escapes measurement. This consists of both illegal (gambling, prostitution, drugs, etc.) and legal activities (babysitting for cash, exchanging services on a barter basis, etc.). While it is difficult to obtain a measure of the relative size of the underground economy, one U.S. estimate suggests that 80 percent of the underground economy consists of unreported income from legal activities.[16] For Canada, the Justice Department's Task Force Report of 1981 set the figure for illegal activities at $8,684 million.[17]

Concentrating only on the legal activities, the general consensus appears to be that higher marginal tax rates have contributed to tax evasion techniques. Table 16 records the combined Federal and provincial marginal tax rates for 1984 (the latest year for which these combined tax rates are available). Clearly, the higher marginal tax rates applicable to higher income earners make it more advantageous for these individuals to alter their activities so as to avoid taxes. By comparison, commodity taxes and the limited use of payroll taxes have not been a significant factor in causing individuals to alter their behavior.

The existence and growth of the hidden economy may be the result of a "disinclination to report taxable income in the face of an increasing real tax rate or decline in real income growth."[18] Table 17 provides some evidence on the personal tax burden. It has increased from less than one percent of personal income minus government transfers to persons in 1946 to more than 16 percent in 1984.

---

[16]Edgar L. Fiege, "How Big is the Irregular Economy," *Challenge*, Nov. Dec. 1979.

[17]Reported in *Alberta Report*, "Life in the Underground," by Lori Cohen and Fay Orr, February 4, 1985, 28.

[18]Rolf Mirus and Roger Smith, "Canada's Irregular Economy," *Canadian Public Policy*, VII:3, Summer 1981, 449.

While measurements of the size of the hidden economy must be treated with caution, underground activities as a percent of GNP have increased significantly over the past few years. When this is combined with the curtailment of indexation and the introduction of a minimum income tax, the hidden economy is almost certain to become even larger.

VIII. DISTRIBUTION OF TAX BURDEN

While the studies of tax incidence make more or less arbitrary *a priori* assumptions about the shifting of taxes and use these assumptions to generate estimates of tax incidence, the results are of some limited use. In fact, table 18 presents these results on tax incidence for 1969 (the latest year for which information is available).

As the table indicates, total taxes are regressive up to $5,000 of broad income (defined as the level of income which would exist in the absence of government activity), proportional from $5,000 to $15,000 and mildly regressive thereafter. Federal taxes are regressive up to $4,000 and roughly proportional thereafter. This Federal pattern is composed of a number of taxes working in opposite directions. The personal income tax is progressive over the entire range of income while the corporate income is regressive up to about $6,000 and, with some variation, progressive beyond. This regressivity over the lower income groups is partly caused by the fact that a portion of the tax is assumed to be shifted forward to consumers and partly by the fact that family units at the lower income levels (probably the retired elderly) own a larger proportion of corporate shares than middle income family earners. Selective taxes, the general sales tax, and import duties (all of which are allocated on the basis of a variant of consumption expenditures) show regressivity throughout most of the income range with some proportionality being displayed over the middle income group. Social security taxes display some progressivity up to the middle income range and regressivity beyond this.

Provincial taxes are regressive up to $5,000, proportional to $15,000, and regressive thereafter. The inclusion of medical hospital insurance premiums and other taxes adds an additional degree of regressivity over the lowest income brackets. Local tax incidence is regressive throughout the measured income scale. Property taxes are the major contributor to this incidence pattern over the entire income range. This general pattern is similar to results found in other studies employing the same assumptions.

One must treat these results with some caution since they are based upon *ad hoc* assumptions about tax shifting. No sensitivity analysis is reported to see how the results would be influenced by alternative shifting assumptions. We know from the work of others that the shifting assumptions are extremely important. For example, St-Hilaire and Whalley found that virtually any incidence pattern (progressive, regressive, etc.) is possible given alternative plausible shifting assumptions.[19] Similarly, Walker found the tax system to be much more progressive than did Gillespie by assuming, following a suggestion by Browning, that sales and excise taxes are borne by factor suppliers rather than consumers.[20] Furthermore, the calculations assume that pre-tax incomes are not influenced by the introduction of taxes. Thus, factor supplies and relative prices are unchanged.[21] At most, the results indicate the broad impact effects of the tax system calculated from the pre-tax and transfer income position.

While table 18 provides some evidence on effective tax rates by income groups for the latest year for which such a study has been published (1969), it may be useful to speculate on whether changes in tax policy since then have lead to greater or less overall regressivity. For example, the tax reform legislation of 1972 may have improved horizontal equity but it did nothing to improve vertical equity. The elimination of estate taxes almost offset the effect of capital gains taxation on high income earners. As of 1985, subject to certain limitations (discussed under personal income taxation), capital gains have been removed from the tax base, thus providing greater benefits for high income *vis-à-vis* low income

---

[19]France St-Hilaire and John Whalley, "Recent Studies of Efficiency and Distributional Impacts of Taxes: Implications for Canada," in Wayne R. Thirsk and John Whalley (eds.), *Tax Policy Options in the 1980s* (Toronto: Canadian Tax Foundation, 1982), 28-64.

[20]Michael A. Walker, "Measuring and Coping with a Progressive Tax System or Robin Hoodery—A Canadian Tradition Past Its Prime" (Spring 1980), 2 *Canadian Taxation* 8-15. Walker's methodology is drawn from Edgar K. Browning, "The Burden of Taxation" (August 1978), 86 *Journal of Political Economy* 649-71. The argument is based on the idea that low-income households cannot be made worse off by taxes that induce higher consumer prices since much of the higher prices will be offset with transfers that are indexed to the price level.

[21]A recent study by J. T. Marshall Lee, "The Effects of Taxes on Resource Allocation and Distribution of Income in Canada: A General Equilibrium Analysis" (Ph.D. dissertation, Queen's University, Kingston, Ontario, 1983) recalculated the tax incidence results of Gillespie using the same data source but allowing factor prices and incomes to be determined in a general equilibrium system. He found incidence patterns not too different from those of Gillespie.

earners. Since 1972, increases in allowable exemptions and deductions have bestowed greater benefits on high rather than low income earners.

In summary, most of the tax changes over the past fifteen years have not improved the income share of the poor relative to the rich. It is more likely that the relative position of the poor has deteriorated.

IX. TAX REFORM

1. Brief History

The first serious attempt at tax reform (however it is defined) culminated in the publication of the Report of the Royal Commission on Dominion Provincial Relations (Rowell-Sirois) in 1940. It proposed some important tax reforms dealing with intergovernmental relations; for example, one important proposal which is still debated is the assignment of certain taxes to one of the two levels of government. Continuing concern and debates over problems with the tax system led to the formation of the Royal Commission on Taxation in 1962. After numerous hearings and an extensive research program, the Royal Commission's Report was published in 1966. Among the major proposals was a massive broadening of the personal income tax base to include capital gains, gifts and inheritances and virtually every other form of money income. As well, the Commission recommended the adoption of the family unit rather than the individual as the basic taxpaying unit. It argued in favor of a top marginal tax rate of 50 percent. It favored the retention of the corporate tax as a withholding tax and a complete integration of the personal and corporate tax. The Commission advocated the replacement of the manufacturer's sales tax by a retail sales tax administered by the province and added onto the existing provincial retail sales tax.

As a result of substantial pressure, the Royal Commission's recommendations were substantially altered, modified, or even dropped. The first changes of any significance appeared in 1972. These included an expansion in the definition of income (unemployment insurance benefits, family allowance payments, one-half of capital gains, etc. were brought into the calculation of total income), increased limits for personal exemptions and a number of new deductions (unemployment insurance premiums, child care expenses, and the general expense allowance). In the ensuing years, additional deductions were introduced (registered home ownership savings plans in 1974, interest income deduction of

$1,000 in 1974 with dividends added to this in 1975, pension income deduction of $1,000 introduced in 1975, and eligible inter-spousal transfers beginning in 1976) and in 1974, one of the most significant changes of all was implemented—the introduction of indexation.

Throughout the late seventies and into the eighties, tax reform was not a major issue. In fact, very little was heard of tax reform until Finance Minister Alan MacEachen introduced his "ill-fated" tax reform budget in 1981 (Nov. 12). Briefly, this budget recommended temporarily capping the indexation scheme; converting the manufacturer's sales tax into a wholesale sales tax; more stringent taxation of employee benefits; reduction in capital cost allowances; limiting the deductibility of investment costs; and taxing accrued interest every three years. Within a few weeks, the public outcry was so great that the government was forced to back away from many of its proposals.

Although MacEachen's budget incorporated a number of the recommendations of the Royal Commission's Report (1966), its overall intent was to collect more revenues rather than to achieve a more equitable tax system.[22]

The Federal government's experience with attempts at tax reform (the Royal Commission in 1966 and the 1981 budget, for example) have not been forgotten. Governments are now much more cautious to introduce new tax measures. The political repercussions of having their proposals rejected are deemed to be too costly politically. A greater attempt is now being made to solicit the views of key academic, business, and labor leaders, prior to the Federal annual budget.

2. Proposals for Reform

Trying to detect consistency in the proposals for tax reform both across different organizations (labor, business, academics, and government) and over time within a specific organization is not an easy task. For whatever reason, views may change. Reforming the tax system to improve the distribution of income may be the prime objective at one time, whereas reforms designed to generate fewer distortions (greater efficiency) may be desirable at another time. Although there are some similarities in the request for tax reform across groups, there are dissimilarities. Perhaps a brief outline of the position of government, academics, business, and labor is useful.

---

[22]Douglas G. Hartle, *Political Economy of Tax Reform: Six Case Studies*, Discussion Paper No. 290, Economic Council of Canada, Ottawa, 1985, 16.

2.1 Government Initiatives

While it is not entirely clear what the Federal government is considering in the way of reform, there is a general consensus that any reform must be approached in a cautious manner in order to avoid the political repercussions, such as those which surrounded the 1981 budget debacle.

The current and accumulating size of the government deficit and the desire to reduce it have caused the Federal government to initiate changes which are designed, primarily, to generate additional revenues. Evidence of this emerged in the May 1985 budget when the government substantially curtailed the indexation scheme and eliminated registered home ownership savings plans as an allowable deduction. At the same time, the government dropped capital gains, up to a specific limit, from the tax base. This elimination of capital gains irritated a number of provincial governments who previously shared in tax revenues from this source, and has subsequently caused a few provincial politicians to suggest that they are considering ways of reintroducing capital gains into their provincial tax base.

Offsetting this elimination of capital gains is the implementation (1986) of a minimum tax proposal. A further announcement in the May budget (1985) suggested that the Federal government was considering the implementation of a value-added tax (VAT) as a replacement for the manufacturer's sales tax. However, on February 4, 1986, Finance Minister Michael Wilson announced that the government was not in the position to consider the introduction of a VAT in Canada. For the moment, then, VAT has been discarded.

The VAT had been presented as an alternative to the manufacturer's sales tax. The manufacturer's sales tax, in its present form, creates a number of serious distortions. These arise because all services and certain goods are exempt from the tax or because differential rates apply to different categories of taxed materials (the general rate is 12 percent, but on tobacco and alcohol it is 15 percent, on building materials and cable TV, eight percent). Further distortions exist because of the stage at which this tax is levied. It provides an incentive for taxpayers to push as many costs and distribution functions as far forward as possible so that their value will escape taxation. As well, in a number of instances, the tax tends to provide favorable treatment of imports versus domestically produced goods.

Because of the large number of distortions, suggestions have been made for shifting the base of the tax to the retail level (*The Report of the Royal Commission on Taxation*, 1966) or more recently, the wholesale level. In fact, a report from the Federal

Department of Finance in 1977[23] recommended that this tax be shifted to the wholesale level.

By shifting the base, the tax would be moved one step closer to the final selling price and hence, would eliminate some (but not all) of the current distortions. Unfortunately, the major recommendation of this Report was never implemented. Furthermore, the recent decision not to introduce VAT suggests that the Federal government will have to seriously reconsider the possibility of moving the manufacturer's sales tax to the wholesale level in order to avoid many of the distortions in the present system.

Corporate taxes, because of their importance in withholding revenues which would otherwise go to foreign treasuries, are not likely to be altered in any significant manner in the foreseeable future. Changes, such as those involving shifts in the capital cost allowance to promote certain types of investment, and changes in the rate structure (as announced in 1986 Budget) will be made if and when these are deemed to be necessary to improve investment activities. Further changes such as the recent elimination of the three percent inventory allowance and the general investment tax credit will be made when it is perceived that such changes can improve the efficiency and fairness of the overall tax system.

Retail sales taxes and a number of excise taxes (some excise taxes are Federal) are the sole responsibility of provincial governments. The only changes that have been implemented in this area recently and that are likely to continue into the future are those which involve base broadening and statutory tax increases.

Probably the greatest number of Royal Commissions and Special Committees (over the past two decades) have been established with the intent of offering proposals for provincial and local tax reform. Virtually all of the reports emerging from these committees or commissions have devoted a major part of their published work to suggestions for reforming the property tax. From this, a number of important changes have emerged. Assessment and administration practices have improved significantly, removal of education financing (elementary and secondary) away from the property tax base and onto provincial revenues has occurred in Quebec and three of the provinces in Atlantic Canada (Nova Scotia is the exception). Where recent changes in this area will lead us is still somewhat of a mystery. However, it does appear as if attempts to improve the assessment system will continue. Whether or not

---

[23]Canada, Department of Finance, *Report of the Commodity Tax Report Group* (Ottawa: Queen's Printer, 1977)

additional provincial governments will remove the funding for education from the property tax base is purely conjecture. As long as provincial deficits continue, it is difficult to imagine any province implementing any major change which may increase their budgetary costs.

2.2 Academic Proposals

While government proposals may involve major changes, a number of them are likely to consist of either minor changes or simple tamperings with the existing system. Academic proposals for tax reform, on the other hand, are almost certain to concentrate on major shifts. The most notable tax reform proposal by academics involves the move toward a consumption-based and away from an income-based tax. In fact, it has been argued that the tax which we call an income tax is largely a consumption tax. If the limits on a number of the savings deductions ($1,000 interest and dividend deduction, limits on contributions to registered retirement savings plans, registered pension plans, for example) were completely removed, the current tax system would approach a consumption tax.

Further support for a consumption, rather than an income tax came out of the MacDonald Commission's[24] recommendations in 1985. In fact, there are some senior government officials who also believe that a switch to a full consumption tax would be desirable.

While no one questions the efficiency gains arising from a move towards a consumption tax, the implementation of this tax will ultimately depend on its acceptance as an equitable tax. At the moment, there is a large segment of the population that does not readily accept, as the index of equality, taxation on the basis of expenditures made rather than on the basis of income received. Only when this attitude is changed is it likely that a fully operational consumption tax will emerge.

2.3 Business and Labor

While it is difficult to find a common stance taken by all types of business or all types of trade unions, there are a few themes that seem to surface. Generally, each of the groups is interested in having someone else pay the tax.

Labor unions have strongly supported the notion of a minimum tax on high income earners. As well, they have frequently advocated greater use of corporate taxes (without understanding the

---

[24]*Report of the Royal Commission on the Economic Union and Development Prospects for Canada*, University of Toronto Press, 1985.

economic effects of these taxes) as a substitute for personal income taxes.

Small businesses have been pushing for a simplification (including fewer required forms to be completed and submitted to governments) of the tax system under which they operate. Corporations have often argued for the more liberal use of allowable expenses including capital cost allowance in order to foster investment.

As one can see, virtually all of these arguments are self-serving and, in fact, often contradictory when all of their implications are presented.

SELECTED BIBLIOGRAPHY

D.A.L. Auld and F.C. Miller, *Principles of Public Finance: A Canadian Text*, Second Edition, Methewn, Toronto, 1982.

Richard M. Bird and N. Enid Slack, *Urban Public Finance in Canada*, Butterworths, Tornoto, 1983.

Robin W. Boadway and Harry M. Kitchen, *Canadian Tax Policy*, Second Edition, Canadian Tax Foundation, Toronto 1984.

Canadian Tax Foundation, Toronto, *Canadian Tax Journal*, six issues annually.

Canadian Tax Foundation, Toronto, *National Finances*, annual publication.

W. Irwin Gillespie, *The Redistribution of Income in Canada*, Gage Publishing Co., Carleton Library, No. 124, Ottawa, 1980.

Douglas G. Hartle, "Political Economy of Tax Reform: Six Case Studies," Discussion Paper No. 290, Economic Council of Canada, Ottawa, 1985.

Harry M. Kitchen, *Local Government Finance in Canada*, Canadian Tax Foundation, Tornoto, 1984.

Douglas J. McCready, *The Canadian Public Sector*, Butterworths, Toronto, 1984.

Table 1
Total Taxes by Level of Government and as Percent of Gross National Product (GNP), Selected Years[1], 1926-84

Year	Federal Level ($ mil.)	Federal Percent of GNP	Provincial Level ($ mil.)	Provincial Percent of GNP	Local Level ($ mil.)	Local Percent of GNP	Total Level ($ mil.)	Total Percent of GNP
1926	355	6.9	110	2.1	252	4.9	717	13.9
1939	470	8.4	234	4.2	284	5.1	988	17.7
1946	2,447	20.6	417	3.5	332	2.8	3,196	26.9
1956	5,313	16.6	1,160	3.6	1,024	3.2	7,497	23.4
1966	9,896	16.1	4,647	7.5	2,477	4.0	17,020	27.6
1976	34,387	18.1	19,250	10.1	7,186	3.8	60,823	32.0
1981	61,414	18.5	36,824	11.1	12,233	3.7	110,471	33.3
1984	77,934	18.5	51,406	12.2	16,000	3.8	145,340	34.5

Source: *The National Finances*, annual (Toronto: Canadian Tax Foundation), and *Economic Review*, April 1985, (Ottawa: Department of Finance.)

[1] For 1966 and subsequent years, Federal taxes include the Canada and Quebec Pension Fund contributions.

Table 2
Selected Taxes and Nontax Revenue as a Percent of Total Revenues for All Levels of Governments, 1970 and 1980

Revenue Source	1970[1]	1980[1]
Personal Income Tax		
Federal	20.0	17.6
Provincial/Local	8.4	11.0
Total	28.4	28.6
Corporation Income Tax		
Federal	7.5	6.7
Provincial/Local	2.4	2.8
Total	9.9	9.5
Property Tax		
Federal	—	—
Provincial/Local	10.9	8.1
Total	10.9	8.1
General Sales Tax		
Federal	7.1	4.5
Provincial/Local	5.6	5.2
Total	12.7	9.7
Motor Fuel Tax		
Federal	—	0.4
Provincial/Local	3.4	1.5
Total	3.4	1.9
Alcohol and Tobacco Tax		
Federal	2.8	1.2
Provincial/Local	0.6	0.7
Total	3.4	1.9
Customs Duties		
Federal	2.5	2.6
Provincial/Local	—	—
Total	2.5	2.6
Payroll Taxation		
Federal	4.1	4.9
Provincial/Local	4.4	3.8
Total	8.5	8.7
Other Taxes		
Federal	1.4	1.3
Provincial/Local	1.6	3.2
Total	3.0	4.5

(Continued on next page)

Table 2 (Continued)
Selected Taxes and Nontax Revenue as a Percent of Total Revenues for all Levels of Government, 1970 and 1980

Revenue Source	1970[1]	1980[1]
Total Taxes		
Federal	45.4	41.2
Provincial/Local	37.2	34.3
Total	82.6	75.5
Nontax Revenue		
Federal	5.9	6.6
Provincial/Local[2]	11.5	17.9
Total	17.4	24.5
Total Revenue		
Federal	51.3	47.7
Provincial/Local	48.7	52.3
Total	100.0	100.0

Source: Data collected and percentages calculated from Statistics Canada, *Consolidated Government Finance, 1979*, Catalogue No. 68-202, Tables 5 and 9 (1980 is the latest year for which detailed data are available).

[1]Fiscal year ended nearest to December 31 for Federal and provincial governments and calendar year ended December 31 for most local governments. The data for 1980 are based on estimates of Federal, provincial, and local governments.

[2]This excludes Federal government transfers.

Table 3
Federal Personal Exemptions in Canada, Selected Years, 1973-86

Status	1973	1976	1979	1983	1986
Basic Personal Exemption	$ 1,600	$ 2,091	$ 2,650	$ 3,770	$ 4,180
Married or Equivalent Exemption	3,000	3,921	4,970	7,070	7,840
Aged, additional	1,000	1,310	1,660	2,360	2,610
Incapacitated, additional	1,000	1,310	1,660	2,360	2,610
Dependent child or other dependent under age 16[1]	300	390	500	710	710
Dependent child or other dependent age 16[1] or over	550	720	910	1,300	1,420
Education deduction[2]	50	50	50	50	50
Dependent's earnings not affecting taxpayer's claim:					
Spouse	300	360	430	570	520[3]
Dependent child or other dependent under age 16[1]	1,100	1,410	1,750	2,440	2,760
Dependent child or other dependent age 16[1] or over	1,150	1,470	1,840	2,570	1,340[3]

Source: Robin W. Boadway and Harry M. Kitchen, *Canadian Tax Policy* 2nd edition, Canadian Tax Foundation, Toronto, 1984, p. 56 for the years 1973 to 1863. 1986 information was obtained from the Canadian Tax Foundation.

[1]The age of the dependent child or other dependent was increased from 16 to 17 in 1979 and to 18 in 1980.

[2]The deduction is $50 per month for each month while enrolled in a post-secondary institution.

[3]Federal government reduced the limits for spouse in 1984 budget and a child or other dependent in 1985 budget.

Table 4
Total Deductions as a Percent of Total Income, Selected Years, 1961-1983

Item	1961	1966	1971	1972	1976	1980	1983
Medical Claims	.7	.7	.2	.2	.1	.1	.1
Charitable Donations	1.5	.7	.5	.5	.5	.5	.6
Standard Deduction[9]	2.1	1.9	1.5	1.4	.9	.7	.5
Registered Pension Plan Contributions	1.7	1.3	1.5	1.5	1.5	1.5	1.5
Retirement Savings Plan Premiums	.2	.3	.6	1.0	1.7	1.8	1.9
Union and Professional Dues	.1	.3	.4	.3	.4	.4	.4
CPP or QPP Contributions[1]	—	1.1	1.0	.9	.8	.8	.9
Tuition Fees[2]	—	—	.3	.3	.2	.2	.2
Unemployment Insurance Premiums[3]	—	—	—	.4	.8	.7	1.1
Childcare Expenses[3]	—	—	—	.1	.2	.2	.2
General Expense Allowance[3]	—	—	—	1.4	1.0	1.8	2.0
Other Employment Expenses[2]	—	—	.5	.6	.5	.4	.4
Registered Home Ownership[4]	—	—	—	—	.4	.3	.2
Interest & Dividend Deduction[5]	—	—	—	—	1.9	2.0	1.7
Pension Income Deduction[6]	—	—	—	—	.5	.4	.4
Eligible Interspousal Transfers[7]	—	—	—	—	.3	.3	.2
Other Deductions	.5	1.3	.7	.6	1.1	1.8	1.8
Total[8]	6.8	7.6	7.1	9.3	12.9	13.9	14.1

Source: Calculated from data in *Taxation Statistics*, Department of National Revenue, Taxation, Ottawa, Annual publication—1983 is the last year for which data are available.

[1]Introduced in 1966.

[2]Introduced in 1968.

[3]Introduced in 1972.

[4]Introduced in 1974 and dropped in 1985.

[5]Interest income deduction introduced in 1974 and dividend deduction introduced in 1975.

[6]Introduced in 1975.

[7]Data for this category were first published in 1976. These transfers include the unused portion of (i) the age exemption; (ii) interest, dividends, and capital gains deduction; (iii) pension income deduction; (iv) deduction for blind persons or persons confined to bed or wheelchair; (v) education deduction (this may also apply to dependents other than spouse).

[8]May not add up to total because of rounding.

[9]As of 1985, no longer allowed.

Table 5
Federal Taxable Income Brackets
Subject to Indexing and Tax Rates, 1982-1986

Rate,	Inflation Factor				
%	1982: 12.2%	1983: 6%	1984: 5%	1985: 4.6%	1986: .8%
			Taxable Income Bracket		
6	First $1,112	First $1,179	First $1,238	First $1,295	First $1,305
16	1,113- 2,224	1,180- 2,358	1,239- 2,476	1,296- 2,590	1,306- 2,611
17	2,225- 4,448	2,359- 4,716	2,477- 4,952	2,591- 5,180	2,612- 5,221
18	4,449- 6,671	4,717- 7,074	4,953- 7,428	5,181- 7,770	5,222- 7,832
19	6,673-11,120	7,075-11,790	7,429-12,380	7,771-12,950	7,833-13,054
20	11,121-15,568	11,791-16,506	12,381-17,332	12,951-18,130	13,055-18,275
23	15,569-20,016	16,507-21,222	17,333-22,284	18,131-23,310	18,276-23,496
25	20,017-31,136	21,223-33,012	22,285-34,664	23,311-36,260	23,496-36,550
30	31,137-53,376	33,013-56,592	34,665-59,424	36,261-61,160	36,551-62,657
34	53,377+	56,593+	59,425+	62,161+	62,658+

Source: *The National Finance, 1984-85,* Canadian Tax Foundation, Toronto 1985, p. 86 for 1982-1985. Unpublished data provided from Canadian Tax Foundation for 1986.

Table 6
Provincial Personal Income Tax Rates, January 1, 1986

Province	Percent of Federal Tax
Newfoundland	60.0
Prince Edward Island	52.5
Nova Scotia	56.5[1]
New Brunswick	58.0
Quebec	—[2]
Ontario	49.2[1]
Manitoba	54.0[3]
Saskatchewan	50.0[4]
Alberta	43.5[5]
British Columbia	44.0[6]

Source: M. Goodman, Checklist, 33 *Canadian Tax Journal,* May-June 1985, pp. 716-717.

[1]This province provides an exemption for low-income taxpayers.

[2]Quebec collects its own personal income tax. The rate schedule in effect ranges from 13 to 33 percent of taxable income subject to a tax reduction of three percent of tax payable.

[3]Manitoba imposes a 20 percent surtax on provincial income tax payable on taxable income over $25,000.

[4]Saskatchewan provides a vanishing tax cut, and a 12 percent surtax on provincial income tax payable in excess of $4,000. It also levies a flat tax of 10 percent on top of its present income tax.

[5]Alberta provides a vanishing low-income exemption.

[6]British Columbia levies a 10 percent surtax on provincial income tax payable in excess of $3,500. It also provides that low-income taxpayers pay no more provincial personal income tax than Federal tax.

Table 7
Corporate Tax Rates, January 1, 1986
(Percent)

Province	Corporate Tax Rate Applicable to Canadian Controlled Private Corporations (small business rate)				Corporate Tax Rates Applicable to Other Corps.			
	Nonmanufacturing and Nonprocessing Profits[1]		Manufacturing and Processing Profits[2]		Nonmanufacturing and Nonprocessing Profits[3]		Manufacturing and Processing Profits[4]	
	Provincial	Combined Federal/Provincial	Provincial	Combined Federal/Provincial	Provincial	Combined Federal/Provincial	Provincial	Combined Federal/Provincial
Newfoundland	10	25	10	20	16	52	16	52
Prince Edward Island	10	25	10	20	10	46	10	46
Nova Scotia	10	25	10	20	15	51	15	51
New Brunswick[5]	9	24	9	19	15	51	15	51
Quebec	3	18	3	13	13	49	5.5	41.5
Ontario[6]	10	25	10	20	15.5	51.5	14.5	50.5
Manitoba	10	25	10	20	16	52	16	52
Saskatchewan	10	25	0	10	16	52	10	46
Alberta	5	20	0	10	11	47	5	41
British Columbia	8	23	8	18	16	52	16	52

Source: Calculated from data in *National Finances 1984-85*, Canadian Tax Foundation, Toronto, 1985, pp. 109-120; "Checklist," by Millie Goodman, *Canadian Tax Journal*, May-June 1985, Vol. 33, No. 3, pp. 714-717; and unpublished data from Canadian Tax Foundation.

[1]The Federal tax rate is 25 percent, however, a 10 percentage point abatement is given to the provinces effectively lowering the Federal rate to 15 percentage points. To this latter figure, the provinces add their own rates to get the combined Federal/provincial rate.

[2]The Federal rate of 20 percent is reduced by the 10 percentage point abatement leaving a figure to which the provincial rate is added to get the combined Federal/provincial rate.

[3]The Federal rate is 46 percent. The combined provincial/Federal rate is obtained by subtracting the 10 percentage point Federal abatement from 46 percent and adding the provincial tax rate.

[4]The Federal rate is 40 percent. The combined provincial/Federal rate is obtained by subtracting the 10 percentage point Federal abatement from 40 percent and adding the provincial rates.

[5]Beginning January 1, 1986, small business corporations with active business income of $100,000 or less are taxed at an effective rate of five percent for a three-year period.

[6]A three-year tax exemption applies for new small business corporations.

Table 8
Withholding Method at 50 Percent Rate with All Corporate Profits Distributed

(a) Marginal tax rate (percent)	(b) Dividend received	(c) Grossed-up dividend added to personal income	(d) Income tax before credit	(e) Tax payable after credit of burden	(f) Total tax tax burden	(g) Additional this method*	(h) Percent of tax burden removed by this method*
0	$500	$750	0	-$250	$250	$250	$50
10	500	750	$75	-175	325	225	50
20	500	750	150	-100	400	200	50
30	500	750	225	-25	475	175	50
40	500	750	300	50	550	150	50
50	500	750	375	125	625	125	50

Source: Robin W. Boadway and Harry M. Kitchen, *Canadian Tax Policy*, Second Edition, Canadian Tax Foundation, 1985, p. 208.

*The calculation of the additional burden removed requires information on the tax burden on $1,000 of corporate source income under a non-integrated system (col. 2 below) with the burden under a fully integrated system (col. 3 below). The additional burden of non-integration (col. 4 below) is obtained by subtracting col. 3 from col. 2. The figures in col. 1 in the above table are obtained by taking the figures in col. (g) of that table as a percent of the figures in col. 4 below.

(1) Marginal Tax Rate (percent)	(2) Tax payable under non-integration ($500 corporate tax plus personal income tax on dividends of $500)	(3) Tax payable under full integration (partnership method)	(4) Additional Tax Burden (col. 2 - col. 3)
0	$500	$0	$500
10	550	100	450
20	600	200	400
30	650	300	350
40	700	400	300
50	750	500	250

Table 9
Withholding Method Under a 25 Percent Corporate Tax Rate with All Profits Distributed

(a) Marginal tax rate (percent)	(b) Dividend received[1]	(c) Grossed-up dividend added to personal income[2]	(d) Personal income tax before credit of $375[3]	(e) Personal tax payable after credit of $375[4]	(f) Total tax burden (col. e plus $250 corporate tax)[5]	(g) Additional tax burden[6]	(h) Percent of tax burden removed by this method[7]
			(dollars)				
0	$750	$1125	0	-$375.00	-$125.00	-$125.00	$133
10	750	1125	$112.50	-262.50	-12.50	-112.50	133
20	750	1125	225.00	-150.00	100.00	-100.00	133
30	750	1125	337.50	-37.50	212.50	-87.50	133
40	750	1125	450.00	75.00	325.00	-75.00	133
50	750	1125	562.50	187.50	437.50	-62.50	133

[1]Dividend received after corporate tax of $250 had been paid on $1,000 of corporate source income.
[2]Dividend received times 1.5.
[3]Marginal tax rate applied to grossed up dividend.
[4]Column (d) minus $375.
[5]Column (e) plus $250 corporate tax.
[6]Tax payable under full integration scheme (column 3 in footnote to table 8) minus column (f).
[7]Figures in column (g) as a percent of the figures in column 4 of the table below. These numbers illustrate the percentage of the additional burden removed by this integration method.

(1) Marginal tax rate (percent)	(2) Tax Payable under non-integration ($250 corporation tax plus personal income tax on dividends of $750).	(3) Tax payable under full integration	(4) Additional tax payable under burden (col. 2 – col. 3)
0	$250	0	$250
10	325	$100	225
20	400	200	200
30	475	300	175
40	550	400	150
50	625	500	125

Table 10
Withholding Method at 50 Percent Rate with One-Half Profits Distributed

(a) Marginal tax rate (percent)	(b) Dividend received	(c) Grossed-up Dividend (1.5 x b)	(d) Capital gains (nontaxable)	(e) Income tax before credit	(f) Tax payable after credit of $125	(g) Total tax burden (f = 500)	(h) Additional tax burden	(i) Percent of burden removed by this method*
0	$250	$375	$250	0.	-$125.00	$375.00	$375.00	25.0
10	250	375	250	$37.50	-87.50	412.50	312.50	30.6
20	250	375	250	75.00	-50.00	450.00	250.00	37.5
30	250	375	250	112.50	-12.50	487.50	187.50	46.4
40	250	375	250	150.00	25.00	525.00	125.00	58.3
50	250	375	250	187.50	62.50	562.50	62.50	75.0

*These figures are obtained by calculating the figures in column (h) as a percent of the figures in column 4 of the footnote to table 2. These numbers illustrate the percent of the additional burden eliminated under the conditions set out in this table.

Table 11
Pension and Savings Deductions, 1983[1]

Income category	Registered Pension Plan			Registered Retirement Savings Plan			Interest, Dividend and Capital Gain Deduction[2]			Pension Income Deduction		
	Percent of all returns claiming deduction	Average claim	Average claim as a percent of gross income	Percent of all returns claiming deduction	Average claim	Average claim as a percent of gross income	Percent of all returns claiming deduction	Average claim	Average claim as a percent of gross income	Percent of all returns claiming deduction	Average claim	Average claim as a percent of gross income
1–$5,000	1.0	$153	6.3	0.6	$527	21.6	28.8	$447	18.4	1.5	$666	27.3
$5,001–10,000	3.0	282	3.8	3.2	816	11.0	42.0	645	8.7	7.2	892	12.0
10,001–15,000	10.8	434	3.5	9.5	1,261	10.2	48.7	654	5.3	12.1	952	7.7
15,001–20,000	29.2	676	3.9	16.3	1,605	9.2	51.4	616	3.5	9.4	956	5.5
20,001–25,000	41.3	911	4.1	22.7	1,871	8.4	55.6	613	2.7	8.0	958	4.3
25,001–30,000	51.0	1,178	4.3	27.8	2,052	7.5	59.3	595	2.2	6.6	959	3.5
30,001–40,000	56.3	1,488	4.3	36.6	2,228	6.5	66.5	617	1.8	6.3	959	2.8
40,001–50,000	57.2	1,987	4.5	47.4	2,461	5.6	75.0	684	1.5	6.7	962	2.2
50,001–100,000	43.7	2,418	3.8	52.6	3,724	5.8	83.0	772	1.2	8.8	950	1.5
100,000+	18.6	3,024	1.7	60.2	5,516	3.1	89.2	895	0.5	10.7	933	0.5
Total	22.4	1,184	6.5	15.2	2,145	11.8	47.3	621	3.4	6.8	936	5.1

Source: Figures calculated from data in Canada, Department of National Revenue, Taxation, *Taxation Statistics* (Ottawa: Department of Supply and Services, 1985), Table 2.

[1] Latest year for which data are available.

[2] As of 1986, capital gains are no longer included in this deduction.

Table 12
Total Personal Savings and Components
as a Percent of Personal Disposable Income,
Selected Years, 1971-83
(Percent)

Plan	1971	1976	1980	1983
Canada Pension Plan/ Quebec Pension Plan	0.9	0.9	0.9	0.9
Registered Retirement Savings Premiums	0.5	1.7	1.9	1.9
Registered Home Ownership Contributions	—	0.4	0.3	0.2
Private Pension Plans	1.4	1.6	1.6	1.5
All Other	3.1	4.6	7.4	8.4
Total Personal Savings	5.9	9.2	12.1	12.9

Source: Calculated from data in Table 2 of *Taxation Statistics*, selected years, Revenue Canada, Taxation, Ottawa and *Economic Review*, Department of Finance, April 1984, Reference Table 14.

Table 13
Per Capita Local and Provincial Revenue by Source, 1980

Taxes	Provincial Amount Per Capita	Provincial Percent of Total	Local Amount Per Capita	Local Percent of Total
Personal income	$ 549.69	21.5	$ —	—
Corporation income	147.35	5.8	—	—
Retail sales	254.94	10.0	—	—
Real property	—	—	355.50	31.4
Business tax	—	—	39.20	3.5
Other	361.37	14.1	1.80	0.2
Total Taxes	1,313.35	51.4	396.50	35.1
Privileges, licenses, permits	63.97	2.5	6.96	0.6
Sales	51.95	2.0	108.39	9.6
Other	614.61	24.0	99.33	8.8
Total Own Source Revenue	2,043.88	79.9	611.18	54.1
Unconditional grants				
Federal	163.57	6.4	—	—
Provincial	—	—	52.33	4.5
Conditional grants				
Federal	351.55	13.7	7.76	1.6
Provincial	—	—	463.09	39.9
Total Revenue	2,559.00	100.0	1,134.36	100.0

Source: Provincial government revenues calculated from data in *Provincial and Municipal Finance, 1983*, Canadian Tax Foundation, Toronto. Local government revenues calculated from data in Table 6-A4 in Harry M. Kitchen and Melville L. McMillan, "Local Government and Canadian Federalism" in *Intergovernmental Relations*, Richard Simeon, Research Coordinator, Vol. 63, University of Toronto Press, Toronto, 1985, p. 253.

Table 14
Utilization of Real Property, Personal Income, and
Retail Sales Taxes, Selected Years, 1933 to 1981

Years	Property tax as a percent of personal disposable income	Personal income tax as a percent of personal disposable income	Retail sales tax as a peprcent of personal disposable income
1933	8.5	1.4	0
1941	4.6	5.6	0.3
1951	3.5	6.3	0.6
1961	5.4	7.9	1.3
1971	5.7	17.0	3.4
1981	4.8	18.0	2.7

Source: Calculated from data in *Historical Statistics of Canada*, 2nd edition, edited by F. H. Leacy (Ottawa: Statistics Canada, 1983) and *The National Finances, 19184-85*, Canadian Tax Foundation, Toronto, 1985, ch. 4.

Table 15
Property Tax as a Percent of Owner-Occupied Equity
by Money Income, 1982[1]

Money Income (dollars)	Ontario	Quebec	British Columbia
3,000—5,999	1.57	2.31	0.90
6,000—9,999	1.59	1.54	1.18
10,000—14,999	2.49	2.03	1.11
15,000—19,999	1.85	2.22	4.26
20,000—24,999	2.51	2.83	1.47
25,000—29,999	2.55	3.66	1.78
30,000—34,999	2.87	3.49	2.32
35,000—39,999	2.75	3.97	1.94
40,000—49,999	2.84	4.14	1.54
50,000—69,999	2.10	3.36	3.38
70,000—99,999	1.70	2.65	1.67
100,000 or more	5.28	2.51	0.82

Source: Calculated from *1982 Survey of Family Expenditure*, Microdata tape, Statistics Canada, Ottawa.

[1]Only three provinces are presented because these are the only provinces for which information is presented separately.

Table 16
Personal Income Tax: Federal and Provincial Marginal Rates (Combined[1]), 1984

Taxable income ($)	Combined marginal rates, percent									
	Nfld.	P.E.I.	N.S.	N.B.	Que.	Ont.	Man.	Sask.	Alta.	B.C.
1	**3.60**	**3.15**	—	**3.48**	**13.00**	—	—	—	—	**0.11**
574	3.60	3.15	—	3.48	14.00	—	—	—	—	0.11
1,239	**9.60**	**8.40**	—	**9.28**	14.00	—	—	—	—	**0.28**
1,245	9.60	8.40	—	9.28	**15.00**	—	—	—	—	0.28
2,016	9.60	8.40	—	9.28	**16.00**	—	—	—	—	0.28
2,027	**25.60**	**24.40**	**25.04**	**29.36**	**23.68**	**24.64**	**16.00**	**16.00**	**16.00**	**16.28**
2,151	25.60	24.40	25.04	25.28	29.36	24.06	24.64	16.00	16.00	16.28
2,477	**27.20**	**25.93**	**26.61**	**26.86**	**30.20**	**25.57**	**26.18**	**17.00**	**17.00**	**17.30**
2,722	27.20	25.93	26.61	26.86	30.20	25.57	26.18	**25.67**	17.00	17.30
2,907	27.20	25.93	26.61	26.86	**31.20**	25.57	26.18	25.67	17.00	17.30
2,981	27.20	25.93	26.61	26.86	31.20	25.57	26.18	25.67	17.00	**24.78**
3,230	27.20	25.93	26.61	26.86	31.20	25.57	26.18	25.67	17.00	24.78
3,937	27.20	25.93	26.61	26.86	**32.20**	25.57	26.18	25.67	17.00	24.78
3,942	27.20	25.93	26.61	26.86	32.20	25.57	26.18	25.67	**24.40**	24.78
4,201	27.20	25.93	26.61	26.86	32.20	25.57	26.18	25.67	24.40	24.78
4,953	**28.80**	**27.45**	**28.17**	**28.44**	**33.03**	**27.07**	**27.72**	**27.18**	**25.83**	**26.24**
5,128	28.80	27.45	28.17	28.44	**34.03**	27.07	27.72	27.18	25.83	26.24
6,509	28.80	27.45	**29.74**	28.44	**35.03**	27.07	27.72	27.18	25.83	26.24
7,429	**30.40**	**28.98**	**29.74**	**30.02**	**35.87**	**28.58**	**29.26**	**28.69**	**27.27**	**27.69**
8,096	30.40	28.98	29.74	30.02	**36.87**	25.58	29.26	28.69	27.27	27.69
8,201	30.40	28.98	29.74	30.02	36.87	28.58	29.26	28.69	27.27	27.69
8,589	30.40	28.98	29.74	30.02	36.87	28.58	29.26	28.69	27.27	27.69
9,662	30.40	28.98	29.74	30.92	36.87	28.58	29.26	28.69	27.27	27.69
9,936	30.40	28.98	29.74	30.02	**37.87**	28.58	29.26	28.69	27.27	27.69
12,062	30.40	28.98	29.74	30.02	**38.87**	28.58	29.26	28.69	27.27	27.69

Table 16 (Continued)
Personal Income Tax: Federal and Provincial Marginal Rates (Combined[1]), 1984

Taxable income ($)	Combined marginal rates, percent									
	Nfld.	P.E.I.	N.S.	N.B.	Que.	Ont.	Man.	Sask.	Alta.	B.C.
12,381	32.00	30.50	31.30	31.60	39.70	30.08	30.80	30.20	28.70	29.15
14,520	32.00	30.50	31.30	31.60	40.70	30.08	30.80	30.20	28.70	29.15
17,333	36.80	35.08	36.00	36.34	43.20	34.59	35.42	34.73	33.01	33.52
17,361	36.80	35.08	36.00	36.34	44.20	34.59	35.42	34.73	33.01	33.52
20,645	36.80	35.08	36.00	36.34	45.20	34.59	35.42	34.73	33.01	33.52
22,285	40.00	38.13	39.13	39.50	46.87	37.60	38.50	37.75	35.88	36.44
24,442	40.00	38.13	39.13	39.50	47.87	37.60	38.50	37.75	35.88	36.44
25,001	40.00	38.13	39.13	39.50	47.87	37.60	41.20	37.75	35.88	36.44
28,830	40.00	38.13	39.13	39.50	48.87	37.60	41.20	37.75	35.88	36.44
29,449	42.50	40.63	41.63	42.00	51.37	40.10	43.70	40.25	38.38	38.94
33,903	42.50	40.63	41.63	42.00	52.37	40.10	43.70	40.25	38.38	38.94
34,665	51.00	48.75	49.95	50.40	57.05	48.12	52.44	48.30	46.05	46.73
35,814	51.00	48.75	49.95	50.40	57.05	48.12	52.44	48.30	46.05	48.11
36,462	51.00	48.75	49.95	50.40	57.05	48.12	52.44	50.14	46.05	48.11
36,984	48.00	45.75	46.95	47.40	54.05	45.12	49.44	47.14	43.05	45.11
39,767	48.00	45.75	46.95	47.40	55.05	45.12	49.44	47.14	43.05	45.11
46,545	48.00	45.75	46.95	47.40	56.05	45.12	49.44	47.14	43.05	45.11
54,381	48.00	45.75	46.95	47.40	57.05	45.12	49.44	47.14	43.05	45.11
59,425	54.40	51.85	53.21	53.72	60.39	51.14	56.03	53.42	48.79	51.12
60,715	54.40	51.85	53.21	53.72	61.39	51.14	56.03	53.42	48.79	51.12

Source: *The National Finances, 1984–85*, Canadian Tax Foundation, Toronto, pp. 98-99.

[1]To identify changes in rates, each new rate is in boldface type.

Table 17
Personal Income Tax as a Percent of Personal Income Minus Government Transfers to Persons

Year	Percent
1946	0.9
1954	7.1
1964	8.8
1974	15.6
1979	14.9
1984	16.1

Source: Calculated from National Accounts data.

Table 18
Tax Incidence: Effective Tax Rates Using the Broad Income Concept, Canada, 1969
(Percent)

Line tax	Family money income class									
	under $2,000	$2,000-2,999	$3,000-3,999	$4,000-4,999	$5,000-5,999	$6,000-6,999	$7,000-9,999	$10,00-14,999	$15,000-& over	Total
Federal taxes										
1 Personal income tax	2.0	2.8	4.0	5.2	6.6	7.5	8.9	11.0	11.2	9.3
2 Corporation income tax	9.3	4.9	3.8	3.5	2.4	3.2	2.5	2.5	4.9	3.3
3 General sales taxes	13.3	7.4	5.5	4.8	4.5	4.4	4.1	3.8	2.6	3.8
4 Selective excise taxes	5.3	2.9	2.3	2.0	2.1	1.9	1.7	1.5	.8	1.5
5 Social security taxes	2.9	2.7	3.4	4.1	4.7	4.1	3.7	2.7	1.2	2.8
6 Customs import duties	4.8	2.6	1.9	1.7	1.6	1.6	1.5	1.4	.9	1.4
7 Succession and estate taxes	.5	.3	.3	.2	.1	.1	.1	.1	.3	.2
8 Total Federal taxes	3.82	23.6	21.2	21.5	21.9	22.9	22.3	23.0	22.1	22.3
Provincial taxes										
9 Personal income tax	.8	1.1	1.6	2.0	2.5	2.9	3.4	4.3	4.3	3.6
10 Corporation income tax	3.4	1.8	1.4	1.2	.9	1.1	.9	.9	1.6	1.2
11 General sales tax	8.9	5.8	4.8	3.5	3.4	3.2	3.0	2.8	1.8	2.8
12 Selective excise taxes	7.2	4.6	3.7	3.8	3.7	3.7	3.4	3.1	1.7	2.9
13 Social security taxes	.3	.2	.3	.3	.4	.5	.5	.3	.2	.3
14 Medical/Hospital premiums	8.9	3.2	2.1	1.6	1.6	1.3	1.1	1.0	.6	1.1
15 Succession and estate taxes	.7	.4	.4	.3	.2	.2	.1	.1	.4	.2
16 Other taxes	5.3	3.1	2.2	2.1	1.8	2.0	1.8	1.8	1.8	1.9
17 Total provincial taxes	33.2	20.2	16.3	14.9	14.4	15.0	14.1	14.2	12.4	13.8
Local taxes										
18 General sales tax	—	—	—	—	—	—	—	—	—	—
19 Property tax	22.8	12.7	7.5	6.1	5.3	5.1	4.7	4.3	3.5	4.7
20 Business tax	1.8	.9	.6	.4	.5	.5	.5	.4	.3	.4
21 Poll taxes	.1	—	—	.1	—	—	—	—	—	—
22 Other taxes	.2	.1	.1	.1	—	—	—	—	—	—
23 Total local taxes	24.8	13.7	8.2	6.6	5.8	5.6	5.3	4.8	3.8	5.2
24 Total all taxes	96.3	57.5	45.8	43.0	42.2	43.4	41.7	42.0	38.3	41.3

Source: W. Irwin Gillespie, "On the Redistribution of Income in Canada; (July-August, 1976), 24 *Canadian Tax Journal* 417-50.
Note: Details may not add to totals because of rounding.

CHAPTER 9

Japan

M. Homma, T. Maeda,
and K. Hashimoto

INTRODUCTION

The purpose of this paper is to present the major features of the current Japanese tax system and to give a brief summary of the main economic analyses carried out by Japanese writers.

The Japanese tax system has all of the major taxes used by other countries, except for a broad-based consumption tax. The national government relies heavily on the individual income tax and the corporation income tax. In fiscal year 1986, the individual income tax and the corporate income tax accounted for 40.5 percent and 30.6 percent of national tax revenue, respectively. Substantial revenues are raised by selected excise taxes at all levels of government. Inheritance and gift taxes are minor sources of revenue.

Japanese local governments are composed of prefectural governments and municipal governments. The major sources of tax revenue at the prefectural government level are the prefectural inhabitants tax and the enterprise tax. In fiscal year 1986, the prefectural inhabitants tax and the enterprise tax amounted to 28.8 percent and 38.4 percent of tax revenue, respectively. The two main tax instruments at the municipal level consist of the municipal inhabitants tax and the fixed assets tax. In fiscal year 1986, the ratio of municipal inhabitants tax to total revenue was 49.4 percent, and that of fixed assets tax 33.4 percent.

As in other countries, there is considerable dissatisfaction in Japan with the present tax system. Japanese income taxes are riddled with special provisions, which produce major inequities and distort economic activity. Tax reform to broaden the income tax bases and lower the tax rates is being actively discussed. In addition, serious consideration is being given to the introduction of a value-added tax in order to reduce the distortionary effects of the indirect tax system.

I. THE INDIVIDUAL INCOME TAX

In Japan, the individual income tax and the corporation tax are treated separately under the Income Tax Law and the Corporation Tax Law, respectively.

1. Outline of the Individual Income Tax

Under the present Individual Income Tax Law, ordinary income is classified into ten categories: interest income, dividend income, real estate income, business income, employment income, retirement income, timber income, capital gains, occasional income, miscellaneous income. The basic procedure for the income tax consists of five steps: (1) adjustment of various types of ordinary income, (2) calculation of adjusted gross income, (3) computation of taxable income, (4) application of tax rates to taxable income, and (5) subtraction of tax credits. The procedure for calculating the individual income tax is summarized in figure 1.

1.1 Adjustment of Ordinary Income

Each ordinary income is adjusted in principle by subtracting from gross receipts the expenses of earning income. There are also some special deductions for the various ordinary income categories.

Employment income includes salaries, wages, allowances, bonuses, and pensions. Expenses cannot be deducted in an itemized manner from gross receipts; instead a special deduction is allowed for employment income, which is computed in accordance with the following table.

Employment income (yen millions)	Deductions (percent)
0.00—1.65	40[1]
1.65—3.00	30
3.00—6.00	20
6.00 and over	10

[1]The minimum deduction is 570,000 yen.

Figure 1
The Basic Formula to Compute Income Tax When Taxpayer Does Not Select Separate Taxation on Interest and Dividend Income

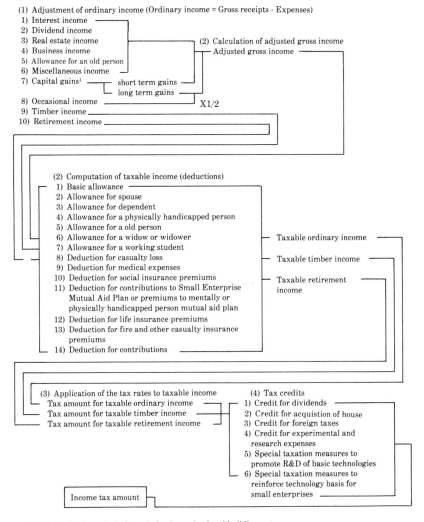

(1) Adjustment of ordinary income (Ordinary income = Gross receipts - Expenses)
1) Interest income
2) Dividend income
3) Real estate income
4) Business income
5) Allowance for an old person
6) Miscellaneous income
7) Capital gains[1] — short term gains
  long term gains
8) Occasional income — X1/2
9) Timber income
10) Retirement income

(2) Calculation of adjusted gross income
Adjusted gross income

(2) Computation of taxable income (deductions)
1) Basic allowance
2) Allowance for spouse
3) Allowance for dependent
4) Allowance for a physically handicapped person
5) Allowance for a old person
6) Allowance for a widow or widower
7) Allowance for a working student
8) Deduction for casualty loss
9) Deduction for medical expenses
10) Deduction for social insurance premiums
11) Deduction for contributions to Small Enterprise Mutual Aid Plan or premiums to mentally or physically handicapped person mutual aid plan
12) Deduction for life insurance premiums
13) Deduction for fire and other casualty insurance premiums
14) Deduction for contributions

Taxable ordinary income
Taxable timber income
Taxable retirement income

(3) Application of the tax rates to taxable income
Tax amount for taxable ordinary income
Tax amount for taxable timber income
Tax amount for taxable retirement income

(4) Tax credits
1) Credit for dividends
2) Credit for acquistion of house
3) Credit for foreign taxes
4) Credit for experimental and research expenses
5) Special taxation measures to promote R&D of basic technologies
6) Special taxation measures to reinforce technology basis for small enterprises

Income tax amount

[1]Capital gains do not include capital gains on land and buildings, etc.

This deduction simplifies tax administration and reduces the cost of compliance for wage earners. Deductions for expenses are not allowed, but there are the following special deductions for small amounts of savings:

1. interest on bank deposits, joint operation money trusts, public bonds, mortgaged debentures and stock investment trusts up to three million yen,

2. interest on postal savings up to three million yen,

3. interest on government bonds up to three million yen,

4. interest income or distribution of profits from employee savings accounts up to five million yen.

Dividend income is calculated by subtracting interest paid on borrowings for the acquisition of shares from gross dividends receipts.

Real estate income is rent from real estate and any initial lump sum payment received for rented houses or land. (Such a lump sum payment is classified as a capital gain if it exceeds half the value of the land.)

Business income includes earnings from business activities or professions such as commerce, manufacture, agriculture, fishing, medical service, actors, musicians.

Occasional income includes gifts received from corporations, prizes, and other income of an occasional nature. Ordinary occasional income is 50 percent of net income after subtracting a special deduction of 500,000 yen.

Capital gains include income from the sale or transfer of assets. Capital gains from the sale of securities are not taxed, except for gains of continuous traders. For tax purposes, capital gains are divided into two categories: capital gains from the transfer of such assets as machines, installments, fishing rights, etc., and capital gains from the transfer of land and buildings. (See below for the tax rates on capital gains.)

Miscellaneous income includes royalties on books, compensation for manuscripts or lectures, and other miscellaneous income not classified in the other categories.

Retirement income includes lump sum pensions, retirement allowances, etc. Lump sum retirement allowances paid by the social insurance system and qualified pension plans are regarded as retirement income. Only 50 percent of retirement income less a special retirement deduction is subject to tax. The special deduction is 250,000 yen a year (with a minimum of 500,000 yen for service of 20 years or less, and five million yen plus 500,000 yen for each year in excess of 20 years).

Timber income includes income derived from the sale or transfer of timber. The amount of timber income equals total receipts less the costs of acquisition, forestation, management and lumbering of the forest, other necessary expenses, less a special deduction of 500,000 yen.

1.2 Calculation of Adjusted Gross Income

Adjusted gross income is calculated by summing each ordinary income except retirement and timber income. However, separate taxation can be chosen for capital gains on land and buildings, dividends, and interest income under the special Taxation Measures Law. Retirement and timber income are taxed independently of adjusted gross income.

1.3 Computation of Taxable Income

Taxable income is calculated by subtracting from adjusted gross income, retirement income, and timber income the personal exemptions and deductions for specified expenditures.

Personal exemptions are divided into the following categories: basic allowance, allowance for spouse, allowance for dependent, allowance for a physically handicapped person, allowance for an elderly person, allowance for a widow or widower, and allowance for a working student. A taxpayer may subtract 330,000 yen as a basic allowance from his ordinary income, retirement income, or timber income, for himself, his spouse, and dependents (390,000 yen for a spouse and aged dependents who are 70 years or older). If a taxpayer is an aged person (over 65), widow, widower, working student, physically handicapped or has a physically handicapped dependent who lives with him, an allowance of 250,000 yen may be deducted from ordinary income, retirement income, or timber income. In the case of a severely handicapped person, the amount is 330,000 yen. However, the allowance for a spouse is not allowed if the spouse's income exceeds 330,000 yen and is employment income, business income, retirement income, or miscellaneous income, or if the spouse's income exceeds 100,000 yen when it is other than earned income arising from assets. Also, if the total of capital income and 10/33 of earned income is over 100,000 yen when the spouse's income is composed of both earned income and capital income, no spouse allowance is allowed.

Deductions are allowed for casualty losses in excess of 10 percent of income, medical expenses in excess of five percent of income, social insurance and life insurance premiums, fire and other casualty insurance premiums, contributions to the small enterprise mutual aid plan, mentally or physically handicapped person mutual aid, and other contributions.

The deduction is limited to two million yen for medical expenses, 50,000 yen for life insurance premiums, and 15,000 yen for fire and other casualty insurance premiums.

A deduction is allowed to a taxpayer who gives contributions to (i) government or municipalities, educational institutions, scientific or other public organizations, which are designated by the Ministry of Finance; (ii) institutions stipulated by the Cabinet Order as making a significant contribution to the promotion of education or science, improvement of culture or social welfare, or advancement of public interest; and (iii) political organizations which meet certain requirements.

If the contributions during a year exceed 10,000 yen, the full amount up to 25 percent of ordinary income may be deducted.

1.4 Tax Rates

Ordinary taxable income is taxed at the progressive schedules shown in table 1. The maximum marginal tax rate is 70 percent. The minimum marginal rate is 10.5 percent. In addition, the maximum marginal rate is four percent under the prefectural individual inhabitant tax and 14 percent under the municipal individual inhabitant tax. Summing these taxes increases the total maximum marginal rate to 88 percent. However, in fact, the total actual effective rate is limited to 78 percent by statute.

Taxable retirement income and taxable timber income are taxed separately from other ordinary taxable income. Interest income and dividend income are also taxed separately from other ordinary taxable income, if the taxpayer selected final settlement at the tax withholding rate of 35 percent. Also, as a temporary special measure, capital gains on land, buildings or right-to-use land are taxed separately from ordinary taxable income. As timber is usually cut at long intervals, the tax on timber income is computed by a divided-by-five, or a multiplied-by-five formula to lessen progressivity.

Capital gains on land and buildings are divided into long-term and short-term gains. Long-term (short-term) capital gains are those derived from transfer of land and buildings used more than ten years (less than ten years). The tax rate is 20 percent of taxable long-term gains and 40 percent of taxable short-term gains up to 40 million yen. Taxable gains above 40 million yen are taxed at somewhat higher rates (see figure 2).

Long-term capital gains on land and buildings up to one million yen are not taxable. Further, there is a 30 million yen deduction of capital gains on the sale of a residence; if this special deduction is taken, the one million yen deduction is not allowed. The total amount of the special capital gain deduction is limited to 30 million yen for each taxpayer.

Figure 2
Separate Taxation of Interest and Dividend Income

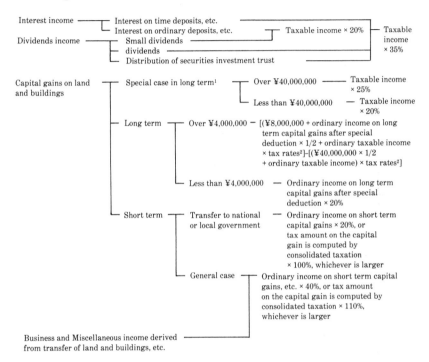

[1]Transfer for the promotion of supply of good quality housing or housing land.
[2]The tax rates shown in table 1 are applied.

1.5 Tax Credits

There are six categories of tax credits: for dividends received; the acquisition of a dwelling; foreign taxes; experimental research expenses; promotion of R&D basic technologies; and reinforcement of the technology basis of small enterprises. If the tax credits exceed the tax before tax credits, a tax refund is not allowed.

The credit for dividends is 10 percent of dividends received for taxpayers with taxable income less than 10 million yen. If a taxpayer has taxable income of 10 million yen or more, the credit is 10 percent of the first 10 million yen of dividend income and five percent of the remaining dividend income.

If a taxpayer constructed or purchased a dwelling after 1986 and borrowed funds from private financial institutions with a repayment period of more than 10 years, the tax credit is one percent of the outstanding repayment at the end of the year (if the outstanding repayment is not less than 20 million yen, the deduction is 20 million yen) in the succeeding three years, when the house is actually available for residence within six days after date of acquisition. However, this credit is not allowed unless the floor space of the house is more than 40 square meters and less than 180 square meters. Also, this credit is not allowed for a year in which the taxpayer's annual income is over 10 million yen.

Foreign taxes similar in nature to the Japanese income tax are creditable in full against the Japanese income tax.

When the annual expenses for research and experimentation exceed the largest amount of such expenditures in any year since 1966, a tax credit of 20 percent of the excess is allowed. This credit is limited to 10 percent of the income tax on business income. The limit on this credit for small enterprises is 15 percent of the years 1985-88.

In addition to the credit for experimental and research expenses, a tax credit is allowed for specific property used in R&D of basic technologies only if a taxpayer chooses to file a blue return (see below). The tax credit is seven percent of the acquisition cost of specified property used for such R&D. This special measure is applicable from 1985 to 1988. The total is limited to 15 percent of the income tax credit for experimental and research expenses and for R&D in basic technologies.

2. Treatment of the Family

The taxable unit under the income tax is the individual. However, the progressive tax rates are applied to the total property income of all family members (such as interest income, dividends income, and rents). Every taxpayer is obliged to pay only his or her own tax, but not the tax payable by the other family members.

3. Current Payment System

The income tax is levied under the so-called self-assessment system. Under this system, the tax liability is determined by the taxpayer's declaration. If the taxpayer fails to file a correct return, the tax authorities assess deficiencies through the "correction" or "determination" procedures. Earners of interest income (including income from original issue discount on bonds bearing no interest), dividends, employment income, retirement income, and remuneration or fees, etc., paid to self-employed persons are not required to file a final return. For convenience of tax collection, the withholding system requires payers with these types of income to withhold the tax at the time of payment and to transmit it to the government.

4. Requirement for Filing Tax Returns

A resident taxpayer submits a final return for a given year between February 16 and March 15 of the following year. However, a taxpayer is not required to file a final return if his or her total income does not exceed the total of the 15 deductions or allowances, or if his or her liability does not exceed the dividend tax credit.

A taxpayer whose gross receipts from employment income is less than 15 million yen is not usually required to file a final return. Such a taxpayer may, but is not required to, file a final return to obtain a tax refund.

5. Blue Returns

The taxpayer who has income from business, real estate, or timber may choose to file a return on a blue form for any taxable year subject to the condition that he keeps proper accounting records. The main privileges granted to an individual taxpayer filing a blue return are (i) he is allowed as expenses as much of wages or income as is deemed reasonable, if paid to relatives living with him in the same household, (ii) he may be regarded as a corporation for tax purposes; and (iii) he is allowed the credit for experimental and research expenses and for R&D in basic technologies.

6. Adjustments for Inflation

An indexation system of income tax purposes has not been introduced in Japan. However, discretionary tax cuts have often been made to adjust for inflation. The minimum taxable floor has been increased periodically. As a result, the Japanese minimum taxable floor is higher than in other countries.

7. Anonymous Accounts

Anonymous accounts are frequently used by taxpayers to conceal their income from the tax authorities, especially income from public bond debentures, loan trusts, and securities investment trusts. Interest and distributions accruing in these anonymous accounts are subject to the withholding tax of 35 percent. Anonymous accounts cannot be used in the tax-exempt saving system.

II. THE CORPORATION INCOME TAX

Japan's corporation income tax is based on the view that a corporation is a collective body of individual shareholders and that the corporation income tax should be integrated with the individual income tax. To prevent double taxation of dividends, distributed earnings are taxed at a reduced rate at the corporate level and a credit for dividends received is provided at the individual level. In addition, dividends received by corporate shareholders are exempt from the corporation income tax when they are distributed as dividends.

1. Major Features of the Corporation Income Tax

The corporation income tax is levied on a corporation's ordinary income, liquidation income, and other receipts. Ordinary income for a corporation is the excess of gross income over costs.

Gross income includes revenues from sales of commodities and manufactures, revenue from sales of fixed assets, interest revenue and other income. Expenses include the cost of sales included in gross income, sales expenses, general administration expenses, expenses specially stipulated in the Corporation Tax Law (such as depreciation expenses, deferred expenses, taxes paid, various kinds of reserves, loss carryforwards, and so on). Though the calculation of corporate net income generally follows regular accounting practice, some adjustments are required or allowed under the Corporation Tax Law. Thus, dividends received and tax refunds are exempt from gross income; compensation, bonuses and retirement allowances paid to directors, entertainment expenses, various reserves, and other items are deductible only within limits.

The tax rate on ordinary corporate income is proportional in principle and is, therefore, different from the progressive individual income tax. (Details are given in the following section.) Tax credits, such as the credit for experimental and research expenses, the investment tax credit for specified equipment, and the tax credit for foreign taxes, may be deducted from the tax on ordinary income.

The procedure for calculating the corporation income tax is summarized in figure 3.

Figure 3
The Procedure for Calculating the Corporation Tax

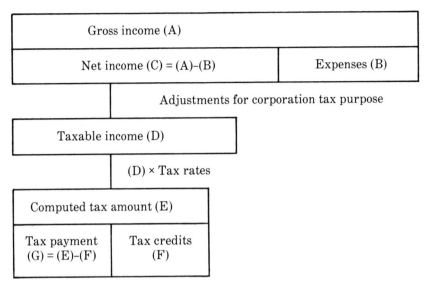

2. Tax Rates

The corporation income tax is levied by the central government at rates of 42 percent on undistributed profits and 32 percent on distributed profits. However, from April 1, 1984 to March 31, 1987, the tax rates were raised to 43.3 percent on undistributed profits and 33.3 percent on distributed profits. For corporations with capital of not more than 100 million yen, the permanent tax rate on profits up to eight million yen is 30 percent on undistributed profits and 24 percent on distributed profits. (For details, see table 2.)

The prefectures levy an enterprise tax of 12 percent of the net income of corporations (with reduced rates for small corporations). In addition, prefectures and municipalities levy a corporate inhabitant tax (which is a form of surtax) on corporations. The standard surtax is five percent of the central government corporation income tax for prefectures and 12.3 percent for municipalities. The enterprise tax is allowed as a deduction in computing the corporation income tax, but the corporate inhabitant taxes are not.

The effective tax rate of large corporations is computed by the following formula:

$$\frac{(70 \times .433 + 30 \times .333)(1 + .173) + 100 \times .12}{100 + 100 \times .12} = .5292$$

where 43.3 percent is the corporation income tax for undistributed profits, 33.3 percent is the corporation income tax for distributed profits, 17.3 percent is the sum of the standard surtax rates at the local government level, and 12 percent is the enterprise tax rate.

3. Treatment of Small Corporations

As noted above, ordinary corporations capitalized at less than 100 million yen are taxed at reduced tax rates both on undistributed and distributed earnings, with larger reductions going to those with taxable income under eight million yen. Further, special depreciation and tax free reserves are allowed for smaller corporations.

In addition to ordinary depreciation, special initial depreciation allowances of 14 percent are provided for plant and equipment newly acquired for more than one million yen by corporations with less than 100 million yen capital and fewer than 1,000 employees; 16 percent for plant and equipment used to develop technology (eight percent for a building); and 21 percent for outlays made for modernization (eight or 16 percent for building).

Dues paid to associations specified by the Financial Assistance Law for modernization of small enterprises are deductible as business expenses.

4. Treatment of Dividends

In Japanese tax law, the corporation income tax is regarded as an advance payment of the individual income tax. A dividends-received credit is provided at the individual level and a dividends-paid deduction is provided at the corporate level, the former eliminating three-quarters and the latter one-quarter of the double taxation of distributed corporate earnings.

The credit for dividends is 10 percent of dividends received for taxpayers with taxable income less than 10 million yen. When taxable income is more than one million yen, the credit of 10 percent is allowed for the part of dividend income which is equal or less than 10 million yen, and five percent for the part of dividends income exceeding 10 million yen.

Dividends received by a corporate shareholder are exempt from corporation income tax, if they are distributed as dividends. If retained, only one-quarter of the dividends received by corporate shareholders is exempt.

III. SAVING AND INVESTMENT

There are numerous tax provisions to promote saving and investment in the Japanese tax law.

1. Saving Incentives

The preferential provisions for saving are as follows:

1. Interest on bank deposits, joint operation money trusts, public bonds, mortgaged debentures and stocks investment trusts is exempt from income tax, up to three million yen of the principal amount of deposits or face value of securities.

2. Interest on postal savings up to three million yen is exempt.

3. Interest on government bonds issued from April 1, 1984 to December 31, 1988 up to three million yen is exempt.

4. Interest income or distribution of profits from employee savings accounts set up under contract with their employers up to five million yen is exempt.

2. Investment Incentives

Reduced rates. The reduced corporation tax rate on distributed earnings and the tax credit for dividends received at the individual level has incentive effects. The reduced rate encourages equity financing, while the dividend tax credit encourages individuals to invest in corporate stocks.

Depreciation. The straight-line method or the declining balance method may be used for depreciation. The depreciation rate and the useful life for each type of asset are legally determined by regulations issued by the Ministry of Finance. The Special Taxation Measure Law allows various special depreciation allowances, tax credits, and tax free reserves, which are targeted to certain industries and specific types of assets. The special allowances are broadly grouped into two categories: initial allowance and accelerated depreciation.

The initial allowances provide a deduction of a portion of the acquisition cost of a qualifying asset in the first year in which such an asset is placed in service. Accelerated depreciation permits certain corporations to depreciate their assets at a faster rate than the rate under ordinary depreciation. Major examples of the accelerated depreciation allowances are shown in table 3.

Tax free reserves. Tax free reserves are also used to encourage specific types of investment and business activities. The most important tax free reserves are: price fluctuation reserves for commodities subjected to extreme price fluctuations; special repair reserves for vessels, blast furnaces, etc.; overseas investment loss reserve; atomic power plant construction reserve; nuclear fuel disposition reserve; security transaction responsibility reserve; and commodity transaction responsibility reserve.

Tax credits. As a substitute for an initial allowance, tax credits were provided for investment in effective use of energy. The tax credit is seven percent of the acquisition cost of machinery and equipment. (The maximum tax credit is 20 percent of corporate tax.)

Research and development expenditures. Special initial depreciation is provided for machinery and equipment under the law on Extraordinary Measures to promote R&D of small enterprises. The allowances are 16 percent of acquisition cost of machinery and equipment and eight percent for buildings.

An incremental investment credit is also allowed for experimental and research expenses. The credit is 20 percent of the excess of covered research and development expenses in the taxable year over the largest amount of such expenses incurred in any year from June 1, 1957 to March 31, 1988. Experimental and research expenses are defined as those incurred in experimental and research work to manufacture products, or to improve design or investment techniques. The credit is limited to 10 percent of the corporation income tax liability.

Special amortization is provided for payments to specified associations which are engaged mainly in research work, including write-off of the full amount in the year of payment.

3. Effects of Incentives on Saving

Ogura (1984) and Yoshino (1984) have completed representative empirical studies on the economic effects of Japan's tax-exempt saving system. Ogura investigated the relation between the individual net saving rate and age, and between the increase in individual financial assets and age. He concluded that the tax-exempt system does not have a strong effect on individual saving.

Yoshino tried to explain the factors determining individual financial assets. Using time series data by income class, he estimated the relation between net increases in the ratio of individual financial assets and net saving to disposable income and the following variables: the financial assets balance, the rate of growth of disposable income, tax payments, the rate of growth of land value, the interest rate on time deposits, and the limit on tax-exempt saving.

He found that the coefficients for the limit on tax-exempt saving are positive and significant in the first and second income quintiles, but insignificant in the third to the fifth quintiles. His explanation is that in the first and second quintiles, most persons attempt to save up to the limit of tax-exempt saving. However, in high income quintiles, taxpayers do not increase their saving because it already exceeds the limit.

4. Effects of Incentives on Investment

Tajika and Yui (1984) provide an econometric analysis of the relation between the special treatment of reserves and depreciation and the rate of growth of capital investment, by industry. Their most important result is that the correlation between the effective corporation income tax and the growth rate of capital investment is positive and significant in the chemical, steel, metalworking, and machine industries, but not in other industries.

Homma, Atoda, Hayashi and Hata (1984) analyze how permanent and temporary changes in the corporation income tax and the investment tax credit affect investment incentives by using Tobin's "q theory." They conclude that, in the typical example case, investment in the first year increases by about 950 billion yen as a result of a five percent cut in the corporation income tax rate (tax cut in the initial year is about 1,400 billion yen). Thus, the induced investment multiplier is about 0.67. They also find that the investment tax credit required to induce additional investment of about 950 billion yen in the first year is about 150 billion yen: in this case the induced investment multiplier is about 6.32. As a result, they conclude that the incentive effect of the investment tax credit is larger than that of an equivalent cut of the corporation income tax rate. On the basis of their simulations of a temporary corporate tax cut, they conclude that:

1. Corporation income tax cuts concentrate investment in the first half of the period in which the cut is in effect. If the period is extremely short, the effect is small. Consequently, temporary cuts in the corporation income tax rate do not stimulate investment.

2. An investment tax credit does not produce such anomalous results. Even a short-run increase in the credit stimulates investment to some degree.

3. The incentive effect of the investment tax credit is larger than that of a corporate rate cut.

4. The incentive effect of an investment tax credit is larger than that of a rate cut in each year of the period during which the corporate tax cuts are in effect.

IV. INDIRECT TAXES

In Japan, various excise taxes are imposed on particular commodities and services. In fiscal year 1986, the revenue from these indirect taxes accounted for 26.2 percent of national tax revenue. Major national indirect taxes are liquor tax (4.8 percent of national tax revenue in fiscal year 1985), gasoline tax (4.1 percent), commodity tax (3.9 percent), stamp tax (3.5 percent), and tobacco excise tax (2.4 percent).

1. Liquor Tax

All kinds of liquor are subject to specific duties in principle. Ad valorem duties are applied when the manufacturing sales price exceeds a certain level. The taxpayers of these taxes are manufacturers or importers. Effective tax rates on retail prices are higher than those on other commodities: 40.1 percent for special-class sake, 14.1 percent for second-class sake, 48.8 percent for beer, 50.3 percent for special-class whiskey, and so on, as of May 1986.

2. Gasoline Tax

The gasoline tax, together with the local road tax, is imposed on gasoline. Although the local road tax is allocated to local governments for road construction, the gasoline tax is appropriated for expenditures in the national budget. The tax is 45,600 yen per kiloliter, as of May 1986; another 8,200 yen is imposed as the local road tax. The taxpayers are refiners or importers.

3. Commodity Tax

Under the present commodity tax system, taxable commodities are divided into two classes. Class 1 includes precious stones, precious metal products, fur products, carpets, etc., and these items are subject to ad valorem tax at the retail stage. The tax base is the retail price, and the tax rate is 10 percent for carpets and 15 percent for the others. Major products of Class 2 are goods for amusements and sports, automobiles, electric appliances, television sets, musical instruments, cameras, furniture, watches, cosmetics, soft drinks, and so on. The ad valorem taxes are imposed on the wholesale prices or imported prices of the commodities. The tax rates range from five percent for coffee to 30 percent for yachts and other items.

4. Stamp Tax

A stamp tax, one of the transaction taxes, is imposed on documents for transfers of assets and contracts. The tax rate rises with an increase in amount stated in the document. For example, while an agreement with the amount less than 10,000 yen is exempt, a tax of 600,000 yen is imposed on the amount exceeding five billion yen.

5. Tobacco Excise Tax

An ad valorem and a specific tax are imposed on cigarettes. Tobacco is classified into six categories with different tax rates; for example, the tax rate on cigarettes is 23 percent of retail price and 582 yen per 1,000 pieces and on pipe tobacco 17.9 percent and 917 yen per kilogram. A tobacco excise tax is levied at the local level (see section VIII).

V. PAYROLL TAXES

As shown in table 4, the social insurance system is financed by general revenues of the national government and premiums in the form of a payroll tax.

The public pension plan, originally a fully funded system, has become a partially funded system because of financial difficulties. Under this system, although operated on a reserve basis, the fund is partially financed on a pay-as-you-go basis. The premium of the national pension system (which covers all citizens except general workers) is a lump sum, 6,740 yen per month. The premium for general workers is 6.2 percent each for the employee and employer (for women, 5.6 percent for the employee and 5.7 percent for the employer) and applies to the employee's standard salary.

All citizens are covered by public health insurance. As in the case of pensions, there are separate systems for general workers and others. The premium rates for the former are 4.2 percent each for employees and employers and that of the latter, 4.616 percent for the employer and 3.457 for the employee. The rates for the latter are fixed by the local governments; in fiscal year 1984, they averaged 103,984 yen.

VI. THE HIDDEN ECONOMY

In Japan, the discussion of the hidden economy has been focused mainly on the equity in income taxation that results from different degrees of compliance of different classes of taxpayers. That is, under the present tax system, income reporting rates (the degree to which income is reported to the tax authority) by employees, the self-employed and farmers differ greatly.

Ishi (1981) has prepared estimates of differential reporting rates by comparing the income reported to the tax authority and income data in national accounts (published by the Economic Planning Agency), which are regarded as reflecting "true income." He estimated that the reporting rates in 1970-78 were only 60-70 percent for business income and 20-30 percent for agricultural income, as compared with 90-100 percent for wages and salaries.

Homma, Atoda, Ihori, and Murayama (1984) point out that Ishi's work contains two problems. First, there are arbitrary factors in the statistical procedures, because the data come from different sources. Second, there is not enough information to estimate the difference between the actual tax liability and what the liability would be if there were no underreporting.

Homma's group insists it is necessary to take account of the actual income distribution and the income tax as it applies to each income level. Accordingly, they examine microeconomic statistical data to estimate differences in income tax burdens among occupations. These estimates are made by comparing income and tax burdens for each occupation on the assumption that the distributions by income classes of employees, the self-employed, and farmers in the tax data approximate the actual income distributions. They conclude that the degree of reporting among the occupations is roughly represented by "10-7-5." This means that the tax authority can "grasp" 100 percent of wage and salary income, 70 percent of business income, and only 50 percent of farm income.

VII. TAXATION OF WEALTH

1. Major Structural Features of Inheritance and Gift Taxes

The inheritance and gift taxes are imposed on transfers of wealth. The inheritance tax is levied on an increase in an heir's net assets resulting from inheritance, bequests, and so on, while the gift tax is levied on an increase in the donee's net assets generated by the gift. Although Japan's inheritance tax was originally an estate tax, it was changed in 1950 to an accession tax on the basis of the Shoup Mission's recommendation. To supplement the inheritance tax, the gift tax was established in 1953.

A basic deduction (20 million yen plus 40 million yen multiplied by the number of heirs) and some exemptions and tax credits are allowed for the inheritance tax. For the gift tax, the basic deduction is 600,000 yen and a spouse allowance is added. The inheritance tax is divided into 14 brackets, with rates ranging from 10 percent on inheritances of less than two million yen to 75 percent on amounts in excess of 500 million yen. The gift tax has 14 brackets with rates ranging from 10 percent on gifts of less than 500,000 yen to 75 percent on the amount of the gifts exceeding 70 million yen.

2. Wealth Taxes

A net wealth tax was introduced in accordance with the recommendations of the Shoup Mission in 1950 to complement the income tax and prevent excessive concentration of wealth. However, this tax was abolished in 1953 because different properties were being reported at different rates. In the present tax system, wealth taxes are confined to the local level where a property tax (levied on fixed assets), a city planning tax and a special tax on land holdings are levied.

3. Effects on the Distribution of Wealth

In Japan, there is no great concern about the effect of the tax system on the distribution of wealth. The Planning Bureau of the Economic Planning Agency (1975) completed studies on the distributional effects of the inheritance and property taxes.

In these studies, the distributional effect was estimated by comparing the Gini Coefficient of the before- and after-tax income distributions. They concluded that the redistributive effect of the inheritance tax is stronger than that of the income tax (see tables 5 and 6).

On the other hand, the fixed assets tax has a negative effect on wealth distribution. This result is attributed to the fact that the tax rate is to a considerable extent a per capita levy, on the principle of benefit taxation.

VIII. DISTRIBUTION OF TAX BURDEN

Table 7 shows the effective rates of national income tax and local inhabitant tax in 1986 for a single family, a married couple and a married couple with two children.

Hashimoto and Hayashi (1982) have estimated the effective rates of all taxes for a married couple with two children in 1977. The estimates are based on the following assumptions:

1. The burden of the individual income taxes falls on the person who pays them.

2. Consumption taxes are borne by consumers.

3. Corporate taxes fall on shareholders (Case I), or half on shareholders and half on consumers (Case II), or entirely on consumers (Case III).

For purposes of these calculations, income includes employee compensation, business income, transfer payments from governments, the corporation tax, and indirect taxes. It excludes current subsidies, social insurance contributions, other personal contributions, and imputed rent.

The results, which are shown in figures 4, 5, and 6, may be summarized as follows:

1. The burden distribution of national taxes is proportional up to the 3,200,000 yen income level and progressive thereafter. On the other hand, the burden of local taxes is regressive as a whole (figure 4).

The burden distribution for all taxes is U-shaped. This results from the progressivity of taxes on income and the regressivity of the taxes on consumption (figure 5).

3. The burden of taxes including taxes on corporations is different for each of the three cases (see figure 6). In general, corporation taxes add to the progressivity of the tax system in the highest class. Case I, in which it is assumed that shareholders bear the corporation income tax, is the most progressive.

Figure 4
Total Taxes as a Percentage of Family Income, 1977
(Not Including Taxes on Corporations)

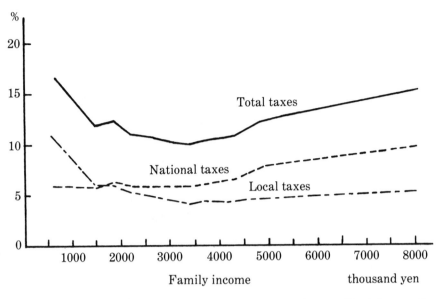

Source: Hashimoto, T. and Y. Hayashi, "Incidence of the Japanese Fiscal Structure," *Kwansei Gakuin University Annual Studies*, Vol. 31, 1982, p. 180.

Figure 5
Total Burdens by Type of Tax, 1977

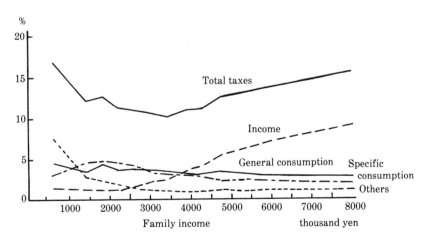

Source: Hashimoto, T. and Y. Hayashi, "Incidence of the Japanese Fiscal Structure," *Kwansei Gakuin University Annual Studies*, Vol. 31, 1982, p. 180.

Figure 6
Total Taxes as a Percentage of Family Income, 1977
(Including Taxes on Corporations)

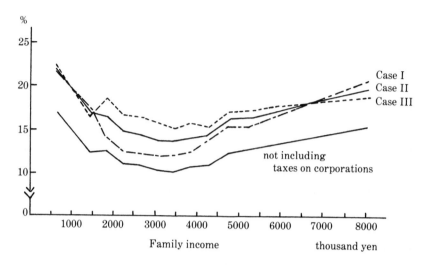

Source: Hashimoto, T. and Y. Hayashi, "Incidence of the Japanese Fiscal Structure,"
Kwansei Gakuin University Annual Studies, Vol. 31, 1982, p. 180.

IX. THE LOCAL TAX SYSTEM

1. Major Taxes Used

At the national level, individual and corporation income taxes
are most important. The prefectural inhabitant and enterprise
taxes are most important at the prefectural level, the municipal
inhabitant and the fixed assets taxes are most important at
municipal levels.

There are two types of local taxes—prefectural and municipal.
The features of the major local taxes are as follows:

1.1 Prefectural Taxes

The prefectural inhabitant tax is imposed on individuals and
corporations. The individual inhabitant tax consists of a per capita
levy and an income levy. The per capita levy is computed independently of the amount of income. The standard tax rates on income
are two percent for annual income of 1,500,000 yen or less and four
percent for annual income of over 1,500,000 yen. The income levy is

imposed on the previous year's income; the base of the local income levy is the same as the national income tax base, although some deductions are lower.

The corporate inhabitant tax also consists of a per capita levy, and a corporate income levy. The tax base of corporation income levy is the amount of the national corporation income tax before deducting income tax credits and the credit for foreign taxes. The standard tax rate is five percent of the national corporation income tax.

The enterprise tax is levied on individuals and corporations. Its tax base is the income of business enterprises. As this tax is based in part on the scale of business activities, we can say it is a kind of taxation of the ability to pay off business enterprises.

The real property acquisition tax is a transactions tax which is imposed on those who acquire land or buildings. The tax base is the market value of the acquired real property and the tax rate is four percent (three percent for houses acquired from July 1, 1981 to June 3, 1989).

The prefectural tobacco excise tax is the same as the national tobacco excise tax except for the tax rates.

The automobile acquisition tax is a prefectural tax which is earmarked for prefectural and municipal road expenditures. The prefectural governments allocate 70 percent of the tax revenue to municipal governments on the basis of the relative square areas and mileage of municipal roads.

1.2 Municipal Taxes

The municipalities levy a municipal inhabitant tax. Except for tax rates, the structure of this tax is the same as that of the prefectural inhabitant tax.

A property tax is imposed on land, buildings, and depreciable business assets. Land and buildings are taxed on the basis of their value as assessed by municipalities, which is between about 30 and 50 percent of the market price and revalued every three years. Although the standard rate is 1.4 percent, relatively poor municipalities may increase it to as much as 2.1 percent.

The municipal tobacco excise tax is the same as the national tobacco excise tax except for the tax rates.

2. Grants by National Government to Local Governments

Japan's national grant system consists of the local allocation grant and the specific purpose grants. In fiscal year 1986, the local allocation grant and the specific purpose grants accounted for 18.6 percent and 18.8 percent of local government revenue, respectively. The remainder was raised by local taxes and debt.

2.1 The Local Allocation Grant

The local allocation grant is an unconditional, general purpose grant from the national government to the local governments. It resembles the general revenue sharing program in the United States. Its major purpose is to ensure every local government sufficient funds to provide a standard level of public services.

The allocation grant equals 32 percent (originally 20 percent and raised several times later) of the total revenue of the individual income, corporation and liquor taxes; 94 percent is distributed as an ordinary allocation grant and the remaining six percent as a special allocation grant.

The ordinary allocation grant paid to each local government depends on its fiscal deficiency, that is, the excess of basic fiscal needs over basic revenue. Therefore, only local governments with basic fiscal needs exceeding their basic revenue can receive it. Basic fiscal needs are defined as the reasonable and standardized fiscal needs arising from the natural, social, and geographical conditions of local governments. These are calculated using the following formula, for the various categories of expenditure (roads, police, education, etc.):

Fiscal needs = unit of measurement x modification coefficients x unit costs.

The modification coefficients take account of special fiscal needs of particular local governments. For example, one coefficient is applied for municipal governments with rapid population growth, since such governments face greater fiscal needs than others. The modification coefficients adjust the standard fiscal needs for population size, scale economies, cold climate, a decline in measurement units, fiscal capacities and others, as well as for population growth.

Basic revenue measures the reasonable fiscal capacity of local governments. The basic revenue of prefectures equals 80 percent of their tax revenue as estimated at the standard tax rates. For municipalities this ratio is 75 percent.

The special allocation grant supplements the ordinary allocation grant. It is provided in the following cases:

1. When there are specific fiscal needs not covered in the ordinary allocation grant (such as election of local assemblymen, and the prevention of epidemics and disease).

2. When the basic revenue is overestimated.

3. When there is an increase in fiscal needs or a reduction in tax revenue after the calculation of the ordinary allocation grant.

2.2 Specific Purpose Grants

There are conditional grants over which the national government exercises strict controls. They are divided into three categories: the national government's contribution, the national government's 100 percent payment, and the national government's subsidy.

The national government's contribution is subdivided into three types. The first type consists of contributions to expenditures for local public services, which local governments are obligated to provide by law for national and local interests, but which need the fiscal assistance of the national government to provide them. Expenditures on education (including salaries and pensions for personnel in compulsory education, and construction of schools), health, welfare (including public assistance and medical expenses under national health insurance), assistance to agriculture and other programs, are covered by this type of contribution. Most of these are matching grants.

The second type is provided for outlays on local public works, which local governments are required by the national government to build. These include matching and nonmatching grants.

The third type covers expenditures resulting from disasters. Although the Local Public Finance Law prescribes that the national government bear all or a part of the expenditures of the first and second type of contributions, it prescribes that the national government bear only a part of the third type.

The national government's 100 percent payment is provided to local governments for activities the national government has entrusted to local governments or their officials. This grant program covers local expenditures on the election of national assembly members, the compilation of statistics and research for the benefit of national government, registration of aliens, administration of health insurance and national pension insurance, and so on.

X. PROPOSALS FOR TAX REFORM

1. Governmental Initiatives

In November 1983, the Tax Commission (the official tax advisory organization for the prime minister) submitted new mid-term recommendations entitled "A Desirable Picture of the Future Tax System." In its mid-term recommendation of 1977, the commission had recommended the reconstruction of the Japanese tax system by the introduction of a general consumption tax (value-added tax of consumption type). However, as a result of strong objections by the general public and defeat of the Liberal Democratic Party in the 1979 election, the introduction of a general consumption tax was delayed. Moreover, in July 1981, the Provisional Commission of Administrative Reform submitted "The First Report on the Reform of the Administrative System" which insisted that the reform of the tax system be achieved by curtailing and rationalizing governmental expenditures, rather than by increasing existing taxes or by introducing a new tax.

In this situation, the mid-term recommendation of 1983 by the Tax Commission emphasized the necessity of curtailing and rationalizing governmental expenditures. However, at the same time the commission argued that the current tax system should be reexamined from the viewpoint of neutrality, equity, and appropriate tax revenue, in order to cope with the changes in society and the economy. The main proposals in the 1983 recommendations were as follows:

1. The personal deductions, basic allowance, and employment income deduction under the national income tax should be raised.

2. The rate of progression of the national income tax should be moderated. (In fiscal 1984 the maximum rate was lowered from 75 percent to 70 percent, the minimum rate was raised from 10 percent to 10.5 percent and the number of tax rate brackets was reduced from 19 to 15.)

3. The "Green Card System" should be introduced to reduce underreporting of interest and dividends income. The "Green Card System" was intended to identify individual depositors in order to enforce comprehensive taxation on interest and dividends income. It was once planned to be introduced to prevent abuse of the nontaxable saving system. Under this system, (1) a taxpayer wishing to benefit from tax-exempt interest on small savings (including postal deposits) is issued a Green Card at his request, (2) the card records the depositor's name, number, and amount of the nontaxable saving, (3) the depositor must present his card to the financial institution, thus providing a basis for checking the amount of his nontaxable saving. Taxable interest and dividends would be taxed under the progressive tax schedules. This proposal was repealed as a result of political pressures in March 1985.

4. Corporations should be taxed at a flat rate, not at progressive rates. The difference between the basic rates and the rates for small corporations, cooperative associations, public interest corporations, etc., should be reduced.

5. The treatment of investment income of public corporations should be examined.

6. The retirement allowance reserve and the bad debts reserve should be reexamined.

7. The special treatment of social insurance benefits in the enterprise tax should be reexamined.

8. Tax accounting should be based on standard bookkeeping practice and registration should be enforced to clarify the obligations of taxpayers included in the system.

9. Differences in tax burdens of various classes of liquor should be reduced and ad valorem taxes should be expanded for commodities having wide price ranges.

10. The list of items subject to commodity taxes should be broadened.

2. Academic Proposals

The research commission of economists, organized by the National Institute for Research Advancement (a Japanese think tank), published a report entitled "Basic Viewpoints for Tax Reform" in 1985. The members of the commission were Professor H. Ishi (Hitostubashi University), Professor M. Ito (Kyoto University), T. Ushijima (Nagoya City University), H. Kaneko (Tokyo University), and S. Fujita (Osaka University). The major reforms recommended in this report were as follows:

1. To achieve equity in taxation, six tax rate brackets with marginal tax rates ranging from 10 to 60 percent should be substituted for the present rates which range from 10.5 to 70 percent.

2. The tax base should be broadened. However, three deductions and allowances should be increased (the personal deduction: from 330,000 yen to 400,000 yen; the basic allowance: from 330,000 yen to 500,000 yen; and the allowance for dependents: from 330,000 yen to 500,000 yen). The commission also recommended that the employment income deduction should remain unchanged, and that the other income deductions should be abolished.

3. The corporation income tax base should be reexamined. Three possible revisions were suggested: (1) The special taxation measures for specific policy objectives should be abolished. Specifically, tax deductible reserves *Junbikin* which are based on generally accepted accounting principles, should be eliminated. (2) In addition to the changes in (1), a part of dividends received should be included in gross income, and no entertainment expenses should be deductible. (3) In addition to (1) and (2), various kinds of tax deductible reserves, *Hikiatekins*, which are not justified by generally accepted accounting principles, should be eliminated.

4. The difference between the basic rate and the reduced rates for small corporations, cooperative associations, and public interest corporations should be reduced.

5. Gains on the sale of depreciable assets should be subject to the capital gains tax on the accrual basis.

6. As the present indirect tax system is composed of various kinds of specific consumption taxes, it lacks neutrality and equity. Therefore, a value-added tax of the type levied in the European Communities should be enacted and earmarked for the financing of the social security system.

In 1985, the Japan Tax Association published a report entitled "The Basic Course of Japan's Tax Reform" which was drafted by Professor T. Hashimoto (Kwansei Gakuin University) and Professor K. Yoshimuta (Nihon University). The report points out that the present tax system is not consistent with the changing needs of society and the economy, and proposes tax reform aimed at equity, simplicity, and an appropriate level of tax revenue. The purposes of the reform are to (1) alleviate the tax burdens of middle-class taxpayers (those with income ranging from four million yen to eight million yen) who feel that they are heavily taxed and whose incentives to work should be stimulated; (2) eliminate tax avoidance and tax evasion by high-income taxpayers; and (3) simplify the income tax system. The major reforms recommended in the report are as follows:

1. The maximum individual income tax rate should be cut from 70 to 50 percent and the minimum rate from 10.5 to 10 percent, and the number of rate brackets should be reduced from 15 to six.

2. The personal deductions (basic allowance, spouse allowance, and allowance for dependent) should be changed either to 300,000 yen (Case 1) or 400,000 yen (Case 2).

3. The employment deduction and the deduction for social insurance premiums should not be changed. The deductions for casualty losses, medical expenses, life insurance premiums, and fire and other casualty insurance should be abolished.

The report estimates that the tax revenue of 11,628.8 billion yen in 1983 would be reduced by 2,379.9 billion yen in Case 1 and by 3,410.1 billion yen in Case 2. However, taking account of the reduction in the number of rate brackets of the local inhabitants tax, tax revenue would be increased by 320 billion yen in Case 1 and reduced by 290 billion yen in Case 2. The before-tax Gini coefficient for employment income would be reduced from 0.3294 (0.3147, after tax) to 0.3219 in Case 1, and to 0.3217 in Case 2. The Gini coefficient for assessment income would be reduced from 0.5211 to 0.4671 in Case 1 and 0.4818 in Case 2.

4. The base of the enterprise tax should be changed from net income (profits) to value added. The purposes of this change are to stabilize the local tax revenue and to tax deficit corporations. The report estimates that a two percent value-added tax would yield about 3,028 billion yen, which nearly equals the present revenue of the enterprise tax. A four percent value-added tax would be sufficient to finance the revenue loss from the proposed income tax reforms.

5. A value-added tax with a uniform tax rate should be introduced. However, zero rating of foods, medical, education, and other expenditures or exemptions for these expenditures is proposed. Also, the liquor, tobacco excise, gasoline, and other taxes would remain. This reform was proposed in order to tax different services and new products equally (the existing commodity taxes are not neutral in this respect); to raise large amounts of revenue; to attain greater horizontal equity in taxation than can be achieved with the income tax above; to simplify consumption taxation; and to coordinate with internationalization of the tax system. The report estimates that a value-added tax would raise about 3,000 billion yen if the tax rate were five percent.

The regressivity of the value-added tax would be alleviated by zero rating of foods and other necessities. Table 8 shows the estimated burden of the proposed value-added tax, by quintiles. Table 9 shows the combined effect of the proposed income tax reforms and the introduction of the value-added tax, also by quintiles.

6. The basic structure of the corporation income tax should not be changed. However, the tax rate should be lowered from 43.3 to 40 percent immediately and to 35 percent in the future, and the years over which depreciable assets are depreciated should be shortened. The report also proposes that the difference between the basic rates and the reduced rates for small corporations, cooperative associations, public interest corporations, etc., should be reexamined.

3. Views of Business on Tax Reform

In January 1986, the Japan Committee for Economic Development (*Keizai Doyou Kai*), one of the major business organizations in Japan, released an interim report on tax reform. The report suggests that the maximum marginal tax rate on individual income tax (including the local inhabitant tax) should be reduced from 78 percent to 60 percent now and to 50 percent in the future, and that the number of rate brackets should be reduced from 15 to 10. The effective corporate tax rate (including that of local tax) should be reduced from 52.92 to less than 50 percent. As resources are not available to finance the proposed changes in the income and corporation taxes, a broad-based indirect tax should be introduced.

4. Views of Trade Unions

The major trade unions (the General Council of Trade Unions of Japan, the Japanese Confederation of Labor, etc.) propose a national tax reform in fiscal year 1986 to reduce income tax by raising the minimum taxable income (1,120 billion yen), reducing progression (500 billion yen), and reducing the local inhabitant tax (180 billion yen). They also propose a tax cut to improve social welfare (500 billion yen). They strongly object to introducing a value-added tax, and to taxing interest income tax on small savings in order to finance tax cuts. They insist that sufficient funds for the tax cuts can be obtained by reducing government expenditures and abolishing special tax measures under the income tax.

5. Prospects for Tax Reform

The U.S. Department of the Treasury Report, *Tax Reform for Fairness, Simplicity and Economic Growth* (November 1984), has greatly influenced discussions of the tax reform in Japan. Japan's tax specialists rate this report highly. The Japanese government also plans a fundamental tax reform in fiscal year 1987. This tax reform will examine the whole system of taxes from the viewpoint of equity and neutrality in taxation.

Japan's tax system has relied heavily on the income tax since the recommendations of the Shoup Mission of 1950. However, the present income tax system has some problems. First, the tax base has been remarkably eroded by the tax exemptions for capital gains on securities, imputed income, interest income from small savings, and other income. Secondly, the progressive income tax has created difficult problems, such as disincentives for labor and distortions from inflation.

There is a great deal of discontent with the high progressive income tax rates in Japan. As noted earlier, the maximum rate of 70 percent (national tax) is higher than those of other countries and there are too many tax brackets. Therefore, the government expects to reduce the maximum rate and to reduce the number of tax brackets in fiscal year 1987. The present tax schedule imposes heavy burdens especially on the middle income class (defined as those with incomes between four and eight million yen) and the proposed reductions in rates are expected to reduce their tax burdens. The revenue reduction caused by the rate reductions is expected to be financed by expansion of the tax base.

In this context, the problem of taxation of interest income is most acute. Although the tax exemption is intended to promote small savings, it is a hotbed of tax evasion by the higher income classes. As a result, a proposal to shift to separate taxation of interest at a low rate has surfaced in order to simplify compliance and administration. Such a tax is not expected to shift investment from bank deposits to other financial assets. Because the anonymity of depositors would be protected, the bankers associations also will not oppose separate taxation. The strongest opposition to this proposal came from the Ministry of Posts and Telecommunications, which is trying to protect the tax exemption for postal savings.

A proposal to substitute a cash flow corporate tax for the present corporation income tax has been made by some economists. However, as this proposal is not supported generally, a fundamental reform of corporation income tax is not expected in the near future. In the framework of the present tax system, the 1987 reform will reduce the corporation income tax rate and expand the tax base by eliminating special tax preferences. It is also expected to raise the reduced tax rates for small corporations to the basic tax rate.

Finally, there has been increasing discussion of the value-added tax as a method of reforming consumption taxes. Japan does not have a value-added tax, and it is different from most OECD countries in this respect. Under the present excise tax system, distortions are inevitable. For this reason, the introduction of the value-added tax is supported by many economists. But the self-employed and trade unions strongly oppose the value-added tax because of its regressive effect, effect on commodity prices, and difficulty of administration.

REFERENCES

Gomi, Y. *Guide to Japanese Taxes*. Zaikeishohousha, 1984.

Hashimoto, T. "On the Local Tax System—'Choice and Burden' of the Local People," *Jichi Sogo Center* (General Center for Local Autonomy), No. 11.

Hashimoto, T. and Y. Hayashi. "Incidence of the Japanese Fiscal Structure," *Kwansei Gakuin University Annual Studies*, Vol. 31, 1982.

Homma, M., N. Atoda, F. Hayashi, and K. Hata. *Setubi Toshi to Kigyo Zeisei (Plant and Equipment Investment and the Corporation Tax System)*. Economic Planning Agency, Economic Research Institute, 1984.

Homma, M., T. Ihori, N. Atoda, and J. Murayama. "Shotokuzei Futan no Gyoshukan Kakusa no Jittai (The Actual Difference of Income Tax Burdens Between Types of Industries)," *Kikan Gendai Keizai*, No. 59, 1984.

Ishi, H. "Kaxei Shotoku Hosoku Ritu no Gyoshukan Kakusa (Differences of Effective Rates of Taxable Income Between Types of Industries)," *Kikan Gendai Keizai*, No. 42, 1981.

Jichi Sogo Center. *Local Tax System in Japan*. Jichi Sogo Center, 1982.

Japan Tax Association. "Showa Zaisei Zeisei Jyuyo Shiryou Shu (Important Statistics of Public Finance and Taxation in the Showa Era)." Japan Tax Association, 1982.

Ministry of Finance. *Zaisei Kin'yu Tokei Geppo (Monthly Report on Fiscal Statistics)*, No. 409, 1986.

National Institute for Research Advancement. "Choikitekina Zeisei no Arikata ni Kansuru Kenkyu (The Study of a Desirable Picture of Long-term Policy on the Tax System)." National Institute for Research Advancement, 1985.

Ogura, S. "Maruyou Seido no Keizaikoka (The Economic Effects of the Maruyou System)," *Keizai Seminar*, No. 348, 1984.

Planning Bureau, Economic Planning Agency. *Shotoku Sisan Bunpai no Jittai to Mondaiten (The Actual Condition and Problem on Distributions of Income and Assets)*. 1975.

Shibata, T., ed. *Public Finance in Japan*. University of Tokyo Press, 1986.

Shoup Mission. *Second Report on Japanese Taxation*. Japan Tax Association, 1950.

Tajika, E., and Y. Yui. "Sengo Nippon no Houjin Zeisei to Setubi Toshi (The Corporate Tax System and Plant and Equipment Investment in Japan After World War II)," *Kikan Gendai Keizai*, No. 59, 1984.

Tax Bureau, Ministry of Finance, *An Outline of Japanese Taxes*, Tax Bureau Ministry of Finance, 1985.

Tax Commission. "Showa 61 Nendo no Zeisei Kaisei ni Kansuru Toshin (Report on the FY 1986 Tax Reform)." Tax Commission, 1985.

Tuji, K., ed. *Public Administration in Japan*. University of Tokyo Press, 1986.

Yonehara, J. *Local Public Finance in Japan*. Center for Research on Federal Relations, The Australian National University, Canberra, Research Monograph No. 36, 1981.

Yoshino, N. "Nippon no Chochiku Kozo no Keiryo Bunseki (Econometric Analysis of the Saving Structure of Japan)," *Zaisei Kenkyusho*, 1984.

Table 1
National Government Individual Income Tax Rates, 1986

Taxable Income (yen)	Tax Rates (percent)
Less than 500,000	10.5
1,200,000	12.0
2,000,000	14.0
3,000,000	17.0
4,000,000	21.0
6,000,000	25.0
8,000,000	30.0
10,000,000	35.0
12,000,000	40.0
15,000,000	45.0
20,000,000	50.0
30,000,000	55.0
50,000,000	60.0
80,000,000	65.0
More than 80,000,000	70.0

Source: *An Outline of Japanese Taxes, 1985*, Tax Bureau, Ministry of Finance.

Table 2
National Government Corporation Income Tax Rates, 1984-87
(Percent)

Size of Corporation and Profits	Permanent Rates	April 1, 1984 to March 31, 1987
Undistributed Profits		
Corporations with capital of		
100 million yen or more	42.0	43.3
Corporations with capital of less than 100 million yen		
Annual income of 8 million yen or more	42.0	43.3
Annual income of less than 8 million yen	30.0	31.0
Distributed Profits		
Corporations with capital of		
100 million yen or more	32.0	33.3
Corporations with capital of less than 100 million yen		
Annual income of 8 million yen or more	32.0	33.3
Annual income of less than 8 million yen	24.0	25.0
Cooperative Associations	n.a.	23.0
Liquidation Income		
Ordinary corporations	n.a.	38.1
Cooperative associations	n.a.	25.8

Source: *An Outline of Japanese Taxes, 1985*, Tax Bureau, Ministry of Finance.
n.a.: not available

Table 3
Major Depreciation Allowances,[1] 1986

Qualified Asset	Allowance (Percentage of acquisition cost)
Depreciation	
Machine conserving energy	30
Electronic machine equipment	30
Qualified plant and equipment	
To prevent environmental pollution	22
Designed not to cause environmental pollution	16
Industrial water-supply equipment	16
Machinery and equipment for recycling which may promote efficient resource use	18
Machinery and other depreciational assets for saving energy	16
Steel vessels[2] used by ocean transport corporations	14
Aircraft[3] used by air transportation corporations	14
Assets used in manufacturing in developing areas, industrial development regions, agricultural areas, mining areas, etc.	
Plant and equipment	16
Buildings	8
Initial Allowances	
Qualified plant or equipment, etc., operated by a corporation employing handicapped individuals[4]	16[5]
Newly constructed facilities for storing petroleum gas	32

Source: *An Outline of Japanese Taxes, 1985,* Tax Bureau, Ministry of Finance.
[1]Except for depreciation allowances for small corporations.
[2]More than 2,000 tons.
[3]Maximum takeoff weight more than 120 tons.
[4]Not less than two percent of its labor force.
[5]For plant, equipment, and trucks.

Table 4
Summary of the Pension and Health Insurance Systems Publicly Operated in Japan, Fiscal Year 1985

Type of Insurance	Members[1]	Managing unit	Contribution (percent) Employee	Employer
Public Pension Union				
Welfare pension insurance	General workers	National government and welfare pension fund	6.2	6.2
			5.6[4]	5.7[4]
National pension insurance	Individuals not covered by other insurance (the self-employed, etc.)	National government and national pension fund	6,740[5] yen	—
Insurance for workers in special occupations				
Seamen's insurance	Seamen	National government	6.8	6.8
Mutual association's insurance	National government workers, etc.	Mutual association	7.7	7.7
	Local government workers, etc.	Mutual association	6.9	6.9
	Private school teachers, etc.	Private school personnel mutual aid association	5.2	5.2
	Agriculture, forestry, and fishery organization employees	Agriculture, forestry, and fishery organization mutual aid association	5.5	5.5
Health Insurance				
Union-managed insurance	General workers	Health insurance union	4.6[2]	3.5[2]
Government-managed insurance	General workers	National government	4.2	4.2
Insurance for workers in special occupations				
Seamen's insurance	Seamen	National government	4.1	4.1
Mutual association's insurance	Public workers and teachers, etc.	Mutual associations	3.2—5.3	—
National health insurance	Individuals not covered by other insurance (the self-employed, etc.)	Local government and national health insurance union	103,984[3] yen	—

Source: T. Osu, *Zusetu Nippon no Zaisei (An Illustration, Public Finance in Japan)*, Toyo Keizai Sinposha, 1980.
[1]Including their families.
[2]Averages for all unions in fiscal year 1983.
[3]The average annual sum of fiscal year 1984.
[4]Contribution rates for women.
[5]Monthly sum.

Table 5
Redistributive Effects of Inheritance Tax
on Income Distribution, Fiscal Years 1963-73

Fiscal year	Gini-coefficient for income distribution before tax	Gini-coefficient for income distribution after tax	Percent change
1963	0.4860	0.4031	17.1
1964	0.4914	0.4158	15.4
1965	0.4689	0.3951	15.8
1966	0.4389	0.3699	15.7
1967	0.4665	0.3951	15.3
1968	0.4490	0.3832	14.7
1969	0.4624	0.3906	15.5
1970	0.4720	0.3978	15.7
1971	0.4853	0.4053	16.5
1972	0.4756	0.4022	15.4
1973	0.4866	0.4031	17.2

Source: Planning Bureau, Economic Planning Agency, *Shotoku Sisan Bunpai no Jittai to Modaiten* (*The Actual Condition and Problems of Distributions of Income and Assets*), Planning Bureau, Economic Planning Agency, 1975, p. 132.

Table 6
Redistributive Effects of Fixed Assets Tax
on Family Income, Fiscal Years 1971-1973[1]

Fiscal year	Gini-coefficient for income distribution before tax	Gini-coefficient for income distribution after tax	Percent change
1971	0.2584	0.2584	0.47
1972[2]	0.2647	0.2657	0.38
1973	0.2666	0.2678	0.45

Source: Planning Bureau, Economic Planning Agency, *Shotoku Sisan Bunpai no Jittai to Mondaiten* (*The Actual Condition and Problems on Distributions of Income and Assets*, Planning Bureau, Economic Planning Agency, 1975, p. 136.

[1] These results were estimated by using Statistics Bureau Management and Coordination Agency, Annual Report on the Family Income and Expenditure Survey, Planning Bureau, Economic Planning Agency.

[2] The numerical value of FY 1972 is the most reliable value owing to the condition of data.

Table 7
Effective Income Tax Rates by Income Classes, 1985
(Percent of income)

Annual Income	Income Tax	Inhabitants Tax	Total
1,000,000 yen			
Single	0.3	0.5	0.8
Married couple	—	—	—
Married couple with two children	—	—	—
1,500,000 yen			
Single	3.3	1.8	5.0
Married couple	0.9	0.9	1.8
Married couple with two children	—	—	—
2,000,000 yen			
Single	4.2	2.3	6.5
Married couple	2.3	1.5	3.7
Married couple with two children	—	0.0	0.0
3,000,000 yen			
Single	4.9	2.8	7.7
Married couple	3.3	2.0	5.3
Married couple with two children	0.4	0.7	1.1
5,000,000 yen			
Single	5.5	3.3	8.7
Married couple	4.0	2.5	6.5
Married couple with two children	1.4	1.2	2.6
7,000,000 yen			
Single	10.7	6.7	13.0
Married couple	9.5	6.2	11.3
Married couple with two children	7.5	5.3	7.9
10,000,000 yen			
Single	14.7	8.3	22.9
Married couple	13.7	7.9	21.6
Married couple with two children	11.7	7.2	18.9
20,000,000 yen			
Single	27.0	11.1	38.0
Married couple	26.1	11.0	37.1
Married couple with two children	24.5	10.6	35.0

(Continued on next page)

Table 7 (Continued)
Effective Income Tax Rates by Income Classes, 1985
(Percent of income)

Annual Income	Income Tax	Inhabitants Tax	Total
50,000,000 yen			
Single	43.3	13.9	57.2
Married couple	42.9	13.8	56.7
Married couple with			
two children	42.1	13.6	55.7
100,000,000 yen			
Single	52.9	15.4	68.4
Married couple	52.7	15.4	68.1
Married couple with			
two children	52.2	15.3	67.5

Source: Ministry of Finance, *Zaisei Kin'yu Tokei Geppo* (*Monthly Report on Fiscal Statistics*), No. 397, 1985. p. 32.

Note: The income tax is the tax amount in 1985. The inhabitants tax is the tax amount in fiscal year 1985.

Table 8
Tax Burden of Value-Added Tax, by Quintiles

Tax Rates	Quintile				
	I	II	III	IV	V
4 percent	0.0189	0.0189	0.0178	0.0169	0.0169
6 percent	0.0284	0.0284	0.0268	0.0283	0.0254

Source: Japan Tax Association, "Wagakunino Zeisei Kaikakuno Kihontekihoko, *The Basic Course of Japan's Tax Reform*, 1985, p. 4.

Table 9
Total Tax Burden, by Quintiles

Tax Rates	Quintile				
	I	II	III	IV	V
4 percent[1]	0.0363	0.0444	0.0506	0.0555	0.0660
6 percent[2]	0.0339	0.0428	0.0499	0.0560	0.0681

Source: Japan Tax Association, "Wagakunino Zeisei Kaikakuno Kihontekihoko, *The Basic Course of Japan's Tax Reform*, 1985, p. 4.

[1] Plus Case 1.

[2] Plus Case 2.

Contributing Authors

(Affiliations as of mid-1986)

Krister Andersson (Sweden) is a member of the staff of the Department of Economics, University of Lund, Sweden.

Laura Castellucci (Italy) is Associate Professor of Public Finance, Faculty of Economics, University of Rome, Italy.

Flip de Kam (Netherlands) is Head, Systems Analysis Department of the Social and Cultural Planning Office, Rijswijk, the Netherlands. He was a member of the Tax Simplification Commission that presented its proposals in May 1986.

Annette Dengel (Federal Republic of Germany) is a member of the staff of the Institut fur Finanzwissenschaft, University of Mainz, West Germany. Translation by Birgit Schneider, Institut des Finances Publiques, Universite de la Sarre, Saarbrucken.

M. Homma, T. Maeda, and K. Hashimoto (Japan) are, respectively, Professor of Economics, Osaka University, Associate Professor of Economics, Oita University, and graduate student in economics, Osaka University.

Harry M. Kitchen (Canada) is Professor of Economics, Trent University, Peterborough, Ontario, Canada.

Jean-Louis Lienard, Kenneth C. Messere, and Jeffrey Owens (France) are staff members of the Directorate of Financial, Fiscal, and Enterprise Affairs, Organization for Economic Co-Operation and Development, Paris, France.

Nick Morris (United Kingdom) is Deputy Director of the Institute for Fiscal Studies, London, England.

Joseph A. Pechman (editor) is Senior Fellow, and formerly Director of Economic Studies, at the Brookings Institution, Washington, D.C., U.S.A.

Index